CLEANING-UP

HAZARDOUS MATERIALS

A Refutation of *Hazardous Materials*
By
Gail Riplinger

Dr. Kirk DiVietro, Th.M., Ph.D.

H. D. Williams, M.D., Ph.D., Editor
The Dean Burgon Society
Box 354
Collingswood, NJ 08108

Published by:

The Dean Burgon Society
Box 354
Collingswood, New Jersey 08108
USA

April, 2010

Copyright © 2010 by The Dean Burgon Society
All Rights Reserved
Printed in the United States of America

REL006100: Religion: Biblical Criticism & Interpretation

ISBN 978-1-56848-068-8

All Scripture quotes are from the King James Bible except those verses compared and then the source is identified.

No part of this work may be reproduced without the expressed consent of the publisher, except for brief quotes, whether by electronic, photocopying, recording, or information storage and retrieval systems.

Address All Inquiries To:
The Dean Burgon Society
Box 354
Collingswood, NJ 08108

Internet Address: www.DeanBurgonSociety.org
E-mail: bft@BibleForToday.org

BIBLE FOR TODAY #3457
Internet Address: www.biblefortoday.org
E-mail: bft@biblefortoday.org

DEDICATION

My association with Dr. D. A. Waite began in the early 1990's when he introduced me to Scrivener's Greek New Testament. It was through Dr. Waite that I was introduced to Logos Bible Research® and was able to provide them with Scrivener's text. For years he has been my friend, teacher, and source of information. I have been privileged to stand behind him and beside him in the ministry of the Dean Burgon Society® and the Bible for Today®. It was at his insistence and with his support that I produced this book.

My association with Dr. Williams and his dear wife Patricia began just a few years ago when they became an integral part of the Dean Burgon Society®. Dr. Williams and Patricia worked tirelessly to edit hundreds of pages of notes and comments which were dictated into the computer. It was their arduous task to figure out that "It is not with the lexicographer's chromatogram a grammar tuitions philologist in etymologists right, it is what the reader selects from what they write." actually meant "It is not what the lexicographers, commentators, grammarians, philologists, and etymologists write. It is what the reader selects from what they write." Without them this book would still be just a file on my computer.

And so it is with great gratitude for their encouragement and help in producing this book, I dedicate it to these three selfless servants of God, my mentor and friend Dr. D.A. Waite, and my editors and friends Dr. & Mrs. H. D. Williams without whom it would not have been possible.

PREFACE

In the pages to follow, Dr. Kirk DiVietro, Th.M., Ph.D., a well trained pastor, theologian, and linguist has done an excellent job pointing out the difficulties that many are having with Gail Riplinger's book, *Hazardous Materials*. In this preface, we will attempt to enumerate the points that he has made. We will also supplement it with several additional thoughts that a number of pastors as well as others have contributed.

Failed Marriages and Charismatic Influence

It is obvious that Mrs. Riplinger is angry, bitter, and hurt as evidenced by the tenor of her words in her work (Psa. 37:8, Pro. 15:1, 18, 16:32, 19:11, 22:8, Ec.7:9). We suspect that the facts recently revealed about Mrs. Riplinger's three marriages and two divorces have significantly influenced the words that she has written (Pro. 14:10, Psa. 64:3, Col. 3:8, Col. 3:19, Heb. 12:15, Jam. 3:14) (see the "Appendix," pp. 285ff, 325).

It is reported that her early experiences in a charismatic church may have influenced the thoughts and opinions that are revealed in her writings. For example, she implies in her writings that the Holy Spirit verbally gave the King James Bible (KJB) translators the English words for the translation just as He gave the prophets and the apostles the original Words in Hebrew, Aramaic, and Greek. But, the KJB translators gave no indication that this is true, and, as a matter of fact, the translators reported the opposite (see their own words in the Preface to the KJB); whereas the prophets and apostles knew that they were receiving inspired Words (cf. 1 Cor. 2, 1 Thes. 1, 2 Pe. 1, 2 Pe. 3, etc.).

The Attempts to Defend a False Doctrine

In addition, it is obvious to many that *Hazardous Materials,* as well as her other writings, are extensive attempts to defend her belief in inspired translations. There is no doubt that she has been responsible for many individuals turning their attention to the King James Bible, but at the same time she has turned many people away from the Hebrew, Aramaic, and Greek Words underlying the King James Bible.

She should abandon her use of sharp words and the reporting of inaccurate facts that frequently appear in her work (q.v.). For example, she claims Dr. Maurice Robinson, who is currently Senior Professor at Southeastern Baptist Theological Seminary, was editor of Berry's interlinear in 1897, which is false.[1] Another example, among many, is her statement that Donald Waite, Jr. said that Scrivener "back-translated" (see Riplinger's statements on p. 634, 637 in *Hazardous Materials*). This is absolutely false. Please compare her comments with (1) Donald Waite, Jr.'s letter in the "Appendix" of this work, p. 306, (2) a radio interview with Donald Waite, Jr. on "Just For Women," aired January 9, 2010, which is available from Bible For Today, and (3) his additional comments on pages 204-208 in this work. The radio program is a **must listen to** discussion to understand how Mrs. Riplinger is confused at best or is manipulating information at worst. We will let you be the judge. But, in the end, there is no excuse for this and it brings into question her entire work, including the facts, the exegesis of Scripture, the quotes of individuals, and the doctrine promoted in her work.

False Doctrine

For example, she claims Jude 3 has nothing to do with the prophets and apostles receiving the Words of God "once" (Jude 3) and she totally misunderstands 2 Tim. 3:16 (see p. 1145 and many other places too numerous to mention). Even her 'logic' becomes convoluted. For example, if her explanation in very small print on page 1145 is read carefully, her logic confirms that *"the words which **were spoken***

---

[1] This incorrect fact was confirmed in a personal email from Dr. Maurice Robinson. The false fact was published by Mrs. Riplinger in a brochure advertising her book, *Hazardous Materials*. See Dr. Robinson's revuttal and testimony in the Appendix, pp 285ff. Also, see her derogatory comments about Dr. Robinson on pages 591, 643, 1013, and 1014 inher work.

PREFACE

before *of the apostles..."* by Paul, Peter, and other apostles, were given *"once."* Of course by extension, this applies to *"the faith,"* which is the doctrine included in *"all scripture,"* which *"was once delivered"* by God to all of the recorders of Scripture. *"The faith," "was once delivered"* (Jude 3) by Words *"given by inspiration"* to serve as a *"foundation"* for translating the Words of God into the languages of the world.

The Proper Exegesis of 2 Timothy 3:16

Dr. D. A. Waite, Th.D. Ph.D. is President of the Dean Burgon Society. He is a SUPERBLY trained linguist.[2] His experience and knowledge probably far exceed any living linguist. He has proclaimed the correct doctrine of inspiration, but it has been ignored, shunned, or despised WITHOUT CAUSE in favor of the opinions of individuals who are poorly trained. He has warned that something is drastically wrong when individuals clearly ignore Biblical principles concerning divorce and remarriage and women teaching men. He has repeatedly warned about the modern heresy of inspiration as defined by Peter Ruckman and Gail Riplinger. His reproofs have gone unheeded by many. As a result, many have fallen into a pit. Their emotions and feelings have ruled over the Words of God. The theological truth concerning theopneustos is present here one more time. Dr. Waite said:

---

[2] Dr. D. A. Waite's interest in the original Biblical languages of Hebrew and Greek led to the following credentials. He received credit in these languages in class hours of credit either at the University of Michigan or at the Dallas Theological Seminary as follows: In Classical or Koine Greek, 66 semester hours; in Hebrew, 25 semester hours; a total of 91 semester hours in combined Biblical languages. In addition to these 91 semester hours, Dr. Waite has received credit for 27 additional hours in other languages, divided as follows: Latin, 8 semester hours; French, 8 semester hours; Spanish, 11 semester hours. The grand total of languages, in terms of semester hours, in addition to the many other related courses taken at schools for work on the author's A.B., M.A., Th.M., Th.D., and/or Ph.D. has been 118 semester hours in languages. This is only 2 semester hours short of a solid 4 year undergraduate course consisting of 120 semester hours required for graduation in most universities today.

The first part of 2 Timothy 3:16 in the King James Bible contains **eight** English words, "**All scripture is given by inspiration of God.**" The Greek text has only **three** Words. **PASA** (every or all) **GRAPHE** (Word or Words written down) **THEOPNEUSTOS** (God-breathed). These three Words refer exclusively to God's miraculous action of His original breathing out of His Hebrew, Aramaic, and Greek Words of the Old and the New Testaments. This miracle occurred one time only and will never and can never be repeated. These Words do not refer to any Bible translation in any language of the world.

THEOPNEUSTOS is a compound adjective which comes from two Greek words, THEOS (God) and PNEUSTOS (an adjective meaning "breathed") PNEUSTOS comes from the verb, PNEO "to breathe." It does not come from nor is it synonymous with the noun, PNEUMA. It comes clearly from the verb, PNEO (to breathe"). **Gail Riplinger and others are totally in error to claim that an adjective (PNEUSTOS) could be taken as a noun (PNEUMA). This is contrary to all Greek grammar, whether classical or Koine. It is clearly false teaching and false doctrine.**

In the Greek text, there is no verb that links these three Words together. The word. "IS" is implied, even though not stated. The adjective THEOPNEUSTOS modifies GRAPHE. All of this GRAPHE has been once and for all THEOPNEUSTOS (God-breathed) and never will God repeat this miracle "breathing out" in any form or in any way. This verse teaches clearly that God "breathed out" all of His original Hebrew, Aramaic, and Greek Words. God did not "breathe out" or "inspire" any other words in any language of the world. It was a unique "breathing out" which God has never repeated, nor will He ever repeat."[3]

Errors and False Doctrine

Now, to whom are you going to listen? Are you going to listen to a man who has a remarkable Christian testimony as well as superb training or to others who have violated doctrines of Scripture and

---

[3] From a personal email that was sent to fully and clearly explain the three Greek Words from the original text on 1/1/2010. It is on file.

PREFACE

twisted them to their benefit concerning marriage, divorce, remarriage, and lying?

The Greek word, theopneustos, is a very technical term. It occurs only ONCE in the New Testament. This is contrary to Mrs. Riplinger's statement on page 1185 in *Hazardous Matierials* that the Greek word "is translated 322 times as "spirit" (i.e. in **spir**ation) and never as the tangible word 'breath…'" Of course, Mrs. Riplinger intended to say the Greek word, pneuma, which she believes is THE underlying word of theopneustos. But, as our expert Dr. Waite has testified in the quote above, that is INCORRECT. Who are you going to believe?

In addition, she is wrong about the number of occurrences of the Greek word, pneuma, or its cognates, which occurs 385 times in 350 verses.[4]

Here is an example to help clarify 2 Tim. 3:16. A certain condition may require a doctor to order two million units of aqueous penicillin to be given intramuscularly. If a doctor tells a nurse that **"all"** of the prescribed injection of penicillin "is given" (e.g., for this condition[5]), he does not mean that it "is given" repeatedly, or in separated amounts, over many hours, days, months, or years (e.g., repeatedly) in many intramuscular sites; but all "is given" "once." When God gave the Words recorded in each book or epistle of the canon, the book *"is given;"* it **is** the Words breathed-out by God to the prophets and apostles to record for a "foundation." The false application of "is given" to translations throughout the centuries must stop. Inspiration of translations is a false doctrine concocted by men to justify a position when they were caught proclaiming a doctrine that cannot be substantiated by the Scripture, by the grammar of passages in question, or by history. *"All Scripture is given by inspiration"* does not mean the Words of God are repeatedly given over and over and over again in translations, which, more times than not, are poor translations.

---

[4] SwordSearcher, Version 5.5.1.3, © 1995-2009 StudyLamp Software LLC, Broken Arrow, OK, US

[5] This illustration is from the treatment of a very common bacterial disease often acquired from fornication. A massive dose of aqueous penicillin "is given" **once** intramuscularly for a cure.

The following is another example of just how ridiculous all of this has become. In light of wrong exegesis of 2 Tim. 3:16 by many, if it is applied to Matthew 28:18, they believe when Jesus said, "*All power **is given** unto me in heaven and earth*" that He meant "all power" is **repeatedly** given unto Him from time to time (just as they believe inspiration "is given" from time to time in translations). Furthermore, those claiming "is given" in 2 Timothy 3:16 applies to "all translations" or "any translation" or "certain translations" or "the King James Bible translation" need to prayerfully consider the effects of this false teaching concerning translations presently existing as well as those currently in progress around the world.

Truncating of Quotes

In order to avoid the many inaccurate statements in Mrs. Riplinger's work, she should abandon the truncating of quotes that contribute to a biased re-creating of an author's intent or purpose. (see Dr. DiVietro's work to follow and the "Appendix" pp. 285-313 for examples).

Riplinger's Potential Influence

The opinions of Mrs. Riplinger need to be addressed. Why? In order to protect those who may be potentially influenced by her views with which we do not agree and to present facts that are contrary to those presented by Mrs. Riplinger. Additionally, following her teaching will lead to the abandonment of the study of Biblical languages, which we believe will seriously affect the proper training of pastors, missionaries, and others in Christian ministries.

Furthermore, several of those individuals presently alive who were accused of various errors, charged with incorrect statements and actions, or quoted incorrectly have contacted us with their comments about and corrections to Mrs. Riplinger's statements. They have proclaimed that there are many serious errors that she has made in her work(s). A few of the claims are listed below. Several individuals have

PREFACE

allowed their statements to be published in the "Appendix" (p. 285ff) to this work by submitting examples and substantiating the evidence.

We would suggest from the evidence in the "Appendix" of this work by Dr. DiVietro beginning on page 285 that Mrs. Riplinger should heed her own advice. She says on page 54 in *Hazardous Materials*:

> "My burden for college students has led me to pray daily that those who lie to them would **repent**, and should they refuse, their lies would be silenced. Perhaps they should pursue *other* jobs where their talent for lying would do no *spiritual* harm. Selling used cars might be the logical position. The Lord *has* chosen to stop several professors and Bible doubters in their tracks, sending some for rehabilitation to used car lots, where lying has strict legal consequences." (my bolding, HDW)

After many months, her former friends to whom she lied about her multiple marriages, informed us that they are still waiting to hear from Mrs. Riplinger on this marriage matter. There is never an excuse for lying, no matter how painful it is. If Mrs. Riplinger did not want to discuss the situation, she should have declared it a personal matter and not to have lied. Questions concerning marriage and divorce are not related to sexual matters. However, because of scriptural admonitions related to pastors, teachers, and deacons concerning marriage, divorce, and remarriage, questions posed to someone professing to teach others doctrinal matters are **very** legitimate that should be honestly answered. Any church and its leaders should have questions for any "teacher" or "author" concerning the area of marriage, divorce, and remarriage if they are teaching their people through books or personal appearances.

A List of Problems

A summary of the comments concerning Mrs. Riplinger that were received are presented below. They are from very successful pastors, missionaries, teachers, authors, and educators. Their names are withheld because of the present prevalent bitterness sweeping Christendom.

CLEANING-UP HAZARDOUS MATERIALS

1. As a woman, she has wrongly assumed the role of a teacher and corrector of theologians. (1 Tim. 2:12)
2. She has become a teacher of men even though she is a woman (and a twice divorced and remarried woman). (1 Tim. 2:11)
3. She seems to desire wrongly to be the "sole" establisher, determiner, or exegete of truth for all believers in this age as demonstrated by the tone of her work(s). (1 Tim. 2:14-15)
4. She has had ethical problems related to lying about multiple marriages and divorces (Col. 3:9) (see the "Appendix" pp. 285ff), but she declares any work by others who have had moral or ethical problems as completely invalid and useless (Jn. 8:7). If this is true, should not her work be declared completely useless also? Perhaps the books written by the Apostle Peter, King David, and others should be abandoned because they were sinners. Have we forgotten that we are all sinners?!
5. The fact is that two divorces and three marriages disqualify her from teaching pastors and others, much less that she is a woman and has lied about the marriages (Jam. 3:14, 1 Tim. 3, Tit. 1). (see the "Appendices") Gail Anne Ludwig is her maiden name. Gail Latessa Kaleda Riplinger would be her name with the three marriages included. (See the "Appendix.")
6. She falsely claims Dr. Scrivener back-translated the Greek text underlying the King James Bible. (See this work and the "Appendix.")
7. She falsely claims Donald Waite, Jr. said that Scrivener back-translated his Greek text. (See p. 357, 634, 637, 640, 962 in *Hazardous Materials*.) (See the "Appendix" and this work for a rebuttal, pp. 204ff and 306ff.)
8. She falsely claims Donald Waite, Jr. used several lexicons that are known to be corrupted to define the words in the footnotes of the Defined King James Bible when in fact he used primarily six dictionaries, but on occasion consulted lexicons in difficult places. (See the "Appendix," page 306ff.)
9. She is not a formally trained linguist, but has concluded that many linguists in the past and present are wrong about most things. (See many places in *Hazardous Materials*.)

PREFACE

10. She attended a charismatic church in the past and many of her conclusions seem to be influenced by that experience.
11. She denies polysemy for some words, but uses polysemy to defend her various positions elsewhere in her work(s).
12. She denies that the underlying Hebrew, Aramaic, and Greek texts of the King James Bible are the preserved Words of God, but uses the Hebrew and Greek words to defend her position(s). (See many places in *Hazardous Materials*.)
13. She truncates quotes to justify her conclusions. (See *O Timothy* magazine, Vol. 11, Issue 8, 1994, Updated Jan., 2008, FBIS, in the Appendix, pp 300ff and Dr. DiVietro's work to follow.)
14. She wrongly claims any good translation in any language is an "inspired" "pure" text, but never gives specifics as to who determines how to judge a translation. Many translations are very poor. In other words, what is the foundation for comparison? Therefore, who becomes the judge of a translation in any language? The DBS believes it is the God-breathed Hebrew, Aramaic, and Greek Words underlying the King James Bible, which must be consulted and used by translators as the final determination of a good translation.
15. She never addresses the issue of the need for a foundation for translating other than the KJB, insisting that no Hebrew or Greek text is necessary (cf. Eph. 2:20). This is insulting to many nationals who are pastors, teachers, and translators and who use the Hebrew, Aramaic, and Greek Traditional Words **and** the best translations of those texts in other languages for their translating work, just as other good translations have done.
16. She declares that "the faith" found in the writings of the prophets and apostles, which is the foundation in Hebrew, Aramaic, and Greek Words, was **not** "once delivered," but repeatedly "given by inspiration" (i.e. new revelations) in translations down through the centuries. Her ilk is comparable to false prophets in the past who proclaim 'new' revelations. Mrs. Riplinger and her followers need to carefully review the scholarly work of F. H. A. Scrivener, M.A., D.C.L. LL.D., *The Authorized Edition of the English Bible (1611), Its Subsequent Reprints and Modern Representatives*. In order to

CLEANING-UP HAZARDOUS MATERIALS

assist those who are intellectually honest, Appendix A of Dr. Scrivener's work is on pages 334ff. If the KJB was 'inspired', why were so many editions and revisions needed?

17. She wrongly uses gematria to support her "proofs."
18. She wrongly claims the description of the Greek tenses and moods in all Greek grammar books is wrong and should be abandoned.
19. She wrongly claims Acts chapter 2 supports her contention that the Scriptures were received and recorded immediately as inspired "translations." She forgot passages such as Acts 2:43, 47 and 1 Cor. 14:5, which reveal that the temporary gifts, such as tongues, were for establishing and edifying the early church (see Dr. DiVietro's comments to follow).
20. She wrongly claims the verb in 2 Timothy 3:16, "is," means any book called the Scripture or a Bible throughout the centuries "is given" by inspiration.
21. Since she does not believe the Hebrew, Aramaic, or Greek Words behind the KJB are the preserved Words of God, in order to establish her false position she claims that translations are given by the Spirit of God just as the words in Hebrew, Aramaic, and Greek were given to the apostles and prophets. We believe this is predicated on her charismatic tendency and misunderstanding of Scripture.
22. She wrongly claims 2 Peter 1:20-21 refers to spoken words of the prophets only and not to the recorded Words of God's revelation to the apostles **and** prophets. Then, how does she explain Jesus' exclamation that His spoken Words, *"the same,"* would judge us in the last day if His spoken words were not recorded (Jn. 12:47-48)? God would be unjust.
23. She wrongly claims that the Words of God in Hebrew, Aramaic, and Greek are not perfectly preserved as God promised; rather, she claims that His Words are only preserved perfectly and kept pure in "good" translations.
24. She wrongly defines "original" as referring to "the original **manuscripts**" only and she does not help others to understand that most authors are referring to "the original **words**" in Hebrew, Aramaic, and Greek. In contradistinction to her claims, those

PREFACE

Words have been perfectly preserved in copies throughout the centuries in the Traditional Text manuscripts, various printed editions, lectionaries, and church elder writings as God promised. The handwritten manuscripts underlying the Traditional Words are virtually identical (see the Appendix, pp. 331ff, for a description of the "Received Text" or "Traditional Text" as used by the Dean Burgon Society).

25. She fails to consider that many false books have been written by the enemies of individuals in order to discredit them or their work. For example, many of the claims by authors past and present concerning King James or Dean John William Burgon are bogus. Consider that many authors have accused King James of being a homosexual, but it has been established that he was not. Others have denied the truths uncovered by Dean Burgon concerning the origin of the Traditional Text. Using spin, they declare that Dean Burgon was simply a noisy, unscholarly believer. Therefore, could many of the quotes, which she uses to destroy trust in lexicographers and their work, be lies by their enemies?

26. She makes an egregious error when she leads others to believe that lexicons serve as the ultimate guide for translators or students of God's Words. There are many things that bear upon a translator's choice of a word while translating, including his own theological bias and interpretation, context, polysemy, cultural history, etc. Lexicons are not "translators," but rather aids to translators. Furthermore, exegetes, translators, students, and teachers of God's words are not bound by lexicons. They are bound by the received Words of God (Jn. 17:8), which, if they are accurately and faithfully translated, carry the authority of God's Words; that is, they are quick, powerful, piercing, and discerning (Heb. 4:12).

27. Mrs. Riplinger is like a Ruckmanite because she teaches that the King James Bible is better than the preserved original Hebrew, Aramaic, and Greek Words. She believes there is no need for learning by using Hebrew or Greek or other tools. If this were true, believers would not have the KJB, because the KJB translators "laboriously" translated the English Bible from the original

language Words in Hebrew, Aramaic, and Greek (see the Preface to the 1611 King James Bible available online at many sites).
28. She falsely claims Wycliffe did not use the Latin Vulgate as the basis for his translation, but that he used Hebrew, Greek, and Old Latin sources. (FBIS News Service, August 29, 2005).
29. There is a poor understanding of the Hebrew, Aramaic, and Greek text called the "Received Texts," "Traditional Texts", or call it whatever you would like that underlies the King James Bible. That foundation and its accurate and faithful translation has been blessed by God in unfathomable ways. Thus, the DBS stands upon that foundation as the fulfillment of the promise of God to preserve His Words. Those Words were received "once" without the need for repeated revisions or editions as the King James Bible has needed. (see the Appendix, pages 331ff)
30. Please see the additional list on pages 9-10 of this work compiled by Dr. DiVietro.

Be Aware of the Following

In light of the comments above and those to follow by Pastor DiVietro, Th.M., Ph.D., many are suspicious of the work of Mrs. Riplinger. This brief analysis of a book that is over 1000 pages is not meant to be complete. It would take several years to look up every reference and to comment on every statement. Dr. DiVietro has commented on those areas that he believes are critical and need to be addressed immediately.

Please be aware that Dr. DiVietro is severely compromised by his current medical and surgical situation that has left him with the inability to type. He was severely injured in Iraq while helping to establish a Baptist church in that country.

Therefore, he has dictated his response to *Hazardous Materials*. Many of the auto-transcribing mistakes have been corrected, but there are surely others. Please be understanding. He has done an excellent job in light of his circumstances. The Dean Burgon Society (DBS) was anxious to get the information included in this book out to others, so please pardon any lingering errors. The DBS is confident that the

PREFACE

general overall theme in Mrs. Riplinger's work is accurately examined and the general inaccuracy is exposed by Dr. DiVietro. It should be very helpful to many who are honestly seeking how to receive *Hazardous Materials* and who are not being emotionally influenced.

Dr. DiVietro's Work Was Not Done In Secret

Mrs. Riplinger was informed that Dr. DiVietro's response to *Hazardous Materials* was in progress. Dr. DiVietro said:

> "Mrs. Riplinger was aware that I was writing this critique. She was told by both myself and a third party. I never hid my disagreement with her assertions. On October 14, 2009, I wrote an e-mail to Mrs. Riplinger asking why her organization was not honoring my order of several items from her catalogue. This email was the last in a series of emails attempting to obtain previous writings of Mrs. Riplinger cited in *Hazardous Materials*. In that email I explained that I knew she knew that I was writing a critique of *Hazardous Materials* and since it included citations from *In Awe of Thy Word* I wanted to check references and be sure that I was not misrepresenting her. I wrote:
>
>> **I know that you have been informed that I am reviewing your book *Hazardous Materials*. I also know that you have been informed that I do not agree with some of your premises.**
>
> Two days later on October 16, 2009, she responded:
>
>> **Should we not work together as scholars and pursuers of truth. If we can work together as brother and sister in Christ, I will be most happy to send you, as a gift, the books /In Awe of Thy Word/ and /The Language of the King James Bible./**

In this case, it is not necessary for you to pay for them.

She ultimately honored her word and some of the materials requested were received but not in the media requested.

Lastly, the work to follow by Dr. DiVietro is based upon the publication of *Hazardous Materials* copyrighted in 2008.

H. D. Williams, M.D., Ph.D., A Vice-President
The Dean Burgon Society

Pastor D. A. Waite, Th.D., Ph.D., President,
The Dean Burgon Society
February, 2010.

TABLE OF CONTENTS

TITLE	PAGE
Dedication	
Preface	i
Table of Contents	xv
Introduction	1
A New Premise	12
Riplinger's Challenges	19
Challenge #1	19
Challenge #2	33
Challenge #3	71
Challenge #4	83
Challenge #5	87
Challenge #6	99
Challenge #7	107
Quote And Comments	119
Appendix	285
To Whom It May Concern by Dr. M. Robinson	285
A Testimony by Mrs. D. A. Waite	289
Gail Riplinger's Lies To Dr. and Mrs. Waite by D. Cloud	300
Gail Riplinger's Lies To The Waites, Part 2 by D. Cloud	304
Setting The Record Straight by Donald Waite, Jr.	306
Defined KJB Footnotes, Author and Editor's Introduction by Donald Waite, Jr.	307
What About Gail Riplinger's New Book? by D. Cloud	311
The Fire of London	313
The Gift of Tongues by Pastor Kirk DiVietro	314
KJB Translator Rules	321
Gail Riplingers Marriage Licenses	325
The Received Text, What Is It?	331

Scrivener's Appendix A	334
Index	379
About the Author	391
About the Editor	395

INTRODUCTION

The Marvellous, Miraculous Book

The Bible is a truly marvelous, miraculous book. It is God's revelation of truth to man. God had many options when he chose to reveal his word. In fact he did so by many different methods. Three times God wrote with his own finger: the Ten Commandments (Exodus 20), Belshazzar's palace wall (Daniel 5), and the dust of the ground (John 8). But that was not his preferred mode of inspiration. Sometimes he spoke through dreams (Joseph, Matthew 1.20) and visions (Daniel 7-9). At others he spoke by illustration (Jeremiah 18). But most often he simply spoke to and through a prophet.

Because most of his revelation was done subtly it was necessary for the hearers to recognize the distinction between the words of God and the words of the prophet. Elijah and Elisha were both prophets of God but neither left a book containing his prophecies. They were not the eternal words of God. Obadiah would write the shortest book of the Hebrew Scriptures concerning Edom, not even Israel, and yet it was recognized as the words of God. Jeremiah's prophecy of 70 years was recognized by his contemporary, Daniel, as the words of God. Either Micah quoted Isaiah or Isaiah quoted Micah (Isaiah 2.4, cf. Micah 4.3) recognizing the voice of God in the other's words. Peter even called Paul's writings *scripture* (II Peter 3.16).

Often when the prophets were writing the words of God they had no idea what the full meaning of their prophecy was. Daniel pleaded with God to understand his own prophecy. Peter wrote,

> "Searching what, or what manner of time the Spirit of Christ which was in them did signify, when it testified beforehand the sufferings of Christ, and the glory that should follow."
> 1 Peter 1:11

And yet the words of the writers of Scripture were quite often written simultaneously by the will and thought of the writers. Paul was responding to questions in I Corinthians. The scribes of Hezekiah gleaned proverbs out of the 3000 written by Solomon (Proverbs 25.1). The history of Israel and Judah was gleaned from various chronicles and secular histories. The amazing thing is that when the ink dried, the earthly Scriptures were exact duplicates of those already written in heaven (Psalm 119.89).

2 Timothy 3:16 Explained

At this point it is important to summarize both Dr. Waite's excellent exegesis of II Timothy 3:16 and Dr. H.D. Williams' comments on the exegesis found in the Preface.

2 Timothy 3:16
All   scripture   is   given by inspiration of God,

Πασα   γραφη   [ἐστιν]   θεόπνευστος

As he told us, the first part of 2 Timothy 3:16 in the King James Bible contains eight English words, "All scripture is given by inspiration of God." The Greek text has only three Words. **PASA** (every or all) **GRAPHE** (Word or Words written down) **THEOPNEUSTOS** (God-breathed). These three Words refer exclusively to God's miraculous action of His original breathing out of His Hebrew, Aramaic, and Greek Words of the Old and the New Testaments. They ARE given because they WERE given. This miracle occurred one time only and will never and can never be repeated. These Words do not refer to any Bible translation in any language of the world.

THEOPNEUSTOS translated "given by God" is a compound adjective which comes from two Greek words, THEOS (God) and PNEUSTOS (an adjective meaning "breathed"), PNEUSTOS comes from the verb, PNEO "to breathe." It does not come from nor is it synonymous with the noun, PNEUMA. It comes clearly from the verb, PNEO (to breathe"). **Gail Riplinger and others are totally in error to claim that an adjective (PNEUSTOS) could be taken**

INTRODUCTION

as a noun (PNEUMA). This is contrary to all Greek grammar, whether classical or Koine. It is clearly false teaching and false doctrine.

In the Greek text, there is no verb that links these three Words together. The word, "IS", is implied, even though not stated. Therefore Mrs. Riplinger's exegesis based on the tense of "is" is another argument from silence! The adjective describes writings that already existed and therefore the implied sense of completion. There is nothing to justify her translation of "are being given" which is necessary if this verse applies to translations. All of this GRAPHE has been once and for all THEOPNEUSTOS (God-breathed) and God will never repeat this miracle "breathing out" in any form or in any way. This verse teaches clearly that God "breathed out" all of His original Hebrew, Aramaic, and Greek Words. God did not "breathe out" or "inspire" any other words in any language of the world. It was a unique "breathing out" which God has never repeated, nor will He ever repeat."

Does Mrs. Riplinger believe God has not completed His revelation? Is there more to come? No, a thousand times No she would protest. The King James Bible is perfect and cannot be improved or changed. Yet her interpretation of II Timothy 3:16 would suggest that at any moment God might decide to change his word and inspire a new version in English. Is He constantly giving inspiration to the King James Bible? Is He re-inspiring it every second of every day?" Of course not.

As Dr. Williams pointed out, if we accept Mrs. Riplinger's interpretation of the Greek tense here and apply it to Matthew 28:18, *"All power **is given** unto me in heaven and earth,"* then He meant "all power" is **repeatedly** given unto Him from time to time (just as they believe inspiration "is given" from time to time in translations). Furthermore, those claiming "is given" in 2 Timothy 3:16 applies to "all translations" or "any translation" or "certain translations" or "the King James Bible translation" need to prayerfully consider the effects of this false teaching concerning translations presently existing as well as those currently in progress around the world. [πνέω 1 aor. ἔπνευσα; in the NT only of the wind *blow*; substantively ἡ πνέουσα (with αὔρα [*breeze*] understood) *the breeze* (AC 27.40) (Friberg, Timothy and Barbara Friberg; Neva F. Miller, *Analytical Lexicon of the Greek New*

Testament. Logos Research.) This explanation is from a personal email that was sent to fully and clearly explain the three Greek Words from the original text on 1/1/2010. It is on file.]

The Divine-Human Cooperation

The Divine-human cooperation was exactly like that of the new birth. Man is required to believe the Gospel yet he cannot effect the new birth. Mary's body was the source of the material for the body of the Lord Jesus (Hebrews 10.5) and yet He was God from eternity (Micah 5.2) and always existent (John 1.1). As He walked this earth, Jesus was a man who always did perfectly the will of God. He was surrendered fully to the Holy Ghost, and yet at the same time, He did what He did in His own power as the second member of the Godhead (the hypostatic union).

We cannot explain Divine-human cooperation. Anyone who has ever tried has been branded a heretic. Anyone who has ever tried to separate the divine from the human has been found deficient. We are not asked to explain them. We are only asked to accept them.

The Preservation of the Words

God not only chose to give His words by Divine-human cooperation, He chose to preserve them the same way. He could have caused the autographs to supernaturally survive the ravages of time and persecution to be housed in museums somewhere like the US Declaration of Independence and Constitution are housed in our national archives. But then like Nehushtan, the brass serpent, we would worship the objects and not the God they reveal. He chose instead to have imperfect men copy those original documents as his process of preservation. In the early days when the Scriptures existed as single books, it was easy for a careful scribe to faithfully copy the content. Most of the New Testament epistles can be copied in a few hours. The Gospels and larger books of the Hebrew Scriptures would have taken longer. Many copyists would have made replicas of the originals. At the same time the words of Scripture were often

INTRODUCTION

memorized. As a result, in the multiplicity of copies the original was preserved and available. Because God promised that He would preserve His words, by faith, we believe that He did so and His original words are still available to us today.

One of the great indications of this truth is an interesting phenomenon. The men who handled the Scriptures had a general reverence for those writings. Even errant readings were preserved lest the proper reading be accidentally omitted. In the Hebrew Scriptures there are what we call the Kethib and the Qere: that which is written and that which is read. In the New Testament we have variant manuscripts which can be compared making the original reading manifest.

It is a sin to purposely avoid knowledge that is positive in understanding the Scriptures. It should be the desire of every child of God to understand exactly what God has said. The present Bible reader is several steps away from the actual words that God spoke into the hearts and pens of the original writers. He is separated from the writing by at least 2000 years and up to 3500 years. He is separated from the writing by an ocean (geography) and 2000 years of language development. He is separated by culture and custom. Mrs. Riplinger seems to infer that the reader should believe it is a sin to attempt to bridge that chasm.

The Hebrew Scriptures were preserved by careful processes. They had the advantage of being the national treasure of a single people. Scribes were carefully chosen. Letters were counted. The first, last, and middle letters were noted. If a manuscript was found faulty it was generally destroyed. The copies of the Scriptures were carefully guarded. Many of the books were memorized. The result is that when the Dead Sea scrolls moved our evidence of the Hebrew text back by almost 1000 years we found no significant differences.

The Christian Scriptures were different. They were produced and written to various audiences throughout Asia Minor and Europe. The Gospel of Luke and the Acts of the Apostles were addressed to a particular individual as were several of the epistles of Paul. These various books were reproduced locally and distributed. Very early in their history they were translated into various languages. Even when variants found their way into the text there were enough other copies of the Scriptures to compare and ascertain the true reading. Since the persecutions of Christians were generally local, in the first 200 years of Christianity there were safe havens for the Scriptures until they had been so widely distributed that even the universal, empire-wide persecutions could not destroy the Scriptures.

Translation of the Scriptures

The Scriptures as they were inspired and first written in the Hebrew Aramaic and Greek originals would do you and me very little good. When the world ceased to speak Greek as its *lingua franca,* God providentially allowed the translation of the Scriptures into the local languages. In the western part of the Roman Empire, this was Latin. These early Latin translations are not the Latin Vulgate of the Roman Catholic Church. They were the language of the people and preachers of the empire. In the East, the Bible was translated into Aramaic, Gothic, Georgian, etc. as it reached beyond the bounds of the Empire and into other peoples. These translations were only as good as the people who did them. God did not re-inspire the Scriptures in those languages. If the translation was accurate, then the people had the words of God in their own language. If the translation was poor, then the people had books which contained the words of God and man.

Over the course of the last 2000 years languages have changed more rapidly and drastically than they did in the 4000 years before Christ. Translations have multiplied with the evolution of language. Each language-group or ethnic group wanted a Bible in their own understandable language. Missionaries and preachers wanted their audiences to have an accurate Bible in their own language. Some translations were made from previous translations. Others attempted to reach back to the original Greek Hebrew and Aramaic texts. Others were a combination of the two.

While God promised to preserve his words, He never promised that every translation or copy of His word would be perfect. The accuracy of translation depends on the qualifications, both spiritually and linguistically, of the translator(s). It depends on the accuracy of the source that is being translated.

INTRODUCTION

Yet, in all this human confusion, God has promised to preserve his words. That means that you and I can find them and have them today. Most simple Bible believers believe that God did in fact preserve the original Hebrew, Aramaic, and Greek, words. Conservative believers like this author believe that those words are contained in the Masoretic Text of the Hebrew Scriptures and the Received Text of the New Testament that underlie the King James Bible. Less conservative believers believe they are contained in the edited eclectic texts produced by modern textual critics.

Translating, Lexicons, and Grammar

The words of God are preserved into English, if one holds an accurately translated form of the proper Greek Hebrew and Aramaic texts. This author believes that the only place that this occurs consistently and accurately in English is in the King James Bible that was first translated in 1611. While critics point to the various 'revisions,' there was no translational revision of the 1611 text. There were several minor revisions of type face, spelling, and incidentals. The text we now use was done in 1769.

In any translation it is necessary for a translator to understand the vocabulary, grammar, and nuances of both languages. The accuracy and acceptability of the translation will be a direct function of the translator(s)'s knowledge. Vocabulary of a dead language, such as Biblical Greek, Hebrew, and Aramaic, is established by one of two methods. It can be established by a traditional lexicon showing the traditional equivalences. Or, it can be established by reading all available literature written in that language and letting the meanings inductively rise out of the language. Once the basic meaning of a word is established, then the translator must seek its specific meaning in the context and use by the author he is translating. In this case it would be God.

Grammar is established the same way. Once a break-through has been made between two languages, then the translator attempts to define the rules of the language. All languages have similar elements: parts of speech, sentence formation, etc. It is the job of the translator to understand the working of the receptor language. When Adoniram Judson went to Burma there was no written language. In order to translate the Bible into Burmese he had to learn the language and then write a dictionary and a grammar. Then, and only then, he could begin his translation of the Scriptures. Whether the grammar and the lexicon are written or mental, translation is impossible without them.

Since languages are in constant flux, it becomes necessary to revise grammars and lexicons. Since the knowledge of the donor languages increase with discovery and study, it becomes necessary to revise grammars and lexicons. Anyone with the most primitive knowledge of languages and translation knows this. These study aids become obsolete. That does not mean that a lexicon written 50 years ago is utterly useless. It just means that the translator must confirm its accuracy and detail before he puts his full dependence on it.

Interpretation

The final step in this chain is interpretation. Interpretation is the work of the student who is studying the text in the receptor language to accurately understand what underlies the words he is reading. For this reason, English speaking Bible students prior to the second half of the 20th century were required to learn Greek and Hebrew, the languages of the inspired words of God. A commentary attempts to fully enlighten the student to the full impact of the original language. By knowing the languages and the tools for understanding them, an interpreter of the Scriptures was able to make an informed judgment on a comment in a commentary.

Modern Bible students are lazy. They have no time for Greek and Hebrew. Bible institutes and colleges marginalize the study of those languages in favor of ministry methodology. If a student will not learn Greek or Hebrew, he is completely dependent on the knowledge of Greek and Hebrew of someone else. As a result, the modern Bible student is woefully unprepared to interpret the Scriptures for himself. He picks a meaning that fits his comfort zone. As a result we have the greatest resources and the least knowledge of any generation of Bible teachers.

INTRODUCTION

Hazardous Materials

We, Bible believing pastors, send our young people away to Bible colleges and institutes only to have them return minus their faith in the authority of the preserved words of God. Instead they quote *scholars* of dubious quality to justify their contemporary theology and methods. Our modern churches are a confused vortex of contemporary versus traditional organizations with contempt for anyone who stands strongly on the authority of Scripture. Even if they do stand strongly on the authority of Scripture the question emerges, *which Scriptures?* There seems to be a new translation every week.

In reaction, pastors have *moved* to the opposite extreme. We would rather teach our students in the church than send them to be destroyed by some college. If the problem is too much confusing information, we will provide a list of 'approved' reference works. We will stand on the King James Bible.

Whenever two strong ocean currents meet there is a whirlpool. That is what produced Paul's Euroclydon (Acts 27). The collision of modern scholarship with traditional simple fundamentalist beliefs has caused a maelstrom. Into this maelstrom of confusion sails Mrs. Riplinger's *Hazardous Materials*. As preachers and Bible students become more and more dependent on Bible study aids, their ministry and authority rest more and more on the authors and quality of those aids. Most of the Bible study aids produced in the last fifty years are non-critical repetitions of former aids. In layman's terms they are plagiaries. Because copyrights have run out, modern authors can copy vast portions of former works and claim them as their own.

The Problems In *Hazardous Materials* Summarized

Hazardous Materials is an attempt to give a way out for those who hold to historic Christian beliefs. Unfortunately it creates more problems than it solves. As this author read the book, I noted the following errors which I will address in subsequent chapters.

1. She bases much of her writing on *ad hominem* attacks.

2. She bases much of her opposition on guilt by association.
3. She bases much of her opposition to the writings and works of the people she rejects on their moral character.
4. She bases much of her opposition to the writings of works of the people she rejects on their theology.
5. She demonstrates a shallow understanding of how languages work.
6. She appears to purposely misunderstand how translations are produced from one language to another.
7. She bases her exaltation of the King James Bible on a false theory of inspiration.
8. She perverts the meaning of Pentecost, ignoring the biblical explanation.
9. She presents very little evidence to support her positive theory. While all of the targets may have been wrong, even willfully wrong, their wrongness does not automatically prove her rightness.
10. She is a woman who violates I Timothy 5, usurping authority and teaching men.

When this author taught in a Bible college as a part-time adjunct professor, he would assign term papers of specific length. He gave very detailed directions for the writing of the papers. He always warned the students that he had a fluff detector. One particular student handed in a six page paper which was reduced to 1½ pages when the fluff was removed. In this writer's opinion, Mrs. Riplinger's tome contains a little legitimate information and a whole lot of intellectual fluff. While many of the things that she says may be true, they have nothing to do with proving her thesis. Although it was 1200 pages long, it took less than three days to read.

The Thesis of *Hazardous Materials*

A, or perhaps the, thesis of this book is that the King James Bible and other translations are inspired words of God. Yet she ignores the very criterion by which she discounts the Greek and Hebrew texts of the Bible—minute differences between printed texts. If this is her criterion, then one must ask which King James Bible is perfect in all of

INTRODUCTION

its minutiae? Is it the 1611 Cambridge or the 1611 Oxford? Is it the 1769 Cambridge or the 1769 Oxford? Since the shapes of letters provide their meaning, is it the original font in which 's' looks like 'f' and 'u' and 'v' have reversed roles? Is it the version where 'J' looks like 'I' or the modern font which changes all these?

If Mrs. Riplinger were arguing that an accurate translation of the Bible preserved all the power and presence of God to the modern vernacular reader, we would agree whole heartedly. But since she is not, we cannot agree. If a person is bi-lingual and the 'Holy Bible' in the two languages are not 100% consistent, then which is the inspired version? If the previous vernacular Bibles are inspired, should not there be a perfect agreement between them in all minutiae? And if not, how can we know which is the inspired copy and which is the uninspired version? Or can a Bible be partially inspired (in the parts that do agree perfectly) and partially uninspired (in the places where it does not)?

Mrs. Riplinger's thesis about the Bible affects her thesis of this book. Since her Bible carries its own inspiration, then all Greek and Hebrew texts are obsolete. All study aids which refer to them are detrimental to the understanding of God's inspired words. And further, she insists, they were written by ungodly men who often were determined to undermine and destroy the power and authority of the King James Bible. Anyone using these corrupting influences, the Greek and Hebrew texts, and/or the Greek and Hebrew language aids, will necessarily be affected in a negative way.

To respond to Mrs. Riplinger's theses, this author will use her own suggestion. In her "Epilogue," she presents seven challenges to anyone who would object to her findings. This author will use her seven challenges as the structure of this review and rebuttal further on in this work.

A NEW PREMISE

The Foundational Thesis of *Hazardous Materials*

From the beginning, let this point be evident. Whenever the proper Hebrew, Aramaic, and Greek texts are translated accurately into English, we have the preserved words of God. On the other hand, this author does not believe that modern translators have or can produce such translations. He would no more trust modern translators, no matter how sincere they are, to translate the Bible than he would trust the present members of the United States Congress to rewrite the United States Constitution. This author is not an advocate of contemporary translations. His English Bible is the King James Bible. He does not find that any modern translation comes up to it in quality or accuracy. While many of its conventions are archaic and difficult to the modern reader, it preserves into English the inspired text better than any other effort.

Hazardous Materials is the sequel to *In Awe of Thy Word*. The latter presents an almost Kabbalistic defense of the inspiration of the King James Bible. The **foundational thesis** of *Hazardous Materials* **is that all study aids are unnecessary and, in fact, detrimental to understanding the Words of God**. According to this thesis, the King James Bible is not the result of translating Hebrew, Aramaic, and Greek originals into English. The King James Bible is supposedly the result of purifying an original inspired Anglo-Germanic version of the Bible (this author will cite specifics later). According to Mrs. Riplinger's theory, on the day of Pentecost God gave the apostles the ability to write the Scriptures in every language of Acts 2 and possibly in every active language in the world of that day.

> "God knew the Greeks, as a nation could not bear the responsibility of preserving the word of God. He immediately provided a safety net in Acts 2 and 1 Corinthians 14:21 to catch the words they were apt to lose. The Acts 2 "Scriptures in tongues," as Wycliffe called them, were created directly by the Holy Ghost and were not man-made *translations* from

A NEW PREMISE

'the' Greek. These "Scriptures" would have quickly been available in Latin, Coptic, Gothic, Celtic, Ethiopic, Arabic, Hebrew and a myriad of other languages." (p.1095)

This writer believes that he understands the following statements from *In Awe of Thy Word*.

"Paul said, "We use great plainness of speech..." (2 Cor. 3.12). Was that verse directed at the Corinthian Greeks only? That verse and others were plain to them but they would not be plain to all, so the Holy Ghost gave the gift of tongues." (p. 494)

"The Holy Ghost inspired the word of God for "every nation under heaven." (Some have not chosen to keep it *widely* in print as Amos 8:11 fortells). All pure Bibles had their matrix in Acts 2:4, 5: "And they were all filled with the Holy Ghost, and began to speak with other tongues, as the Spirit gave them utterance ... every nation under heaven." (p. 542)

Mrs. Riplinger seems to say that Paul did just not write a Greek original of Romans, which was then translated into other languages. Instead, Paul wrote a Latin version to the Romans, a Greek version to the Greeks, an Aramaic version to the Syrians, etc. These were not translations of the inspired original. Each was separately and equally inspired to the people of that language group. As the modern languages developed, the inspired version was carried along at each stage of development. Various editors would *purify* the inspired version into the contemporary version of the language.

At other times she does say that in the apostolic age, the Bible was translated into the various languages of the world under the inspiration of the Holy Ghost.

"The words on the cross spoke, not just in Hebrew and Greek, the languages of the original scriptures, but in Latin. This signifies the opening of "the faith among all nations" (Rom. 1:5). The word of God was given in the "language" of "every nation under heaven." The Bible, once complete, was translated so that each man could have a Bible "in his own language" (Acts 2:4, 5, 6, 7).

> All of these vernacular Bibles, written during the first centuries after Christ, were destroyed during the persecution of Roman Emperor Diocletian in A.D. 303." (In Awe of Thy Word p.620)

According to Mrs. Riplinger the English Bible was a refinement of the Gothic Bible.

> "Gothic was a major world language spoken at the time of Christ. It was spoken as early as the "300's B.C. [300 years *before* Christ]. "Goths had been recruited in increasing numbers into the Roman army." "[T]heir relations with the adjacent Roman empire were close ... receiving diplomatic subsidies and sending soldiers to fight" for Rome...
> The Gothic language was then one of those spoken in the book of Acts chapter 2, when the disciples "were all filled with the Holy Ghost, and began to speak with other tongues ... of every nation under heaven." "Every man heard them speak in his own language " (Acts 2;4, 6, 7). Those unnamed Christians who received this Gothic gospel message, took it to the Goths, obeying Christ's command to "Go ye into all the world, and preach the gospel" (Mark 16: 15) ... "unto the uttermost part of the earth" (Acts 1:8)."(Ibid. p.621)
> "The original New Testament was complete before A.D. 100; the Gothic Bible must have been translated *immediately* to fill the need of the nearby Gothic Christians..."(Ibid. p.622)
> "The original Latin and Gothic Bibles from Acts 2 carried Christ to Europe. As languages continued to be confounded by divergent dialects, God gave each of these languages his words, "forever settled in heaven," which would judge people in the last day (John 12:48). As language changed, Holy Bibles were "given" and "purified" (2 Tim. 3:16, Psalm 12:6, 7) to fit the linguistic need. The Italic, Gallic, Celtic, and Old Saxon editions came forth. As will be demonstrated, *new* New Testaments have usually been birthed from previous vernacular New Testaments. For example, the pure Old Latin Bible became the Romaunt, Provençal, Vaudois, Toulouse, Piedmontese, and Romanese Bibles." (*Hazardous Materials* p. 1105)

Supposedly Tyndale and Luther didn't actually translate the Bible. They just updated the language of their inspired version into their contemporary vernacular.

As a result of this process every *Holy Bible*, Mrs. Riplinger's term for the authoritative Bible in a given language, is free standing. The meaning of its words does not extend back past the production of that Bible. The reader should determine the meaning of the words of Scripture by using methods described in *In Awe of Thy Word*, for example, simply reading ten words before and ten words after. These *Holy Bibles* are made up of Holy Ghost given "holy separate from sinners' vocabulary." It would be sacrilege to try to define or expand on them to make them more understandable to the modern reader. These words must never be changed.

Facts Do Not Support Her Thesis

Can this thesis be supported by facts? It would be nice if it could be. But unfortunately it rests on a very weak foundation. It has been a basic premise of Bible study that if an idea is new it's not true and if it's true it's not new. The fact of Bible translation cannot be reasonably denied. Even the King James translators, whom Mrs. Riplinger so admires, freely admitted that their work was a translation.

"Translation Necessary

But how shall men meditate in that, which they cannot understand? How shall they under-stand that which is kept close in an unknown tongue? as it is written, Except I know the power of the voice, I shall be to him that speaketh, a Barbarian, and he that speaketh, shall be a Barbarian to me. [1 Cor 14] The Apostle excepteth no tongue; not Hebrew the ancientest, not Greek the most copious, not Latin the finest. Nature taught a natural man to confess, that all of us in those tongues which we do not understand, are plainly deaf; we may turn the deaf ear unto them. The Scythian counted the Athenian, whom he did not understand, barbarous; so the Roman did the Syrian, and the Jew (even S. Jerome himself calleth the Hebrew tongue barbarous, belike because it was strange to so many) so the Emperor of Constantinople calleth the Latin tongue, barbarous, though Pope Nicolas do storm at it: so the Jews long before Christ called all other nations, Lognazim, which is little better than barbarous. Therefore as one complaineth, that always in the Senate of Rome, there was one or other that called for an interpreter: so lest the Church be driven to the like exigent, it is necessary to have trans-lations in a readiness. Translation it is that openeth the window, to let in the light; that breaketh the shell, that we may eat the kernel; that putteth aside the curtain, that we may look into the most Holy place; that removeth the cover of the well, that we may come by the water, even as Jacob rolled away the stone from the mouth of the well, by which means the flocks of Laban were watered [Gen 29:10]. Indeed without translation into the vulgar tongue, the unlearned are but like children at Jacob's well (which was deep) [John 4:11] without a bucket or something to draw with; or as that person mentioned by Isaiah, to whom when a sealed book was delivered, with this motion, Read this, I pray thee, he was fain to make this answer, I cannot, for it is sealed. [Isa 29:11]"

To assert that the King James Bible was a purification of the proto-Anglo version of the Scriptures and not a translation is just not accurate. The translators were very clear that until and unless the Scriptures were brought from the dead languages of Hebrew, Aramaic, and Greek into readable English, the English speaking person was at the mercy of the learned 'clergy.' They did not claim their work to be a 'purification' of the proto-English; but were quite forward that they translated, and especially from the Greek and Hebrew originals. They made no pretense. They refer to the many sources which they used as corroborative materials but they were consistent in their claim that their translation came from the Greek and Hebrew. They were willing to admit that they built on the foundations which came before them, but also stated that they considered and retranslated every word of the Greek and Hebrew texts. The entire text of their "Introduction" may be found in many places on the internet.

A NEW PREMISE

The Fire of London, 1666

Much to our chagrin, the notes of the King James Bible translation committee along with the specifics of the Greek, Hebrew, and Aramaic texts that they translated are lost to history. They were destroyed in a fire that devastated London in the year 1666 (see the Appendix, pp. 313ff). The notes of John Boyce (spelled in various ways) have been recovered and do give some insights into the translation but do not give us all the specifics.

The Argument From Silence Is Invalid

No strong argument can ever be made from silence. Mrs. Riplinger is not free to assert that the translators did not avail themselves of such lexicons, grammars, commentaries, and word studies as were available to them in that day. In the book *In Awe of Thy Word* she states that the translators did use lexicons and grammars. She admits that they were intimately familiar with written grammars. She extols their extensive libraries of ancient Greek and Latin writings. Her primary issue is the quality of these aids. In *Hazardous Materials*, this fact is quietly neglected or diminished leaving the impression that they made no use of these materials.

She cannot assure us with surety and guarantee that every King James translator was born again, filled with the Spirit, and divinely manipulated at every moment of the translation project. We can only judge the result.

History does testify to the success of the effort which culminated in 1611. It exceeded the expectations and hopes of its translators. The King James Bible has ascended to the top of the English Bibles. While others have come and challenged it for a generation, they are relegated to the dusty shelves of libraries while the King James Bible is still in the hands of those who dearly love the Words of God. After each challenge, it emerges the favorite and re-exerts its pre-eminence. Without apology this author still believes it to be the most accurate and trustworthy preservation of the Words of God in the English language.

He does not however believe that it was specially and directly inspired in 1611 and then purified in 1769.

Some Translations Only Contain The Words of God

Any place the proper texts of the Old and New Testaments are accurately translated, we have the words of God. While other translations contain the Words of God, in this writer's opinion, the KJB is the only extant translation to accurately translate the correct Hebrew and Greek texts from Genesis 1.1 through Revelation 22.21, from "In the beginning God. . ." to the last Amen.

Mrs. Riplinger provides the framework for her own refutation. She asks leading questions. Unlike a good lawyer, she does not realize that you should never ask questions of a witness if you don't know his response in advance. And so, she asks and this author answers her challenges.

RIPLINGER'S CHALLENGES

CHALLENGE #1

Quote: "Define *the specific* text indicated when you say "in *the* Greek" or "in the Hebrew," with full bibliographic information." (p. 1193)

The Differences in Texts

Although various editors have taken in hand to print the Greek New Testament, every one of them has some controversial reading(s). Are there any variations in the various printings of Mrs. Riplinger's books? If there are (and the writer knows there are), which is the authoritative version? Do the variations mean that nothing she says has any value? Of course not.

Mrs. Riplinger is right when she says that no two printed Greek texts or Hebrew texts are perfectly identical. She takes several chapters in her attempts to prove what is common knowledge. HOWEVER, what she has NOT SAID is far more important than what she said. The main differences between primary printed Textus Receptus Greek texts, purporting to be the underlying text of the King James Bible, are very minor.[6] The primary differences between Scrivener and Stephanus are the names of books of the New Testament and the reversal of punctuation (e.g., commas for colons). This author is not aware of any scholar who asserts that the titles of the books are inspired. Scrivener often used short titles while Stephanus used longer titles. It is not the

---

[6] This author wrote the computer codes for both the Stephanus 1550 and the Scrivener's Texts for Logos. He has detailed notebooks of both of these texts compared to the United Bible Society 2nd Edition Greek New Testament. He further presented a paper to the Dean Burgon Society annual meeting demonstrating that that many of the differences are in titles of books and subscripts at the end of books. He writes from personal tedious research.

title of the books but the content of the books that concerns the translator. Differences of titles do not equate into inaccuracies.

There are a few minute differences separating the various printed texts. Some are intended while others are typographical differences. Scrivener was quite candid about his work. He explained that it was his intention to provide the Greek text that was translated into the King James Bible, Cambridge. He stated that he chose the last printed edition of Beza as his base. He stated that there were 190 places where the King James Bible did not follow the Beza text.[7] He put a disclaimer, stating specifically that there was room for correction even in his work, since it was done after the fact and without the benefit of the original notes of the 1611 translators.

A research paper that this author presented to the DBS in the 1990's was an examination of the 190 readings. The author was able to locate the vast majority of the variants between Beza and the KJV that were found in Stephanus. Some of the remaining differences, especially spellings of names, were because of King James' rule that they were to use traditional proper names. Ultimately, there were only 30 readings that could not be explained with the resources in my possession. Mrs. Riplinger is making a big deal about how untrustworthy Scrivener's text is, when in fact there are very few true variants.[8] These variants are readily noticeable by reverse translation of the King James Bible!

The Real Issue:
What Do You Mean by Hebrew or Greek Text?

The real issue is what the phrase "in the Greek" or "in the Hebrew" refers to in the quote above. The vast majority of readings in the various printed Received Text editions are identical. If there is no variation in the Greek or Hebrew passage that is being translated, then

---

[7] All variations from Beza's text of 1598, in number about 190, are set down in an Appendix at the end of the volume, together with the authorities on which they respectively rest. (Scrivener's Annotated Greek New Testament: Dean Burgon Society Press, 1999, p. ix.)

[8] The present list is probably quite incomplete, and a few cases seem precarious. (Ibid. p. 656)

RIPLINGER'S CHALLENGE #1

the commentator can know the source of the English translation with surety. The commentator is referring to the words which God clearly inspired.

No bibliography is necessary. It appears that Mrs. Riplinger has to major on minutiae to justify her attacks on the Greek and Hebrew basis of the Scriptures.

In this author's opinion, Mrs. Riplinger clouds the truth when she says that the Greek manuscripts were not the final authority. She is also clouding the truth when she obscures the record of the printed editions of the Greek New Testament. She is right when she says they were not the final authority. The **published** editions of the Greek text were not the final authority, but the Greek text was!

Corroborating Evidences

The translators of the King James Bible did compare manuscripts of the Greek New Testament against various early **translations**. They did not use the vernacular versions of the Scriptures in place of the Greek text. By back translating these early vernacular versions, it was possible to reasonably arrive at the Greek words which underlie their text. The conjectured source is then compared to the various readings extant in the Greek manuscript record. This comparison then helps to establish the authenticity of the given reading in Greek.

They also used another source to determine the proper Greek text, the lectionaries of the various churches. These lectionaries contain daily or weekly readings that took the reader through the Scriptures over the course of 1-3 years. They do not include every verse of Scripture, but the Scriptures they do include give the translators another method of verifying the correct Greek text.

In every case that this author is aware of, the translators had at least one Greek manuscript with which those comparisons agree. These early documents were used to verify the proper reading when the Greek manuscripts were divergent. The authority of these corroborating sources rests in their **antiquity** and **not** special inspiration. The writer is not aware of anyone outside the Riplinger camp that suggests the vernacular versions were inspired.

Riplinger Cites Her Own Work As Documentation

It is interesting that Mrs. Riplinger demands bibliographic information when **she does not even include a bibliography at the end of her book.** She does not include an index of authors or subjects to facilitate the easy location of quotes and statements. This is not her only inconsistency. When she does provide documentation it is most often difficult to read. At times her documentation indicates secondary or tertiary quotations not easily available to be consulted and read and thereby verify their context and intent. She also often quotes her own work as an authority. At other places, she sends us back to an obscure source so that we cannot check the context. She asks us to go against 2000 years of accepted truth, (i.e., the New Testament was written in Greek).

As we have demonstrated, she makes the assertion that the New Testament was equally inspired in languages other than Greek with or without translation. Her primary documentation is her own writing.

This is a glaring example of modern faulty rhetorical theory. Today in any debate, an assertion is assumed true unless the opposition is able to prove it false. This is precisely what Mrs. Riplinger is doing. She has made a seemingly outlandish assertion, which can neither be proven nor disproven, since all the participants are dead.

Where is the original preserved Gothic text so that we may see that it is perfect in all its readings? Do all Gothic manuscripts agree perfectly? Do they agree perfectly with the King James Bible? Where are the Itala manuscripts so that we can compare them and demonstrate perfect agreement among them? Do they agree perfectly with the King James Bible? What do we compare them against to know that they are perfect? Has she provided us a catalog of the Itala manuscripts with full bibliographic information? How about the Aramaic? Or the Gothic? By her reasoning if all these vernacular manuscripts are not identical in their text they are not reliable witnesses of the Scriptures.

RIPLINGER'S CHALLENGE #1

The Only Complete and Reliable Texts

The only manuscript history which is complete and against which we compare texts is the Greek text of the New Testament and the Hebrew text of the Old Testament. This is not coincidence. This was not some late development. The generation of the Renaissance was especially thrilled to gain access to the Greek texts and to be able to compare them against the Latin translation of the Roman Catholic Church. They were thrilled to restore an accurate Bible to the world.

Erasmus was not a higher critic. Nor was he a faithful Roman Catholic. He took on the Roman Catholic powers of the day when he published his first Greek New Testament complete with a parallel Latin translation. The opposition of the Roman church came because his Latin challenged the *Clementine Vulgate* of his day. He took his life in his hands to do so.

Riplinger Makes Tyndale a Liar

The fugitive community at Geneva translated the Bible. They used the Greek text. Tyndale claimed to have translated the New Testament comparing it to the Greek and German. That's the title of his work, yet Mrs. Riplinger would seem to call him a liar and plagiarist by claiming that his work simply purified an extant English Bible.

The Basis of Challenge #1

The basis of this challenge is Mrs. Riplinger's assertion that:
1. The Greek and Hebrew text were primarily ONLY for the Jewish people and the land of Greece respectively,

and

2. These texts have been hopelessly tampered with and are totally unreliable for the student of the inspired words of God.

> "The old serpent which is the devil knows the power of the word of God and he has sought to counterfeit. **The great**

counterfeiter has latched on to the ultimate counterfeit, the so-called originals." (Emphasis mine) (p. 18)

Truth Versus Counterfeit

By definition, the original text of the Scriptures cannot be counterfeit. The true must exist before there can be a counterfeit. No one counterfeits $30 bills! And if the original words of the Scriptures still exist, why should we ignore them? Mrs. Riplinger appears to be preparing us for a long journey, which will result in rejecting any reference to the Hebrew or Greek texts that underlie our King James Bible. She says,

> "The saga now continues at a deeper level in this encyclopedic book, *Greek and Hebrew Study Dangers, The Voice of Strangers: The Men Behind the Smokescreen, Burning Bibles, Word by Word*. The Lord, the "expert in war" (1 Chron. 12:33), **allowed me to forge this new comprehensive weapon which can put to silence the ignorance of foolish men who question the King James Bible at every turn of a page of Greek and Hebrew reference materials.**" (Emphasis mine) (page 21)

> "Taken together, *New Age Bible Versions* and the book you hold in your hand create a complete **examination of Greek and Hebrew study dangers.**" (Emphasis mine)

> "THE MOST EGREGIOUS Greek study dangers are found in the critical Greek text made popular by Westcott and Hort and seen today In the Nestle-Aland and United Bible Society's Greek text. Several chapters will document the collusion of B.F. Westcott and C.J. Vaughan, the child molester, who together with other Revised Version translation committee members, corrupted the scriptures and first penned many of the words seen today in new versions, as well as lexicons such as *Vine's Expository Dictionary of the New Testament*." (Page 22)

This author agrees that the Westcott Hort text, whether in its original form or in its present form (Nestle-Aland 27th edition, or the

United Bible society Greek New Testament Fourth Edition) is a distortion and perversion of God's word. This author does not support the modern perversion in any of its forms. Taking advantage of the Greek and Hebrew texts does not automatically undermine one's faith in the accuracy and authenticity of the King James Bible.

The *Textus Receptus*

> "The good Greek text, variously referred to as the *Textus Receptus*, Majority Text, and Byzantine text, is popularly accessed today in only three editions, which have varying levels of accuracy." (Page 22)

The words *Textus Receptus* refer to the Greek text as it was commonly received at the beginning of the Reformation, which found its way into the King James Bible. This Greek text found its way to print under Erasmus in 1516. A Roman Catholic version of the Greek text was done by Cardinal Ximenes called Complutensian Polyglot, which was published in 1521. Erasmus published several more editions of this Greek New Testament which he tweaked in various places. One major tweak was the inclusion of I John 5:7, a major Trinitarian verse. There are several myths about his inclusion of this verse. A few years later in the 1550s, Robert Stephens, (also known as Robert Stephanus, and Robert Étienne) published several editions of the commonly used Greek New Testament in Paris, France. In the 1580s and 90s, Theodore Beza published several editions of the Greek New Testament in Geneva Switzerland. In 1633 the Elzevirs published an edition on the continent in which they included in the preface the words from which the name of *Textus Receptus*[9] came. However, the *Textus Receptus*, or the *Received Text*, or the *Traditional Text* did not originate in 1633 when the Elzevirs used this Latin term (as many Critical Text Fundamentalists and others have written). These Words go all the way

---

[9] Textum ergo habes, nunc ab omnibus receptum, in quo nihil immutatum aut corruptum damus. ([The] text therefore now by all men received in which nothing has been changed or corrupted.) (Introduction of the Elzevir Greek NT)

back to the original Greek New Testament as originally written and to the times of the apostles.

What the KJB Translators Used

Not one of these many published Greek texts is the exact text underlying the King James Bible In every point of minutia. The translators had these various printed editions (except Elzevir) plus other printed Greek manuscripts in addition to manuscript versions of the Latin and other corroborative works. But they did not slavishly follow any one of them. They included corroborative works, which as stated above, included early translations and the writings of the early church fathers as well as lectionaries of the early Greek church in their deliberations.

Out of this volume of documentary evidence, in addition to building on previous English translations, the King James Bible emerged. Within a generation, it had captured the imagination of the English-speaking Christian world. It stood unchallenged for over 150 years. Even after its challenge by Westcott and Hort, it continues to be the best-selling book and most commonly used Bible among Christians who speak English. No one observing the facts could deny that God has placed his blessing on the King James Bible. It has been responsible for great spiritual movements in the English-speaking world.

Inspiration

Does this mean that God separately inspired this particular translation of the English Bible? Mrs. Riplinger says, "Yes!" Others of us say, "No!" Inspiration, θεοπνευστος (THEOPNEUSTOS) means "God breathed." What were the words that God placed into the mouths and pens of those he moved on to write in the Scriptures?[10] What words contain the very breath of God? What words did God speak out? What words contain the very Spirit of God? What words were recorded

---

[10] 2 Peter 1:21 "For the prophecy came not in old time by the will of man: but holy men of God spake *as they were* moved by the Holy Ghost."

RIPLINGER'S CHALLENGE #1

in heaven from eternity before they were transferred to earth by inspiration? What form did they take when they entered human experience?

Is there any question that the Old Testament was given primarily in Hebrew with a few chapters given in Aramaic? Is there any question that the New Testament was given in Greek? This has been the position of Christians from the beginning. It was not until recently, when Mrs. Riplinger and others of her persuasion began to teach the inspiration of the 1611 King James Bible, that this was even drawn into question.

An Example

Riplinger says,

> "The wonders of this language (Hebrew), the pictorial elements in its letters (just like Chinese), and its impact on other languages (such as English) have generated much deserving study. However - The Old Testament *in Hebrew,* is **a book *of* the Jews and *for* the Jews.**" (bolding mine, KD) (p. 904)

> "Old Testament study and translation has been ill affected by six or more corrupters:
> Corrupt Manuscripts
> Corrupt marginal **notes**, which have crept into the text or which are followed instead of the pure text; pure readings in the text which have been discarded and moved into the margin in certain manuscripts.
> Corrupt **Printed Editions** (German, British & Jewish)
> Corrupt **vowel** points in either text or margin
> Corruptions in the Old Testament **versions** in other languages
> Currently available Hebrew **Lexicons** (Hebrew-German, Hebrew-Latin, and Hebrew-English) *all* of which were created by liberals based on pagan sources and corrupt texts." (p. 971)

> "In reading the Hebrew texts of the TBS and B&FBS editions, which I have been accessing as needed for nearly 20 years **(never of course for study, but only to prove**

errors in the corrupt versions), I discovered that the TBS[11], B&FBS[12], and Hendrickson/Green[13] editions are not as pure as God's rain from heaven, nor as pure as those living waters purified seven times for Holy Bibles (e.g. KJB). What I discovered, although not a word-for-word collation of the *entire* Hebrew Bible, is enough to resign these texts permanently to the shelf and thank God that Christians have a Holy Bible that they can love, read and trust completely.

Although we have been told that the TBS (Ginsburg) and B&FBS (Letteris, Hendrickson, and Green) texts are the word-for-word, letter-for-letter ben Chayim text, they are not. Ginsburg's misrepresentation has become the party line, and is partly a lie.

Lie #1: Ginsburg said, "The text itself is based upon that of the *First* edition of Jacob ben Chayim's Massoretic Recension, printed by Bomberg, at Venice, in the year 1524-5."

Lie #2: Ginsburg said, "No variations, however strongly supported by Hebrew Manuscripts and Ancient Versions, are introduced into the Text itself"..."All variations are relegated entirely to the margin."

The Truth: Omitted Verses in ben Chayim

1.) The original ben Chayim Hebrew Bible wrongly omitted Joshua 21:36, 37.

"Jacob b. Chayim was the first who omitted these verses in the *editio princeps* of his Rabbinic Bible with the Massorah of 1524-1525.

Of course these two verses *do* belong in the Bible and are exhibited in most of the Hebrew manuscripts. The King James Bible rightly includes these two verses. This proves that the KJB translators DID NOT follow the ben Chayim exclusively." (p. 1015-1016)

This is an argument from silence. What she does not tell us and what this author does not know is, did ben Chayim include these verses in subsequent editions? If he did, then it is probable that the first edition omission was an oversight or typesetting error. If it wasn't an oversight or typesetting error then was it not in the manuscript or

---

[11] Trinitarian Bible Society
[12] British and Foreign Bible Society
[13] Jay Green's Hebrew-English Interlinear

RIPLINGER'S CHALLENGE #1

edited text he was using yet he came to believe them genuine? Unless Mrs. Riplinger provides proof that no edition of ben Chayim's writings includes these verses her criticism of Ginsburg in this particular area is inaccurate and prejudicial.

> "The KJB translators had access to manuscripts and printed Bibles which included these verses. They were included in the earlier Bomberg press's *edition princeps* of the Rabbinic Bible in four parts edited by Felix Pratensis, Venice, 1516-17, who "utilized the printed editions of his predecessors" for the text. They were in the second quarto edition of the Bible, Bomberg, Venice, 1521. They were in The Bible, Bomberg, 1525-1528 (quarto), which is a fusion of ben Chayim's and Pratensis's texts. This 1525 edition quickly reinstates the two verses taken out by ben Chayim. Ginsburg says of the 1525 edition that "The text as a whole is substantially that of Felix Pratensis," a monk who dedicated his edition to the Pope. It was popular "at the time of the Reformation." One copy has "notes in the handwriting of Luther," who also used the Brescia edition of 1494." (p. 1016-1017)

It is nice that Mrs. Riplinger assigns good textual judgment to the King James Translators but how does she know that they did not make these verses up out of thin air? Without their original notes on these passages we cannot say for certain from which manuscript or printed text they got those verses and what made them judge them legitimate. This author happens to agree with her that they had good cause to include and translate these verses but that does not change the *known* facts.

Riplinger Uses Reverse Translation

Since she recognizes that these verses did exist in other printed Hebrew texts, all that was necessary to say was that the printed Hebrew texts, which she has referenced, have some errors. The only way she knows those verses belong in the Hebrew text is **because of reverse translation.** She condemns it for others but preserves the process for herself. She saw the English, conjectured the Hebrew and sought until she found it. There is nothing wrong with that process!

Yet later she will condemn the Scrivener Text of the Greek New Testament for the same process. This seems to be an inconsistent application of her principles.

Denigration of the One and Only Inspired Revelation

> "Easily shattered is myth that there exists only one Greek text or that one can carelessly say, "The Greek says. . ." (page 578) (This is Mrs. Riplinger's wording, not mine, KD)

This *myth* is not easily shattered because it is not a myth! At least not in any informed, rational person's mind. **God gave one and only one inspired revelation.** Those parts of that revelation that were given in Greek had a single text as their source. He did not inspire several Greek texts. One must not confuse the text which is the original words and a printed edition of the text which is the work of man.

The exact Greek text of the King James Bible was destroyed in the fire of London (1666). What Mrs. Riplinger appears to refer to is that every extant printed text of the Greek text has variations from every other printed Greek New Testament and from the King James Bible. Because of that, the student of the Scriptures must be careful before he announces "In the Greek this says ...".

Ultimately, it would appear that she does not wish for care in dealing with the Greek manuscripts and texts. She wishes for repudiation of the Greek text. She does not believe that there is an accurate, divinely- inspired, inerrant, infallible Greek text of the New Testament. She cannot differentiate between the efforts of man and the works of God. She isolates the student from any anchor for his Bible and leaves him with the simple declaration that the King James Bible was inspired and rests on no Greek text.

The Second Part of the Challenge

The second part of the challenge must also be addressed. This author is admonished to provide "full bibliographic information." This

RIPLINGER'S CHALLENGE #1

is of particular interest since Mrs. Riplinger does not provide a comprehensive bibliography of her own work. Many of her documentary notes referred to her own works rather than to a confirming second source. She may protest that no one else has done this research and therefore no one else is qualified to provide corroboration but this is poor scholarship. If it is true, it is not new. And if it is new, it is not true. Does she ask us to believe that contrary to every author before her, she alone has discovered the truth? Does she truly want us to believe that the King James Bible has no basis in the Greek or Hebrew text because she says so? Is this not the way cults come into being? The founder discovers 'the restored Gospel' or some other truth neglected since the days of the apostles. Having restored the lost truth, they become the sole authority in theology (i.e., Charles Russell, Ellen G. White, Herbert W. Armstrong, etc.)

Documentation Must Be Able To Be Checked

The ability of the reader to check and confirm documentation is essential for peer review of a scholarly work. If that documentation is subjectively interpreted by the author, then the conclusion based on that documentation can be false. The reader must be able to determine if quotes have been "cherry picked" or twisted in application. There is some basis for believing that these flaws have found their way into Mrs. Riplinger's work. The sheer physical size of her tome overwhelms. Repetitions and restatement of her earlier written works make up large parts of the volume without making any significant addition to its arguments. The documentation is often printed in almost unreadable size at the end of a given paragraph. The net effect is to discourage anyone trying to objectively verify her citations and justify her conclusions.

This author freely concedes that any printed edition of the Greek or Hebrew text of the Bible will have some variations. And by definition those printed editions are not the infallible, inerrant **Word of God. BUT** in the readings that have universal support are clearly and irrefutably the **WORDS OF GOD.** Some of the variants within the published editions are minute and others extremely significant.

CLEANING-UP HAZARDOUS MATERIALS

Most of the differences within the Textus Receptus printed editions make absolutely no difference in the English translation of the text of the Bible. The training and prejudices of the editor as well as the accessibility of confirming manuscripts and evidence and the accuracy of the type setter ALL are involved in producing variant readings. But that does not change the facts. The King James Bible was translated from the Greek and Hebrew texts that were in the hands of the translators. If we believe that the King James Bible accurately brings the words of God into English, then we must believe in the integrity of its source texts.

There are many other places in *Hazardous Materials* that can be cited to establish that this is Mrs. Riplinger's position: God has not preserved His Hebrew, Aramaic, and Greek Words. Many quotes appear in the "Quote and Comments" section. The author has no desire to bore the reader with unnecessary tedium. He can skip that section if he has reached an understanding of what Mrs. Riplinger is intending to do.

Questions We Must Ask

The reader must ask the question, "Why has God preserved the Greek and Hebrew texts of the Bible, if they are of no value to the modern student?" "Why did the King James translators, as well as the other major translators of the 16th century, claim to have translated from them if they were not important?" And if they were the source of the King James Bible, "Is there no value in studying those texts? Can no insight be gained into the words of the King James Bible?"

The study of the Greek and Hebrew texts of the King James Bible does not necessarily include RETRANSLATING the King James Bible. What it does do is remove ambiguity from confusing grammar and/or phrasing. It gives a fuller understanding of the words used to bring the meanings of the inspired words into English. It is obedience to the command to:

> "Study to shew thyself approved unto God, a workman that needeth not to be ashamed, rightly dividing the word of truth." (2 Timothy 2:15)

CHALLENGE #2

Quote: "Give the Christian testimony of the man whose English mind and English mouth created the so-called English equivalents in your Greek lexicon. (This testimony must be from the originator of the word, not the copy-cat who plagiarized it)" (p. 1193)

Another Thesis in *Hazardous Materials*

This challenge focuses on the testimony of the compiler of lexicons and study aids. It appears that the purpose of *Hazardous Materials* is to denigrate and destroy the authority and usefulness of any Bible study aids based on the Greek or Hebrew texts. In her first challenge, Mrs. Riplinger attempted to state that the published Greek and Hebrew texts have no legitimate authority.

Ad hominem Attacks Do Not Disqualify Compilers

In this challenge, she assassinates the character of the compilers of Hebrew and Greek lexicons, word studies, and grammars in an attempt to destroy the authority of these aids. The vast majority of *Hazardous Materials* is *ad hominem*[14] attacks on the authors and the objectivity and accuracy of their conclusions. Ad hominem attacks, or attacks on the person, do not automatically infer that their research is flawed. One must find flaws in the work, not the worker, if the research is to be rejected. Mrs. Riplinger chose not to provide examples of inaccurate definitions or grammar in the works of her targets.

---

[14] Main Entry: 1ad ho·mi·nem Pronunciation: \(')ad-'hä-m?-?nem, -n?m\ Function: adjective Etymology: New Latin, literally, to the person Date: 1598 1 : appealing to feelings or prejudices rather than intellect 2 marked by or being an attack on an opponent's character rather than by an answer to the contentions made (http://www.merriam-webster.com/dictionary/ad%20hominem)

Bible Translation is Different

When it comes to **Bible translation,** the character of the translator is absolutely germane to the discussion. The Bible is clear that it is a spiritual book and can only be spiritually discerned.[15] A computer can provide a list of synonyms for any given Hebrew or Greek word, but God had a single thought in mind when He gave His words to man. A translation of the Bible is only valid when the translator chooses words in a receptor language which accurately produce the meaning and nuance of the Author as he expressed it in the original language. Simple technical equivalence is not enough.

If one is going to reproduce an historic building then he must build according to the original plan and specifications. His dimensions must be the same as the original. His materials must be the same as the original. His colors and decorative treatments must be the same as the original. It will be even more genuine if the techniques are reproduced. If any element of the original is changed, then the result is not an exact replica of the original. If every element has been accurately reproduced, then the replica is exact. The rebuilder does not have the luxury of inserting his artistic expressions. He is to reproduce the original building.

The character of the man driving the nails into the wood does not affect its perfection as long as he uses the right number of the right kinds of nails in the right places. The character of the workman at the lumber yard is not relevant as long as the lumber supplied meets the exact specifications. In the same way, the character of the lexicographer is irrelevant, unless it can be proven that his lexicon distorts the true meaning of a given word.

---

[15] 1 Corinthians 2:12–14 "Now we have received, not the spirit of the world, but the spirit which is of God; that we might know the things that are freely given to us of God. Which things also we speak, not in the words which man's wisdom teacheth, but which the Holy Ghost teacheth; comparing spiritual things with spiritual. But the natural man receiveth not the things of the Spirit of God: for they are foolishness unto him: **neither can he know *them*, because they are spiritually discerned.**"

RIPLINGER'S CHALLENGES #2

Guilt By Association

Hazardous Materials is extremely successful in assassinating the character of every compiler of a Greek lexicon. While it attacks virtually every established authority in Greek and Hebrew, this author has chosen a single example.

An Example: James Strong

James Strong of Strong's Concordance

1. Strong was a member of the Westcott and Hort **Revised Version Committee** (RV) of 1881 and worked in masterminding this corrupt version.
2. Strong was also a member of the ***American Standard Version*** **Committee**, finally published in 1901. It said Jesus Christ was a creature, not the Creator.
3. On these committees, Strong joined Unitarians (e.g., Thayer), a child molester (Vaughan), followers of Luciferian H.P. Blavatsky (e.g. Ginsburg, Schaff), and a horde of Bible critics (e.g., S. R. Driver), who together changed nearly 10,000 words of the text.
4. ***Strong's Concordance*** **definitions are often the very vocabulary of these corrupt versions and also the Koran.**
5. Strong also gathered his definitions from Gesenius' corrupt *Hebrew Lexicon*. His work also accesses the corrupt lexicons of Liddell-Scott, Thayer, Brown, Driver, and Briggs. All merit chapters in this book.
6. Strong's Greek text is not always that which underlies the King James Bible.
7. Strong's various definitions may not give anywhere near a literal translation of the Greek.
8. Some of the latest editions of *Strong's Concordance* are not even Strong's original. In the Greek and Hebrew lexicons in the back section, they contain even more corrupt definitions from new version editors. In the main body of the concordance, which originally was correct, new editions omit important KJB usages of the word 'Jesus' in order to match corrupt new versions. (p. 161)

It is important to note several distortions in this attack on James Strong's character. The first is guilt, and therefore incompetence, based on association. Several mentions are made of his inclusion with demonstrable heretics on the committees of the Revised Version (RV) and American Standard Version (ASV). She multiplies the effect of her accusation by including the repulsive moral character of Vaughan.

Yet, she would use his concordance (see p. 200, her work)! Why use the work of this terribly flawed scholar? Is no fine Christian capable of compiling an accurate concordance? Can we possibly expect that a man of such low moral character (sic) would accurately locate each English word, and accurately provide the Greek or Hebrew source word (Strong's Numbers)[16]? Would the heretics and child molesters he associated with not disqualify his Concordance like it disqualifies his lexicon? Could it be that Mrs. Riplinger has a double standard?

Mystical Speculation

Mrs. Riplinger is apparently appalled at the mystical speculations of many of the compilers of lexicons and word studies. Yet she advocates a mystical perfection of the Scriptures. She cites the following phenomena as if they somehow prove the inspiration of the King James Bible and the genuineness of the I John 5.7:

---

[16] In the original Strong's Lexicon the numbering is flawed. There is an omission of 100 numbers by apparent oversight.

RIPLINGER'S CHALLENGES #2

Jesus is not only "the first and the last," he is "in the midst" of the New Testament in 1 John 5:7 (Matthew 14:24, 25; 18:2; Luke 5:19, 6:8, nine; 24:36 "Jesus himself stood in the midst. John 8:9, 8:59; 18:19 "Jesus in the next," 20:19; 20:26.	
Count the number of *letters* in the first verse of the KJB	44
Count the number of *letters* in the last verse of the KJB	+44
Count the number of *letters* in the I John 5:7 in the KJB	88
When the letters in the first and last verse are totaled, they equal the same number of letters in 1 John 5:7.	
Count the number of *vowels* in the first verse of the KJB	17
Count the number of *vowels* in the last verse of the KJB	+17
Count the number of *vowels* in the I John 5:7 in the KJB	34
When the number of vowels in the first and last verse are totaled, they equal the same number of vowels in 1 John 5:7.	
Count the number of *consonants* in the first verse of the KJB	27
Count the number of *consonants* in the last verse of the KJB	+27
Count the number of *consonants* in the I John 5:7 in the KJB	54
The number of consonants in the first and last verse equals the same number of consonants in 1 John 5:7	

A man named Ivan Panin did extensive numeric analysis of the Bible. His work was used by **fringe elements** to demonstrate the divine authorship of the Scriptures. He even used math to decide on the textual readings when there was controversy.

> "This verse has seven Hebrew words having a total of 28 letters 4 x 7. The numeric value of the three nouns "God", "heaven" and "earth" totals 777. Any number in triplicate expresses complete, ultimate or total meaning.
>
> Also tightly sealed up with sevens are the genealogy of Jesus, the account of the virgin birth and the resurrection. Seven occurs as a number 187 times in the Bible (41 x 7), the phrase "seven-fold" occurs seven times and "seventy" occurs 56 times (7 x 8).
>
> There are 21 Old Testament writers whose names appear in the Bible (3 x 7). The numeric value of their names is divisible by seven. Of these 21, seven are named in the New

Testament: Moses, David, Isaiah, Jeremiah, Daniel, Hosea and Joel. The numeric values of these names is 1554 (222 x 7). David's name is found 1134 times (162 x 7).

Eight is the number of new life or "resurrection". It is the personal number of Jesus. When we add together the letter values of the name Jesus in the Greek we get 888. Jesus was called The Christ, the numeric value of this title is 1480 (185 x 8). He was Savior which has the value 1408 (2 x 8 x 88).[17]

While there are many phenomena in the Scriptures, we do not have the luxury of using it anecdotally for textual criticism or definition. Which language should we use, Greek or English? Panin proved the Greek text DIFFERENT from the source of the KJB which is divinely inspired and proven by numerics?[18]

Using the same false gematria scheme, Bullinger demonstrated that some of the eclectic text readings were required. For example, the number of verbs in an epistle is always a multiple of seven which justified the addition or subtraction of a verb in question. These Kabbalah-istic schemes can be worked for any book. They border on the nonsense of the Bible codes and have as much validity. Far from being proud of her discovery, the author thinks Mrs. Riplinger should be ashamed of her method. If it was revealed to her by *the spirit,* one might admonish her to try that spirit.

More Attacks By Mrs. Riplinger

Henry Liddell

"Dean Liddell and "the don's wives seem content to allow this stammering clergyman to photograph their daughters completely nude, though only when they were very young [pre-teens]". Liddell and his coterie provided the children and Dodgson, the pedophile, provided the camera. (p.206)

---

[17] http://www.biblebelievers.org.au/panin2.htm
[18] Panin, Ivan, *The Last Twelve Verses of Mark: Their Genuineness Established:* Grafton, Mass., 1910

RIPLINGER'S CHALLENGES #2

Henry Liddell (1811-1898), the Real Humpty Dumpty

"Henry Liddell's upbringing, or lack of it, makes it all too clear why he grew up to be a man who wanted to make the Church of England "broader and more liberal" through his Greek-English Lexicon (Encyclopedia Britannica, New York: Encyclopedia Britannica, Inc., 1911, vol. 16 p. 588). When all too tender to think for himself, he was shuttled off to "the rough discipline" of boarding school for brainwashing. Liddell's mother and father traded parental guidance for training in the pagan Greeks. There, students "were obliged to learn all the Odes and Epodes of Horace by heart, and to be able without book to translate them ... " (Henry L. Thompson, Henry George Liddell, London: John Murray, 1899, pp. 2, 7). The diet, no doubt, was a mix of gruel paste and "Greek plays ... Satires ... and Plato's Apology." He said the school had, "not much of religion in it ... " and "was not a place to foster religious impressions ... " There, the heartless dead skeleton of Church of England formality was given a shroud of liveliness with the lurid tales and wicked plays of the twice dead pagan Greeks. With no indication of his own spiritual awakening, Liddell says that at "fifteen years of age, I was confirmed with others by Bishop Bloomfield" (Thompson, pp. 11, 10)."(p.207)

"Liddell chose to surround himself with imps and wimps from Satan's inner circle of mind-molders and nation-makers.

"George **Eliot** (aka Mary Ann Evans) (pantheist and libertine)
Arthur **Stanley** (consoler of Luciferian Annie Besant, Revised Version host and translator)
John **Ruskin** (Socialist, racist, New World Order Utopian, fascist, alleged pedophile, and member of the Metaphysical Society and Sidgwick's Society for Psychical Research (contacting the dead through séances)
Charles **Kingsley** (universalist, whose endorsement appeared in Darwin's *Origin of the Species*)
Benjamin **Jowett** (pantheist and heretic)
Max **Müller** (professed atheist, lecturer on Hinduism, author of *Theosophy* (1893), who had a "generous estimation" of Luciferian, Madame. Blavatsky)
"**C.L. Dodgson** (pen-name, **Lewis Carroll**, alleged pedophile and author of Alice *in Wonderland*, a book named

because of Dodgson's prurient 'interest' in Liddell's child, Alice.
"Robert **Scott**: member of Westcott and Hort's vile Revised Version Committee of 1881 (Pp. 221-222)

R.C. Trench

"R. C. Trench's official portrait shows him donning the 'X' medallion, like the Masonic Grand Scottish Knights of St. Andrew, the 'X' Club, and the Skull and Bones." (p. 359)

"He had established himself as a critic of the KJB quite early. He was preceded only by petty Catholic priests and a posse of Unitarians poised at re-crucifying Christ. Trench followed immediately on their heels and was one of the *very* first to secularize the meanings of Bible words." (p. 361)

"These men cared little for Fathers or Schoolmen [Christianity], but a great deal for Wordsworth and Coleridge, Goeth, and Shiller, Kant, and Schelling [all anti-Bible and Christianity]. These were the men with whom the future Archbishop [Trench] chiefly associated..." "In Jewish, Mahometan [Mohammed, **Muslim**], and even **Pagan** legends he [**Trench**] **found a spiritual significance**; while in such poems as his 'lines written on a picture of the Assumption [of the **Virgin Mary**] by Murillo.'... His poetry remained always free from partisanship..." (Bromley, P. 244; see also M. Trench, *Richard Chenevix Trench Archbishop: Letters and Memorials*, London: Kegan Paul, Trench & Co., 1888, vol. 1, PP. 8-9)." (p. 363)

Moulton

"Deissmann added that it was only *probable* that Jesus *understood* Greek. (Deissmann to Moulton, 19 February 1908) (*The Origin and Scope of Moulton and Milligan's Vocabulary of the Greek New Testament* ... , G. H R. Horsley, John Rylands Library, Manchester, Bulletin, Vol. 76 (1) 1994)."

"James Hope Moulton Approves Pagan Religions
"Moulton published four books on Zoroastrianism and Parsism: *Early religious poetry of Persia* (Cambridge University Press, 1911), *Early Zoroastrianism* (the Hibbert

Lectures; London: Williams & Norgate, 1913), *The teaching of Zarathushtra* (Bombay: P.A. Wadia, 1917), and *The treasure of the Magi* (published posthumous, London: Oxford University, 1917)* (The Origin and Scope of Moulton and Milligan's Vocabulary of the Greek New Testament ... , G.H R. Horsley, John Rylands Library, Manchester, Bulletin, Vol. 76 (1) 1994).

"Zoroastrianism is a religion from Iran which worships a God named Mazda. It professes a dualism wherein Mazda is in competition with an evil god named Angra Mainyu. Fire worship is often associated with this religion also. Of this religion Moulton says it "nowhere includes what is untrue" (James Hope Moulton, *The Treasure of the Magi: A Study of Zoroastrianism*, London: Humphrey, Milford, 1917, p.211). His writing entitled, *Syncretism in Religion as Illustrated in the History of Parsism* (Zoroastrians in India) (1908) speaks of his belief that all religions are good; he, like Westcott, believed that God approved of such religions and that Christ was just the icing on the cake that they needed, "Moulton was a pacifist. For some time, in fact he was vice-president of the London Peace Society ... " (The Origin and Scope of Moulton and Milligan's Vocabulary of the Greek New Testament..., G. H. R. Horsley, John Ryland's Library, Manchester, Bulletin, Vol. 76 (1) 1994).

"In 1915 he went to India to lecture on and pursue his studies of Zoroastrianism" and to travel, "lecturing to the Parsis on Zoroastrianism." The Lord saw fit to sink his sinking view of the Bible, as "He lost his life through submarine action on the return journey in 1917" at the young age of 54 (Moulton, *The Treasure*, p. x; Oxford Dictionary of the Christian Church, 2nd ed.). The book, *The Treasures of the Magi* was posthumously published by J.N. Farquhar with help from "the Right Reverend Dr. Casartelli, Roman Catholic Bishop of Salford," whose "friendship" with Moulton the book's Foreword concedes (Moulton, *The Treasure*, p. xiii)." (p. 410-411)

"Moulton's books, such as *The Treasure of the Magi: A study of Modern Zoroastrianism*, are a defense of the religion of Iran, not a criticism of it."
"*If* Moulton *was* a Christian, he was a very confused one." (p.411)

CLEANING-UP HAZARDOUS MATERIALS

Thayer

"The plot thickens. Ask any follower of Vine, Berry or Thayer: 'Where where did *Thayer* get *his* lexicon?' As Thayer's subtitle indicates, he translated German Karl Grimm's Latin-Greek Lexicon into English (Lexicon Graeco-Latino in livres Novi Testimonti, 1862, 1867 at al.)." (p. 331-332)

"Thayer was a Unitarian, and the errors of this sect occasionally come through in the explanatory notes." (p. 333)

"Every word in *Thayer's Lexicon* is shadowed by his worldview. One who does not have Christ indwelling cannot understand spiritual things. His particular animosity to Jesus Christ, the Trinity, the blood atonement, and the *need* for salvation through faith makes him a double threat." (p. 334)

"In the opening pages of *Thayer's Lexicon*, he lists the names of well over 300 pagans and philosophers whose writings he consulted to give hints as to 'meanings' and usages of Greek words." (p.337)

"The *Dictionary of Heresy Trials* not only cites Thayer, it devotes an entire chapter to the heresy trials of Philip Schaff, the ASV/RV chairman whose handpicked thugs, such as Thayer and Strong, help him wrench words from the Holy Bible." (p. 348-349)

She makes similar attacks on Robert Scott, Vincent, Bauer, and the other compilers of lexicons and word studies, and all are subjected to the same *ad hominem* attacks. Were they pillars of their communities? Not necessarily. Were they born again, washed in the blood, fundamentalists? Not according to their testimony, life styles, or writings. Are their works valuable in our searching of the Scriptures? Absolutely! Are they our final authority? Absolutely NOT!

RIPLINGER'S CHALLENGES #2

Do Missionaries Use Only Saved People?

Can a missionary learn a language only from saved people? If he can, we must discard Adoniram Judson. He went to Burma and learned Burmese. He reduced the language to written form. He compiled a grammar and a lexicon. Then and only then did he begin a true spiritual ministry in Burma and won his first convert. Can God speak through unsaved lips? If he cannot, then we must discard the amazing ministry of David Brainard, proposed son-in-law to Jonathan Edwards and missionary to the Indians at the Forks of the Delaware. For six years Brainard preached to the Indians through a drunken interpreter.

A Translator Must Be Saved

There has been a twisting of a valid spiritual principle. An unsaved man is incapable of accurately translating the Bible. Would this author let his word be the final word in exegesis of the Scriptures? NEVER. Will he throw away every book not written by someone who sees eye to eye with him on every issue? Not on your life.

This author's library is filled with books of every sort. There is American Literature, Ancient literature, Karl Marx, Ellen G. White, Charles Taze Russell and Judge Rutherford, Billy Graham, Abraham Lincoln, Ulysses Grant, Jefferson Davis, George Washington, and Conspiracy books, Social Science texts, philosophical writings ancient and modern, and the list goes on. This author is not afraid of ideas which contrast his own. This author is not so arrogant as to believe HE ALONE is the source of truth as some do. And this author tries to be consistent.

Whose Books Do We Discard?

If one were to accept Mrs. Riplinger's thesis, then he would be forced to discard every volume not consistent with her teaching. But then would he not still be allowing the "works of man" to influence his understanding of the Words of God, so her works must go as well. He has to start in Genesis and define every word of the King James Bible using only the King James Bible. But then his conclusions would form a LEXICON and he would have to discard it. Where does the spiral end? Where all such spirals end, in frustration!

When a person studies the King James Bible they cannot compare it to the modern eclectic renditions of the Greek and Hebrew texts. The modern original language texts have been altered by textual critics in thousands of places. This author knows that the editors protest that they have not altered anything major, but this is far from the truth. When one translates their texts many doctrines of the Scriptures are affected in various ways.

When a person studies underlying texts of the King James Bible, he must understand grammar of both the King James Bible and of the underlying Greek, Hebrew, or Aramaic. Contrary to popular belief the language of the King James Bible was not the language of every day conversation. It was a literary language which had its own grammar and vocabulary. This literary language employed in both the King James Bible and the writings of men like William Shakespeare are given credit for establishing modern English.

"In The Beginning[19]

INTRODUCTION

"...The two greatest influences on the shaping of the English language are the works of William Shakespeare and the English translation of the Bible that appeared in 1611. ...Literary scholars have heaped praise upon it. Nineteenth-century writers and literary critics acclaimed it as the "noblest monument of English prose." In a series of lectures at Cambridge University during the First World War, **Sir Arthur Quiller-Couch** declared that the King James Bible was "the very greatest" literary achievement in the English language. The only possible challenger for this title came from the complete works of Shakespeare. (p.1)

"...The King James Bible was a landmark in the history of the English language, and an inspiration to poets, dramatists,

---

[19] Allister McGrath, *In The Beginning,* Doubleday, New York, 2001.

artists, and politicians. The influence of this work has been incalculable." (p.1)

"...The King James translators seem to have taken the view-which corresponds with the consensus of the day-that an accurate translation is, by and large, a literal and formal translation.

"No other book has so penetrated and permeated the hearts and speech of the English race as has the Bible. What Homer was to the Greeks, and the Koran to the Arabs, that—or something not unlike it–the Bible has become to the English."[20]

"The King James Bible, along with the works of William Shakespeare, is regularly singled out as one of the most foundational influences on the development of the modern English language. It is no accident that both date from the late English Renaissance, when English was coming into its own as a language." (p. 253)

There was virtually universal agreement in the nineteenth and early twentieth centuries that the King James Bible had made a massive contribution to the development of the English language in general, and English prose in particular. The "noblest monument of English prose" was recognized as being of decisive importance in the molding of English. (p.254)

FACTORS IN THE SHAPING OF MODERN ENGLISH

1. The King James Bible established norms in written and spoken English
2. The northern and other colloquial dialects did not significantly impact the King James Bible is written in a standard literary language, free from the confusing variations of local dialects.(P258)
3. The King James Bible was published within a window which allowed it to exercise a substantial and decisive influence over the shaping of the English language. (P.258)
4. One of the most fundamental contributing factors to this willingness to accept and use verbal immigrants at this formative period was the influence of the King James Bible...

---

[20] Quoted from Albert Stanburrough Cook, Professor of English Language and Literature at Yale University in the 1920s.

    a. The many Hebraic phrases and idioms have become so common in normal English use that most modern English speakers are unaware of their biblical origins.
    b. They have become assimilated into English, and made the way for other words and idioms to migrate into English making most welcoming to words whose origins lie elsewhere.(p. 259)
    c. About 93 percent of the words used in the King James Bible (including repetitions of the same word) are native English, rather than Latinisms or other linguistic imports. English was no longer dependent on 'classical language' for future development. (p. 262)
5. William Rosenau concluded that:
"The [King James Bible] has been–it can be said without any fear of being charged with exaggeration–the most powerful factor in the history of English literature. Though the constructions encountered in the [King James Bible] are oftentimes so harsh that they seem almost barbarous, we should certainly have been the poorer without it."
Rosenau argued that the King James Bible possessed a penetrative force that could best be demonstrated by observing how its turns of phrase came to be absorbed, often unconsciously, within everyday English.(p.263)
6. It preserved pronouns, verbal endings, and other already obsolete spellings which preserved enrich the language: thou, thee, ye, -est, -eth, etc. (pp. 265-276)

    In the same way Koine Greek was not common slang. It was not the language of the "hood." It consisted of the local indigenous thought patterns being expressed in the vocabulary and grammar of the Greeks. It encompasses various local formal dialects of Greek complete with grammatical rules and idioms. Biblical Greek consisted of Hebrew thought patterns expressed in Greek vocabulary and grammar.

    It is very wrong to try to render the formal, concise concepts of the Scriptures in crude, vulgar, contemporary speech. "Whereby we cry Abba Father" cannot be accurately translated "We can call God Daddy." A translator must catch the impact of the original language and match it to its equal in the receptor language with as much literal expression as possible.

Without the use of lexicons, grammars and word studies this is virtually impossible. Unfortunately very few men who compiled these works in the past were Christians by the definition of Scripture. Most were professional churchmen but not necessarily men who had been born again by the Spirit of God (John 3). They were schooled in philosophy and classical language but did not understand Koine Greek as a formal dialect. Much of the scholarship came out of Germany where it was tempered by rational Christian atheism. It was not until the time of A.T. Robertson and Adolf Deismann that Biblical Greek was finally recognized as a Koine dialect.

If the author understands Mrs. Riplinger correctly, she objects to the use of Greek and Hebrew study aids for the following reasons:

1. Modern lexicons and study aids are just plagiarisms and revisions of the work of these people and carry the same stain.
2. Lexicons and grammars are constantly under revision so they are not authoritative.
3. The original authors and compilers of lexicons (and other study aids) have flawed character and theology.
4. The author/compilers of lexicons, grammars, and word studies were associates of perverts and heretics. Therefore their work is unreliable.
5. Lexicons and word studies come from modern flawed translations of the Bible and therefore are flawed.
6. Modern Bibles are the results of flawed lexicons, grammars, and word studies and so are flawed.
7. Lexicons and grammars constantly need to be updated and revised. By the time they go to print they are already obsolete.
8. The King James Bible defines itself. No external study aids except a concordance are necessary.

Misunderstanding the Value of Study Aids

Mrs. Riplinger's objection to these study aids seems to rise from her apparent failure to grasp the value of the Greek and Hebrew sources of the Bible. She finds the Greek and Hebrew origins of Scripture both flawed and irrelevant. They seem to appear to her as unnecessary nuisances. In addition, she counts the lexicons, grammars, and other original language aids invalid because of the moral character of their authors and/or their association with unsavory characters.

Ad hominem attacks are attacks on the author rather than the work. One of the primary reasons Mrs. Riplinger discounts all modern study aids is because of the flawed character of their originators. Her comments on pages 12-13 lay the ground work for these attacks.

> "Who was the dorm supervisor who allowed (encouraged?) the worst episodes of sexual violence in British boy's school history? Who was the pedophile who was dredged out of hiding to join the dorm supervisor on the Revised Version Committee? Who took their words and placed them in that best-selling 'Bible Dictionary' on your bookshelf? Who harbored and befriended another well known pedophile who became one of the suspects in the 'Jack the Ripper' case? Who went to the meetings where Luciferian Madam Blavatsky spoke? Who used her serpent logo on his books criticizing the King James Bible? Who denied that the blood of Christ saves? Who defines the word Lucifer like Jesus Christ? Who was on the Westcott and Hort RV committee? Who was on the ASV committee? Who used RV amd ASV words to define KJB words? Who was a Unitarian and denied the Trinity and Christ's blood atonement? Who thought Christians were heretics and pagan Gnostics were superior? Who thought pagans Zoroastrianism was a forerunner of Christianity? Who copied all of his definitions from the men who embraced the aforementioned abominations? Who was charged with heresy, even by his liberal denomination? Who was discharged from his college teaching position for heresy? Why are Christians trusting Greek and Hebrew study tools created by these men who have this kind of record – even above their Holy Bibles?

The reader can be assured she intends to answer these probing questions in the pages that follow.

RIPLINGER'S CHALLENGES #2

"If you use Greek and Hebrew lexicons and grammars others than those exposed in this book, know for certain that their definitions contain the same errors as those discussed in this book, because they were taken from one of these authors." (p. 36)

In chapter 1 under *Lexicon Death Certificate,* Mrs. Riplinger soundly condemns all modern lexicons etc. as vehicles to undermine and destroy the King James Bible. The reader might justly ask, "What is a lexicon?" The dictionary responds:

"a book containing an alphabetical arrangement of the words in a language and their definitions : DICTIONARY"
"**a:** the vocabulary of a language, an individual speaker or group of speakers, or a subject **b:** the total stock of morphemes in a language."

The reader might justly ask, "What is wrong with knowing what a word means?" A lexicon is just a dictionary! I am sure that most lexicons of the English language (Dictionaries) are not solely compiled by Bible believing Christians. Does that diminish their value?

What Corrupts the Heart?

What is so nefarious about an alphabetical list of words in a language with their definitions? A lexicon is no more evil in its concept than Webster's Dictionary! Yet, Mrs. Riplinger treats them as if they as evil and corrosive as sulfuric acid. They are to be avoided at all costs. No one who uses them could possibly remain uncorrupted. But wait! On Page 598 she calls this author "one true believer, Dr. Kirk DiVietro" and he avails himself of lexicons daily! Perhaps this leads us to another more valid conclusion. It is not the lexicon that corrupts but the heart! If the heart is corrupted, it will seek corrupted definitions. If the heart is right, it will find legitimate elucidations of the God-breathed words of Scripture.

Her reasoning continues like this: 'If an author is corrupt, then all of his work will be corrupt. And so, if a corrupt author accuses a corrupt work of being corrupt he is in essence, declaring the corrupt to be accurate and hence condemning his own opinion.'

This reasoning introduces an endless cycle of confusion to confuse and frustrate the reader. Instead of actually judging a work on its substance, the King-James-Bible-Christian should just read his Bible and ignore all the arguments.

One of her first arguments against lexicons is that they change.

> "Modern lexicographers can clearly see the bald errors in today's lexicons. Lexicographers inform us that "the life of a printed dictionary has been approximately twenty years." Soured and moving past the expiration date are all dictionaries used by Christians, including *Strong's Concordance Greek and Hebrew Lexicon, Vine's Expository Dictionary of the Old and New Testament,* Moulton and Milligan's *Vocabulary of the Greek New Testament,* Perschbacher's *New Analytical Greek Lexicon,* Kubo's *The Reader's Greek English Lexicon of the New Testament,* Vincent's *Word Studies in the New Testament,* Wuest's *Word Studies in the Greek New Testament,* Zodhiates *Hebrew-Greek Key Study Bible and Complete Word Study Dictionary.* Kittel's *Theological Dictionary of the New Testament,* Bauer, Danker, Arndt and Gingrich *Greek-English Lexicon of the New Testament,* the Greek-English lexicons of Thayer, Liddell-Scott-Jones and all of the others." (p. 67)

> "Given the ever-changing series of scholars, Chadwick says that any *printed* lexicon is subject to error." (p. 68-69)

Riplinger Condemns Any Revision, Even Her Own

This is a pretty comprehensive list. By design it includes virtually every lexicon and word study used in the ordinary study of the original Greek and Hebrew texts. But is *revision* a sign of a fatal flaw? If it is, then every writer who has ever released a second or subsequent edition of a work in which any change has been made is condemned. Mrs. Riplinger has foolishly condemned any revisions of her own works in the past, present, or future. If she discovers any new data to support her thesis, her new work will invalidate not only the original work, but the revision.

All literary work is subject to review, revision, and re-release. The only thing invalidated by a revision is a conclusion specifically revised in the new release. Revision does not invalidate the unchanged portions of the work.

Lexicons must be updated as more data becomes available. When English becomes a static language, no longer changing, and when every ancient source has been exploited, and all of the data is collected and interpreted, then and only then will a lexicon become fixed in stone. This is the meaning of the comment that they expire. It is wrong to assert that after twenty years we should discard an aid which contains information on the definition, use, and implications of the original languages.

Lexicons Should Be Revised

In like manner lexicons can and should be revised and updated as new information becomes available. If they were not then critics like Mrs. Riplinger would be pointing to obvious errors as the basis of rejecting them.

Scholars grow old, die, and are replaced by new younger scholars. The new scholars build on the work of their predecessors, hopefully, weeding out errors and updating information. Scholars also cross geographical borders. A lexicon written in German does not help English speaking people unless it is translated into English. In the process of translation, quite often revisions are made. There is no inherent dishonesty involved in the process. Yet, Mrs. Riplinger sees a lexicon which makes a generational or geographical leap to be inherently flawed and evil.

> "Did God express his opinion of the **German** to English Bauer, Arndt, and Gingrich *Greek-English Lexicon of the New Testament and Other Early Christian Literature?*" In 1952 its tentative notes made a trip to Germany. The ship which carried them, the *Flying Enterprise*, sank and the notes

> were buried in Davy Jones locker...Back to the drawing board. (p. 81)

First, in the quote above, Riplinger seems to be implying every untoward experience of man can be interpreted as God's disapproval. How wrong can a person be?! Second, was it necessary for God to express his opinion of the German to the English-speaking authors of this lexicon? No. God didn't have to inspire the lexicon. As long as the lexicon analysis of the Greek language is correct, the lexicon fulfills its purpose. Mrs. Riplinger's seeming demand that all lexicons be directly inspired of God in the language of the reader is absurd.

> "If one hopes to translate (plagiarize with permission) German lexicons, fluency in German is a must. Danker worked with Arndt and Gingrich in translating the **German** lexicon of Bauer (who in turn worked from **Latin**-Greek dictionaries) and recently worked with Bauer's **German** revision by Kurt Aland. Danker admits that there are "**hazards** in semantic [word] transference from one language to another." He says, "The capacity of German for formation of compounds can lead to **semantic falsification** when features in the context of a specific Greek term become embedded in the receptor glossing term, without determining the specific meaning of the source term." Yet he cites several **German**-based lexicons as sources of his definitions, such as those by Nazi war criminal Gerhard Kittel as well as those of Baltz and Schneider." (pp. 81-82)

The Very Reason We Need Lexicons

These comments play on the stereotypical anti-Semitism of mid-20th century Germany. Unless one can demonstrate a clear anti-Semitism in the lexicons, this prejudicial quote is without merit.

Danker's admission that NO TWO languages have exact verbal equivalence is **the very reason we need lexicons**. This is not a reason to reject all lexicons. Translation is only possible when the set of concepts under the umbrella of a word in a source language intersects the concepts under the umbrella of the receptor language. The primary purpose of a lexicon is to present the full set of ideas represented by the donor language vocabulary. The assumption is that the reader is familiar with his own language and will be able to pick the proper word in the receptor language.

The non-equivalence of two languages is the reason the lexicography is an art and not a science, although science is involved. The compiler of a lexicon does not make up definitions. He discovers and compiles them from many sources. The person utilizing the lexicon is responsible for applying the lexical work.

Riplinger is Right

Would it be preferable that all lexicons, dictionaries, and grammars, were done by born again, Spirit-filled, well-educated, universally read authors? Of course. Is that a practical reality? NO! Therefore, we are often forced to use the work of someone who is not of that spiritual ilk. We ignore their postulations and accept only their concrete data. If we find that a root definition is inalterably biased by their theological and philosophical positions, then we reject the definition. If facts can be gleaned from a work, even when surrounded by error, a discerning reader is able to make good use of a bad book.

> "In the end scholars simply want the reader to "make his or her own decisions about the meanings of words" rather than take definitions dogmatically from a lexicon." (p.69)

Absolutely! Only a harsh critic would assert that the authors of lexicons start out to change the meanings of words and make accurate translation impossible. This is projecting. The reader should make his/her own decision with the following caveat. If a person is not able to make an intelligent decision based on personal knowledge and experience, then they are making decisions based on pragmatism and emotion. The problem is not with the lexical aids. The problem is with those who use them.

The Reason(s) the Church Needs Teachers

"When a Greek word is defined in a lexicon, it is invariably the Greek word in the corrupt Greek text of Westcott-Hort, Nestle-Aland and the United Bible Society, not the Greek word seen in Received Text Bibles and any edition of the *Textus Receptus*. **Since most who use these tools do not know the differences between these two text types *at every point* and cannot *really* read the Greek words, they will be unaware that they are being given the definition of the *wrong* Greek word!** For example, Rev. 15:3 says, "King of saints" in the KJB and the Received Text. The corrupt texts and modern versions say either "King of ages" or "King of nations." Therefore the lexicon's definition will be given for the Greek word *aion* (e.g. ages, NIV) or *ethnos* (e.g. nations, NASB), not the Greek word, *hagios* (saints, KJB). For this reason alone, all lexicons and Bible study 'helps' should be buried to prevent the spread of their deadly hazards. This includes *all* lexicons as well as *all* Greek grammar books. Complete autopsies of their dead works follow in this book." (my emphasis) (p.70)

The first part of this comment lays the blame for inaccuracy on the undereducated reader of the study aids. This can only be corrected by proper education in textual matters and then in Greek/Hebrew language.

The example presented is more heinous and purposely deceptive. Any inquirer trying to discern a *deeper meaning* of Revelation 15:3's "King of saints" (ὁ βασιλεὺς τῶν ἁγίων [HO BASILEUS TON HAGION]) should see huge red flags if the definition they find says *King of ages* (ὁ βασιλεὺς τῶν αἰων [HO BASILEUS TON AION]). The same would apply to *King of nations* (ὁ βασιλεὺς τῶν ἐθνῶν [HO BASILEUS TON ETHNON]). If he is not astute enough to recognize these substitutions, he should not be teaching.

It was this kind of "bait and switch" in the UBS 2nd edition of the Greek New Testament that pushed this author into his textual studies. As a total novice in the study of the Greek language and the Greek New Testament, he discovered the absence of several words from I John 5.13. There was no way to make the reading of the UBS 2nd create the

RIPLINGER'S CHALLENGES #2

King James Bible reading. Since there were no italics in the KJB, he knew there had to be another Greek text that contained the missing words. He searched until he found it. Shame on anyone who is a teacher that would not recognize an obvious corruption such as this illustration!

This leads to another ostensible flaw in Mrs. Riplinger's reasoning. At times she says that lexicons mistranslate the Bible. Lexicons do not translate verses. People do. You may use a lexicon to translate, but the ultimate result is a function of the human mind and will. One does not look up Revelation 15:3 in a lexicon. They look up the Greek word ἅγιον [HAGION], ἔθνος [ETHNOS], or αἰών [AION].

To make the error Mrs. Riplinger uses as an illustration, the reader would have to be totally unfamiliar with Greek and totally dependent on an interlinear which uses the Westcott-Hort based modern text that pretends to be the underlying Greek text of the King James Bible. The reader would have to be unobservant and fail to recognize the obvious substitution. The reader would have to take the Greek word to an analytical lexicon where he would find the lexical form. Finally, he would then look up the lexical form in a lexicon and determine the meaning.

A person this unfamiliar with Greek or Hebrew rarely has the determination to follow this full process. Usually they just look up the Strong's number. The Strong's number, which is based on the vocabulary of the King James Bible, for these three words is DIFFERENT and would not lead them to a false lexical definition. Her illustration is invalid.

Misunderstanding the Development of Lexicons

On pages 74 and 75, Mrs. Riplinger objects to the concept of building on another's work. All language and therefore all language tools are built on the past. It is not plagiarism to revise an earlier work and update it based on new knowledge and new understanding as long as one gives credit to the original author. In the field of language tools, there have been very few which were written independent of any previous work. Therefore, by necessity, virtually all modern Greek

CLEANING-UP HAZARDOUS MATERIALS

lexicons, dictionaries, and word studies start from some former work and revise. Revision does not disqualify a work. It is the accuracy of the revision that qualifies the work.

> "New version editors and naïve Bible students look to lexicons or what they think are 'advanced' insights. How shocking to discover that lexicons often take their 'meanings' from corrupt bible versions themselves." (p.77-78)

This is an ostensible assumption by Mrs. Riplinger not supported by facts. Can she prove the average KJV reader wants 'advanced insights'? They should want to know what the KJV translators thought was the proper meaning of the words which underlie our King James Bible. Can she prove that new version editors mechanically look to lexicons to do their work? Can she prove that quality lexicons work backwards from Bible translations? The obvious answer to these rhetorical questions is no. Does Mrs. Riplinger want a lexicon created from the King James Bible? She advertizes one that is partially created by her philosophy and methodology.

Lexicons are compiled BEFORE translation and are one type of aid in translation. It does not work the other way around. The translation of a lexicon from a language other than English may follow the publication of a version of the Bible translated using that lexicon, but the lexicon comes FIRST! It is intellectually disingenuous for a person to say that lexicographers take their meanings from translations of the Bible unless the person is specifically writing a lexicon of that particular version, in which case the lexicon would be of little objective value.

Distorting the Facts

> "Newman admits he borrowed English words from the **Revised Standard Version**, the **Goodspeed** translation, and the **Good News Bible New Testament**." (p.78)

This is an example of a distortion of the facts. Newman did not produce a general lexicon. His is a lexicon of words in a specific translation of the New Testament. It follows that he made an alphabetical list of the Greek words used in the version(s) he had as a focus and then provided lexical meanings. This writer does not have access to this volume, but is reasonably sure that its introduction will identify the Greek text from which it is derived. He assumes that is where Mrs. Riplinger got her information.

Taking her word as true, one may reasonably assume Newman wrote a lexicon specifically to define words AS THEY WERE USED IN MODERN TRANSLATIONS. This is quite different from the major lexicons like Arndt & Gingrich, which attempt to define any Greek word used in **ANY** Greek context including the New Testament.

> "Newman based his lexicon on W.F. Moulton and Geden's A *Concordance to the Greek Testament* which is based on the adulterated Greek texts of "Westcott and Hort, Tischendorf and **the English Revisers [Revised Version]**." (p. 78)

Again, READ THE TITLE AND INTRODUCTION. Newman was defining words USED IN THE MODERN TRANSLATIONS as evidenced by the fact that he used a concordance of those works. If a student is TOO LAZY to know the character of the research tools he uses, then his conclusions will always be flawed. We cannot burn all books to prevent incompetent use.

An Inflammatory Quote

> "Newman's is typical of all lexicons: 1.) It takes its English 'definitions' from corrupt bible versions. This pattern used by all lexicons will be thoroughly documented in this book. 2.) It is based on the corrupt Westcott-Hort Greek text (Aland-Metzger, UBS), not the *Textus Receptus*, and 3.) It copies its definitions from an earlier lexicon, which copied its definitions from one earlier than that - all the way back to Liddell-Scott. Therefore Metzger's definitions, some admittedly coming from Newman, came originally from the corrupt text and the vilest new versions in print. Yet how many naïvely look to Metzger's *Concise Greek-English Dictionary* definitions for the 'original.'" (p. 78-79)

CLEANING-UP HAZARDOUS MATERIALS

YOU DON'T LOOK TO A DICTIONARY TO FIND THE ORIGINAL TEXT! This generalization is totally unwarranted and inflammatory. It reverses the process. Translations come from lexicons. The DEFINITIONS in lexicons do not come from translations. Only secondary lexicons come from translations. Secondary resources rarely carry objective weight. Even then, the Greek and/or Hebrew words may come from a corrupted text, but the lexical definitions, if properly derived, will give a proper base meaning of the word translated. Quality lexicons are not arranged by reference. They are alphabetically arranged.

A Lexicon is Not Evil if it Depends on Earlier Works

All lexical works depend on previous work. It is impossible for any one person to acquire all of the data necessary to create a lexicon from scratch. It is much easier to take an earlier lexicon and revise and correct it.

> "Did God express his opinion of the **German** to English Bauer, Arndt, and Gingrich *Greek-English Lexicon of the New Testament and Other Early Christian Literature*?" (p.81)

Modern Greek-English lexicons are traced from Rome (Greek-Latin lexicons) to Germany (Greek-German lexicons) to English (Greek-English lexicons). Mrs. Riplinger finds this woefully evil since the path led through Germany. She invokes the image of the Axis powers on page 82 and points us to further proof of German anti-Semitism coloring the definitions in any works translated from German on pages 535 and following. The other implication is even more reprehensible to Mrs. Riplinger. Some of the Germans borrowed from Latin-Greek lexicons! Surely the Roman Catholic Church has twisted and corrupted the meanings.

One must NEVER FORGET **it is the quality of a work and not its origin that determines its usefulness.** On earlier pages Mrs. Riplinger rues the fact that lexicons get their definitions from commentaries, which get their verbiage from translations of the Bible, which get their vocabulary from lexicons, which get their definitions from common usage as listed in word studies, which get their definitions from commentaries, etc., *ad infinitum*. There is nothing sinister about this process. There is nothing wrong with translating a good work into English.

And it does not even matter that it might have come from a Latin-Greek lexicon. Latin and Greek are related like English and French. A Latin-Greek lexicon written when both languages were in use by the academic and theological community is of great value in lexical studies. It is the antiquity and fraternity of the work that makes it valuable, just as the Septuagint provides a treasure trove for finding the Hebrew thoughts behind the Greek words of the New Testament. The Septuagint is not an accurate translation of the Hebrew Bible, nor is it a pre-Christian work. Still it was produced by Hebrew people who spoke both languages.

No wise student takes their documentation, definition, or direction from just one work. There is a reason this author has a library of thousands of books. Many of them are language study works. While no one of them is inerrant, one can gain an overall sense of the meaning of the word phrase or grammatical structure by comparing the various articles on those matters. It is helpful to have access to the works which are referenced in the development of the definition.

Translating is a Complex Process

One does not translate a version of the Bible by simply comparing the Greek vocabulary or Hebrew vocabulary to a single word list. Translation is far more complex. If a translator is bound to a lexicon for his translation he is not qualified to translate. It is for this reason that this author does not accept the work of most modern translation committees. A language student knows that he does not really know language until he can dream in that language. There are not many today who dream in biblical Greek or Hebrew.

CLEANING-UP HAZARDOUS MATERIALS

Riplinger's False Premise

Bible translations do not provide the definitions for a lexicon. **The process is the exact opposite.** Mrs. Riplinger's continuing restatement of this false premise implies either total incompetence or willful deceit on her part.

Was it necessary for God to express his opinion of the German to the English-speaking authors of this lexicon? No! God does not inspire lexicons. This author is not aware of any English scholar who spontaneously taught himself Greek without any aids or teachers. He is not aware of any born-again American Christian who took the time and effort to scour the ancient works personally until he understood the implications of every given Greek or Hebrew word. He is not aware of any American, with these qualifications, writing a lexicon of the words used in the King James Bible as they were used in their contexts.

As long as the lexicon analysis of the Greek or Hebrew language is correct, the lexicon fulfills its purpose. Mrs. Riplinger's demand that all lexicons be inspired of God is absurd.

> "If one hopes to translate (plagiarize with permission) German lexicons, fluency in German is a must. Danker worked with Arndt and Gingrich in translating the **German** lexicon of Bauer (who in turn worked from **Latin**-Greek dictionaries) and recently worked with Bauer's **German** revision by Kurt Aland. Danker admits that there are "**hazards** in semantic [word] transference from one language to another." He says, "The capacity of German for formation of compounds can lead to **semantic falsification** when features in the context of a specific Greek term become embedded in the receptor glossing term, without determining the specific meaning of the source term." Yet he cites several **German**-based lexicons as sources of his definitions, such as those by Nazi war criminal Gerhard Kittel as well as those of Baltz and Schneider." (p. 81-82)

RIPLINGER'S CHALLENGES #2

No Two Languages Have Exact Verbal Equivalence

Of course it is necessary to know German if one is to translate a German lexicon into English. Danker's admission that NO TWO languages have exact verbal equivalence is true and the very reason we need lexicons. That a foundational lexicon is a translation of a German original is not a reason to reject all lexicons later derived from it.

Translation is only possible when the set of concepts under the umbrella of a word in a source language intersects the concepts under the umbrella of the receptor language. The primary purpose of a lexicon is to present the full set of ideas represented by the donor language vocabulary. The assumption is that the reader is familiar with his own language and will be able to pick the proper word in the receptor language.

Translation is Not an Exact Science

Translation is not an exact science. No two languages have one-to-one correspondence of vocabulary and grammar with any other language. The non-equivalence of two languages is the reason the lexicography is an art and not a science, although science is involved. The compiler of a lexicon does not make up definitions. He discovers and compiles them. The person utilizing the lexicon is responsible for applying the lexical work.

The Beginning of a Rant

"All Bible study dictionaries are based in great part on the definitions in the first Greek-English lexicon by Henry Liddell and Robert Scott, although this is not expressly written on most of them. The Liddell Scott *Greek English Lexicon* is the whorish MOTHER of all harlot lexicons.... One can merely trace the history of each definition or new version word, which I have done, and see that it springs from Liddell-Scott the first Greek-English lexicon." (p. 83)

This statement begins a long and oft repeated rant condemning all lexicons because of the weakness of character of Henry Liddell. *Ad hominem* attacks have been dealt with. Liddell, with the assistance of Robert Scott, is responsible for producing the foundational Greek-English lexicon upon which most subsequent lexicons are built.

The errors of judgment by these two men and those who compiled the lexicons upon which they leaned are precisely why there have been so many revisions of Liddell-Scott. It needed them! Subsequent scholars had the good sense to see the need to make them. One does not condemn the hospital because it is full of sick people. A good hospital takes sick people and fixes them. A hospital is considered good if its sick people come out healthier than when they went in.

> "The Liddell-Scott Lexicon (and from it all Bible study tools, new bible versions, and lexicon authors) gathered its word meanings from the same crumbling Greek ruins which show God's judgment upon that ancient Greek empire and no less upon the German nation which likewise relied on the pagan Greeks to support their shaky German-Latin lexicons. Such Greek sources include the bawdy plays, both tragedies and comedies, the pagan myths, as well as the political and anti-God philosophical writings of the ancient Greeks who lived during the centuries before and after the time of Christ." (p. 90)

Where else would one find the definitions of words as they were used in the time of the writing of the New Testament? To the best of this author's knowledge no one is old enough to span that gap and speak from experience and personal knowledge. Anyone, with an even cursory understanding of languages, knows that unless you learn a language by total immersion into a society speaking that language; it is necessary to have some vocabulary and grammar aids.

Definitions in Lexicons
Depend on Their Use in a Language

Lexicons of other languages are created the same way that dictionaries (lexicons) are made of the English language. Words are defined by their use. Definitions do not come from lexicons. Lexicons come from definitions.

When this author comes upon a word or grammar structures that he does not understand, he goes first to his lexicons, grammars, grammatical analyses, and word study books. He then goes to the on-line Perseus Project[21] which is sponsored by Tufts University where all extant Greek texts are computerized with a search engine. He quite often does a search for the word or structure and examines how it was used by the early Greeks because God took the words from the language as they were used in the days of the writing of Scripture and charged them with his own meanings. Before this 'one true believer' can comprehend God's usage, he needs to first understand their usage. To deny him that resource is to deny him full understanding.

> "All lexicon authors, like Danker, tell their readers that they consult the godless ancient Greek authors "Plato, Thucydides, Herodotus, Aeschylus, Sophocles and Euripides" to determine the meaning of Bible words. As a graduate student in Classical Greek Danker studied "Plato, Aristotle, Pindar, Thucydides..." His second year textbook was Aristophanes' *Clouds*. Did this Greek author's "rollicking wit" provide the key to understanding the Bible? Danker said that he had a "special interest in Homer, Pindar and the Greek tragedians." Chadwick quips,"
> "it is hardly possible to be sure now what exactly Homer meant in some of his formulae; he may not have known himself."
> "Truer words were never spoken. If we can not be sure what Homer meant (and Homer himself did not know), why are we using his writings to define Bible words?" (p. 90-91)

Let's think about this for a moment. When the King James Bible was translated, the English language was still in the process of being birthed. In fact, as noted earlier in this work, the King James Bible and the plays of William Shakespeare are given credit for establishing modern English. The words used in the King James Bible are the same words used in the Shakespearean plays. To gain the general meaning of

---

[21] http://www.perseus.tufts.edu/hopper/

any given word or to see how it was used in non-biblical English, it is perfectly proper to note its use by William Shakespeare and his contemporaries.

Biblical Greek is a dead language. According to Mrs. Riplinger Greek had evolved into a new level by the year 600. The Greeks of Greece no longer spoke what is known as Koine Greek. Actually, even that is irrelevant. There is no one today that speaks historic Greek, koine, classical, or Byzantine. Modern Greek is an amalgam of Turkish and the remnants of Greek mixed with a little Slavic influence.

It is not biblical Greek. It has the same alphabet but a different vocabulary and a different grammar, just as modern English differs from Chaucer. Most modern English-speaking people could not begin to intelligently read Chaucer in its original form. To understand Chaucer one has to go back and trace the development of words, observing how they are used in contemporary contexts. For convenience those words are often arranged into a lexicon.

We Define Words by Usage

In 2009 the word *gay* does not have the same meaning that it had in 1909. Three hundred years from now, it may well have another meaning. The only way a future translator or commentator would be correct in his definition of *gay* would be to isolate the word as it is used right now and apply that knowledge to his work. The philological and etymological development of the word may or may not be important to our understanding. But they are worth examining. It is absurd to assume that we can understand biblical Greek in a vacuum.

The Bible was not written in a vacuum. It was written using words they were common to both the writer and the reader. If they were not, they would not have been understandable even by their original addressees. Is it reasonable for Mrs. Riplinger to object to us learning the meanings of those words the same way a child of that day would have learned them?

RIPLINGER'S CHALLENGES #2

A Thought From Absurdity

"Some Greek-English lexicons and Bible study tools generate their definitions by studying the works of the early Catholic church 'Fathers,' secular writers such as Philo and Josephus and a swarm of first through third century heretics. The lexicons imply that some of these men are 'Christian' writers, but their heresies make them very unsound sources for determining Christian meanings." (p. 92)

Again, these comments originate from a vat of sublime absurdity. The early church fathers wrote theological treatises in Greek, the same Greek that the New Testament was written in. Although many were heretics, word usage, grammatical structure, and other translational issues can be learned from their writings without absorbing their heresies. Yes, Clement of Alexandria, Origen, and many of the Eastern fathers were consumed with Greek philosophy. Often their doctrines do not match the Scriptures. Many if not most modern heresies and cults find their origin in Origen. Origen was given credit for merging Christianity and Gnosticism successfully. Clement of Alexandria was his teacher. This author would not go to Clement or Origen or to the other early Eastern fathers for theology. However, this author does have their works in both English and Greek so that he can gain some insights into the everyday working of the Greek language.

It would be easy for this author to make *ad hominem* attacks on Mrs. Riplinger. It seems her blind prejudice causes her to make, what he considers, some very foolish statements. When the world spoke Latin, the Roman Catholic Church continued writing in Greek. Once vulgar language developed and people no longer understood Latin, they continued writing in Latin.

Riplinger's Inconsistencies

Even though we reject the theology and the attendant biases in their writings, there is much knowledge of the Greek language to be gleaned from the Latin-Greek works of the Catholic Church. In subsequent chapters, Mrs. Riplinger will conjecture that God gave at least parts of the New Testament in Latin contemporary with the Greek. She would have us believe that Latin is consistent with the inspired Greek texts and yet will deny us concrete parallels between Greek and Latin of the same age. Her argument at this point is inconsistent.

> "The ancient pagan Greeks never wrote a Greek-English dictionary. What they would have said in English is anyone's guess. Any English-speaking person who gives an English definition of an ancient Greek word is simply guessing. Definitions are 'guessed' by looking at the word in context, examining ten words before and ten words after. The context must be the one in which the word is used, not that of another author. A discussion about 'love' by *Playboy* founder, Hugh Hefner, or even the Inquisitor Pope Innocent III, will not elicit the definition of 'love' used by Jesus Christ in the Holy Bible. Even within the work of one author, a word may have several different meanings depending upon each individual context. Yet, in their drive to secularize the Bible, lexicographers and new version editors toss their own rules to the wind and refuse to define Bible words using only the context of the Bible. They plunge God's pearls into the murky mire of paganism." (p. 100)

How Are Bible Words Defined?

Mrs. Riplinger's comment that all King James Bible words are defined by the King James Bible is very difficult for this "one true believer" to accept. She asserts that many KJB words are defined by reading 10 words before and 10 words after. One might find the ENGLISH definition of an ENGLISH word that way (in virtually any large English work) but there is no way that the KJB translators translated the KJB in a vacuum. They could not comprehend "the originall greeke" by this method.

The first task in translating from one language to another is to determine the base word in the original language. It is looked at in its various native contexts. Each use is noted and analyzed. When the general analysis is complete, the basic meaning is inductively determined. The translator-linguist then attempts to understand how that word's base meaning grows into its contextual meaning. This builds a sphere of meaning and use of this word. The better the linguistic skills of the translator-linguist, the more comprehensive his examination, the more accurate the conclusion will be.

Once the English equivalences for a Hebrew or Greek word are determined, THEN translation can begin. The same process has to occur in the English vocabulary (or other receptor language). The definition and nuance of English words also extend from a basic meaning. The fullness of an English word with its synonyms has to be determined.

The same process must be applied to the workings of the language or grammar. How do parts of speech work in both languages? How do sentences form? Is the language inflected so that word morphemes determine the grammatical use of a word, or is it analytical; that is, does the word order determine use? Are there parts of speech that do not appear in one language or the other? Are there grammatical and/or usage idioms which violate the normal use of a word or phrase?

When both the language and the grammar are understood, then and only then can translation begin. The translator will have a list of definitions and grammar of both languages. It may be written or it may be mental, but it must exist before translation begins. The quality of the translation will be proportionately accurate as to the fullness of understanding of both languages by the translator. Quality translations do not and cannot come from a simple superficial use of written lexicons and grammars.

The Reason the KJB is a Superior Translation

The Divine providence which produced the King James Bible is evident. Without the distractions of modern life, scholars became fluent in Bible languages. They were not dependent on a written lexicon or grammar book to understand the classics of the spiritual and secular libraries. They had deep understandings of all necessary languages. To defend his doctorate at Harvard, Cotton Mather stood before a board of professors. The professors would read to him from the Greek or Hebrew Bible and without notes he had to orally produce a Latin translation of the passage. Many of the King James Bible translators knew many languages and could study in multiple languages. Such was the common scholarship of their day.

Not only did they have the use of the necessary languages, the King James translators had the benefit of a virgin language. Modern English was in large part created and standardized by the King James Bible and the writings of men like William Shakespeare. The English of the King James Bible was a literary language which was understood by all but spoken by none. It was crafted to carry literary intent with a minimum of ambiguity. As such it was inflected rather than analytical. Word order mattered far less than in modern language because of the use of identifying morphemes within a word. This allowed the 16th century Bibles to follow closely the word order of the Greek text. In Greek, the order of words in a sentence determines the emphasis of the word rather than the use of the word. The most emphasis applied to the word or grammatical idiom appearing either first or last in a sentence. The inflection of the literary 16th century English allowed the translators to parallel the Greek giving the same emphases to English translation.

The translators of the King James Bible, being uniquely qualified for their work, also had a hundred years of foundation to build on. The 16th century translations of the Bible, Tyndale, Coverdale, Bishop's Bible, Geneva Bible, etc., were basically good accurate translations. This gave them a rich treasure trove to draw from. To a large degree, their translation by committees canceled out personal theological biases and idiosyncrasies. Because they were not inventing the wheel from scratch, they were able to concentrate on making a better wheel. They were able to put emphasis on the poetic effect of the King James Bible. They were able to focus on nuance and implication. They were able to produce an English masterpiece that has transcended the development and diversification of the English language.

The King James Bible was released in 1611, just nine years before the Mayflower sailed to America. Never again would English be a single language. As English speaking nations arose in the United States, Australia, India, etc., it divided into local dialects. By 1885 when the Revised Version was released, it was necessary for the 1901 American Standard Version to also be created. English "English" didn't mean the same things as American "English." The only way a modern English translation can have universal acceptance is to water down the translation into a rough paraphrase with multiple ambiguities. The accuracy and magnificence of the Words of God must be muddled for uneducated readers.

Understanding the King James Bible

These providential realities created the King James Bible, and make it possible for the modern reader to use some of Mrs. Riplinger's methodology for understanding it. Because Hebrew used parallelisms of thought for poetry and rhetoric, many difficult Bible words do in fact have their definitions in simpler words just a sentence away. The English reader unfamiliar with Greek and Hebrew can spend a lifetime exploring the Scriptures with understanding. He does not need to feel that he is incapable of understanding the Scriptures. BUT at the same time there is nothing to be feared in knowing the Greek and Hebrew.

Since the King James Bible is an accurate translation of the texts from which it comes, reading those texts with understanding can produce the same deep reverential respect for the Words of God that the KJB translators had. Read with the right attitude and disposition, the result will be the same as reading the King James Bible with one ADDITION. The qualified fluent reader of the Greek and Hebrew will come away with a deeper understanding of the English. The wise student will be looking for elucidation, not correction. He will be dredging the channel, not digging a new river bed.

One can often determine the specific meaning of words by context. We define God's words by examining all the uses of that word in the Bible. One could interpret and understand God's word by Mrs. Riplinger's method, but they could not produce a translation from one language to another with it. It is wrong to equate translation and interpretation.

In the Bible discussion of tongues, the KJB uses 'interpretation' in the same way that it is used of dreams in the Old Testament. It is used to mean making understandable the incomprehensible. In modern usage they are not the same. To translate is to provide a one-to-one correspondence between a Greek or Hebrew sentence and an English sentence which accurately reflects it. To interpret is more concerned with application. How is the passage to influence doctrine, practice, or faith?

CHALLENGE #3

"Give one Bible verse that states that these man-made lexicons and critical editions are in authority *above* the Holy Bible. One will be sufficient." (p. 1193)

The Oft Used "Straw Man"

No one with any knowledge of languages and translation would make such a foolish statement. This is a charge Mrs. Riplinger has made throughout her book. This writer has never seen any statement anywhere else that says a lexicon holds authority greater than the Holy Bible. Where can that statement be documented? Or, is it a statement created as a straw man with a steel backbone?

Questions of this sort are common to those who criticize Bible Christianity. The Muslim demands, "Show me one verse where Jesus says, "I am God." The Muslim knows that there is no verse with that specific language in the Bible. The Jehovah's Witness says, "Show me one verse where Jesus says, "I am God." The Jehovah's Witness knows there is no such verse in the Bible. The same challenge is raised against the words *rapture, trinity*, and several other theological terms and concepts. That does not mean that the Bible does not teach those truths. It is not necessary for God to say something in our self-determined wording. Theological conclusions rise from comparing Scripture to Scripture, taken in their context, and letting the truth crystallize. These theological conclusions are married to defining words.

Riplinger Misunderstands the Source For Lexicons

Mrs. Riplinger presents a malignant concept of lexicons. She thinks that lexicons are inherently evil. She thinks that lexical definitions somehow mechanically replace intelligent translation. That evil is compounded if the lexicon is a completely original work by an

English speaking compiler who goes directly from Greek (or Hebrew) to English.

> "A Greek lexicon, which held up Plato and the Greek myths as *the* source for meaning and truth, *higher* than the Holy Bible, could not help but place Greek philosophy on a pedestal shadowing the Bible itself. The backfire of Liddell's lexicon, and the path it provided to the mysticism of Greece, fueled the mystical views already nascent in the Anglican Church." (p. 233)

> "Do not interpretations belong to God?" (Genesis 40:8)

> "Studying the *English* Bible will reveal how God uses English words to speak to the English reader's mind and heart. A lengthy trip to the libraries of Greece, via Germany and Rome is not necessary. The Holy Bible is a living book, and like all living things, it lives in the light of daily use, not in dusty libraries." (p.719)

In her etymological world, the compiler of a lexicon must not use any source except the Bible in his compilation of the lexicon.

> "The Liddell-Scott Lexicon (and from it all Bible study tools, new Bible versions, and lexicon authors) gathered its word meanings from the same crumbling Greek ruins which show God's judgment upon that ancient Greek empire and no less upon the German nation which likewise relied on the pagan Greeks to support their shaky German-Latin lexicons. Such Greek sources include the bawdy plays, both tragedies and comedies, the pagan myths, as well as the political and anti-God philosophical writings of the ancient Greeks who lived during the centuries before and after the time of Christ." (p. 90)

In her world, the words of the Bible are special words without earthly connection. Searching the everyday use of the word in its contemporary literature is fraught with danger.

> "Liberal lexicographers have from the very beginning set out to strip the Holy Bible of its 'holy' 'separate from sinners' vocabulary by replacing these holy words with the words of

sinners. **The English definitions and translation choices in lexicons are highly secularized, that is, they are "the words which men's wisdom teacheth," not those special "separate from sinners" words which God instilled early in the English Bible."** (Emphasis mine) (p.101)

The Reason God Chose
The Hebrew, Aramaic, and Greek Words

This author does believe Psalm 12:6-7.

"The words of the LORD are pure words: as silver tried in a furnace of earth, purified seven times. Thou shalt keep them, O LORD, thou shalt preserve them from this generation for ever."

God carefully chose every word He used in writing the Scriptures. Each word of the Hebrew and Greek texts was tried in the furnace seven times before it found its way into Holy Writ. One of the reasons He chose the words so carefully was so that they could be translated into every language of man with accuracy. This is why the Bible is the most translated book in history.

The Bible was written in a Divine-human cooperation. It is wholly the work of God and still men were used to do the work. The virgin birth was a Divine-human cooperation. Jesus Christ was a man carried to term in the womb of Mary. He has all the attributes of man. He probably looked much like Mary and her family. His flesh was real. He had a human soul, a human mind, and a human spirit. He was a man. And, yet he was completely God.

The hypostatic union in Jesus Christ was a Divine-human cooperation. He was not half God and half man. He was both fully God and fully man. When he walked on the water, was it because it was a man fully controlled by the Spirit of God who was performing a miracle for and through Him? Or, was it because he was God the Son, Creator of the world, overriding the laws of nature? The answer is, Yes! And yet, He was and is one person.

The salvation of a sinner is a Divine-human cooperation. Salvation is a work of God. *"By grace ye are saved..."* (Eph. 2.5) and *"Salvation is of the Lord"* (Jonah 2.9). And yet the Bible is clear that man must make a meaningful decision to receive God's salvation. He is completely responsible for his own salvation or damnation.

> "That if thou shalt confess with thy mouth the Lord Jesus, and shalt believe in thine heart that God hath raised him from the dead, thou shalt be saved. For **with the heart man believeth** unto righteousness; and with the mouth confession is made unto salvation. For the scripture saith, **Whosoever believeth** on him shall not be ashamed. For there is no difference between the Jew and the Greek: for the same Lord over all is rich unto all that call upon him. For **whosoever shall call upon the name of the Lord shall be saved.**"[22]

God did not create the vocabulary of the Scriptures in a vacuum. The Hebrew and Greek were not "Holy Ghost" dialects created specifically to write the Bible. In fact, quite the opposite is true. The student of Scripture who is familiar with Greek and Hebrew can differentiate the styles of the various writers. He can do so because the fishermen write like fishermen. The doctors write like doctors. The shepherds write like shepherds. The learned students of the law write like learned students of the law. Each writer wrote with the words most familiar to him. He used them in their contemporary sense, but charged with meanings from above.

The Bible is a Divine-human cooperation. It is as foolish to protest the compilation of lexicons of ancient languages as it is to protest the compilations of modern English dictionaries. Comprehensive, unabridged, dictionaries are simply English lexicons. The compiler traces the development of the word from its source in an early language or form of English to the present. Then, he provides the primary definition of the word. Finally, he lists the meanings of the word in its various contexts with its nuanced meaning. A dictionary or lexicon does not create definitions. It records them!

---

[22] Romans 10:9–13

Not only does Mrs. Riplinger demand that a lexicon avoid the secular use of a word, she also demands that the compiler do his work directly from the ancient language to English. Any building on previous lexicons immediately invalidates his work.

> "If one hopes to translate (plagiarize with permission) German lexicons, fluency in German is a must. Danker worked with Arndt and Gingrich in translating the **German** lexicon of Bauer (who in turn worked from **Latin**-Greek dictionaries) and recently worked with Bauer's **German** revision by Kurt Aland. Danker admits that there are "**hazards** in semantic [word] transference from one language to another." He says, "The capacity of German for formation of compounds can lead to **semantic falsification** when features in the context of a specific Greek term become embedded in the receptor glossing term, without determining the specific meaning of the source term." Yet he cites several **German**-based lexicons as sources of his definitions, such as those by Nazi war criminal Gerhard Kittel as well as those of Baltz and Schneider." (pp. Page 81-82)

Of course, it is necessary to know German if one is to translate a German lexicon into English. We have already discussed Danker's admission, in this quote, that NO TWO languages have exact verbal equivalence is true and the very reason we need lexicons. Just because a lexicon is a translation from the German original is not a reason to reject all lexicons later derived from it.

God's Principle in Scripture Still Stands

God did record a verse which codifies the principle Mrs. Riplinger is looking for.

> "So they read in the book in the law of God distinctly, **and gave the sense**, and **caused them to understand the reading**."[23]

---

[23] Nehemiah 8:8

There is a historical context to this verse. Judah had spent 70 years in Babylon. The children and grandchildren of those who had been carried captive from Judah were more fluent in Aramaic than in Hebrew. Since the Scriptures were written in Hebrew, Ezra and his affiliates, who were fluent in both Hebrew and Aramaic, publicly read the Scriptures **in Hebrew** and then gave a running translation/interpretation in Aramaic so that the audience could understand.

This author realizes that they did not write a lexicon, at least the Bible does not tell us that they did. But Ezra and his affiliates performed the function of a lexicon. Conversant in both languages they gave the Hebrew words and explained them in Aramaic, using accurate contemporary Aramaic terminology, so that their audience could understand. That has been happening in synagogues ever since. One of the tasks of a young man in his *bar mitzvah* is to read in Hebrew and give the sense in his common language. In Rabbinical schools and seminaries, students are taught the meanings of the Hebrew words so that they can explain the meaning to their audiences. The purpose was to complete their understanding, not to obscure and alter it. This is the only purpose of a lexicon. Lexicons do not translate. They are used by translators. Lexicons do not exegete Scriptures. But lexicons are used by those who exegete Scriptures.

Another Absurd Statement

Often Mrs. Riplinger makes the statement that we have to choose between the King James Bible and lexicons. That is like saying we much choose between a refrigerator or the screw driver they used to put the door on. This imagined conflict is totally absurd. Is she sure that the *Holy Bible* she reads is produced only by Spirit-filled Christians? Was each pressman a child of God? Was the type setter a child of God? Was the maker of the press and the ink a child of God? Were all the proof readers and book assemblers children of God? Were those who tanned the leather for its covers and made the thread to bind the pages truly born again? Is she sure every one of them was fully controlled by the Holy Ghost while her copy was created? Her demand in this challenge is just as absurd.

RIPLINGER'S CHALLENGES #3

A lexicon is a neutral tool for translation. It does not translate. If the lexicon is written by an incompetent scholar then the lexicon will be of very limited value. Even then a blind dog can find a bone once in a while. If the lexicon has been carefully researched and created by a scholar or team of scholars, and is an accurate representation of the words as they are used naturally in the secular context and in their historical context, then the lexicon can be of great help in understanding what the **English** of the King James Bible means.

A Shallow Thought

Mrs. Riplinger's problem is that she does not seem to understand (either willfully or in genuine ignorance) the use of lexicons. She does not understand their value. Even if we were to accept Mrs. Riplinger's contention, as shallow as it is, that every word of the King James Bible can be defined by the King James Bible in its fullness, the results would still be a **LEXICON**. It would just be hers. And even though she has a demonstrably flawed moral past (two failed marriages before her present marriage) like some of those she criticizes, if the criticism is accurately done, it would be legitimate. But we would be placing Mrs. Riplinger's understanding of Bible words above the Scriptures, according to her logic.

Nehemiah 8:8 in its context answers the challenge of this question. This author does know what it teaches. And it provides the rebuttal to this question.

In her own words, Mrs. Riplinger provides her summary of the value of study aids.

> "Where Is All This Leading?
> What is the result of the use of Greek and Hebrew study tools? They–
> Elevate the English words in lexicons by unsaved liberals above the English words in our Holy Bible.
> Demote the words of the Holy Bible resulting in a lack of confidence in it.
> Establish an elevated priest-class of a few Greek and Hebrew scholars and insight a rebellious anarchism in the

pews, where *everyman's* own interpretation, taken from stacks of software, supersedes that in the Holy Bible
Give false doctrines and the heresies of history past a voice (e.g. hell dissolved, women deacons, the end of the 'world' updated to the end of the 'age,' Jesus reduced to a servant, not a Son, et al.)
Bring Christians in contact with pagan and secular interpretations, thoughts, views, heresies, and translations.
Provide a dangerous shortcut which leads Christians to believe that understanding the Bible is a linguistic feat, not a time when they meet with God as they "labour in the word" (1 Tim. 5:17). "Let the word of Christ dwell in you richly in all wisdom; teaching and admonishing one another..." (Colossians 3:16). This has been replaced by solitary surfing in dangerous tides of software, books, and on the web.
Lead to time spent away from the Holy Bible.
Isn't it strange that only the current weak and carnal Laodicean-type church has had wide access to Greek and Hebrew study tools (Revelation 3:14)? Could it be they are weak for this very reason? The martyrs throughout history loved the word of God and actually died rather than re-define it." (pp. 1195-1196)

The Difference Between Meditation and Studying God's Words

There is a vast difference between time spent hearing the voice of God through His word and studying to understand and then preach or teach the word of God. When a person is in their private time with the Lord, lexicons and study aids have little play. Quietly meditating on the word allows God to speak to the heart. It is not necessary to know every nuance of the word. In the quiet of the hour, one submits to the Spirit of God allowing the words to sink in. Unless the hearer has no understanding of the words he reads, there is no reason to look away from the Bible he holds in his hands. Even then, he does not want to get sidetracked by dictionaries etc. But, when he stands before an audience and presents the Word, that same reader should be as certain as he can that he has a right understanding. He is under the admonishment:

"My brethren, be not many masters, knowing that we shall receive the greater condemnation." (James 3:1)

Translating and Interpreting

Contrary to Mrs. Riplinger's assertion, translation is not interpretation. Translation is part of interpretation but it is not the same thing. She cited Joseph in Genesis 40:8, which says,

> "And they said unto him, We have dreamed a dream, and *there is* no interpreter of it. And Joseph said unto them, **Do not interpretations** *belong* **to God?** tell me *them*, I pray you."

as the basis for claiming that translations are divinely inspired! This verse has NOTHING TO DO with Bible translation. Joseph was giving the MEANING of the dream. Pharaoh spoke Egyptian. There was no reason to move the language of the dream to another language.

Interpretation is conveying meaning. If that involves conveying meaning from one language to another, then and only then, interpretation is a synonym for translation. It is Biblically wrong to make the two exact equivalents. It is true that in I Corinthians the use of unknown languages (not necessarily unknown to the speaker) was forbidden unless:

> "How is it then, brethren? when ye come together, every one of you hath a psalm, hath a doctrine, hath a tongue, hath a revelation, hath an interpretation. Let all things be done unto edifying. If any man speak in an unknown tongue, let it be by two, or at the most by three, and that by course; and let one interpret. But if there be no interpreter, let him keep silence in the church; and let him speak to himself, and to God." (1 Corinthians 14:26–28)

There is no special implication that this had to be the supernatural gift of tongues. The context does not say it is. But it is the speaking of an unknown language in a public meeting where the majority do not speak that language. Paul forbade the speaking of unknown languages in public meetings unless there was someone there who could translate and interpret what was being said.

Even with proper translation-interpretation, speaking in unknown languages (tongues) was to be kept at a minimum. It was discouraged if the speaker knew the language of the majority. The purpose of speaking in a public church meeting is communication, not showing off.

To build a case for the separate inspiration of translations, Mrs. Riplinger takes this contextually limited definition of interpretation and imposes it on Joseph's use, instead of following her own principle of interpretation. The interpretive principle of first mention is a legitimate principle. The first time a word is used (not a letter as in her kabbalah-like mysticism of *In Awe of Thy Word*) establishes its meaning. That meaning is expanded in later uses in the Scripture, but the word will not change its basic meaning. For example in Exodus, leaven is a type of sin. It does not suddenly become a positive thing when used of the kingdom of God in Matthew 13. It remains a type of sin.

The Proper Use of Study Aids

As this author has constantly asserted, a proper use of study aids increases the knowledge of the Word of God, enhances understanding, and does not in any way threaten the authority of the Word of God. Rather than rail against the tools of understanding, perhaps we need to perfect their use.

Too much preparation and training of men of God is lazy and sloppy. Students are not taught discernment. They are not taught proper use of study aids. And if taught, they do not take the time to learn what is taught. Hermeneutics, the science of scripture interpretation, is one of the most neglected subjects. It is replaced by methodology in most Bible colleges and Bible institutes. Students are woefully unprepared for their primary responsibility. How can one be a minister of the Gospel of Jesus Christ, if he cannot even discern God's words properly?

An Allegory That Fits Riplinger's Reasoning

Railing against tools is like saying cars are evil because they are made on an assembly line staffed by people who live in sin. Many are fine moral people, but some are living in adultery, others are drunkards, some are gamblers, and others thieves. People can get hurt by cars. If a person sticks their hand into the running engine, he can be burned or cut, leaving permanent scars and wounds. Many people buy cars that are too expensive for them and ultimately have them repossessed, which ruins their credit. And when a car is driven carelessly or by a person who does not know the basic rules of driving or by a person under the influence of drugs, people can be hurt or killed. And if a Christian has an accident which kills an unsaved man, he is responsible for sending that man to hell. And, cars wear out! Every year car manufacturers rethink their product and improve it. That means cars are never right! They are horrible! Besides, driving in a car keeps you from reading your Bible and hearing God's voice. Cars should never be used by Christians. They are straight from the pit of hell! As some would reason!

> "Where no oxen are, the crib is clean: but much increase is by the strength of the ox." (Proverbs 14:4)

CHALLENGE #4

"Give one Bible verse that says that the New Testament was originally written to the Greeks only." (p. 1193)

No one, absolutely no one of any learning, asserts that the New Testament was only written to the Greeks. Mrs. Riplinger's challenge appears to be purposely misleading. The question should be: "Is it reasonable and accurate to believe that the New Testament was originally written in Greek?" And, the answer is, "Yes, it is both reasonable and accurate to believe the 27 New Testament books were originally written in Greek."

Riplinger's Thesis:
God Inspired One Bible Per Language

This challenge opens the door to discuss Mrs. Riplinger's thesis that God provided totally independent directly inspired original versions of each New Testament book in more than one language. The New Testament for the Hebrews was in Hebrew, the New Testament for Greece was in Greek, the New Testament for Rome was in Latin, etc. She says there is one and only one inspired Bible per language. This inspired version is the "Holy Bible" for that language group. She contends that once God has inspired a language version, there is nothing to be gained from further study of the "original" languages. She says,

> "An upcoming chapter on R. C. Trench will explain the Biblical directive for having only one Bible translation in each language. Only God can place the proper translation equivalency in the proper context. This chapter has proven the absolute necessity of having one inspired Holy Bible for each language. God would not inspire Greek originals (which few would ever see) and cast the translation of the great mass of Holy Bibles (which billions would see) to a panoply of opinions." (pp. 114-115)

The fact is Paul did write in Greek. To the best of our knowledge so did the other New Testament writers. Their works were circulated in Greek. Textual scholars can point to the emergence of translations of the Greek into local vulgar languages. The various ancient language manuscript record points to translations, not to inspiration. By Mrs. Riplinger's thesis, the Old Testament books would have been placed into inspired languages immediately after Pentecost also. There is no evidence of immediate inspiration in multiple language translations of the Hebrew, Aramaic, or Greek.

Her Thesis Does Not Stand Up to Historical Records

Why did the Apostles write in Greek? Was their target only the cities in the southern extremity of the Balkan Peninsula? No! Greek was the language of the common man in the world of their day. Alexander the Great spread the Greek language from the Balkan Peninsula to the Indus River. His power extended through the mid-east and all the way to Egypt and its boundaries. History records this fact. Greek was the language of Egypt. Greek was the language of the Middle East.

> Koine Greek arose as a common dialect within the armies of Alexander the Great. Under the leadership of Macedon who colonized the known world, their newly formed common dialect was spoken from Egypt to the fringes of India.[24]

Greek was the language of culture in Rome itself. Rome was not an innovator. She was an assimilator. Roman religion and culture were mere adaptations from Greece. Suetonius, a Roman historian, in his book, *The Twelve Caesars,* records how Greek was the language of art and culture in Rome. He records how Augustus and even Nero (who is given credit for putting both Peter and Paul to death and who was contemporary with them) was accomplished in Greek and performed plays and speeches in that language.

---

[24] Andriotis, Nikolaos P. History of the Greek Language.
http://en.wikipedia.org/wiki/Koine_Greek

RIPLINGER'S CHALLENGES #4

Speaking of Augustus Caesar, Suetonius says,

> "He had ambitions to be as proficient in Greek as in Latin and did very well at it. Yet nobody could describe him as ignorant of Greek poetry because he greatly enjoyed the Old Comedy, and often put plays of that period on the stage." (p. 96 in *The Twelve Caesars*)

Speaking of Nero:

> "He often sang at Neopolis, for several consecutive days, too; and even while giving his voice a brief rest could not stay out of sight, and after bathing went to dine in the orchestra where he promised the crowd in Greek that, when he had drowned down the drinker to you give them something to make their ears ring." (p. 223 in *The Twelve Caesars*)

> "It was strange how amazingly tolerant Nero seemed to be of the insults that everyone cast in the form of jokes and lampoons. Here are a few examples of verses, in Greek." (p. 237 in *The Twelve Caesars*)

> "He kept moaning about his cowardice, and moderated: 'How ugly and vulgar my life has become!' and then in Greek: 'This certainly is no credit to Nero, no credit at all,' and: 'Come pull yourself together!'" (p.245 in *The Twelve Caesars*)

And why wouldn't Greek be commonly spoken in Rome? The vast majority of its residents were slaves taken from the empire. Almost every noble Roman home had a pedantic slave from Greece to teach culture and history to their recognized heirs. Latin may have been the language of government and business, but Greek was the language of the common man.

> "Greeks were especially prized slaves for both their cultural refinement and education. Greeks with the ability to educate the Roman youth or with knowledge of medicine were expensive and highly sought after. By the late empire, the predominant house slaves in Rome came almost entirely

from the east (and all its various ethnicities), as Western Europe and Africa were almost exclusively of citizen class."[25]

Greek, the Universal Language of Biblical Times

The Greek New Testament was not written just to the inhabitants of Greece. God gave it to the world in a language which was universally understood throughout the world that they knew. At that time, no other language known to man was capable of containing all the concepts in the New Testament, especially the epistles, with the accuracy of the Greek language. Its basis in philosophical language allowed the elevation of biblical principles from the illustrative Hebrew language and narrative into an accurately abstract language that could be easily translated into any other language.

(1)There is no verse in the New Testament that says the New Testament in Greek was only addressed to the Greeks. There doesn't need to be, because it wasn't. It was addressed to the world and was therefore written in the language of the world. The fact that early translations appear in history and are useful for verifying the Greek text is testimony to the divine choice of Greek as the language of the New Testament. (2) Nor is there any indication in the New Testament of inspiration of translations.

The discussion of inspiration is dependent on the definition of the word. *Inspiration* comes from 2 Timothy 3:16:

> "All scripture is given by inspiration of God, and is profitable for doctrine, for reproof, for correction, for instruction in righteousness:"

The only other appearance of *inspiration* is in Job 32:8

> "But there is a spirit in man: and the inspiration of the Almighty giveth them understanding."

Mrs. Riplinger's interpretive method is not sufficient for us to gain a full understanding of this English word.

---

[25] http://www.unrv.com/culture/roman-slavery.php

CHALLENGE #5

"Give one sentence from a professional linguist or professional translator that proves *scientifically* that a Greek word *must* be translated differently from that of the KJB. There are hundreds of different translations of the Bible because translation is not a science." (p. 1193)

There is no need for the services of a professional linguist or translator. Nobody says that a Greek word has to be translated differently from that which appears in the King James Bible. The true Bible student's purpose in using a lexicon, word study, or other translation aid is **not to correct the King James Bible. It is to understand the King James Bible**.

Riplinger Has No Use For Original Languages

Mrs. Riplinger's statement attempts to find legitimacy in the overuse of references to the original languages. This author can remember a seminary student appealing to the Hebrew to show that a *well* was *a hole in the ground from which water was drawn*. It had no purpose except to prove that the preacher had taken Hebrew 101. But she goes far beyond protesting overuse. She would have NO USE of original languages.

"Preachers who do not know Greek and Hebrew often think that they can appeal to Strong's Lexicon. They trace the word in English, get its number and turn to the Lexicon in the back. They find a whole list of meanings and are under the impression that they may freely choose anyone of the listed meanings. Often their selection is based on a desire to escape a difficult passage or to prove some "shock" doctrine.

One of the worst examples of this kind of false scholarship is found in racists who want to demonstrate a difference between lightest skinned people and the darker skinned peoples. This quotation from *Proof: God's Chosen Are White Adamic Christians "Verboten"*, obtained from the Ku Klux Klan in Pennsylvania takes this principle to an absurd extreme.

> "Adam - The First White Man
> Adam is translated from the Hebrew word 'AWDAWM' and means White Man. The basic derivative means: "Ruddy complexion, show blood in the face, transparent white skin." The skin of the black and yellow races is not transparent nor is it with mongrels. Even the ability to blush (show blood in the face) is confined to the White Race.
>
> "This is caused by your sub-conscious which only God controls, as He breathed His Living Spirit into Adam who passed it on to you, his White descendants. You are an infinitesimal projection of your Creator, so when you do or say something embarrassing, your sub-conscious rushes excess blood to your face. The colored races, not having been endowed with God's Spirit, have no abstract sense of right or wrong, consequently are never embarrassed.
>
> "NON-WHITES EXISTED BEFORE ADAM
>
> "When referring to Adam. the Hebrew always says 'THE AWDAWM" (the White Man). When speaking of his descendants, the Hebrew just uses the word "AWDAWM" (White Man). Another word from the Hebrew is "ENOSH" which is used to imply an inferior, evil or wicked man, and is also used when referring to a pre-Adamic man.
>
> "Psalms 10: 18: "To judge the fatherless, and the oppressed, that the ENOSH MAN may no more oppress." Proverbs 28: 5: "Evil men (ENOSH MEN) understand not justice, but they that seek the Lord understand all things. "A third Hebrew word for man is "ISH" (female "ISHA").
>
> "Most translators completely ignore these words and use the word MAN for all three of them.
>
> "In the first Chapter of Genesis we find the word "day." This is incorrectly translated from the Hebrew word "YOME," which, like the Greek word "EON," means ERA or AGE, not a twenty-four hour day.

The definition of Adam upon which all of this race baiting hate speech rests is drawn directly from the Strong's Definition. Similar distortions of the creation story words augment the lunacy. Day (יֹם YOM-not YOME) is turned into ages. Enosh (אֱנוֹשׁ-ENOSH) is not an inferior form of man. It is the source of the word ISH (אִישׁ ISH) the common word for a man as opposed to a woman. But by cherry picking meanings and giving them spin, the racists are able to justify their hatred.

Where are the Autographs?

Some people, like Mrs. Riplinger, say that the use of Greek study aids (or Hebrew) indicate that the King James Bible is not accurate nor the authoritative Word of God. They tell us that it is wrong and self-defeating to assert that the Bible was verbally inspired in its autographs and then to say that there is question about the authenticity of certain passages. They say it moves the inspired words of God two degrees away from the present-day Christian.

The autographs of the New Testament books have not been available to the churches for almost 2000 years. The autographs of the Old Testament books have not been available since the destruction of the temple by Nebuchadnezzar when the ark containing the actual tables of the 10 commandments was captured. If the autographs of the other Hebrew books were stored in the temple they were lost at that time too. If they were not, then those autographs were gone long before.

This author agrees with Mrs. Riplinger, those autographs have long returned to the dust from which they came. They no longer exist, and even when they did exist, few people ever saw them. There was never a time when the sixty-six autographs of Scripture were together in one place at one time.

Where are the Words on the Autographs?

The *Words* on those autographs are much different. The *text* of the autographs is made up of the words that were on those original manuscripts. Although the original material on which the Words "given by inspiration" were written have dissolved into the dust, the Words in Hebrew, Aramaic, and Greek have been preserved. Those Words are living. They are the very Words of God himself. They never disappeared. They were copied and copied and copied again. Although any given Greek manuscript (handwritten copy of the Bible) will have human errors when the manuscript evidence is compared, it is possible to determine the original words of any given book. Thus, the living words of God are preserved.

The Best English Translation

We believe that the translators of the King James Bible used the right texts (words that appeared on the autographs of the New and Old Testaments) and accurately translated them. The King James Bible was the result of over one hundred years of prayerfully attempting to produce an accurate translation of the Bible for the English speaking world. They did not do it alone. They built on the work of their predecessors. Tyndale, Coverdale, Matthews, the Bishops Bible, and the Geneva Bible were previous attempts to bring the words of God accurately into the English language. They never truly established themselves like the King James Bible.

Much of the language of the King James Bible is borrowed from these predecessors. Where those versions had been accurately translated, the King James translators saw no reason "to reinvent the wheel." So the King James Bible has wording from Wycliffe, Tyndale, Coverdale, and the Geneva translators. We believe that the Holy Ghost guided these godly men in their selection of the Hebrew, Aramaic, and Greek Words and the translation of them. The result was a Bible that has dominated the English-speaking Christian world ever since. This "one true believer" does not believe the Holy Ghost inspired the King James Bible, but we do believe He providentially oversaw the entire process that produced the King James Bible so that it preserved His Word accurately and powerfully into English.

Other translations have come and gone. Many of them are only found on the dusty shelves of an old library or in a computer program that attempts to revive them but not in the common use of common Christians.

The Bible we use is a translation of the Hebrew, Aramaic, and Greek text now extant. We agree with Mrs. Riplinger's example of Luther who protested Zwingli's constant use of other languages in the pulpit. To take the hearer one further degree from the inspired word

RIPLINGER'S CHALLENGES #5

with statements like "In the Greek it says" or "What the Bible really says" is inaccurate, unnecessary and counter-productive. These statements cause our hearers to lose faith in their own Bible. They discount the Bible doctrine of preservation.

The Responsibility of Pastors and Teachers

The careless use of the Greek and Hebrew, and the aids associated with them, in the pulpit is dangerous. If it does not affect the faithful old saint in the pew, it certainly does affect the next generation of Christians and preachers. They look down with impudence at anyone who is not so proficient as they in their knowledge of languages.

What are the rules which will give us maximum benefit for our effort? Through over 35 years of ministry, this author developed a set of rules for his own use of the Greek and Hebrew in study and public ministry.

As a Christian, this author's main responsibility is to be a soulwinner. This author is to bear fruit (Jn. 15:4-5), as other Christians. As a pastor, he is to lead, watch over, protect, and shepherd the flock entrusted to him. As a preacher, he is to spend time studying the Word, so that when he preaches, he preaches truth. This author is to educate and then motivate those whom God has given to him to lead.

Every good educator knows that he must go into a teaching session over prepared. One seeks to fill himself with knowledge of the subject to be taught and teaches from the overflow. The pulpit ministry is no different. This author must over-learn, over-study, and over-prepare before he is ready to teach or preach. This author is dealing in eternal truth and does not have the luxury of being wrong or misunderstood. If his audience thinks that he is simply passing on what he read in a book that they can read, then they have little respect for what he says. Either the preacher does a line-by-line comment from his own Holy Ghost attended studying on the Scripture or he gives a book report on the last commentary he read.

Knowledge of Biblical languages is important at the studying stage. We may use them to find the true thrust and importance of the passage under consideration. We can't be sure that we are looking at the passage correctly. We may use them to find the idea being emphasized by the Holy Spirit. Understanding the words of the King James Bible accurately should be the emphasis of Bible teaching or preaching. The learned Bible preacher will use the original language to find illustrations and points of elucidation, which will make the hearer more prone to remember and apply the message. The preacher should use references to original languages to clear ambiguities and paradoxical statements in the English language. He should use them to become knowledgeable about the passage or subject under consideration.

This study should remain in the study. References to original languages should be kept to a minimum, because the hearer begins to believe that unless he can read Greek or Hebrew he cannot understand the Scriptures. This impression must never be left by the speaker. The truly educated man is the man who uses the tools at his disposal to take a difficult problem and resolve it into manageable, understandable units. The good teacher is the man who can take a complex truth and reduce it to understandable terms without diluting or abridging it. He bends to the level of his hearers and lifts them step by step toward his own.

The Pastor's Duty to Apply the Message

Hearers don't need to know HOW the preacher came to his conclusion. They want to know the conclusion. They are not interested in the process. They need the product. They want their heart lifted from the mundane and placed in the presence of God. They want to know how to live and what decision to make. They don't care how the pastor got his divine wisdom; they just want to tap it. They want to sense that the preacher has spent time in the presence of God and have come back to take them there.

The preacher must learn to differentiate between the product and the process. Share the process only with those who express a genuine interest in it. Keep direct, annotated references to Greek and Hebrew to a minimum. Use them publicly only when absolutely necessary. It is

RIPLINGER'S CHALLENGES #5

the preacher's job to give his hearers confidence in their knowledge of the words of God

It is not necessary to retranslate the Bible. That has been done and has been done well in the King James Bible. There are some difficult passages where a public appeal to the originals is helpful. There are also passages where the language of translation has evolved over time and needs to be defined by the original text.

English is not a static dead language. Some English words mean different things in the 21st century than they meant in 1611. While it is not necessary to retranslate the King James Bible, it is sometimes necessary to provide the meaning of the word in 1611 to make it correctly applicable. There may be times when it is helpful to clear up a passage, but it is not necessary to retranslate it.

The Defined King James Bible

One of the tools which are appropriate in this area is *The Defined King James Bible*, which footnotes any archaic English word in the text of the King James Bible with a dictionary meaning at the bottom of the page. It makes no attempt to replace or retranslate the King James Bible. It uses the 1769 revision of the 1611 King James Bible Cambridge edition, which most of us use as the King James Bible.

Why is the KJB's Grammar Sometimes Difficult?

Most of the difficult grammar in the King James Bible is a direct result of an accurate translation of the original readings in which God used difficult grammar in the Greek or Hebrew. A perfect example is Romans 5:15:

> "But not as the offence, so also is the free gift. For if through the offence of one many be dead, much more the grace of God, and the gift by grace, which is by one man, Jesus Christ, hath abounded unto many."

This sentence is "impossible" in English. The only way to fully exegete it is to refer to the Greek grammar. It is a Greek idiom, which indicates that there are similarities between two proposals but there are also demonstrable differences.

There are theological words such as *propitiate,* which had no source in an English word. Wycliffe took a Latin word and created an English word. Without a lexicon of the New Testament, no one would know what it means.

What is the Goal of a Preacher/Teacher?

Remember that the goal of the preacher/teacher of the Scriptures is to bring men to the standard. It is not to bring the standard back to the men. It is not the goal nor should it be the goal of the teacher/preacher to retranslate the Bible. It is his job and goal to raise men to the place where they can understand it.

Each generation's knowledge is the empirical capstone of all knowledge that has gone before. Learn to build on knowledge rather than try to create it. In the long run, you will save time and misery. Unless one spends years of specialized study in languages, the teacher will not have sufficient proficiency in the Greek and Hebrew to take theology directly from the originals. The devil will throw you tidbits and ego inflating revelations, which will lead the teacher down a thousand rabbit trails. When all is said and done, the teacher will come to the ultimate conclusion: "If it's true, it's not new. And if it's new, it's not true."

A Practical Test

There is a practical test of when to use the original languages in study and presentation. It is fairly simple:

DETERMINATION:

Have a reason to check the Hebrew or Greek text. In the beginning of ministry, Hebrew or Greek study takes a considerable amount of time. If one spends time studying the Hebrew or Greek text he will feel obligated to use it in his message. Be sure that there is a reason to appeal to the Hebrew or Greek text.

RIPLINGER'S CHALLENGES #5

Go to the Hebrew or Greek text if there is a **word, phrase, or grammatical form** which one does not easily understand. Go to the Hebrew or Greek text to see if a deeper meaning is escaping from the English text. Go to the Hebrew or Greek text looking for an illustration to let the light in. Go to the Hebrew or Greek text to fine-tune a thought. Go to the Hebrew or Greek text if you have time to be curious.

TRANSLATION:

Accurately translate relevant words or units. Focus on the part of the text which drew you to the original language text. Translate that part along with its immediate context. Be accurate. Use multiple lexicons. Verify any difficult grammar by appealing to several grammars. Be accurate. Use an analytical lexicon if necessary to determine the specific grammatical use of the word and its implycations. Determine the usage of the word(s) under consideration. If necessary diagram the sentence. Write an English translation as a smooth English sentence. Compare the translation to the English text. If the translation is not equivalent to the KJB reading you have made a judgment error. Go back and find it. If your translation is equivalent to the KJB, then go to the next step. If not, assume that you have missed something and go back and restudy. You have not properly translated the passage until it does.

EVALUATION:

Use only that which legitimately adds to the study. What matter of significance did you discover by your study? It really doesn't matter that a verb is aorist or perfect in its tense if the English text already conveys the proper tense. It doesn't matter if a word is translated 200 times by the same English word if this is one of the 200 times. It isn't news if a dog bites a man, but if a man bites a dog, that's news.

There are two reasons an audience rebels against "In the Greek it says ...". They rebel if the speaker is trying impress them with his intelligence and education. They rebel if the reference is unnecessary. Evaluate. Evaluate. Evaluate. Is it true? Is it necessary? Is it helpful?

APPLICATION:

Use the findings in the least obtrusive manner. The final step is application. How will one use what one has learned? Remember **the hearers are interested in the product not the process**. They want truth. They want to have their hearts lifted to God. They want to have their lives purified. They don't want to hear how the preacher learned what he is telling them. Find a way to present the truth with as few references to "In the Greek" as one can. Preaching is proclaiming truth. Let them ask after the service, if they want to know how the preacher learned what he has just preached.

Occasionally it is necessary to say "In the Greek..." If one is dealing with a controversial subject, and a particular Greek word or grammatical device is the determining factor, then a reference to Greek is in order. For example, the Bible word *wine* does not always refer to beverage alcohol. If one is teaching the Bible doctrine of abstinence one must establish this fact. One must define the Greek οἰνός [OINOS] and publicly examine its usages in Scripture.

If one is building a sermon around a particular Greek definition, one must present that definition. For example, in preaching on "Jesus wept" the words "he groaned in his spirit" (v.33), and "groaning in himself" (v.38), is the middle form of ἐμβριμάομαι (EMBRIMAOMAI). The central stem is BRIMAOMAI. This is the same as the stem of BRIMSTONE. The middle voice indicates that he stirred himself. "He stirred a tempest of brimstone in his spirit."

The whole story hinges on this situation. In the midst of all the grief and woe caused by Lazarus' death Jesus "stirred himself into a furious rage." His tears were not tears of sorrow; they were tears of rage! Anger at sin and the pain it caused to those He loved. Jesus commanded Lazarus to come forth as a commander commanding his troops in battle. The anger stirred here was the anger that carried the man Jesus Christ to the cross without hesitation. The definition and voice of ἐμβριμάομαι as well as some other words is central to the message. They must be identified. Far from correcting the King James Bible, this example elucidates with wonderful clarity.

If an illustration rises directly out of the ancient usage of a particular word or idiom, it may be necessary to refer directly to the Greek. For example, the word βαπτίζω [BAPTIZO], translated *baptize* in English, has been assigned various theological meanings. To the Roman Catholics, it means *sprinkling*. To the Greek Orthodox, it is the *immersion 3 times forward of a naked baby*. To the Mennonites, it is *affusion* or *pouring*. To the Baptists, it is *immersion after salvation*.

RIPLINGER'S CHALLENGES #5

To the hyperdispensationalists, it is a spiritual work of God. In a papyrus fragment, we read about a "submerged boat" that is baptized. In other places, we read that the word is used of cloth submerged in a dye vat. In every ancient usage, βαπτίζω is associated with immersion. This understanding allows us to authoritatively say that baptism does in fact mean the temporary immersion or dipping of a person underwater and then lifting them up again. It is a picture of the death, burial, and resurrection of Jesus Christ (Romans 6:1-3) at the command of Jesus Christ after salvation.

The Proper Use of Scholarship

All of this discussion can be summarized in the simple statement "Scholarship is a wonderful servant but a terrible master." The challenge is to use scholarship to make one a more effective, more accurate, more informative communicator of God's truth. Use it to build people's faith in the word of God. Use it to build their interest in the Word of God. Use it to whet their appetite for the Word of God. Don't use it to build the ego. Don't use it to prove the education. Don't use it to establish their ignorance. Don't use it to correct the Scriptures. Use it, don't abuse it.

CHALLENGE #6

"Give one spiritually edifying insight found in the ancient Koine Greek New Testament (not the English in a lexicon) that cannot be found in the English Bible or another widely available vernacular Bible." (p. 1194)

If one takes the database of vernacular Bibles, the proper translation and any insights will naturally be contained in that database. By removing "lexicons" from our database, Mrs. Riplinger's hermeneutics require that the responder has a perfect knowledge of the Greek language as well as Gothic, Aramaic, and etc., any language in which a vernacular version appears.

Example 1

In the previous response to question #5, I provided two examples where appeal to the original language clarifies an ambiguous statement. The insight that flows from John chapter 11 (above) is priceless and does not appear in the King James Bible or any other vernacular version with which I personally am aware.

Example 2

The words Jesus spoke on the cross, "It is finished," have a far greater impact than just to say, "I did what I came to do." "The plan has been completed." Knowing the Greek behind the English does not correct it in any way. The Greek super-charges the English, deepening its impact.

This sentence is a single word in Greek, τετέλεσται [TETELESTAI]. It is a verb written in the perfect tense. The perfect tense indicates an action which has been completed in the past which creates a condition still true. When Jesus spoke this word He was saying, "The grand scheme of redemption has been completed. The sacrifice for sins has been made and sinners may now be forgiven. This sacrifice will never need to be repeated. It is done once for all."

This truth is echoed in I Peter 3:18,

> "For Christ also hath once suffered for sins, the just for the unjust, that he might bring us to God, being put to death in the flesh, but quickened by the Spirit:"

It has another echo in Hebrews 10:12,

> "But this man, after he had offered one sacrifice for sins for ever, sat down on the right hand of God;"

This is a wonderful truth. Once for all, Jesus died for the sins of mankind. He poured out his precious blood and his righteous soul[26] for our sins, it was enough. Nothing more had to be done. Nothing would ever have to be done again. This great truth moved the hymn writer to pen the words:

> "My sin, O the Bliss of this glorious thought,
> My sin, not in part but the whole,
> was nailed to the cross and I bare it no more.
> Praise the Lord, Praise the Lord, O my soul.

God's word is marvelously constructed. The words were carefully chosen. There are many synonyms for ideas in both Hebrew and Greek as well as English. One multi-faceted concept is sin. Unless we know the meaning and nuance of the Greek or Hebrew word used in a passage, we do not grasp the full impact of what God wants us to know.

---

[26] Isaiah 53:10 " . . . when thou shalt make his soul an offering for sin, . . .Isaiah 53:12 . . . because he hath poured out his soul unto death: and he was numbered with the transgressors; and he bare the sin of many, and made intercession for the transgressors."

Example 3

The words used by the Holy Spirit in the writing of the Scripture are pregnant with meaning. God speaks of *sin* in the New Testament, using three related Greek words: ἁμαρτὶα [HAMARTIA], ἁμαρτήμα, [HAMARTEMA], and ἁμαρτάνω [HAMARTANO]. Much insight into the nature and character of sin can be gained by analyzing the Hebrew sources of and the Greek synonyms for these words.

The verb ἁμαρτάνω [HAMARTANO] appears in classical Greek meaning "I miss." "So a hundred times in Homer the warrior ἁμαρτεί who hurls his javelin but fails to strike his foe; so τῶν ὁδαν ἁμαρτάννειν (Thucydides) is to miss one's way." The classical sense is preserved for us in Biblical Greek in Judges 20:16 where we read "Among all this people there were seven hundred chosen men lefthanded; every one could sling stones at an hair breadth, and not miss וְלֹא יַחֲטִא: [`aji(x]y: al{ïw] which in the Septuagint is translated (οὐ διαμαρτανόντες) [OU DIAMARTANONTES]. From this we learn that to sin is to miss a target.

Most of the other words for sin in Greek have this concept in mind but give us a better idea of how the target is missed. In Romans 3:23 God says that the sin is missing the mark by falling short. We have neither the strength nor skill to get the arrow all the way to the target. It is because of this understanding of sin that God is merciful. He sees sinful men as victims of their own natures, incapable of pleasing him, and therefore He provided the means of forgiveness.

Example 4

The synonyms *trespass* and *transgress* are used almost interchangeably. They come from two Greek synonyms παραβῆσις [PARABASIS] and παραπτώμα [PARAPTOMA]. *Parabasis* means *to go beyond*. *Paraptoma* means *to go beside*. The nuance of the first is that when we sin we come to a NO TRESPASSING sign placed there by God. With full knowledge we step across the line and refuse to come back. In contrast, *paraptoma* has the idea of walking along the bank of a river on a hot day and falling in. We enjoy the water and don't want to come out.

These understandings which rise from the Greek help us to get a better grip on Romans 5:12-15,

> 12 Wherefore, as by one man **sin (hamartia)** entered into the world, and death by sin; and so death passed upon all men, for that all have sinned **(hamartia)**:
> 13 (For until the law sin **(hamartia)** was in the world: but sin **(hamartia)** is not imputed when there is no law.
> 14 Nevertheless death reigned from Adam to Moses, even over them that had not sinned **(hamartia** - fallen short) after the similitude of Adam's transgression **(parabasis** - willful stepping across the line), who is the figure of him that was to come.
> 15 But not as the offence **(paraptoma** - fall), so also is the free gift. For if through the offence **(paraptoma** - fall) of one many be dead, much more the grace of God, and the gift by grace, which is by one man, Jesus Christ, hath abounded unto many

Sin, the moral falling short of God's perfection, entered into human experience when Adam willfully disobeyed God's command not to eat the fruit of the tree of the knowledge of good and evil. After Adam's initial, willful transgression of the known law of God, men continued to sin. How do we know? They all died and death is the result of sin. But, they didn't sin the same way Adam did. They couldn't. There were no specific commands for them to transgress (*parabasis*) but they still sinned (fell short). By his willful transgression (*parabasis*) Adam and the whole human race fell (*paraptoma*) and now we are sinners by nature and sinners by choice.

There are other synonyms for sin, each with its own nuance and implications. Rather than examine each in detail here, let the reader note the full impact of Romans 3:23 when every Greek and Hebrew word that is translated sin is applied.

> "For all have sinned, and come short of the glory of God." Romans 3:23

For all have sinned.
For all have missed the mark.
For all have committed acts of sin.
For all have perverted something good.
For all have been corrupted.
For all have disregarded God's will.
For all have disregarded God's person.
For all have deviated from God's will.
For all have gone beyond God's will.
For all have willfully crossed God's boundary for behavior.
For all have acted treacherously toward God.
For all have done wicked things.
For all have acted foolishly.
For all have become guilty.
For all have incurred God's wrath.
For all have been carried captive.
For all have been provided a sin offering.[27]

Example 5

John wrote, *"If we confess our sins, he is faithful and just to forgive us our sins, and to cleanse us from all unrighteousness."* (I John 1:9). The word translated "confess" (ὁμολογίζομαι - [homologizomai] means "to call by the same name." In order to call sin what God calls it and be completely cleansed, we must know what God has called it. Understanding the words for sin heightens our ability to do so.

Similar to the interpretation, yet significant differences of meaning for sin, is the set of synonyms for the Word of God used in Psalm 119. These synonyms center around a trip down the highway.

---

[27] Examples 3 & 4 are from Trench, R. C. (2003). *Synonyms of the New Testament.* (9th ed., improved.) (239). Bellingham, WA: Logos Research Systems, Inc. (§ lxvi. ἁμαρτία, ἁμάρτημα, παρακοή, ἀνομία, παρανομία, παράβασις, παράπτωμα, ἀγνόημα, ἥττημα.)

Example 6

In 2 John 9–10, we read:

"Whosoever transgresseth, and abideth not in the doctrine of Christ, hath not God. He that abideth in the doctrine of Christ, he hath both the Father and the Son. If there come any unto you, and bring not this doctrine, receive him not into your house, neither bid him God speed:"

On its face, the verse says that a Christian should not invite into their home a person who has a wrong understanding of the doctrine of Christ. He should not receive that person, nor should he wish God's blessing on that person.

The Greek grammar of that verse agrees with this translation of the King James Bible. It also adds further insight. The clause "receive him not into your house" is present imperative with a negative. It is a negative command. Don't Do It! It is in the present tense which implies ongoing action. If it were in the Aorist tense it would imply, "Don't start letting them in!" The negative present imperative implies, "STOP letting them in!"

Many make excuses for those who subscribe to bad teaching on the nature of Jesus Christ. They call them Christian brothers and want to extend fellowship and unity to them. The command is to stop fellowshipping with them and not to start with any others. Break your ecumenical and personal Christian fellowship with anyone who would reduce the deity of the Lord Jesus Christ. Stop calling those who reject the physical bodily resurrection, the virgin birth, or the sinless human life of Jesus Christ. If they don't have the doctrine of Jesus Christ correct, reject them and withhold any parting blessing.

Many Insights to be Gained From Studying

Far from contradicting or correcting the Bible, there are other insights to be gained by the study of the Greek and Hebrew origins of the King James Bible. Exploring these texts does not threaten faith in the Word of God. It does not discover 'mistakes' or 'errors' in the King

RIPLINGER'S CHALLENGES #6

James Bible. In fact, the King James Bible becomes even more magnificent as this writer sees how the English was so carefully crafted to point to these deeper understandings. Because of his work on the Greek New Testament of the King James Bible, this author can with reasonable accuracy determine the tense of Greek verbs which lie behind English verbs.

Perhaps Mrs. Riplinger has a method for determining these truths. This author does not. He needs to see the exact words which God used to reveal Himself to us in their original setting to fully grasp what God has said.

Since the challenge involves the use of vernacular versions, it is appropriate to consider what she says about them and examine the validity of her statements. What are vernacular versions? The dictionary definition of vernacular is:

> **ver nac u lar** \vər)-a-kyələ\ **adj** [L *vernaculus* native, fr. *verna* slave born in the master's house, native] 1601 **1a:** using a language or dialect native to a region or country rather than a literary, cultured, or foreign language
> vernacular **n:** a vernacular language, expression, or mode of expression.[28]

Vernacular simply means a Bible or book written in the language of a country. There is no guarantee that a vernacular version of the Bible is the perfectly and separately inspired words of God.

---

[28] Merriam-Webster, I. (2003). Merriam-Webster's collegiate dictionary. Includes index. (Eleventh ed.). Springfield, Mass.: Merriam-Webster, Inc.

CHALLENGE #7

"Give one Bible verse that says to "understand," "study," "search," "preach," or "teach" the Bible involves using another language. It is a shame that David did not speak Hebrew. In the Psalms he said five times, "Give me understanding." David not only spoke Hebrew, he wrote a part of the Hebrew text. Yet he said such things in Psalm 119:34, 73, 125, 144, 169 as,
"Give me understanding"...
"Give me understanding"...
"Give me understanding"...
"Give me understanding"...
"Give me understanding"... (p. 1194

Study to shew thyself approved unto God, a workman that needeth not to be ashamed, rightly dividing the word of truth." (2 Timothy 2:15)
Search the scriptures; for in them ye think ye have eternal life: and they are they which testify of me. (John 5:39)

These verses tell the reader to do his best to understand the Scriptures. There is no prohibition against using the original languages. In fact, knowing the historic view that the Hebrew Scriptures are the authoritative OT Scriptures to a Jew, and knowing that whenever New Testament writers quote the Hebrew Scriptures they made a translation from the Hebrew, it would be hard for Timothy or any other Jewish recipient of this command not to access the Hebrew Scriptures.

"Give me one Bible verse that tells me to "understand," "study," "search," "preach," or "teach" the Bible without using another language? A look at the context of the passages cited reveals that "Give me understanding" has nothing to do with translation. It involves application. It was David's prayer that he would gain the mind of God. He wanted a full comprehension of God's promises, His judgments, His precepts, etc.

The writers of Scripture did not always fully understand what they had written. Daniel, David, and others asked God to help them understand what He had revealed through them and others. That is very different than understanding the full meaning of the words of Scripture.

When Jesus told those around him to search the Scriptures, was He telling them to search the Scriptures in Aramaic since that was the language of the area? Or, was He telling them to search the Scriptures in Hebrew which they no longer spoke? Or, was He telling them to search the Scriptures in Greek? Or, some other vernacular translation?

The Jews of Jesus' day as well as today believe that the ultimate revelation of God in perfection appears only in the Hebrew text of the Scriptures. In the synagogues they still do what Ezra did. They read the Scriptures (in Hebrew) and give the sense thereof (in English) causing them to understand. And so, in my mind and the minds of those who give the Scriptures an honest reading, yes, we are commanded to study the Scriptures and that may include the languages and texts from which they came.

Mrs. Riplinger asked for a single verse that tells us to appeal to another language to understand the Scriptures. It is not difficult. Many times the writer of a passage of Scripture quotes Jesus or someone else speaking in one language and explains what the word meant in Greek. Those who appeal to the original language of the Scriptures to fully understand them are only doing what writers of Scripture did. Here are a few.

> Nehemiah 8:8 "So they read in the book in the law of God distinctly, and gave the sense, and caused them to understand the reading."

This statement was a clear reference to Hebrew in the explanation of the Scriptures to the new generation of Hebrews. Many of those who were returning from Babylon did not speak Hebrew. Or, if they did understand Hebrew, their understanding was imperfect. Ezra and his helpers used their knowledge of Hebrew and the Scriptures to bring the truth to their generation.

> Genesis 28:19 "And he called the name of that place Bethel: but the name of **that city was called Luz at the first.**"

Judges 18:29 "And they called the name of the city Dan, after the name of Dan their father, who was born unto Israel: howbeit the name of **the city was Laish at the first.**"

Matthew 1:23 "Behold, a virgin shall be with child, and shall bring forth a son, and they shall call his name Emmanuel, **which being interpreted is, God with us.**"

Mark 5:41 "And he took the damsel by the hand, and said unto her, Talitha cumi; **which is, being interpreted, Damsel,** I say unto thee, arise."

Mark 15:22 "And they bring him unto the place Golgotha, **which is, being interpreted, The place of a skull.**"

Mark 15:34 "And at the ninth hour Jesus cried with a loud voice, saying, Eloi, Eloi, lama sabachthani? **which is, being interpreted, My God, my God, why hast thou forsaken me?**"

John 1:38 "Then Jesus turned, and saw them following, and saith unto them, What seek ye? They said unto him, Rabbi, **(which is to say, being interpreted, Master,)** where dwellest thou?"

John 1:41 "He first findeth his own brother Simon, and saith unto him, **We have found the Messias, which is, being interpreted, the Christ.**"

Acts 4:36 "And Joses, who by the apostles was surnamed Barnabas, **(which is, being interpreted, The son of consolation,)** a Levite, and of the country of Cyprus,"

Hebrews 7:2 "To whom also Abraham gave a tenth part of all; first being by interpretation King of righteousness, and after that also King of Salem, which is, King of peace;"

In each case, the writer defines a phrase or the name of a place from its original language. God caused them to write these words so that we would know specifically what they were talking about. He wanted us to have the sounds of the original language but he also wanted us to know what was being said. What is this other than a LEXICON?—'Giving the meaning of a word in an original language in the vocabulary of a donor language, so that the reader of the donor language understands perfectly the reference.'

When a Bible-believing speaker or writer wants the writer to grasp the fullness of what God has said, he can and should appeal to the original languages of the Scriptures. These words are the very breath and spirit of God. If the writer does not undercut the authority and accuracy of the King James Bible; and if the writer increases the depth of understanding, he has only done what God did in His Word.

Why did God preserve the Hebrew Scriptures? Obviously because they are part of his revelation to mankind. What are their primary value? They give context and meaning to the truths of the New Testament.

There are many people mentioned in the New Testament who are presented to us in the Hebrew Scriptures. If a person were handed the New Testament, he would be forced to ask, where is the rest of this book? Who is Adam?, Abraham?, Jacob?, Moses?, David?, Isaiah?, or Daniel? What did they do? What is their value to what I am reading now? Imagine reading Romans 4, the great chapter on justification by faith and not knowing about Abraham or David. The Hebrew Scriptures are a LEXICON of men.

There are many concepts mentioned in the New Testament that find their roots in the Hebrew Scriptures. We know that every theme of Scripture has its seed in Genesis 1-3, and its first developments in Genesis 1-11. Nothing new is introduced after that. Each of those themes has a particular vocabulary. New Testament words get their meanings from Old Testament events and institutions.

Atonement starts with the covering of skins in Eden and the promise of the deliverer. Atonement means to cover. The same Hebrew word was used in the covering of Adam and Eve's nakedness, the pitch that coated the arks of both Noah and Moses, and ultimately the blood that covered the sins of Israel. How could one know the full meaning of the Greek word for atonement without the LEXICON of the Hebrew Scriptures?

Propitiation is another of those concepts. There was no word in English to express the thought of the Greek word. Using Mrs. Riplinger's methodology we know that propitiation is tied to sin. It has something to do with its forgiveness.

> Romans 3:25 "Whom God hath set forth to be a propitiation through faith in his blood, to declare his righteousness for the remission of sins that are past, through the forbearance of God;"

RIPLINGER'S CHALLENGES #7

> 1 John 2:2 "And he is the propitiation for our sins: and not for ours only, but also for the sins of the whole world."
> 1 John 4:10 "Herein is love, not that we loved God, but that he loved us, and sent his Son to be the propitiation for our sins."

There is nothing in the English *propitiation* which gives the full meaning of the Greek, especially since it was invented to carry a concept not known to English. We can see that it is part of the forgiveness of sins, and is on the basis of the shed blood of Jesus. We can see that it is the outpouring of love from God toward sinful men and that it affects both saved and unsaved men. But we cannot and do not know the fullness of its meaning without our lexicon.

A survey of the usage of the word in the Septuagint allows us to make the connection to its Hebrew root. The Greek word ἱλασμὸς [HILASMOS] is used consistently to translate the Hebrew word for the Mercy Seat of the tabernacle and temple. It was the place where the blood of the Yom Kippur sacrifice was sprinkled to gain God's forgiveness for the year. It was the place where God's righteous, holy anger against sin was satisfied and God was rendered forgiving toward His people. Thus, in Christ, the holiness and justice of God is completely satisfied so that He can forgive men without being inconsistent with His own nature.

There are many other examples this author could point to. The reader of the Scriptures can either spend the time to compile a list of every use of an English word and go through Mrs. Riplinger's convoluted method for definition. Or, he can make long lists of Greek words and then compare them to every use of the Hebrew word(s) from which they come and then draw his own conclusions. OR, he can pick an accurate Lexicon where the work has already been done and look up ἱλασμὸς and apply its meaning. Or, he can pick up a Word Study (Vine, Vincent, Wuest, etc.) and find its implications there.

Mrs. Riplinger asserts with sarcasm that the only reason a pastor or preacher will not agree with her is pride. Mrs. Riplinger proceeds to point out what she considers prideful responses to her book in a preemptive strike against anyone who might criticize it.

In her own words:

CLEANING-UP HAZARDOUS MATERIALS

> √ Some of this is too dry to read and my flesh is too lazy to 'work ' through it. It would be easier simply to call Dr. 'so-and-so' and see what he thinks.' [If he has made his living using Greek lexicons, do not count on him to thoroughly read the material or to have a humble reaction to it if he does. He has too much to lose.] (p. 1192)

The writer has read the book **in total three times**. He has read the portions cited in this work multiple times in their full context. He has carefully considered its arguments and is ready to refute that which needs to be refuted. Although he has four post-graduate degrees and can be called Dr., he much prefers the title *Pastor, Preacher,* or *Brother DiVietro*. He freely uses Bible study aids. In 30+ years of ministry as a pastor and part-time college professor, he has NEVER once corrected the King James Bible. He has never once invited anyone to question its meaning or authority.

Mrs. Riplinger has no basis for accusing "one true believer" of laziness, pride, or carelessly handling her ideas. She launched a pre-emptive strike because she knew her thesis would provoke legitimate refutation.

> √ 'I am a solid fundamental Christian, therefore I could not be wrong about *anything*. God wouldn't give *this* author this information *before* giving it to me.' [Maybe it was given to this disabled author, with a heart for 'helps,' because you were rightfully busy doing important things which this author cannot do.] (p. 1192)

For 35+ years of being a Christian, this "one true believer" has been shown errors in his faith and practice. When the Scriptures confront him, he adjusts his doctrine and practice to the Scriptures. Mrs. Riplinger is not inspired of God and does not speak with the authority of Scripture. In the arena she has chosen, she is in direct violation of the Scriptures, "But I suffer not a woman to teach, nor to usurp authority over the man, but to be in silence." (I Timothy 2:12).

Perhaps God did not mean what He said or say what He meant in this passage. One wonders why these words are not Holy Ghost inspired, separate from sinners, perfect words. There is not one thing in either the lexicons or Mrs. Riplinger's scheme of defining Bible words which contradicts its plain teaching. Mrs. Riplinger has NO BUSINESS correcting pastors and teachers. She has violated the Scriptures.

In each of her works, she bewails her humble disabled status. This "one true believer" works in constant pain from spinal arthritis and stenosis. Muscular-skeletal degeneration has resulted in torn bicep tendons. His left knee has permanently damaged ligaments. He has eye problems. He is not seeking sympathy. He is just as disabled or more so. It does not in any way increase his spiritual perception or accuracy. Mrs. Riplinger has called him "one true believer" and yet now she insults and derides him, accusing him of pride and laziness because he disagrees with the teaching of her works. Let him answer clearly.

No, Gail, I do not for one second believe "it was given to the disabled author, with a heart for 'helps,' because you were rightfully busy doing important things which this author cannot do." I believe you have given yourself to speak with false authority on things you do not seem to understand. I believe you are destroying the credibility and ability to fully comprehend God's revelation of a generation of sincere young preachers.   I believe you are doing irreparable damage by the things you have written.

> √ I must quickly skim for some small error to prove this wrong. I couldn't have been wrong all these years. I must find something somewhere in the book to show that I know something that this author does not seem to know.' [This may be a test of your humility. "Humble yourselves therefore under the mighty hand of God..." (1 Peter 5:6),] (p. 1192)

It was not necessary to *skim through* looking for errors to refute. In this "one true believer's" opinion, virtually every page of the book was filled with them. Not necessarily errors of fact, but errors of judgment. Errors of citation. Misleading statements. Non sequitor and *ad hominem* attacks. Errors of either ignorance or distortion.

This book is not a test of humility. It is a test of discernment. This book is what Mrs. Riplinger requested. This "one true believer" has attempted to answer her seven challenges. Perhaps she needs to humble herself under the mighty hand of God. I would not want to stand before God with the results that her writings have on young zealous preacher-boys. She stands to imprison an entire generation in bars of ignorance.

> √ What will so-and-so think? Will this put me "without the camp" or denomination I currently follow?' [Maybe God has plans for *you* to help them]. (p. 1192)

This writer is an independent Baptist in a secluded part of the country. He is not affiliated formally with any Baptist fellowship. He has no camp or denomination to follow. He has no local fellowship and has never determined truth by a majority vote. His only loyalty is to the Word of God and the God of the Word.

It is beneath contempt to assume that any preacher holds doctrine just to get along. Our problem is not over-education and over-dependence on study aids. We live in the day which Hosea foresaw when "My people are destroyed for lack of knowledge" (Hosea 4.6). We are falling under the condemnation of Amos 8:11, "Behold, the days come, saith the Lord GOD, that I will send a famine in the land, not a famine of bread, nor a thirst for water, but of hearing the words of the LORD;" and it is reasoning like Mrs. Riplinger's that is getting us there.

Brilliant (with sarcasm) creative exegesis of the Scriptures is being made because preachers do not avail themselves of the study aids. This author has heard Psalm 1:1 *"Blessed is the man that walketh not in the counsel of the ungodly,* **nor standeth in the way of sinners,** *nor sitteth in the seat of the scornful"* preached that Christians should not stand in the way of sinners getting saved. To anyone with even a basic knowledge of Hebrew and English, the clear intent of the passage is that Christians have no business standing around in regular fellowship with sinners. This is what results from Mrs. Riplinger's seeming contempt for honest, intelligent study of the Scriptures. This author could cite a hundred other examples. People are starving for the words of God and ignorance is keeping them away from a table spread in splendor.

> √ I don't believe that Greek and Hebrew study is wrong (although I have not read this book, documenting its problems, nor can I refute it).' ["He that answereth a matter before he heareth it, it is folly and shame unto him" (Proverbs 18:13)]. (p. 1193)

This author reels at the arrogance of this statement. To assume that just because someone has an informed disagreement with her radical, unsupportable thesis, he must do so because he has not intelligently considered the issue. It is no different from Lenin saying that Communism must be a dictatorship until the majority of people can be brainwashed into it. Her thesis falls on its face because it has an unsound foundation, bricks without straw, and *"untempered morter."*[29] Perhaps, every one of these assumptions which she makes is based on her ego and supernatural revelation.

God wants us to know what He meant by what He said. Any tool that helps us more perfectly understand what He has said can and should be used. Yes, there are waters of scholarship fraught with danger. Yes, those who did most of the research were unsaved and some were unsavory. Yes, there are errors of scholarship which need correction and/or omission. Yes, there are some clear attempts to unseat the King James Bible. But do we stop eating mushrooms because some are poisonous? Do we not spend money because some is counterfeit? Do we not learn to read because some have used writing to advance sin through bad philosophy and pornography?

Or, do we learn how to use the tools God has provided us? Can we not simply ignore any reference to "the better manuscripts," "the oldest manuscripts," and "other manuscripts?" Can we not simply compare what is said against the Scriptures and discern that the author has an untoward motive in a particular statement? Can we not glean from their work that which is positive, that which elucidates, that which enhances our understanding of God's word?

It is just as dangerous to have bad doctrine because of ignorance as it is to have bad doctrine because of heresy and apostasy. If you are wrong, it does not matter why you are wrong. You will miss the mark

---

[29] Ezekiel 22:28

of God's perfect will. You will miss the joy of the fullness of God's revelation.

The most perfect example of this is Mrs. Riplinger's twisting of the application of Pentecost. She goes far beyond the Scriptures in her assertions and assumptions. Is her prejudicial interpretation any different from those which she exposes (Brown, Driver, Briggs, Thayer, Bauer, etc)? The reader may ask, what is wrong with her interpretation and application of Pentecost?

Mrs. Riplinger completely misrepresents the gift of tongues as given on the day of Pentecost. She also misrepresents the gift of interpretation. God knew that people would pervert the meaning of tongues and so He gave several complete chapters of His word to their nature, purpose, and use. None of these match Mrs. Riplinger's assertions.

The apostle Paul and the prophet Isaiah were very clear as to what the gift of tongues was. Neither of them said that the gift of tongues was given for the production of the Scriptures in non-Hebrew languages. The gift of tongues was a SPEAKING gift not a WRITING gift.

Mrs. Riplinger argues from silence and uses out of context distorted texts to make it appear that God says what she said. The following dissertation on tongues presents the biblical perspective on tongues. (Please see the "Appendix," p. 310ff.) The purpose of Pentecost WAS NOT to provide each language group with an independently inspired co-equal version of the inspired words of God.

The gift of tongues was not a revelatory gift at all. The gift of tongues was a sign to Israel that they were on the edge of missing the will of God and His refreshing. This gift spontaneously ended when the Gentiles began to dominate the churches and the Gospel of Jesus Christ was being preached in Gentile languages naturally. The Greek word in 1 Corinthians 13:8 παύσονται - [PAUSONTAI - *shall cease*] is in the future middle indicative form indicating *they will temporarily stop by themselves*. Why did God use this form? Is it because Paul may in fact be the prototype of the 144,000 of the tribulation? After the church is raptured, Israel will be without the sign of tongues. Might not God restore the gift to credential them in an extreme time?

Whether He will or will not, the gift of tongues is nowhere described in Scripture as a supernatural inspiring power which allows a person to produce various translations.

QUOTES AND COMMENTS

(Editor's note: In this section, the author, Dr. DiVietro, a pastor for many years, has selected various representative quotes from *Hazardous Materials* and has commented upon them. These were Dr. DiVietro's personal notes and spontaneous reactions that the editors have decided to publish along with the material previously included in this work. On occasion, the reader is referred to pages in the book for confirmation or examples.)

Quote 1

"Whose tongues were set on fire of hell, burning Bibles word by word? The flame is burning yet today and fanned by the books and software which give their dead authors breath. What dangerous men concocted the hazardous words and texts used today in the corrupt new versions..." (p. 12)

My Comments: The tenor of this book is established on the very first page of the introduction. Of course, Mrs. Riplinger begins her book stating her thesis. There is nothing wrong with that. This opening sentence is clearly intended to capture the reader's attention and draw him into the discussion. If Mrs. Riplinger could develop her thesis cogently, then this rebuttal would not be necessary. However, I find her arguments and assertions woefully inadequate. As you will see, she does not understand many things important to the student of God's Words (2 Tim. 2:15).

Quote 2

"Who was the dorm supervisor who allowed (encouraged?) the worst episodes of sexual violence in British boy's school history? Who was the pedophile who was dredged out of hiding to join the dorm supervisor on the Revised Version Committee? Who took their words and placed them in that best-selling 'Bible Dictionary' on your bookshelf? Who harbored and befriended another well known pedophile who became one of the suspects in the 'Jack the Ripper' case? Who went to the meetings where Luciferian Madame Blavatsky spoke? Who used her serpent logo on his books criticizing the King James Bible? Who denied that the blood of Christ saves? Who defines the word Lucifer like Jesus Christ? Who was on the Westcott and Hort RV committee? Who was on the ASV committee? Who used RV and ASV words to define KJB words? Who was a Unitarian and denied the Trinity and Christ's blood atonement? Who thought Christians were heretics and pagan Gnostics were superior? Who thought pagan Zoroastrianism was a forerunner of Christianity? Who copied all of his definitions from the men who embraced the aforementioned abominations? Who was charged with heresy, even by his liberal denomination? Who was discharged from his college teaching position for heresy? Why are Christians trusting Greek and Hebrew study tools created by these men who have this kind of record – even above their Holy Bibles?" (p. 12)

My Comments: The last question of this paragraph is the basis for this rebuttal. The majority of this book is in the form of *ad hominem* attacks on the people who produced the various lexicons, word studies, grammars, and other language aids used by Bible students to study and understand Hebrew and Greek original texts of the Bible. Fundamentalists are often subject to *ad hominem* attacks. We are outraged, and rightly so, when someone attacks us personally instead of the things that we write or teach. We are outraged, and rightly so, when we are painted with a broad brush and accused of things because of association. Neither personal flaw nor association with undesirable people disqualifies an objective consideration of the matter of language. Could we ask similar questions about someone? Yes, such as, who lied about her marriages? Who was married just months after her second divorce? Whose personal life and resume are filled with questions? Who spun the facts to favor a flawed doctrinal position? Should we go on?

Quote 3

"**This author learned many things while researching this book. I trust that all who find this book in their hands will not assume that they have nothing left to learn.**" (not my bolding, KD) (p. 16)

My Comments: Having read her book thrice, Mrs. Riplinger takes the position that if anyone disagrees with her it is simply because they are ignorant of the facts and/or guilty of pride, which will not allow them to agree with her. Nothing could be further from the truth. This is both insulting and untrue. There are some things that she says that cannot be documented or proven. There are some things that she says that appear to be purposely distorted. There some things that she says that are simply not true. If Mrs. Riplinger is not aware of her flaws and does not hire a fact checker to verify her assertions, or if she purposely misrepresents the truth, she should not be writing on such a delicate matter. One must earn the right to be believed. It is not assumed. The sheer volume of the book almost intimidates the reader, especially the novice in this field. He gets lost in the "facts" and arguments and is overwhelmed. Certainly (he is expected to reason), "Mrs. Riplinger has done her homework and knows what she is talking about. I cannot argue with her conclusions so she must be right."

This author is not a novice. By Mrs. Riplinger's own words, he is "one true believer"[30] and a scholar worthy of citation. By so designating this author, Mrs. Riplinger has given him the tacit right to objectively consider what she has written and offer correction and comment (2 Tim. 4:2-3, 2 Tim. 3:16-17). His comments will not support a contemporary translation or version of the Scriptures. Neither will they support a critically corrected Hebrew or Greek text such as the United Bible Society (UBS) or Nestle-Aland (NA) Texts. His comments will seek to put quotes into their context and remove distortions by Mrs. Riplinger.

---

[30] Page 598

Quote 4

"The "old Serpent, which is the devil" knows the power of the word of God and he has sought to counterfeit it. The great counterfeiter has latched on to the ultimate counterfeit, the so-called 'originals.'" (p. 18)

My Comments: What does she mean by "originals?" Is she referring to the original **manuscripts** or the original **words**? By definition, the original words of the Scriptures **cannot** be counterfeited (Psa. 112:5-6, Mat. 4:4, 24:35, 1 Pe. 1:23-25, etc., etc., etc.).

Furthermore, the truth must exist before there can be a counterfeit. And if the original **words** of the Scriptures still exist, and they do still exist, why should we look for other texts? Mrs. Riplinger is preparing us for a long journey, which will result in her enticing all to reject any reference to the Hebrew or Greek texts which underlie our King James Bible.

Quote 5

"The saga now continues at a deeper level in this encyclopedic book, *Greek and Hebrew Study Dangers, The Voice of Strangers: The Men Behind the Smokescreen, Burning Bibles, Word by Word.* The Lord, the "expert in war" (1 Chron. 12:33), allowed me to forge this new comprehensive weapon which can put to silence the ignorance of foolish men who question the King James Bible at every turn of a page of Greek and Hebrew reference materials...Taken together, *New Age Bible Versions* and the book you hold in your hand create a complete examination of Greek and Hebrew study dangers." (p. 21)

My Comments: *Hazardous Materials* is the third of a trilogy on the King James Bible written by Mrs. Riplinger. Here she draws them together for us. The trilogy includes *New Age Bible Versions, In Awe Of Thy Word,* and this tome *Hazardous Materials.* This author converted *New Age Bible versions* from Mac® format to IBM® WordPerfect® format for Mrs. Riplinger. He created both a subject index and a Scripture index for the volume. He has been her friend. When an article appeared in the *Baptist Tribune* published by the Baptist Bible Fellowship, Springfield, Missouri, he contacted the editor and asked why we attack our friends. He was placed in correspondence with the author of the article. After several interchanges he supplied information to the education committee of the Baptist Bible Fellowship. Approximately a year later the author of the article was dismissed from his position on the faculty of the Baptist Bible Theological Seminary. Although it was not mentioned as the specific reason for his dismissal our correspondence was at least part of the deliberation. This author has been Mrs. Riplinger's friend. But, her inappropriate logic must be answered.

Quote 6

> "THE MOST EGREGIOUS Greek study dangers are found in the critical text made popular by Westcott and Hort and seen today in the Nestle-Aland and United Bible Society's Greek text. Several chapters will document the collusion of B. F. Westcott and C.J. Vaughan, the child molester, who together with the other Revised Version translation committee members corrupted the scriptures and first penned many of the words seen today in new versions, as well as in lexicons such as *Vine's Expository Dictionary of the New Testament.*" (p. 22)

My Comments: I do agree that the Westcott/Hort text, whether in its original form or in its present form (Nestle-Aland 27th edition, or the United Bible Society Greek New Testament Fourth Edition), is a distortion and perversion of God's word. I do not support it in any of its forms. The charges against the child molester may or may not be true. If she has any documented police records proving the accusation, it would be most helpful. Finger pointing often occurs by one's enemies. For example, certified official records are available concerning the multiple marriages of Mrs. Riplinger (see the "Appendix," 325ff, in this work).

CLEANING-UP HAZARDOUS MATERIALS

Quote 7

"The good Greek text, variously referred to as the *Textus Receptus*, Majority Text, and Byzantine text, is popularly accessed today in only three editions, which have varying levels of accuracy." (p. 22)

My Comments: The words *Textus Receptus* refer to the Greek text as it was commonly received at the beginning of the Reformation. This Greek text found its way to print under Erasmus in 1516. A Roman Catholic version of the Greek text was done by Cardinal Ximenes called the *Complutensian Polyglot* which was published in 1521. Erasmus published several more editions of this Greek New Testament, which he tweaked in various places. One major tweak was the inclusion of I John 5:7, a major Trinitarian verse. There are several myths about his inclusion of this verse. A few years later in the 1550s, Robert Stephens, (also known as Robert Stephanus, and Robert Étienne) publish several editions of the commonly used Greek New Testament in Paris, France. In the 1580s and 90s, Theodore Beza published several editions of the Greek New Testament in Geneva, Switzerland. In 1633 the Elzevirs published an edition on the continent in which they included in the preface the words that became Textus Receptus.

Not one of these many published Greek texts was the exact text of the King James Bible in every point of minutia. The translators had all of these printed editions (except Elzevir) plus various Greek manuscripts, versions of the Latin translations in printed and manuscript form, and other corroborative works. These corroborative works include early translations such as the Peshitta, an early Syrian and/or Aramaic text from the second century, and the writings of the early church fathers as well as the lectionaries of the early Greek church. Lectionaries are Scripture portions for reading when the churches met. Out of this volume of documentary evidence, in addition to the previous English translations such as the Tyndale Bible (1526), the Geneva Bible (1599), and the Bishops Bible (1568), the King James Bible emerged. Within a generation, it had captured the imagination of the English-speaking Christian world. No major generally recognized translation has been able to challenge its supremacy. Even after it was

QUOTES AND COMMENTS

challenged by the apostate and heretical men, Westcott and Hort, the KJB's various editions continue to be the best-selling book and most commonly used Bible among Christians who speak English.

No one observing the facts could deny that God has placed his blessing on it. Alone, it has been responsible for the great spiritual movements in the English-speaking world. Does this mean that God separately inspired this translation of the English Bible? Mrs. Riplinger says yes. Others of us say no. Inspiration, θεοπνευστος (THEO-PNEUSTOS) means "God breathed." What were the words that God moved His "holy men of old" to record in the Scriptures? What words contain the very breath of God? What words did God speak out? What words were recorded in heaven from eternity before they were transferred to earth by inspiration? What form did they take when they entered human experience? The Old Testament was given primarily in Hebrew with a few chapters given in Aramaic. The New Testament was given in Greek. This has always been the position of Christians **from the beginning.** It was not until Mrs. Riplinger and her mentor, Peter Ruckman, began to teach the inspiration of the 1611 King James Bible that this was even considered or proclaimed with any seriousness. For example, Papias, (c. 140 A.D.) was cited by Irenaeus (c. 202 A.D.), who was a disciple of Polycarp (c. 70-156 A.D.) and Polycarp was taught by the Apostle John. Concerning the four Gospels, Papias said that the Gospel of Matthew was written in the Hebrew tongue. How can Riplinger challenge these facts?

Quote 8

> "**New King James Version (NKJV):** the resident evil and heresy in the *New King James Version* (NKJV), or any modern version which *claims* to be translated from an edition of the *Textus Receptus*, lies in their editor's use of lexicons, all of which are corrupt. For this reason the English Bible, which saw its seventh and final purification in the King James Bible, can never be updated (Psalm 12:6, 7)." (p. 29)

My Comments: It is very superficial and wrong to state that the use of lexicons is the reason why the New King James Version strays from the truth. In the majority, the New King James Version takes word for word from the original. It changes about 4% of the text to justify a new copyright. Words like *forever* are changed to *eternal* and vice versa. Very little of the New King James Version is the result of appeals to lexicons. This statement by Mrs. Riplinger is totally unsupported by fact.

Quote 9

"Knowing this, God simply gave us the perfect English translation for every word. Why wouldn't he? He also defined each word within the Bible itself." (p. 32)

"If you use Greek and Hebrew lexicons and grammars other than those exposed in this book, know for certain that their definitions contain the same errors as those discussed in this book, because they were taken from one of these authors." (p. 36)

"The reader will find that *all* Greek and Hebrew dictionaries lexicons and grammars use the corrupt Greek text..." (p. 38)

My Comments: This sequence of quotes, and especially this last sentence, begins **a major sub-thesis** of Mrs. Riplinger's book. She does not feel that it is necessary to look at any book other than the King James Bible to discover the dictionary meaning of the King James' words.

There is a further corollary by her in her writings that every difficult word in the King James Bible contains the definition of that word within the word. As an example she explains how *sheol* is the word normally translated *pit* or *hell*. She sees the letters **sh**eol (hole) and **sheol** (hell) in the word *sheol*. By her own rules of defining words here *sheol* could also be a **she**ol. The very idea is absurd and Kabalistic.

Quote 10

QUOTES AND COMMENTS

"(For 22 years I have been examining such materials-*uninterrupted*-for at least eight hours a day. No Greek professor or translator has had that time latitude. I began at the age of 13 with a private tutor of classical language. By the time I was 18, I was hired to teach English to Greek-speaking immigrants. For over 30 years I have waded through thorny Greek briars to rescue tangled sheep, brought near the precipice of unbelief by Greek and Hebrew study tools. There is nothing about the Greek New Testament that I did not see before most of my critics were born, as I am now in my sixties)." (p. 42)

My Comments: This author is only a few years younger than Mrs. Riplinger. He has spent most of his ministry utilizing Greek and Greek tools as well as Hebrew and Hebrew tools. **He did not experience this apostasy** she proclaims. He is as convinced as he ever was that the Bible is the Words of God. He is just as convinced that the King James Bible is the most reliable translation of God's words, which preserves them into the English language. He has never wavered in this belief.

Mrs. Riplinger's hyperbole is totally unwarranted. She is not the only person with extensive experience in the Greek New Testament. This author has a bit of a problem believing her claim that she spent five days per week, eight hours per day reading the Greek New Testament. Even to a student of the word, it seems a bit excessive and unreal.

Quote 11

"Greek and Hebrew lexicons, infected by the unhealthy minds of their authors, have contaminated modern bible versions, Bible study tools, and Bible dictionaries with their hazardous material." (p. 60)

We will return to this same statement repeatedly in this book. **Mrs. Riplinger seems to have a problem keeping her *facts* straight.** On one page, she will assert that the lexicons are the source of the translation and on others she will assert that the translations are the result of the lexicons. She can't have it both ways. Perhaps in her next edition of this book she will make up her mind and rewrite her thesis consistent with that decision.

Quote 12

"Typical is one chapter called "Lexical Evolution and Linguistic **Hazard**" by Frederick Danker, editor of the *A Greek-English Lexicon of the New Testament and Other Early Christian Literature*, a highly corrupt lexicon followed by many new versions and Bible study tools. Danker confesses, "lexicography is more of an art than a craft..." (p. 61)

My Comments: Yes, lexicography is an art as well as a science. To create a lexicon, you must discover the foundational meaning of a word by examining its use in works of literature in that original language near the time of your target. A lexicon of modern Greek would not aid in the translation of the Scriptures. One needs to find how Greek words were used the time of the New Testament. As the compiler of a lexicon is able to examine greater volumes of ancient usages, he is able to better approximate the meaning. Words are not static. Nor are they usually limited to a single definition. Both context and genre affect the meanings.

This is not to say that lexicography is impossible. The meanings of the words of the Greek New Testament have been generally determined. A survey of most Bible translations will show agreement in the vast majority of renderings. It is not lexicography which produces corrupt translations. **It is a corrupt text and/or corrupt translators that produce a corrupt translation.** The translation of Philippians 2:6 is a perfect example.

Philippians 2:6:
1. (KJV) Who, being in the form of God, **thought it not robbery** (ἁρπαγμὸς **harpagmos)** to be equal with God:
2. (NIV) Who, being in very nature God, did not consider equality with God **something to be grasped,**
3. (NASB) who, although He existed in the form of God, did not regard equality with God **a thing to be grasped,**

QUOTES AND COMMENTS

4. (NKJV) who, being in the form of God, did not **consider it robbery** to be equal with God,
5. (NRSV) who, though he was in the form of God, did not regard equality with God **as something to be exploited,**
6. (ESV) who, though he was in the form of God, did not count equality with God a thing **to be grasped,**

Now let's check the lexicons:

1. The Analytical Lexicon of the Greek New Testament:

    ἁρπαγμός, οὐ, ὁ (1) literally *something seized and held, plunder,* (2) figuratively in PH 2.6 of Jesus' equality with God οὐχ ἁρπαγμόν; (a) possibly, as not forcefully grasping something one does not have *something not to be seized, not a prize to be seized*; (b) probably, as not forcefully retaining something for one's own advantage *something not to be held onto, not a piece of good fortune.*

2. The Complete Word Study Dictionary: New Testament

    725. ἁρπαγμός harpagmós; gen. *harpagmoú,* masc. noun from *harpázō* (726), to seize upon with force. Occurs only in Phil. 2:6: "Who [Christ], being in the form of God, thought it not robbery [*harpagmón*] to be equal with God." His truly being in the form of God could not render His claim of equality with God as robbery. The Lord did not esteem being equal with God as identical with the coming forth or action of a robber (*hárpax* [727]). The trans. meaning of *harpagmós,* robbery, is necessary here.

3. Dictionary of Biblical Languages With Semantic Domains: Greek (New Testament)DBL Greek:

    772 ἁρπαγμός (*harpagmos*), οὗ (*ou*), ὁ (*ho*): n.masc.; ≡ Str 725; TDNT 1.473—**1.** LN 57.235 **plunder**, something taken by force (Php 2:6+), for another interp, see next; **2.** LN 57.236 **retain by force**, here the focus is on the holding of something by force (Php 2:6+)

4. The Exegetical Dictionary of the New Testament:

"ἁρπαγμός, ὁ harpagmos robbery(?) *1. ἁρπαγμός occurs in Phil 2:6 and **nowhere else in the NT**. It is very rare in secular Greek and does not appear in the LXX or the Apostolic Fathers. The meaning which predominates in secular Greek, **robbery**, is out of the question for Phil 2:6. For this reason it is proposed that equating it with ἅρπαγά is linguistically possible, and it is translated accordingly (Abel, Grammaire 110; BAGD s.v.; W. Foerster, TDNT I, 473f.), although there is no example of this in non-Christian sources. ἅρπαγμα is (1) plunder or booty, or (2) a chance occurrence, lucky break, or blessing. W. Trilling"

5. A Greek-English Lexicon of the New Testament and Other Early Christian Literature:

   "ἁρπαγμός, ου, ὁ (quite rare in secular Gk.; not found at all in the Gk. transl. of the OT). **1. robbery** (Plut., Mor. 12A; Vett. Val. 122, 1; Phryn., Appar. Soph.: Anecd. Gr. I 36. Also Plut., Mor. 644A ἁρπαγμός) which is next to impossible in Phil 2:6 (W-S. §28, 3: the state of being equal w. God cannot be equated w. the act of robbery)."

6. Greek English Lexicon of the New Testament Based on Semantic Domains:

   "ἁρπαγμός, ου m a plunder: 57.235 b something to hold by force: 57.236"

7. Moulton & Milligan: Vocabulary of the New Testament

   "ἁρπαγμός 725 ..."a gift to be eagerly seized" (Gildersleeve, who compares Phil l. c.), "the keen-sought prize" (Myers). This comes very near to the meaning res rapienda (rather than res rapta) by which ἁρπαγμόν seems best explained if really equivalent to ἅρπαγμα "spoil, prize." Against the solitary profane instance of ἁρπαγμός, in Plutarch 2. 12 "τὸν ἐκ Κρήτης καλούμενον±., "seizure, rape," may be set a very close parallel also Quoted by Lightfoot, οὐκ ἐστίν ἁρπαγμὸς ἡ τιμὴ (from a catena on Mk 10:41ff.). Without

QUOTES AND COMMENTS

discussing the crux interpretum, we might supply a list of the -μός nouns parallel to ἁρπαγμός in formation, as found in NT, such as may be cited to support the practical identity of ἁ. with ἅρπαγμα, and its distinctness from it, respectively.

8. Enhanced Strong's Lexicon:
   "**725 ἁρπαγμός** [*harpagmos* /har·pag·**mos**/] n m. From 726; TDNT 1:473; TDNTA 80; GK 772; AV translates as "robbery" once. **1 the act of seizing, robbery. 2** a thing seized or to be seized. 2A{plain booty to deem anything a prize.
   "The passive sense gives a different meaning to the passage: 'Who *though* He was subsisting in the essential form of God, *yet* did not regard His being on an equality of glory and majesty with God as a prize and a treasure to be held fast, *but* emptied himself thereof."

9. TDNTA:
   "harpázō [to seize], harpagmós [something to be grasped] harpázō. a. "To steal" b. "to capture" c. "to snatch," d. "to seize," e."'to take by force," f. "to catch away" (in visions)."

10. Word Studies in the New Testament:
    Thought it not robbery to be equal with God (οὐχ ἁρπαγὰν ἡγήσατο τὸ εἶναι ἴσα Θεῶ/). *Robbery* is explained in three ways. 1. *A robbing*, the act. 2. *The thing robbed*, a piece of plunder. 3. *A prize*, a thing to be grasped. Here in the last sense.[31]

Having surveyed the lexicons on this important and controversial verse, we find that with an almost unanimous voice they agree that the concept of harpagmos is ROBBERY. It is not the fault of the lexicon or lexicography that the verse is mangled in modern translations. Without non-biblical literature we would have no way to define this word that appears only once in the Scriptures. The change from "robbery" to "a

---

[31] M. R. Vincent, (2002). *Word Studies in the New Testament* (3:432). Bellingham, WA: Logos Research Systems, Inc.

thing to be grasped" is based on a biased editorial decision not firm lexical principle.

This demonstrates the principle that lexicons in and of themselves do not translate. They provide information about a word that allows a translation. Translation is the result of the theology and bias of the translator. This last fact is why translation must be done by informed Spirit-filled translators if it is to be reliable and accurate.

Quote 13

"Lee's prop to bolster bookshelves bowing with bad Bible study tools is to patch them with *even more* decaying materials from secular Egyptian papyri. Lee will take the time-worn faces of Moulton and Milligan and engrave a few more lines from scrawled Egyptian inscriptions, then add a new dusty jacket scrawled on the sands of the Sahara." (p. 64-65, see p. 62 for who "Lee" is)

My Comments: The vitriolic rhetoric of this quote, and others like it, add NOTHING of substance to the argument. There is tremendous value in learning how a word is used in non-biblical literature. God did not often invent words to be used in the Scriptures. He used words that occurred in the languages of Hebrew, Aramaic, and Greek that were contemporary to the recording of the words *"given by inspiration of God,"* which were known to the writers. This is not to say that God did not charge extant words with HIS meanings. He did! But, before one can appreciate His adoption and adaptation of a term, it is helpful and often necessary to know its normal secular use.

In chapter 2 of *Hazardous Materials*, "Lexicon Death Certificate," it is most interesting that Mrs. Riplinger condemns soundly all modern lexicons etc. and uses the words of the very men she hopes to condemn, to condemn. If an author is corrupt, then the truth will seem corrupt. And so if a corrupt author accuses a corrupt work of being corrupt, he is, in essence by Mrs. Riplinger's logic, declaring the corrupt to be accurate and hence condemning his own opinion. Clearly she has introduced an endless cycle of confusion to confuse the reader and

QUOTES AND COMMENTS

leave the reader desiring to just read his Bible and ignore all the arguments

Quote 14

"Modern lexicographers can clearly see the bald errors in today's lexicons. Lexicographers inform us that "the life of a printed dictionary has been approximately twenty years." Soured and moving past the expiration date are all dictionaries usually used by Christians, including *Strong's Concordance Greek and Hebrew Lexicon,* Vine's *Expository Dictionary of the Old and New Testament,* Moulton and Milligan's *Vocabulary of the Greek New Testament,* Perschbacher's *New Analytical Greek Lexicon,* Kubo's *A Reader's Greek English Lexicon of the New Testament,* Vincent's *Word Studies in the New Testament,* Wuest's *Word Studies in the Greek New Testament,* Zodhiates' *Hebrew-Greek Key Study Bible and Complete Word Study Dictionary.* Kittel's *Theological Dictionary of the New Testament,* Bauer, Danker, Arndt and Gingrich *Greek-English Lexicon of the New Testament,* the Greek-English lexicons of Thayer, Liddell-Scott-Jones and all the others." (p. 67)

My Comments: Lexicons must be updated as more data becomes available. When every ancient source has been exploited and all of the data is collected and interpreted, then and only then will a lexicon become concrete. This is the meaning of the comment that they expire. It is wrong to assert that after twenty years we should discard an aid that contains information on the definition, use, and implications of the original languages.

By including this comment, Mrs. Riplinger condemns any revisions of her own works in the future. If she discovers any new data to support her thesis, her new work will invalidate not only the original work, but the revision. She knows that all literary work is subject to review, revision, and re-release. The only thing invalidated by a revision is a conclusion specifically revised in the new release. It does not invalidate the unchanged portions of the work.

In like manner, lexicons can and should be revised and updated as new information becomes available. If they were not, then Mrs.

Riplinger would be characteristically pointing to obvious errors as the basis of rejecting them.

Quote 15

"Given the ever-changing theories of scholars, Chadwick says that any *printed* lexicon is subject to error—" (p. 68)

My Comments: Now there is a surprise! Scholars grow old, die, and are replaced by new younger scholars. The new scholars build on the work of their predecessors, hopefully, weeding out errors and updating information. Scholars also cross geographical borders. A lexicon written in German does not help English-speaking people, unless it is translated into English. In the process of translation, quite often revisions are made. There is no inherent dishonesty involved in the process.

Would it be preferable that all lexicons, dictionaries, grammars, etc. were done by born again, Spirit-filled, well-educated, universally-read, unsoiled authors? Of course! Is that a practical reality? NO! Therefore, we are often forced to use the work of someone who is not of that spiritual ilk. We ignore their postulations and accept only their concrete data. If we find that their root definitions are inalterably biased by their theological and philosophical positions, then we reject the work. If facts can be gleaned from a work, even when surrounded by error, a discerning reader is able to make good use of a bad book.

Quote 16

"In the end scholars simply want the reader to "make his or her own decisions about the meanings of words" rather than take definitions dogmatically from a lexicon." (p. 69)

My Comments: Absolutely! Only a harsh critic like Mrs. Riplinger would assert that the authors of lexicons start out to change the meanings of words and to make accurate translation impossible. The reader should make his/her own decision with the following caveat. If a person is not able to make an intelligent decision based on personal knowledge and experience, then they are making decisions based on pragmatism and emotion. **The problem is not with the lexical aids. The problem is with those who use them.**

Quote 17

"When a Greek word is defined in a lexicon, it is invariably the Greek word in the corrupt Greek text of Westcott-Hort, Nestle-Aland and the United Bible Society, not the Greek word seen in our Received Text Bibles and any edition of the *Textus Receptus*. Since most who use these tools do not know the differences between these two text types *at every point* and cannot *really* read the Greek words, they will be unaware that they are being given the definition of the *wrong* Greek word! For example Rev. 15:3 says, "King of saints" in the KJB and the Received Text. The corrupt texts and modern versions say either "King of ages" or "King of nations." Therefore the lexicon's definition will be given for the Greek word *aion* (e.g. ages, NIV) or *ethnos* (e.g. nations, NASB), not the Greek word, *hagios* (saints, KJB). For this reason alone, all lexicons and Bible study helps should be buried to prevent the spread of their deadly hazards. This includes *all* lexicons as well as *all* Greek grammar books. Complete autopsies of their dead works follow in this book." (p. 70)

My Comments: The first part of this comment lays the blame for inaccuracy on the under-educated reader of the study aids. This can only be corrected by proper education in textual matters and then in Greek/Hebrew language.

The example she gives is more heinous and seemingly purposely deceptive than a lexicon. Any inquirer trying to discern a *deeper meaning* of Revelation 15:3's "King of saints" should see huge red flags if the definition they find says *King of nations*. The same would apply to *King of ages*. It was exactly this kind of scholastic incongruity in I John 5.13 that drove me as a Greek 101 student to investigate and learn the issues around Bible texts and translation. Shame on anyone who would not recognize an obvious corruption such as her illustration.

In addition, lexicons do not translate verses. You do not look up Revelation 15:3 in a lexicon. You look up the Greek words ἅγιον, ἔθνος, or αἰών. To make the error Mrs. Riplinger indicates, the reader would have to be totally unfamiliar with Greek and totally dependent on an interlinear that uses the Westcott-Hort based modern text as the underlying Greek text instead of the King James Bible's underlying Greek text. The reader would have to take the Greek word to an analytical lexicon where he would find the lexical form. Finally, he would then look up the lexical form in a lexicon and determine the meaning. A person this unfamiliar with Greek or Hebrew rarely has the determination to follow this full process. Usually they just look up the Strong's number. The Strong's number for these three words is DIFFERENT and would not lead them to a false lexical definition. Her entire illustration is invalid.

Quote 18

"New version editors and naïve Bible students look to lexicons for what they think are 'advanced' insights. How shocking to discover that lexicons often take their 'meanings' from corrupt bible versions themselves." (p. 77-78) (See pages 74-78 in *Hazardous Materials*)

My Comments: On pages 74 and 75, Mrs. Riplinger objects to the concept of building on another's work. All languages, and therefore all language tools, build on the past. It is not plagiarism to revise an earlier work that is updated and based on new knowledge and new understanding if the new work credits the old work. In the field of Bible and language, there have been very few who have actually accomplished anything in lexicons and dictionaries. Therefore, by necessity, virtually all modern Greek lexicons, dictionaries, and word studies start from some former work and revise. In itself, this does not disqualify a work. It is the accuracy of the reviser that qualifies the work.

The quote above from pages 77-78 is an assumption by Mrs. Riplinger that is not supported by facts. The average KJB reader doesn't want 'advanced insights.' They want to know what the KJB

QUOTES AND COMMENTS

translators thought was the proper meaning of the words which underlie our King James Bible.

Lexicons are compiled BEFORE translation and are the basis of translation. It does not work the other way around. The translation of a lexicon from a language other than English may follow the publication of a version of the Bible translated using that lexicon, but the lexicon comes FIRST! It is intellectually disingenuous for a person to say that lexicographers take their meanings from translations of the Bible unless the person is specifically writing a lexicon of that particular version. **NONE** of the major lexicons are written as a lexicon of a particular version.

Riplinger then goes on to cite several authors who infected more Bibles.

Quote 19

"One of the fired professors, Heber R. Peacock picked Barclay M. Newman, Jr. to compile *A Concise Greek-English Dictionary of the New Testament.* Newman's methodology is typical.
"Newman admits he borrowed English words from the **Revised Standard Version,** the **Goodspeed** translation and the *Good News Bible New Testament.*" (p. 78)

My Comments: This is an example of a purposeful distortion of the facts. Newman is not a general lexicon. It is a lexicon of words in the New Testament. I do not have access to this volume, but I am sure that its introduction will identify the Greek text from which it is derived. This is a lexicon specifically to define words AS THEY WERE USED IN MODERN TRANSLATIONS. This is quite different from the major lexicons like Arndt & Gingrich which started from the secular usage of the words used in ANY Greek New Testament.

Quote 20

"Newman based his lexicon on W.F. Moulton and Geden's *A Concordance to the Greek Testament* which is based on the adulterated Greek texts of "Westcott and Hort, Tischendorf and **the English Revisers [Revised Version]**." (p. 78)

My Comments: Again, READ THE TITLE AND INTRODUCTION. Newman was defining words USED IN THE MODERN TRANSLATIONS as evidenced by the fact that he used a concordance of those works. If a student is TOO LAZY to know the character of the research tools he uses, then his conclusions will always be flawed. We cannot burn all books to prevent incompetent use.

Quote 21

The following is a significant quote from the book:

"Newman's is typical of all lexicons: 1.) It takes its English 'definitions' from corrupt bible versions. This pattern used by all lexicons will be thoroughly documented in this book. 2.) It is based on the corrupt Westcott-Hort Greek text (Aland-Metzger, UBS), not the *Textus Receptus*, and 3.) It copies its definitions from an earlier lexicon, which copied its definitions from one earlier than that—all the way back to Liddell-Scott. Therefore Metzger's definitions, some admittedly coming from Newman, came originally from the corrupt text and the vilest new versions in print. Yet how many naïvely look to Metzger's *Concise Greek-English Dictionary* definitions for the 'original.'" (p. 78-79)

My Comments: The statement above is **a significant quote** from Mrs. Riplinger's book. Newman is not typical of all lexicons. This generalization is totally unwarranted and inflammatory. Again, it reverses the process. Translations come from lexicons. Only secondary lexicons come from translations. Even then while the Greek and/or Hebrew words come from a corrupted text, the lexical definitions, if properly derived, will give a proper base meaning of the word translated. Lexicons are not arranged by reference. They are alphabetically arranged.

All lexical works and dictionaries depend on previous works. It is impossible for any one person to acquire all of the data necessary to create a lexicon from scratch. It is much easier to take an earlier lexicon and revise and correct it.

Mrs. Riplinger's next complaint or condemnation against modern study tools is that they have passed through Germany. She invokes the image of the axis powers to slander the **American lexicographers** on the following pages. Again, it is the quality of the work and not the origin of the authors that determines the usefulness of a lexicon or dictionary. On earlier pages Mrs. Riplinger rues the fact that lexicons get their definitions from commentaries that get their verbiage from translations of the Bible and translations of the Bible that get their vocabulary from lexicons that get their definitions from word studies that get their definitions from commentaries etc. *ad infinitum*. There is nothing sinister about this process.

No wise student takes their documentation, definition, or direction from just one work. There is a reason. I have a library of over five to six thousand books. Many of them are language study works. While no one of them is inerrant, one can gain an overall sense of the meaning of the word phrase or grammatical structure by comparing the various articles on those matters. One does not translate a version of the Bible by simply comparing the Greek vocabulary or Hebrew vocabulary to a single lexicon. If in fact the translator is bound to a lexicon for his translation, he is not qualified to translate. It is for this reason that I do not accept the work of most modern translation committees. I once was told by a language student that you do not really know language until you can dream in that language. I'm not sure that there are many who dream in biblical Greek or Hebrew.

The implication that a lexicon would deceptively attach the definition of the Greek word to the English of the Bible version, as Mrs. Riplinger directly implicates, is ludicrous. It demonstrates either total incompetence or willful deceit on her part. Her comment in this field is inflammatory and absolutely inaccurate. (For example, consider her comment concerning translations using saints, nations, and ages in quote 16.)

CLEANING-UP HAZARDOUS MATERIALS

Quote 22

"Did God express his opinion of the **German** to English Bauer, Arndt, and Gingrich *Greek-English Lexicon of the New Testament and Other Early Christian Literature?*" (p. 81)

My Comments: Was it necessary for God to express his opinion of the German to the English-speaking authors of this lexicon? No. God didn't have to inspire the lexicon. As long as the lexicon analysis of the Greek language is correct, the lexicon fulfills its purpose. Mrs. Riplinger's demand that all lexicons be inspired of God is absurd.

Quote 23

"If one hopes to translate (plagiarize with permission) German lexicons, fluency in German is a must. Danker worked with Arndt and Gingrich in translating the **German** lexicon of Bauer (who in turn worked from **Latin**-Greek dictionaries) and recently worked with Bauer's **German** revision by Kurt Aland. Danker admits that there are "**hazards** in semantic [word] transference from one language to another." He says, "The capacity of German for formation of compounds can lead to **semantic falsification** when features in the context of a specific Greek term become embedded in the receptor glossing term, without determining the specific meaning of the source term." Yet he cites several **German**-based lexicons as sources of his definitions, such as those by Nazi war criminal Gerhard Kittel as well as those of Baltz and Schneider." (pp. 81-82)

My Comments: Mrs. Riplinger is playing on the stereotypical anti-Semitism of mid-20th century Germany. Unless she can demonstrate a clear anti-Semitism in the lexicons, this prejudicial quote is absolutely meaningless.

Danker's admission that NO TWO languages have exact verbal equivalence is the very reason we need lexicons. This is not a reason to reject all lexicons. Translation is only possible when the set of concepts under the umbrella of a word in a source language intersects the concepts under the umbrella of the receptor language. The primary purpose of a lexicon is to present the full set of ideas represented by the donor language vocabulary. The assumption is that the reader is familiar with his own language and will be able to pick the proper word in the receptor language.

The non-equivalence of two languages is the reason lexicography is an art and not a science, although science is involved. The compiler of a lexicon does not make up definitions. He discovers and compiles them. The person utilizing the lexicon is responsible for applying the lexical work.

Quote 24

"**The Liddell-Scott *Greek English Lexicon:***
"All Bible study dictionaries are based in great part on the definitions in the first Greek-English lexicon by Henry Liddell and Robert Scott, although this is not expressly written on most of them. The Liddell-Scott *Greek English Lexicon* is the whorish MOTHER of all harlot lexicons..." One can merely trace the history of each definition or new version word, which I have done, and see that it springs from Liddell-Scott, the first Greek-English lexicon." (p. 83)

My Comments: On subsequent pages, Mrs. Riplinger goes into a long rant condemning all lexicons because of the weakness of Liddell-Scott. However, that is precisely why there have been so many revisions of Liddell-Scott. It needed revision! Subsequent scholars had the good sense to see the need to make them. One does not condemn the hospital because it is full of sick people, especially if they come out better than when they went in.

Quote 25

"The Liddell-Scott Lexicon (and from it all Bible study tools, new bible versions, and lexicon authors) gathered its word meanings from the same crumbling Greek ruins which show God's judgment upon that ancient Greek empire and no less upon the German nation which likewise relied on the pagan Greeks to support their shaky German-Latin lexicons. Such Greek sources include the bawdy plays, both tragedies and comedies, the pagan myths, as well as the political and anti-God philosophical writings of the ancient Greeks who lived during the centuries before and after the time of Christ." (p. 90)

My Comments: Pray, where else would one find the definitions of words as they were used in the time of the writing of the New Testament than in the secular writings of the same era? Anyone, with an even cursory understanding of languages, knows that, unless you learn a language by total immersion into a society, in order to speak that language, it is necessary to have some vocabulary and grammatical aids.

Lexicons of other languages are created the same way that dictionaries (lexicons) are made of the English language. Words are defined by their use. Definitions do not come from lexicons. Lexicons come from definitions.

My own practice when reading the Greek New Testament and coming upon a word or grammar structures that I do not understand is to go first to my lexicons, grammars, grammatical analyses, and word study books. I then go to the Perseus Project, which is sponsored by Tufts University, where all extant Greek texts are computerized with search engine. I quite often do a search for the word or structure and examine how it was used by the Greeks because God took the words from the language as they were used in the days of the writing of Scripture, but He charged them with his own meanings. Before I can comprehend his usage, I need to first understand their usage. Denying me that resource is to deny me full understanding.

Quote 26

"All lexicon authors, like Danker, tell their readers that they consult the godless ancient Greek authors "Plato, Thucydides, Herodotus, Aeschylus, Sophocles and Euripides" to determine the meaning of Bible words. As a graduate student in classical Greek Danker studied "Plato,

Aristotle, Pindar, Thucydides, ..." His second year textbook was Aristophanes' *Clouds*. Did this Greek author's "rollicking wit" provide the key to understanding the Bible? Danker said that he had a "special interest in Homer, Pindar and the Greek tragedians. Chadwick quips,
"...it is hardly possible to be sure now what exactly Homer meant in some of his formulae; he may not have known himself."
Truer words were never spoken. If we can not be sure what Homer meant (and Homer himself did not know), why are we using his writings to define Bible words? (p. 90-91)

My Comments: Let's think about this for a moment. When the King James Bible was translated, the English language was still in the process of being birthed. In fact, the King James Bible and the plays of William Shakespeare are given credit for establishing modern English. The words used in the King James Bible are the same words used in the Shakespearean plays. To gain the general meaning of any given word or to see how it was used in non-biblical English, it is perfectly proper to note its use by William Shakespeare and his contemporaries.

Biblical Greek is a dead language. According to Mrs. Riplinger Greek had evolved into a new level by the year 600. The Greeks of Greece no longer spoke what is known as Koine Greek. Actually even that is irrelevant. There is no one today that speaks historic, koine, classical, or Byzantine Greek. Modern Greek is an amalgam of a Turkish and the remnants of Greek mixed with a little Slavic influence.

It is not biblical Greek. It has a different vocabulary and a different grammar, just as modern English differs from Chaucer. Most modern English speaking people could not begin to intelligently read Chaucer in its original form. To understand Chaucer one has to go back and trace the development of words observing how they are used in contemporary contexts. For convenience, those words are often arranged into a lexicon.

We define words by usage. In 2009 the word *gay* does not have the same meaning that it had in 1909. 300 years from now it may well have another meaning. The only way a **future** translator or commentator would be correct in his definition of *gay*, would be to isolate the word as it is used **right now** and apply that knowledge to his work. The philological and etymological development of the word may or may not be important to our understanding. But they are worth examining. It is absurd to assume that we can understand biblical Greek in a vacuum.

The Bible was not written in a vacuum. It was written using words they were common to both the writer and the reader. If they were not, they would not have been understandable even by their original addressees. How can Mrs. Riplinger object to us learning the meanings of those words the same way a child of that day would have learned them? She is being unreasonable and unrealistic in her demands.

Quote 27

> "Some Greek-English lexicons and Bible study tools generate their definitions by studying the works of the early Catholic church 'Fathers,' secular writers such as Philo and Josephus, and a swarm of first through third century heretics. The lexicons imply that some of these men are 'Christian' writers, but their heresies make them very unsound sources for determining Christian meanings." (p. 92)

My Comments: Again, these comments originate from a vat of sublime absurdity. The early church fathers wrote theological treatises in Greek and the New Testament was written in that same Greek. Although many were heretics, word usage, grammatical structure, and other translational issues can be learned from their writings without absorbing their heresies. Yes, Clement of Alexandria, Origen, and many of the Eastern fathers were consumed with Greek philosophy. Often their doctrines do not match the Scriptures. Many if not most modern heresies and cults find their origin in Origen. Origen was given credit for merging Christianity and Gnosticism successfully. Clement was his teacher. I would not go to Clement or Origen or to the other early Eastern fathers for theology. However, I have their works in both English and Greek so that I can gain some insights into the everyday working of the Greek language.

I hate to be pejorative, but Mrs. Riplinger's blind prejudice causes her to make some very foolish statements. When the world spoke Latin, the Roman Catholic Church insisted on writing in Greek. Once vulgar languages developed and people no longer understood Latin, the official language continued to be Latin even in the Catholic Churches Mass.

Even though we reject the theology and the attendant biases in their writings, there is much knowledge of the Greek language to be gleaned from the Latin-Greek works of the Catholic Church. In subsequent chapters, Mrs. Riplinger will **conjecture** that God gave at least parts of the New Testament in Latin that was a contemporary language with the Greek. She would have us believe that Latin is consistent with the inspired Greek texts and yet she will deny us concrete parallels between Greek and Latin of the same age to be used in the construction of a lexicon. She is inconsistent.

Quote 28

"The ancient pagan Greeks never wrote a Greek-English dictionary. What they would have said in English is anyone's guess. Any English-speaking person who gives an English definition of an ancient Greek word is simply guessing. Definitions are 'guessed' by looking at the word in context, examining ten words before and ten words after. The context must be the one in which the word is used, not that of another author. A discussion about 'love' by *Playboy* founder, Hugh Hefner, or even the Inquisitor Pope Innocent III, will not elicit the definition of 'love' used by Jesus Christ in the Holy Bible. Even within the work of one author, a word may have several different meanings depending upon each individual context. Yet, in their drive to secularize the Bible, lexicographers and new version editors toss their own rules to the wind and refuse to define Bible words using only the context of the Bible. They plunge God's pearls into the murky mire of paganism." (p. 100)

My Comments: Mrs. Riplinger's comment that Bible words are defined by reading 10 words before and 10 words after in the English Bible, the KJB only, borders on insanity. Rarely are the words of scripture defined that way. We define God's words by examining **all** the uses of that word in the Bible. But even that can be very fallible because only the English word is examined. We can still misunderstand what God is saying, if the English words or phrasing are ambiguous. How many of us have confessed to not understanding the phrasing in a passage in English. At times, it takes diligent study. What too many are doing lately is believing what at commentary says, rather than digging it out ourselves.

God did the not give the New Testament to Matthew, Mark, Luke, John, Paul, Peter, James, and Jude in 20th century English. He did not give it in 17th century English. It came from other languages: specifically, Hebrew, Greek, and Aramaic. The English Bible came from other languages. Even if I were to accept Mrs. Riplinger's absurd conjecture that God gave his word simultaneously by inspiration in each of the 14 languages of Pentecost, or even in the 70 languages of Genesis 10 and 11, still English in the 16th century, much less the 21st century, was not one of them. Proto-English did not exist. Therefore, unless God **directly dictated** the Bible in 1611 in a second round of inspiration, the translators (and notice we call them translators and they called themselves translators) converted the language of the Bible from some source other than the English into English.

Unless they too were gifted with tongues in the same context that Mrs. Riplinger assigns to the apostle Paul, they had to learn those languages. And, they've learned them from grammars, lexicons, word studies, comparing them to the Latin; reading pagan works; reading heretics; or being taught by someone who had gone through that process. English is not an original language and it is not a primary language, and as a matter of fact, it is not even a secondary or tertiary language. Therefore, there were several intermediates between the original inspired texts of the Scriptures and the 1611 King James Bible.

Quote 29

"The words of the King James Bible are often higher, 'special' words, not defiled or defined by worldly use. Danker dislikes these, calling them "churchly" words; lexicographers avoid them, calling them "ecclesiastical" words. These include words such as 'hell,' 'heaven,' 'preach,' 'grace,' 'gospel,' 'mercy,' 'lust,' 'carnal,' 'charity,' 'salvation,' 'sanctification,' 'heathen,' 'heresy,' 'superstition,' 'heretick,' 'redemption,' 'righteousness,' 'salvation,' 'repent,' 'judgment,' 'covetousness,' 'ungodly,' and 'tribulation.' One will be hard pressed to find these words in most new versions and Bible study tools. Liberal lexicographers have from the very beginning set out to strip the Holy Bible of its 'holy' 'separate from sinners' vocabulary by replacing these holy words with the words of sinners. The English definitions and translation choices in lexicons are highly secularized, that is, they are "the words which men's wisdom teacheth," not those special "separate from sinners" words which God instilled early in the English Bible." (p. 101)

My Comments: Where do I start? The vocabulary of modern Bible versions **is not the results of lexicons**. It is the result of the false premise that the Bible can be made understandable to the unsaved masses. Modern translators are trying to reduce the difficulty of readability just like insurance companies have been forced to reduce technical language in their documents. Instead of teaching men to understand the technical language of the Bible, they water it down. This philosophy has nothing to do with the lexicons. It is a theological and philosophical bias of the translator.

Modern men are lazy. Most of them don't even know what a dictionary is. This includes preachers. Any discipline has its own special vocabulary. Nuclear physicists speak in terms which are understandable primarily by other nuclear physicists. Doctors use medical terms that are only understandable by other doctors. They don't do this to purposely obscure what they are talking about. The nature of their work demands an accuracy in language to avoid disaster.

I agree with Mrs. Riplinger that there are certain words that need to be in the Scriptures. I also agree that modern translators are repulsed by them, so they try to simplify them. In their simplification, they often pervert and lose the meanings God intended. Loving-kindness is not the same as mercy. Sacrifice is not the same as propitiation. Assembly is not the same as church. The list goes on. Still, the problem is not the lexicon. The problem is the translator and his philosophy.

CLEANING-UP HAZARDOUS MATERIALS

A good translator strives for accuracy at the same time he strives for understandability. If one has to suffer, let it be readability not understandability. One can always get a dictionary to define and understand difficult words. But once a concept is watered down it is no longer the same concept.

In every discipline there is the development of specialized terms, which gained meaning and universality through the years. For some reason modern theologians and especially translators want to break that rule when it comes to the Bible. Each new team of translators seems to want to establish their own independent originality and so reinvent theological terms. Perhaps this is done because a certain amount of text has to be changed in order to gain a copyright. So, we change eternal to everlasting, everlasting to eternal; we change charity to beloved, love to charity, will to shall, and shall to will etc. etc. etc. We drop terms like propitiation. We drop terms like repentance, salvation, born again, only begotten, etc., etc. We change words and other terms that have had established meaning for centuries. Instead of making the Bible clearer, they introduce new terms that are so ambiguous that only the informed clergy are qualified to interpret.

Tyndale's plowman can now read the Bible, but the 'bible' he reads has been stripped of all its precious contents. Reading is reduced to a high schooler's recounting of Salvific history. Unfortunately for Mrs. Riplinger, what they write has absolutely nothing to do with her *Hazardous Materials*. Using the same *Hazardous Materials* I could justify the translation of the King James Bible without any difficulty. It is not WHAT THE LEXICOGRAPHERS, COMMENTATORS, GRAMMARIANS, PHILOLOGISTS AND ETYMOLOGISTS WRITE, IT IS WHAT THE READER SELECTS FROM WHAT THEY WRITE.

Just as a student attending a college can choose faculty and courses to reinforce his or her own belief, or they can choose faculty and courses which introduce revolutionary untried concepts. Students can attend Harvard University and graduate with a phenomenal education or can attend four years get a diploma and know less than when they went in. Again, the result is not the sole function of the process. The student subjective application of what is available is the single most determining factor in his or her production thereafter.

Quote 30

"(Reading grade level is dependent upon the number of syllables in a word. As unusual, lexical substitutes have many more syllables than their corresponding KJB words. In this case 'grace,' a one syllable word, is replaced by 'generosity,' a five syllable word. Consequently, new versions, which use the words in lexicons, are always a higher reading grade level than the KJB.)" (103)

My comments: While reading grade level may include the number of syllables in a word it is not solely dependent on the number of syllables in a word. Again, hyperbole and distortion replace clean thinking and accuracy.

There seems to be a constant confusion between translation and lexicography in Mrs. Riplinger's work. A lexicon does its best to present the basic meaning of the word. Lexicographers cannot suggest meaning in a vacuum or from one work or for one period of time. A lexicon gives several of the common uses through the centuries. Translation involves the intelligent, contextual application of a lexical meaning.

The theology of the translators of modern versions has much more to do with the word selection in the translation than the lexicons. If the translators are literalists, then the translation will come out similar to the New American Standard Bible (NASB), which I do not recommend, primarily because it is based upon the wrong text. If the translators accept *dynamic equivalence* as their primary philosophy of translation, then the result will be similar to the New International Version (NIV). If the translators want to be accepted as intellectuals, the vocabulary they choose will be stilted and difficult. If they want to be seen as simplifier's of the Scripture, then the result will be the New English Bible (NEB) or something similar. The translation is always more a function of the theology and philosophy of the translators than it is of the lexicons.

CLEANING-UP HAZARDOUS MATERIALS

Quote(s) 31

"The same phenomenon occurs with the Hebrew Old Testament. In the KJB the single Hebrew word *sheol* is translated 31 times as 'hell,' 31 times as 'grave,' and 3 times as 'pit.' All three words correctly describe a pit, the depth of which varies. All men are buried in a grave or a pit, but all men do not go to hell. The context reveals where the person might be going and the KJB relays that information. The word sheol contains both the word 'hole' (**s**he**ol**) and the word 'hel' (**shel**ol). (In German 'hell' is 'holle'; have you ever heard of a bad place referred to as a 'hell hole'?). All go to a hole; some go to a hole called 'hell; it just depends how far down you ride the elevator of the pit—just to a shallow grave or down to the deep "enlarged" pit in the center of the earth (Isaiah 5:14)." (p. 108-109)

"*The Language of the King James Bible* traces the etymology of the word *(s)heol* back to the Hebrew word **Hel**el, meaning Lucifer. The words *helel* and *(s)heol* are related to 'burning' and 'shining' (like the hot sun). It is seen in English as 'hell,' in Greek as 'helios,' in Middle English as 'helle' and in Danish as 'helvede.' Many new versions and lexicons join the Jehovah Witness sect and refuse to translate the word *sheol*, just as they refuse to translate the Greek word 'hades' in the New Testament. They simply leave the Hebrew word *sheol* and the Greek word *hades* untranslated and carry its letters into English (to transliterate). They do not transliterate *ouranos* (heaven). Why? It is not as hot!) (p. 109)

My comments: Since the KJB supposedly finds its definitions within the transliterations of the Greek and Hebrew, didn't they do that with οὐράνος [OURANOS]? Or, does this nifty little trick only work for certain words? Is Mrs. Riplinger as biased as the editors of the lexicons and translators of the new translations of the Bible?

Quote 32

"Kohlenberger's *The Greek-English Concordance to the New Testament with the New International Version* lists **12**

QUOTES AND COMMENTS

different Greek words which are translated as the one English word, "destroy (ed)," in the NIV. Most are not varied morphological forms of the same word and are not even from the same lemma (stem). These numbers are very typical of nearly every sentence in the NIV and other new versions." (p. 111)

My comments: This phenomenon is not unique to modern translations. All one has to do is to appeal to either the *Englishman's Greek Concordance* or *Young's Analytical Concordance* and he will find that the King James translators did the same thing. Context determines the ultimate choice of words in translation. Lexicons only give the base meaning. Greek words have synonyms. English words have synonyms. Proper translation takes place when the exact meaning of the Greek word in its context is matched with the proper English word. Sometimes a single Greek word can have several proper English translations. Sometimes an English word can have several different Greek sources. This does not make a translation suspect. In fact, attempts to match one English word with one Greek or Hebrew word results in an awkward, inaccurate, almost non-understandable translation. Mrs. Riplinger is apparently hoping that the King James reader does not know that the King James Bible does the same thing.

Quote 33

"The New Testament has approximately 5,170 lexical items, which could potentially have scores of thousands of English equivalents. But only one of these equivalents is "holy, harmless, undefiled, separate from sinners, made higher" and is perfect for each context (Hebrew 7:26). Who, but God, can choose which word fits in which context? Because of these wide varieties of options, none of the hundreds of English translations of the Bible are the same. The Bible says, "let one interpret" (1 Corinthians 14:27)." (p. 113)

My comments: Here we go with one of Mrs. Riplinger's more absurd arguments. While I believe the KJB is the most accurate trustworthy blessed translation of the Scriptures into the English

CLEANING-UP HAZARDOUS MATERIALS

Language, I also believe any place the proper Greek/Hebrew text is translated accurately (according to lexical definition, grammatical construction, and biblical context), we have the words of God in the English language. English has changed in 400 years. Words like *prevent* and *let* have changed meanings. It is possible to restate verses containing those words in modern English without changing the words of God.

Quote 34

"It is absolute blasphemy for an undergraduate Bible school student to be told to make a translation of a chapter of the Bible. The possibilities are endless; the assault upon the word of God is akin to the crucifixion. Using the available lexicons and grammars, he will merely replicate the translation errors exposed later in this book. More seriously, he will be following the serpent, as Adam did, to think "Yea, hath God said?"" (p. 113)

My comments: How else is a student to learn Greek? It is not the process that is wrong. It's just incomplete. This was exactly the method by which I taught myself Greek. However, after completing my own translation, I compared it to the King James Bible. I asked myself, "what did I miss?" If my translation was different from the King James Bible translation, I would note the lesson. From the beginning, my study in Greek was to discern what lay behind the English of the King James Bible. It was never to correct the King James Bible. It was to understand the Bible better so that I could preach, teach, and apply the Words accurately.

Quote 35

"An upcoming chapter on R.C. Trench will explain the Biblical directive for having only one Bible translation in each language. Only God can place the proper translation equivalency in the proper context. This chapter has proven the absolute necessity of having one inspired Holy Bible for each language. God would not inspire Greek originals (which few would ever see) and cast the translation of the great mass of Holy Bibles (which billions would see) to a panoply of opinions." (p. 114-115)

My comments: It really doesn't matter what R.C. Trench explains. Especially, since it will be Mrs. Riplinger and not R.C. Trench that does the explaining. This is one of Mrs. Riplinger's misdirective quotes. Like a magician she is skilled at creating false impressions. She is referring not to the words of R.C. Trench, but to Gail Riplinger as she attempts to self verify an outlandish statement. Despite the danger of 'one true believer' being declared a heretic by Mrs. Riplinger, let me state clearly that I believe wherever the inspired Hebrew, Aramaic, or Greek Words are accurately translated, we have the Words of God. Notice several key words. **Inspired**: the words that God himself spoke; **accurately**: brought into English (or another vernacular language) with the same intended definition, implication, and grammatical emphasis as the original inspired words. While I believe that the only place where I can consistently and confidently believe that I am reading the accurately translated inspired words is in the King James Bible, I do believe that it is possible to elucidate and clarify the King James Bible words by appealing to the original inspired words.

Lest Mrs. Riplinger or any other reader attempt to distort what I would say, let me be clear. When I say the original inspired words, I am not talking about the physical autographs of Biblical writings. I am talking about **the words** which appeared **on** those original autographic writings, which God has preserved for us to this day.

Quote 36

"The definition can be gathered: 1.) from the word next to the word in question, 2.) from several words away, or 3.) by taking 10 words or so from either side of the word. Observe the following 'meaning' or definition which is formed by examining most of the usages of the word 'hell' in the Bible." (p. 116-117)

My comments: This principle is fine for general reading. It is also applicable to English. However, since the Bible was not written in

English, it is totally inadequate for creating lexicons or other study aids for the Bible.

Someone at some time had to determine what the English equivalent to the Hebrew and Greek words of the Scriptures was. Whether these equivalents were compiled into a formal lexicon or not, there was consensus on these equivalents within the translating committee of the King James Bible. These equivalents did not come as the result of Mrs. Riplinger's methodology. They came from familiarity with the Greek and Hebrew as well as many other ancient languages. For example, Dr. Lancelot Andrews, Dean of Westminster, and Chairman of the Westminster group of ten men, was conversant in 15 languages and had prepared his own devotional in Greek.

Quote 37

(On page 118, Mrs. Riplinger appeals to the fact that:)

> "The pagan Greeks describe *hades* (NIV, NKJV, ESV, HCSV, et al.) as a cold, dreary place in which to read and muse." (p. 118)

My comments: Subsequently, she tries to apply that definition to the modern translations of the Bible. This is a perfect illustration of twisting the facts. The word *"hades"* unquestionably appears in the Greek text of the New Testament. To pretend that it is not the source of our word hell is absurd. In order to begin to discover the Biblical definition of hell, it becomes necessary to determine the original meaning of *hades*. But that is not the end. Having determined that *hades* was the Greek word for the domain of the dead, we now go to the Bible and use Biblical context to determine God's usage of the word. The word *hell* was chosen from its Germanic roots because it was closest in meaning to *hades*. The word indicated the afterlife. Once the word was chosen, then its meaning is determined from its Bible use, not ancient Norse mythology.

QUOTES AND COMMENTS

Quote 38

"When working with books other than the Bible, lexicographers do not define words in contexts written by someone other than the original author." (p. 119)

My comments: This simplistic statement could **not** be further from the truth. There is a difference between the lexical meaning of the word and an author's use of the word. **Again**, the lexical definition is determined first and then the author's particular usage is determined.

Quote 39

It is unscholarly to define Bible words using the pagan Greeks or the liberal and confused Catholic 'fathers.' The context in which to define Paul is Paul, not Plato...The King James Bible's built-in dictionary holds the 'meaning' and 'definition' for every Bible word." (p. 120)

My comments: It is not just not unscholarly; it is the only way to determine a base meaning for a word. Once an individual has determined its use in secular language and determined that base meaning, then it is possible to examine the author's use in its context, to determine its specific meaning, and thus to properly translate it. Every book's vocabulary can 'in the main' be defined in the same method that Mrs. Riplinger would apply to the Scriptures. But it only works in the language of that book. And it only provides an approximate definition.

Les Miserables was originally written in French. A reader might deduce unfamiliar words using Mrs. Riplinger's process, but they could not bring this great work from French to English using that process. Mrs. Riplinger must know that. And thus is born her absurd theory that the Bible was given simultaneously in the independent languages of every nation through the gift of tongues. She believes and will state this theory in future pages.

CLEANING-UP HAZARDOUS MATERIALS

Quote 40

(On pages 122 to 123, Riplinger dismisses every Greek grammar as tainted, illegitimate, and inaccurate:)

> "If professional Greek grammarians recognize problems in Greek grammar textbooks, why are professors presenting such material as if it were woven from the veil of the temple?" (p. 123)

My comments: Is Mrs. Riplinger so naïve as to think that a grammar of the English language is static? Certainly she knows that language is a dynamic subject. The basic grammar of Greek is not in question. The nuances of the koine dialect are still not totally understood. As we build our understanding of koine idiom, of course books on grammar are going to evolve. But that does not mean they are without value. Once again the student, and not the grammar textbook that he uses, is the determinant of his accuracy. If I have a basic understanding of the Greek idiom, I can then observe it in its context throughout the New Testament and determine its implication. A grammar simply gives me a starting point, which I would not have if I discarded it. Flexibility demands a fulcrum or else it is simply freefall.

Is Mrs. Riplinger trying to have us believe that there is no passage in Scripture that is ambiguous in English and which needs clarification? And where is this clarification to come from if we cannot appeal to the language text from which the King James Bible was translated? And how will we understand that text if we do not have a basic understanding of the grammar of that language? And if I do not have a basic understanding of the grammar, where will it come from if it is not from a grammar textbook (or notes from a life mentor).

On the subsequent pages, Riplinger discusses the flux in understanding of Greek verbs. That does not change the implication of those verbs. The primary reason for this flux in understanding seems to be a desire to change the translation of the Scripture. For instance, one major New Testament grammarian would now have us to believe that since John used the perfect tense so often that he could not have meant the implication of the perfect. His "confusion" stems from his own

QUOTES AND COMMENTS

desire to denigrate the implication of the perfect for his own purpose and not from any objective observation.

There is a basic understanding of the Greek grammar. While small items are still argued, there is no need to discount all Greek grammar books as useless.

Quote 41

"The life of the Bible is shown in its verbs and Satan's scribes have pointed their "hurtful sword" at the Bible's very heart. The errors, heresies, and faulty translations in Greek grammars will be examined throughout this book...Students are also not taught that all Greek grammar books are based on the corrupt Nestle-Aland or the UBS Greek texts, with verb frequency counts and other particulars varying from the *Textus Receptus* and its historic translation." (p. 126)

My comments: If a student is too lazy to read the preface and introduction to discover the focus of a grammar book, then he is not qualified to use it. However as in lexicons, if the Greek reading of a grammar book does not match the Greek of the New Testament in the Textus Receptus, then you ignore it! There's no great mystery. Compare the words. If they don't match it doesn't apply. I have a general rule. Any time any reference book says "the better text" or some equivalent term, I immediately discount and ignore its conclusion at that point. There is nothing wrong with a grammar or lexicon that intelligent use cannot and will not override.

Quote 42

"In their English translation all Greek grammars ignore the inflected endings on Greek verbs." (p. 127)

My comments: Where do I start? This statement is patently false on its face. No grammar book that I know ignores the inflected endings on Greek verbs! What Mrs. Riplinger is referring to is that modern English uses the pronoun *you* for both the singular and plural second person. Each grammatical use indicates singular and plural to the student. Just because it does not use 17th-century *thee, thy, thine,* and *ye* does not mean that it ignores inflected endings. Mrs. Riplinger's comments are absolutely blatant distortions of the truth. Yes the use of 17th-century pronouns removes ambiguity. But, since they are no longer in use, one cannot expect texts on grammar to use them either. Perhaps she has not read how that the word *anow* was removed from the 1611 edition by the 1769 and in all subsequent versions because it was obsolete. I wonder if Mrs. Riplinger uses a 1769 or the actual 1611?

Quote 43

"Errors in Greek grammars are not limited to verbs. Prepositions provide another pathway away from the straight and narrow path. The English translation of prepositions can open the door to every heresy imaginable. For example, in *Essentials of New Testament Greek* by Ray Summers *dia* (by, through, et al.) is incorrectly translated as "through" in John 1. 'Through' can mean 'by means of' and is best expressed succinctly in this context as 'by.' But Summers blasphemously translates it as "through" and that denies Christ is God..." (p. 128)

My comments: And Summers' translation is wrong in John 1:3! This does not change the fact that Greek prepositions have several implications in English. Should grammarians lie? The specific meaning in a given passage is determined by context and context alone and context includes the entire Bible! It is a judgment call. And, I believe that the KJB translators made the right judgments. While Summers can disagree with their translation, he cannot with any authority, other than his own opinion, say that they were wrong. Again, if a student is not wise enough to understand this, then he or she should not be using a grammar book.

Quote 44

"Memorizing the misdirected English translations of verbs in any current Greek grammar will be as fruitful as memorizing a medical textbook from the 1700s..." (p. 130)

My comments: One small fact, grammars do not translate! It is their job to tell us what grammatical forms imply, not what words mean.

Quote 45

"**Sanskrit**: Robertson applauds the work of New Ager Max Müller. Like him, he believes that the discovery of the Indian Sanskrit language "revolutionized" grammar. This linguistic switch from a Hebrew origin of language to an Indian origin mirrored the late 18th century shift from Western Christianity to Eastern mysticism and from creationism to evolution. Robertson brought the new theory of the 'Indo-European' origin of language which "revolutionized grammatical research" in his mind. Robertson admits that "the Old View" that "Biblical Greek is thus a language by itself" was subject to a "full revolt." He joined those who were "against the theory of a Semitic or biblical Greek." He says, "The old view of Hatch is dead and gone". (p. 132-133)

My comments: On this page, Mrs. Riplinger is appalled that scholars no longer consider Hebrew the original human language. She would have us reject all philological studies to the contrary. There is nothing to be gained by insisting that the languages of the Bible were pure Holy Ghost languages, given specifically for the writing of the Bible. Neither is there anything lost in recognizing a gradual development of languages. The inspiration and preservation of the scriptures is in no way related to either, UNLESS one is trying to build a foundation for the theory that there is no human reason for learning the specific languages of the Bible.

CLEANING-UP HAZARDOUS MATERIALS

Quote 46

"Imagine, a Christ-rejecting Unitarian like Thayer, giving English interpretations from a German grammar. That does not sound like the 'original' Greek to me." (p. 133)

My comments: Just because a grammar was written in Germany and translated into English does not mean that the grammar is of German grammar origin. The analysis of the Greek language is the subject, not a statement of origin. Once a grammar is translated into English, it is no longer German. If the observation is valid, it does not matter who first discovered it. We use many works that come from other countries and languages. Are they not valid because an American did not develop them? Is Victor Hugo's *Hunchback of Notre Dame* or Solzhenitsyn's *Gulag Archipeligo* less than great works of literature because they were not authored in English?

Was the New Testament written in Greek or not? If it was and if a grammarian makes a correct observation, then the honest student is forced to accept that observation. Neither the translation nor the aids in translation change the 'original Greek' that Mrs. Riplinger fears so much.

Quote 47

"The harsh allegations about the dated character of both lexicons and grammars proves only that there is no agreement among the last four centuries' finest minds – I said 'minds' not hearts. There are no authorities, outside of God's word, merely *opinions*, like Adam's, Eve's, and Satan's." (p. 135)

My comments: Quote 47 above pertains to a comment by Mrs. Riplinger about A. T. Robertson's comments on a Greek idiom. Her comments about lexicons and grammars were based upon taking Robertson's commentary out of context and were twisted to say that no lexicons and grammars have any value. The study of languages is always in flux. There are certain details which evolve with time. To

QUOTES AND COMMENTS

build a lexicon or the grammar of a living language is always a temporary work. Dead languages are different. A dead language is frozen in time. However, until every aspect of definition and usage is discovered and established, there are and will be differences of opinion.

The honest student knows that. He seeks a utilitarian knowledge of the language which will allow him to fully appreciate the Bible he now holds in his hand. Mrs. Riplinger would take that away from him. By extension, she would deny him the use of commentaries and teachers' guides since they too are the works of man. Each of us should simply read and meditate on the scriptures and the Holy Ghost will give the meanings. Using her philosophy there should be perfect understanding with unanimity among all 'true Bible students' who follow her methodology. Right!

Quote 48

"No one seeking to define a word, should ever define it with a more difficult, longer, less-used word. But this is what is done. I have cringed every time I have heard teachers define Bible words for over 30 years. The definition given is usually the word in the modern versions!" (p. 141)

My comments: Is she kidding? When working with another language, a word can rarely be fully translated by one English word. It is essential to charge an existing English word with all of the impact of the Greek or Hebrew word. While the translation will contain one English word, the Greek or Hebrew thought behind it is most often represented by more than one original word. The reader who wants to grasp the fullness of God's revelation wants to know the full meaning of the English word he sees in his King James Bible. He is not troubled when he sees a lexicon try to give the fullness of the original word.

Quote 49

"The English derivative 'porn,' we are told, will help us to understand the English words 'whore' and 'fornication', but it actually mis-defines it. The real English root for 'forn' is much more descriptive as it describes the *actual* 'arching over,' (e.g. fort, fortify) which *porn* does not entail. The word 'fornication' may really come from the words *fornax* and *furnus*, meaning 'to burn.' This perfectly parallels the Bible verse, "[F]or it is better to marry than "to burn" (1 Cor. 7:9)." (p. 145)

My comments: Whether Mrs. Riplinger likes it or not, the Greek origin of the words 'whore' and 'fornication' is 'porneia'. I do not see what her reference to 'arching over' has to do with the Greek source of the word unless she is referring to the positions of human bodies during sexual intercourse. Even if Mrs. Riplinger is right about the source of the English word, it does not change the meaning of the Greek and Hebrew words. Having read the book multiple times, I know that she is subtly building her case for a Bible inspired in English, separate from the Hebrew and Greek words which God actually breathed-out and preserved through the millennia. **Her** theory about an inspired English Bible is the only thing that legitimizes her absurd statements here.

Quote 50

"The only thing that is being learned when Greek tools are consulted is that the English Bible is not *quite* right. The implicit question arises in the listener's heart – 'if the Greek word means 'such and such,' why didn't the KJB say that? Oh...my Bible is wrong...'" (p. 148)

My comments: Mrs. Riplinger has already recognized me as "one true believer" and so I speak from belief not doubt. The student must be discerning. If the commentator is fleshing out the English words of the King James Bible, attempting to charge the English words with the full implications of the original Hebrew or Greek words, then there is no challenge to the accuracy of the King James Bible. Can Mrs. Riplinger honestly say that 'let' or 'prevent' or a plethora of other KJB words have not changed in meaning in the last 400 years? Does she honestly expect the normal modern reader to understand the word

QUOTES AND COMMENTS

'superfluidity' or 'lasciviousness' without some explanation? If she is an honest commentator, she must acknowledge that there are times that appealing to the original languages gives the reader or hearer a more accurate understanding of a passage and does not at all challenge his confidence in his Bible. Is Mrs. Riplinger's view of the scriptures so fragile that it cannot stand the light of truth?

Quote 51

"Metzger thinks that even the 'originals' contain errors. In Metzger's *A Textual Commentary on the Greek New Testament*, he says that Matthew penned "erroneous spelling" in the 'original' edition, in both Matthew 1:7 and 10, in the genealogy of Christ." (p. 149)

My comments: Knowing Dr. Metzger's flawed view of Scriptures, I can easily ignore his comments on any given subject. However, Dr. Metzger has had more influence over the text of Scripture than any other American scholar in the last 50 years. His textual commentary is not intended to interpret the Scriptures. It explains WHY THE MODERN TEXTUAL COMMITTEES CHOSE A GIVEN READING IN THE MODERN ECLECTIC TEXT. One does not look to Metzger to explain the scriptures. One does not look to Metzger to understand the scriptures. One only looks at Metzger to see the manuscript evidence for the reading the modern textual critics substitute for the Received Text reading. He has no other value.

Quote 52

"Most new versions are based upon the Greek text created in the 1950s by Metzger for the United Bible Societies. He admits that the "German word for "butcher" is Metzger." He is well-named, because his Greek text carves, chops, and grinds to mincemeat nearly 8,000 words from the Received Text." (p. 150)

My comments: While it is true that Metzger has been instrumental in attempting to replace the Greek New Testament with a modern mess, there is no reason for the *ad hominem* attack on him. There is no relevance in the German meaning of his last name.

Quote 53

"In the transformation of the RSV the into the NRSV, Metzger joined Jesuit priest, George MacRae, S.J., secular Jew, Harry Orlinsky, Lucceta Mowry, and others "in eliminating masculine-oriented language" and coming up with "the least unsatisfactory rendering." (p. 155)

My comments: We know he is heretical in his beliefs about the Bible. Why does this surprise us? No KJB believer puts any value in the modern versions or the people who create them.

Quote 54

"Philip Schaff denied the inspiration of the Bible and only chose committeemen who agreed that the Bible had *never* been inspired; he called 'inspiration,' "the moonshine theory of the inerrant apostolic autographs"." (p. 163)

My comments: On page 163 in the quote above, Mrs. Riplinger is talking about the ASV committee. Again, we know Philip Schaff was heretical in his belief on the Scriptures. We do not accept his theology, conclusions, or translation. His work on church history is invaluable. No other work has compiled so much information on the history of Christianity. The Bible-believing Christian has to read between the lines to see the true churches and Christians since it is written from the traditional Catholic-Protestant perspective. But it is still a valuable reference work despite the heresies of its author.

QUOTES AND COMMENTS

Quote 55

"God will not promote a bible that teaches heresy. The RV/ASV Committee included several Unitarians..." (p. 171)

My comments: I agree. That is why all those 'bibles' eventually find an obscure dusty library shelf for a home while the KJB continues to live in constant use.

Quote 56

"If Strong intends to use a translation that still needs to be translated (i.e. using a transliteration of Greek words, such as a 'Hades' or 'demon'), why did he not leave the KJB's transliterated words such as heresies (*hairesis*), heretic (*hairetikos*) Jesus (*Jesus* in Heb. 4:8 & Acts 7:45) or martyr, (*martur*)? Strong's ASV omits what his fellow committee members called "fearful" terms and "excessive conservatism," such as the words 'heresies,' 'martyr,' 'hell,' and 'devils'." (p. 174)

My comments: Mrs. Riplinger is correct in this. Modern translators do not have the courage to translate key words of Scripture. This does not invalidate the Strong's Concordance, one of the most used concordances in modern Christianity. The problem with the lexicon at the back of the concordance is not its 'liberalism.' The problem with the lexicon is that unlearned people use it incorrectly! Just because a single Greek or Hebrew word has many correct translations does not mean the reader is free to pick whichever definition fits his fancy. Without knowledge of the languages, Strong's lexicon can be a very dangerous thing.

Quote 57

"Where does James Strong get his definitions? He gets some of them from the Koran! He believes the higher critics' false theory that the Hebrews got their Bible words, not from God, but from the neighboring pagans." (p. 188)

My comments: It is statements like this that make me doubt the veracity of Mrs. Riplinger's claim to knowing classic languages. She does not demonstrate that knowledge if she has it. Lexical definitions are determined by studying usage in the language. Since the Hebrew Scriptures are the only major literary work of ancient Hebrew, when meanings were not evident, scholars turned to languages in the area that were known to be related to Hebrew. Semitic languages are very similar. There is value in tracing a given 3 letter consonantal root of a word through various languages. While the definition may not be the biblical definition, it gains insight into the meaning of the root. To say that they found definitions in the Quran is foolishness. Since it is a major source of old Arabic where it used the same roots as the Hebrew text, it is helpful in the study of words. It was used just as Egyptian, Aramaic, and Babylonian texts were used. It HELPS in the understanding of Hebrew words. It does not define them.

I suspect that this is a crude attempt to delegitimize the study of surrounding Semitic languages (and non-semitic languages for loan words from Egyptian *et al.*) to help to discern the meanings of Hebrew words. Since the Bible is the only large source of ancient Hebrew words, scholars do look to neighboring languages to find common roots and common words to confirm and/or define the words in the Hebrew Bible they translated. There is nothing sinful or anti-God in that process. They are not saying that the work of the Bible is a human work although some might. What they are saying is that languages do not exist in a vacuum. Countries next to each other with different languages often have an intermixing of the two, particularly languages from a common source. Latin contains the basic Latin morphemes modified by their vulgar use. Would it be wrong, if I did not know a word in English, to look at the word in German and Swiss and Italian and Spanish to attempt to define a word in those languages that is the exact equivalent of the word in English? That is all they are doing.

QUOTES AND COMMENTS

Quote 58

"Strong's encyclopedia charges that Lucifer is not Satan, but Lucifer is Jesus Christ. It quotes one "Dr. Henderson," whom Strong notes, "justly remarks in his annotation:"
"The application of this passage [Isaiah 14:12] to Satan, and to the fall of the apostate angels, is one of those gross perversions of Sacred Writ..." (p. 189)

My comments: The question is not should the word *Hallal* (הֵילֵל) be translated Lucifer or morning star. The question is WHO is being described here. *Hallal ben shachar* (הֵילֵל בֶּן־שָׁחַר) no matter how it is translated means *the bringer of the morning*. The passage clearly indicates that a person is being addressed. *Hallal ben shachar* is a proper title of this person. The only question remaining is how to translate it. Lucifer means light bearer or light carrier. The Morning Star announces the morning and would be a legitimate translation if the Lord Jesus himself did not bear this appellation.

The translators of the King James Bible were limited by the rules of translation given them by King James. They were to maintain the usage of formal names which had been established in previous translations. Since there is absolutely no reason to change Lucifer into Morning Star, they retained it.

The difficulty that Mrs. Riplinger is referring to is the modern attempt to eliminate Lucifer or a Satan as a person. **This comes not from the Greek or the Hebrew but from the unregenerate heart of the commentator.** Jesus is the only true Morning Star. Satan may have been the anointed cherub. Jesus never was. Satan was cast from heaven, as Jesus tells us he was. But Jesus was never cast from heaven. It is wrong when there is ambiguity to create a contradiction in the Scriptures where none exists. By translating Lucifer, rather than Morning Star, King James translators avoided any ambiguity or contradiction. They were completely justified in the translation.

Coming back to the modern translators, lexicographers, and commentators, their choice of the word Morning Star is a clear indication of their unregenerate heart and willful distortion of the Scriptures. That being said, they still may be accurate in some of their lexicography and or grammatical statements. It behooves the student to either learn enough of the underlying languages or stick strictly with the King James Bible. Our problem is ignorance, not heresy.

Quote 59

"He cites several who chide the KJB translators' "superstitious adherence to the Masoretic text..." In upcoming chapters, readers will learn that modern Hebrew 'scholars' construct word meanings based upon the secular and distorted usage of surrounding pagan nations...Strong's Encyclopedia directs the reader to one of the most extreme works of the higher critics, "Ewald's *Hebrew Grammar*". The encyclopedia denies that the original Hebrew text had vowel points, saying "the vowel sounds formed no part." This belief often enables Strong to write *his own* Bible, "when a change of the points [vowels] would give a better sense..." (p. 196-197)

My comments: I have already addressed the use of other languages to help in the understanding of biblical Hebrew. I will not repeat. A new issue though is addressed in this passage. Did the biblical Hebrew, when given by God, include vowel points? This is a major issue because the same tri-consonantal root in Hebrew can indicate totally different words, grammatical usages, and/or part of speech, based on the vowel assigned to it.

This issue is rather tricky. Most ancient languages of the ancient Middle East do not include vowels in their written forms. That does not mean that the languages were without vowels. One cannot have a language without vowels. Consonants begin and end syllables and words. Vowels make the basic sound of the word. When God gave the 10 Commandments to Moses, He gave them to him in written words and spoken words. Frankly, we do not know if the original written text of the Scriptures included vowel points, but the words clearly included vowels. There are some biblical bases for believing they were part of the original.

QUOTES AND COMMENTS

There are those who contend that the vowel points were original and were later removed by Kabalistic Jews so that they could introduce mystical ambiguities into the Hebrew text. There are also those who contend that the Cantor of the Jewish synagogue is the historic preservationist of the original verbalization of the Hebrew text. Those who believe the vowel points were original lean on the meaning of the word translated tittle in the New Testament. They say that tittle means *hireq*, the smallest of the Hebrew vowel points, and that Jesus was in fact verifying their inspired source. They point to the fact that Jesus said *"Man shall not live by bread alone but by every word that precedeth out of the mouth of God."* The argument goes, without vowels, it is impossible to divide the Hebrew text into definite words.

This is not a new theory. However, because of archaeological evidence, it has fallen into disrepute. It has been revived and is a growing conviction among conservatives who believe in the inspiration and preservation of every word of the Scriptures. There can be no room for ambiguity or error.

Quote 60

"The front matter of his concordance, in which Strong lists the PLACES where a given word is used, is still perhaps the most valuable tool Christians have to "compare spiritual things with spiritual." (p. 200)

My comments: Wow! Suddenly the author's prejudices, inaccuracies, and other foolishness does not affect the validity of his work. In every other case an author's personal flaws, associates, organizational affiliations, and other defects removes all credibility from his work. But now, because Mrs. Riplinger needs the Strong's Concordance to do her only acceptable method; Strong becomes a hero.

Quote 61

"Even the reformer Philip Melancthon said,

"[I]t is a duty to abide by the pure and simple meaning of Holy Writ, as, indeed, heavenly truths are always the simplest; this meaning is to be found by **comparing Holy Writ with itself**. On this account we study Holy Writ, in order to pass judgment on all human opinions by it as a universal touchstone." (p. 202)

My comments: Melanchthon was a German. Suddenly being a German is not a fatal flaw! In fact, somebody translated Melanchthon into English before Mrs. Riplinger could make the quote. (Unless she is fluent naturally in German and then we have to take her word for it.) And I bet they used a lexicon and grammar books. What heretic could have done that? Was he saved? Can we trust him? Or was she dependent on some devious, deceptive, demoniac for this quote?

Seriously, I agree with Melanchthon. But being a Renaissance writer and friend of Martin Luther, I know that Melanchthon was not limiting himself to Luther's translation. His statement is a foundational hermeneutical statement. The best way to interpret the Scriptures is to compare Scripture with Scripture. But the point is lost. Translation is not interpretation. Interpretation depends on sound translation.

Quote 62

"Liddell and Scott took the first *big* English bite from this tree of "knowledge." At the bottom of every Greek-to-English New Testament Lexicon lies the residue of the pagan Greek civilization. Stirred up by Robert Scott and Henry Liddell in 1843, this scum is mixed with their cooked-up English definitions and served today as spiritual food to starving baby Christians...Their poison spreads from generation to generation, as *Vine's Expository Dictionary* tells readers it follows Thayer's *Greek-English Lexicon*, which in turn informs readers that it followed Liddell-Scott's *Greek-English Lexicon*...[S]oftware developers have taken Liddell and Scott's definitions for Greek words and passed them off as their own. Only Logos Bible Software of Bellingham, Washington, brings them out of the closet, boldly parades their 'Greek Pride,' and names Liddell and Scott on their CD-Rom version of the 9th unabridged edition of the *Greek-English Lexicon.*" (p. 205)

QUOTES AND COMMENTS

My comments: Henry Liddell and Robert Scott established a primary Greek English lexicon. This lexicon serves as the foundation for most modern lexicons. It was not perfect. Neither is any modern lexicon. This is the reason there is more than one in circulation. Two things affect the accuracy of the lexicon: (1) the understanding of the original language and (2) the current state of the receptor language. While the original language does not change as our understanding of the language becomes more complete, lexicons which are used to translate it must also be revised. As the language we speak changes, definitions that were clear in the past become ambiguous or inaccurate. There is no shame nor is there any fatal flaw in the concept of lexicons just because they change.

No reputable lexicon ignores the past. A new lexicographer may legitimately use Liddell-Scott as a beginning point. He may legitimately replace wrong definitions and/or update them. Lexicons are not inspired of God.

Quote(s) 63

"The lexicon's English definition for 'bird' may be 'good.' Their pagan definition for 'soul,' 'spirit,' 'heaven' and' 'hell' will be 'evil.'" (p. 206)

"Dean Liddell and "The don's wives seemed content to allow this stammering clergyman to photograph their daughters completely nude, though only when they were very young [pre-teens]". Liddell and his coterie provided the children and Dodgson, the pedophile, provided the camera." (p. 206)

"Liddell and Scott, at the baby-faced age of 23, began working on *the first* (of its kind) Greek-English lexicon in 1834." (p. 209)

The evil purpose of the whole lexicon is openly admitted in a Liddell letter. He "regrets" to see a mind "running too much to **pure** theology." (p. 209)

My comments: Someone has to be first. There is nothing wrong with a lexicon which attempts to find the usage of a word in secular society. The Bible was not written in a special "Holy Ghost language" as was once thought. God did not invent a new language for the Bible. He had the writers write from their normal vocabulary which is why we can discern between John and Luke, *et al.* A lexicon is valuable because it brings together the various uses of a word in the original language. A comprehensive lexicon shows the meaning in various significant contexts and usages. The educated Bible translator or commentator then uses that information in the Bible context to translate the word as it has been selected and charged with meaning by God.

Quote 64

"As Liddell mocks the Bible's words, a "monster" mocks him. He admits,
"Behold the monster, as he has been mocking my waking and sleeping visions for the last many months.'"
The monster takes the form of the Greek letter Π (pi).
"In July 1842 he writes to Scott: 'You will be glad to hear that I have all but finished Π, that two-legged **monster**, who must in ancient times have worn his legs a-straddle, else he could never have strode over so enormous a space as he has occupied and will occupy in Lexicons.'" (p. 211)

My comments: The two quotes, numbers 62 and 63, contained what I consider one of the most absurd arguments I have ever seen. Mrs. Riplinger appears to have taken a statement completely out of context and produced an entire "theology".

On the next page, see quote 63, Mrs. Riplinger proceeds to identify "π" (Greek *pi*) with some kind of mystical power and occultic implication. Nothing could've been further from the truth. It is obvious to anyone with an objective eye that he is talking about the sheer volume of the words beginning with *p* in the Greek language. It was obviously "the hump" of his work. The frequency and diversity of vocabulary of Greek words started with the remainder of the Greek

QUOTES AND COMMENTS

alphabet is dwarfed by that which precedes it. However, Mrs. Riplinger continues:

Quote 65

"Liddell's mind was entombed in the ancient world of Greek myth, art and architecture. He saw the Greek letter π (Pi) come to life as the Greek statue called, The Colossus of Rhodes, one of the seven wonders of the ancient world. The statue represents the pagan Greek sun god, *Helios*, from whence we get the English word 'hell'. This 'god of hell' can only be the devil. He was represented in the statue about 110 feet tall, whose widely spread legs once straddled the harbor of the Greek island of Rhodes, many affirm. The pose represents the occupation and spreading dominion of the pagan sun god, Baal, always represented by the circular shape of the sun (and from which we get the word-'ball'; the football goal posts connecting the horizon line over which the kicked ball 'sets.')" The arms and legs of Liddell's sketch also depict radii of a circle; the monster's left (evil) eye is the circle's center point. (The circumference of a circle equals p [the monster] times the radius squared.) The pagan temples of the Greek gods were built using π (3.14), since they thought it was a magical number." (p. 213) **[All above emphases including brackets and small print are Mrs. Riplinger's]**

My comments: This is ridiculously absurd. Hell comes from a Norse word 'hel' not Helios. *The Barnhart Concise Dictionary of Etymology* under "Etymology and Germanic Mythology" says,

> The modern English word Hell is derived from Old English hel, helle (about 725 AD to refer to a nether world of the dead) reaching into the Anglo-Saxon pagan period, and ultimately from Proto-Germanic *halja, meaning "one who covers up or hides something".[32] The word has cognates in related Germanic languages such as Old Frisian helle, hille, Old Saxon hellja, Middle Dutch helle (modern Dutch hel), Old High German helle (Modern German Hölle), Norwegian and

---

[32] Robert K. Barnhart, (1995) *The Barnhart Concise Dictionary of Etymology*, page 348. Harper Collins ISBN 0062700847

> Swedish helvete (hel + Old Norse vitti, "punishment"), and Gothic halja[3]. Subsequently, the word was used to transfer a pagan concept to Christian theology and its vocabulary[3] (however, for the Judeo-Christian origin of the concept see Gehenna).
> The English word hell has been theorized as being derived from Old Norse Hel.[3] Among other sources, the Poetic Edda, compiled from earlier traditional sources in the 13th century, and the Prose Edda, written in the 13th century by Snorri Sturluson, provide information regarding the beliefs of the Norse pagans, including a being named Hel, who is described as ruling over an underworld location of the same name.

The word 'ball' comes from:

> Etymology: Middle English bal, prob from Old English *beall; akin to Old English bealluc testis, Old High German balla ball, Old Norse bo?llr, Old English blawan to blow[33]

So much for Mrs. Riplinger's scholarship. She seems to be making this up as she goes, purposely distorting things to fit her thesis.

Quote 66

> "His biographer wrote of Liddell's **unending task of correcting**" the Lexicon. So many errors, a lifetime would not permit them to be fixed. Yet this dorm room project of pimple-pocked preppies is used as THE authority to correct the Holy Bible. Even when he was in his eighties, "He still worked, as has been recorded, at the Lexicon, making many corrections throughout..." (p. 214)

My comments: Anyone who has ever attempted to write a work on the level of a lexicon knows that constant proofreading and revision is essential. While I may not agree with Liddell's conclusions in every case, I can find no fault with him trying to be as accurate as possible.

---

[33] http://www3.merriam-webster.com/opendictionary/

QUOTES AND COMMENTS

Quote 67

"Lost in Translation: German to English? Latin to German? Greek-English Lexicons give the false impression that they go from the 'original' Greek right into English, supposedly taking today's reader even closer to the ' originals' and the mind of God. In fact *all* Greek lexicography comes first through *German Lexicons*, the cesspool of Higher and Lower Biblical Criticism. The Liddell lexicon was based upon one used "in Germany for the old epic Greeks" (p. 215)

My comments: No, that is not what the term Greek-English implies. The term implies that an English reader can look up a Greek word and see its English equivalent(s). The title implies the **RESULT** not the **PROCESS.** The reason that modern lexicons are based on German lexicons is because no Americans had done the work to produce one independent of the German original. Why reinvent the wheel? Americans did not invent the wheel but they took the wheel already invented and modified the technology to produce some of the greatest machines the world has ever known.

In the same way, English speaking scholars took the best the world had to offer them and modified them to English use. In the process, definitions were updated. After 200 years and various revisions, they are truly Greek-English lexicons which can take the reader back to the original Greek. This has nothing to do with the Greek manuscripts. It refers to the Greek words as used in common discourse when koine was a living language.

Quote 68

"There, we can trace the words as they travel from the *pagan* Greek mind, blinded by looks at Catholic-touched Latin-Greek lexicons, shadowed by the dark forest of German unbelief, then stagger into the dorm room of a wine-blushed English *student*, who was not a native speaker of German. English words devised this way are not pure, holy, nor given by inspiration, the words which God uses to describe his words." (p. 216)

NO ONE claims that lexicons are inspired of God! When I was in Romania and preached, my sermon was translated. When I was in Jordan and preached, my sermon was translated. When I was in Canada and preached, my sermon was translated. In all three cases, the translator used words as defined in every day usage to translate. He was not looking for Holy Ghost inspired words, just the right ones. We prayed for success and accuracy. But there was no Holy Ghost lexicon for him to refer to. Did God use my words through an Arabic translator? Yes. Did he use them through a Romanian and a French translator? Yes. But the translation did not come from a Holy Ghost lexicon. And when there were questions about what I meant, the translator asked and I explained in MORE THAN ONE WORD until he got the concept.

Quote 69

"Liddell's ungodly circle of like-minded friends is brought back to life through the medium of his official biography, *Henry Liddell*, which was sanctioned by his wife and written by a friend and admirer. Liddell chose to surround himself with imps and wimps from Satan's inner circle of mind-molders and nation-makers.
George **Eliot** (aka Mary Ann Evans) (pantheist and libertine)
Arthur **Stanley** (consoler of Luciferian Annie Besant, Revised Version host and translator)
John **Ruskin** (Socialist, racist, New World Order Utopian, fascist, alleged pedophile, and member of the Metaphysical Society and Sidgwick's Society for Psychical Research (contacting the dead through the séances)
Charles **Kingsley** (universalist, whose endorsement appeared in Darwin's *Origin of the Species*)
Benjamin **Jowett** (pantheist and heretic)
Max **Müller** (professed atheist, lecturer on Hinduism, author of *Theosophy* (1893), who had a "generous estimation" of Luciferian, Madame Blavatsky)
C. L. **Dodgson** (pen-name, **Lewis Carroll**, alleged pedophile and author of *Alice in Wonderland*, a book named such because of Dodgson's prurient 'interest' in Liddell's child, Alice; ...

QUOTES AND COMMENTS

Robert **Scott**: Member of Westcott and Hort's vile Revised Version Committee of 1881." (p. 221-222)

Mrs. Riplinger's 'shotgun' approach to guilt by association occurs throughout her work. Some of my professors from college have since fallen into sin. Does that invalidate all that they have taught me? I have had friends who disappointed me and acquaintances that were guilty of heinous sin. Does that mean whatever I say has no validity? NO. A reference work's credibility rests on its substance, not on the associations of its author(s). Wrong associations may prevent me from fellowshipping with a person, but it will not automatically discredit his work. Dr. Graham has affiliated with undesirable religious leaders. In his latter years, he has embraced positions he would never have embraced in his youth. I cannot be a part of any evangelistic effort by Dr. Graham, but that does not mean I cannot appreciate what he has said and done in the past. He wrote some excellent books. Those things which he rightly said are still right, even if he no longer holds some of those positions. There are others who share this condition. William Spafford, writer of the hymn, *It Is Well With My soul,* denied the existence of hell in his latter years, but I still sing that great hymn. Guilt by association is another red herring.

Quote 70

"As a youth, Liddell had read this *very* philosophy expressed by Plato, who taught that each man's soul was a small part of the Soul of the World and was therefore divine." (p. 224)

My comments: Let us concede that Henry Liddell was not a fundamentalist. He may not have even been saved. The real question is, is his concordance accurate and useful? Does it have flaws? Yes. Does it in some ways reflect his heresies? Yes. Has it been revised? Yes. Can it serve as a starting place for an accurate lexicon of KJB words? Yes.

Quote 71

"Liddell's *Lexicon* had broken down long-standing meanings for Bible words...What a relief for all to discover that the burning hell of the English Bible is merely a seven gated Assyrian amusement park! O, how a lexicon, with dark pagan Assyrian mythology, sheds light upon the English Holy Bible." (p. 230)

My comments: Does the Bible use *sheol* in the Assyrian sense? NO! God describes the true *sheol* in the Bible. BUT *sheol* did represent, to all who used the word in common conversation, the place of the dead. So the reader of the Bible starts his understanding of *sheol* there. Then as the scriptures describe the true *sheol*, hell, we understand what the afterlife is like for the unsaved man or woman.

Quote 72

"Liddell and Stanley allowed the participation of Unitarians on the RV committee." (p. 231)

My comments: And we totally reject them and the Revised Version (1885). It is filled with their prejudices and theological speculations. It is obvious to any who compare life to Scripture that by this time the Anglican Church was infiltrated by 'Bible scholars' who spent more time trying to destroy the Bible than believing and preaching it. Anyone who has studied the Revision committee of 1885 knows their characters and character.

Quote 73

"A Greek lexicon, which held up Plato of the Greek myths as *the* source for meaning and truth, *higher* than the Holy Bible, could not help but place Greek philosophy on a pedestal shadowing the Bible itself. The backfire of Liddell's lexicon, and the path it provided to the mysticism of Greece, fueled

QUOTES AND COMMENTS

the mystical views already nascent in the Anglican Church." (p. 233)

My comments: Quote: "A Greek lexicon, which held that Plato of the Greek myths as *the* source for meaning and truth, *higher* than the Holy Bible, could not help but place Greek philosophy on a pedestal shadowing the Bible itself." Committees do not depend on lexicons. Those of the 1885 committee were the ones who compiled the lexicon in question. The lexicon did not tell them to omit or change the readings of the Hebrew or Greek texts. Their prejudice did. The lexicon did not prevent them from allowing the context of Scripture to give the full meaning of the Greek and Hebrew words, their prejudice did. Mrs. Riplinger is placing the blame on the wrong villain.

Quote 74

"Eavesdropping on one of Ruskin's lectures shows Liddell's doting student desperate to actually "burn" the Bible and its doctrine of punishment. Ruskin said,
"How wholesome it would be for many simple persons, if, in such places (for instance) as Acts xix.19, we retain the Greek expression, instead of translating it, and they had read – "Many of them also which used curious arts, brought their **bibles** together, and **burnt them** before all men...""
Of course the KJB translates the word *biblos* correctly and contextually into English, as "books," not "bibles," in Acts 19:19. (p. 236-237)

My comments: This example proves the point. The word Βίβλος [BIBLOS] means book. The word *Bible* is a transliteration of the word. It is an interpretation of a deficient Hebrew idiom "the book of books" meaning the ultimate Book, as Elohim means "the mightiest of the mighty" or "God." Mrs. Riplinger is correct in saying they were wrong to translate βίβλος [BIBLOS] Bible in this context. It shows blatent disregard and hatred for the words of God on the part of the translators. But what does the Liddell-Scott lexicon say?

179

βύβλος and βίβλος (v. sub fin.), ἡ, **the Egyptian papyrus, Cyperus Papyrus**, Hdt.2.92, A. Supp. 761, Str. 17.1.15: in pl. , **stalks of papyrus**, PTeb. 308.7 (ii A.D.), Thphr. HP 4.8.4, Hdt. 2.96, Plot. 2.7.2.
b. in pl. , *slices of the pith* used as writing-material, Hdt. 5.58, Hermipp. 63.13:
3. roll of papyrus, book, Hdt. 2.100, A. Supp. 947, etc. : heterocl. pl. , βύβλα, τά, AP 9.98 (Stat. Flacc.); esp. of sacred or magical *writings*, βίβλων ὅμαδον Μουσαίου καὶ ρφέως Pl. R. 364e, cf. D. 18.259, Act.Ap. 19.19, PPar. 19.1 (ii A.D.); ἱεραί β. OGI 56.70 (Canopus, iii in B.C.); β. ἱερατική PTeb. 291.43 (ii A.D.); so of the Scriptures, ἡ β. γενέσεως οὐρανο καὶ γ ς Lxx Ge. 2.4, etc. ; ἡ β. *the Sacred Writings*, Aristeas 316; β. Μωυσέως ψαλμ ν, προφητ ν, Ev.Marc. 12.26, Act.Ap. 1.20, 7.42; β. ζω ς Ep.Phil. 4.3: pl. , of magical *books*, Act.Ap. 19.19, Ph. 2.522, Pl. Plt. 288e.
4. a division of a book, Plb. 4.87.12, D.S. 1.4, etc. ; αἱ β. the nine *books* of Hdt. , Luc. Herod. 1.
II. β. στεφανωτρίς *flowering head of papyrus*, Theopomp.Hist. 22c, Plu. Ages. 36. [, A. Supp. 761.] (βύβλος, βύβλινος, βυβλίον, etc. , are the original forms: βιβλ- seems to have arisen in Attic. by assimilation in βιβλίον, and is found in earlier Attic. Inscrr. , cf. IG 2.1 b, etc. , and prevails in Ptolemaic papyri; Inscrr. vary, βυβλία Test.Epict. 8.32 (iii/ii B.C.); βιβλία IG 5(1).1390.12 (Andania, i B.C.); in Roman times βυβλ- was restored.)[34]

Now, just where does this lexicon tell the translators to translate βιβλός Bible? It doesn't. That translation was not dependent on the Liddell lexicon.

Quote(s) 75

"He permitted his children to become quite involved with *two* men who were alleged pedophiles...Yale University Press's

---

[34] Liddell, H. G., Scott, R., Jones, H. S., & McKenzie, R. (1996). *A Greek-English lexicon.* "With a revised supplement, 1996." (Rev. and augm. throughout) (333). Oxford; New York: Clarendon Press; Oxford University Press.

QUOTES AND COMMENTS

definitive two-volume biography of Ruskin, by Tim Hilton, asserts that "he was a paedophile." Ruskin's autobiography, *Praeterita*, details, in part, his relationships with Liddell's young daughters." (p. 240-241)

"As a homosexual, "Rhodes had no wife and children..." (p. 244)

"Liddell's lexicon took away his faith and carried him instead to the feet of the Utopian dreamers, Plato and Aristotle. **The Lexicon bars him forever from ever reading the English Holy Bible** as *it is*." (p. 251)

My comments: Why? Showing word development does not contradict its contextual usage.

Quote 76

"Liddell's constant companions were the wicked god-men of the Greek myths." (p. 255)

My comments: This is blatantly false. Just because an English speaking person reads Shakespeare, does it make him as bawdy as the great bard? How about reading the Hash eaters like Poe and Coolridge? Does that make the person drug addicts? Reading the literature of a language gives insight into the meanings of words.

Quote 77

"There was much Evangelical and Anabaptist dread and protest about what the college's Greek class was doing to destroy the faith of students." (p. 258)

My comments: Because of the UNBELIEF of the Greek teachers, not because Greek causes apostasy. I am a Christian because of the New Testament. I am a Baptist because of the Greek New Testament.

Quote 78

"Imagine having THE standard Hebrew-English Lexicon (Gesenius, Brown, Driver, and Briggs) edited by a man who scorns what he calls, "the old Hebrew belief in a personal Jehovah." (p. 260)

My comments: Knowing his prejudice, I 'eat the meat and spit out the bones.'

Quote 79

"...Müller's passion for India's pagan Hinduism shifted the entire focus of Oxford's linguistic, religious, and historical study. Müller ripped their roots from the Hebrews and planted them deep in the mountains of India, far from God's truth and too close to the Hindu *deies* (Sanskrit for devils),...instead of the previously assumed Hebrew root. From this 'new' root, it's 'meaning' was re-cast." (p. 261)

My comments: Is Hebrew the original language of man from which all other languages are derived? That is something only God can answer. After Babel, God confused the tongues and caused men to separate into language groups.

Whether Mrs. Riplinger likes it or not, there are clear similarities between the Indo-European languages, and even closer similarities among the Semitic languages. Having learned French in high school and Greek in college, I was able to develop a working knowledge of Latin, and a smattering of Spanish, Portuguese, Romanian, and Dutch. Learning Hebrew in college let me learn some Arabic without great difficulty. There are similarities of morphemes, phonemes, and grammar that aid in the learning of related languages. If Sanskrit demonstrates itself to be the common denominator from which the others diversify, then big deal. In no wise does it affect the translation of the Bible or the faith of its readers.

QUOTES AND COMMENTS

Quote 80

"Müller's and Blavatsky's minds were nearly mirror images; his beliefs, as seen in his *Collected Works*, are identical to those found in her books, the *Secret Doctrine* and *Isis Unveiled*. They believe that primordial Hinduism was the first, truest, and purest religion." (p. 263)

My comments: Once again we take the guilt by the association tact.

Quote(s) 81

"For the ongoing correction of his Lexicon, Liddell needed a native-speaking German friend to help him access the German lexicon (Passow), of which his was essentially a mere translation. Müller was that go-between. "Liddell's German knowledge," though weak, no doubt helped him converse with his German underling." (p. 268)

"Mueller suggests that to understand the *highest* philosophies, we study not only "Sanskrit," which is an Indian dialect, but "Vedic Sanskrit," which is the unique Sanskrit used in the Vedas, which are the Hindu 'scriptures'." (p. 271)

My comments: David Brainard, proposed son-in-law to Jonathan Edwards and missionary to the Indians along the Delaware River, preached to the Leni Lenape (the Delaware Indians) for years through the tongue of an unsaved, drunken Indian translator. Is that any different? If Müller knew German and Liddell, so be it. Neither one was saved, but they both understood languages and provided a Greek-English lexicon.

Quote 82

"Liddell's biographer said that he was very involved with the upbringing of his children and that, "nothing was complete without his co-operation and approval". (p. 271)

My comments: My question is exactly this: "Why would *he* cooperate and "approve" of having his daughter 'baby sat' and photographed in immodest poses by a known pedophile, Charles Dodgson, alias Lewis Carroll, who has been alleged to be the infamous Jack the Ripper?" (p. 271) Perhaps something is not true here!

Quote 83

"Scott had the dubious distinction of being *liberal* enough to be selected to be on the Westcott and Hort Revised Version Committee of 1881. After all, it was his and Liddell's *English wine-washed* words which were now going to jump from *their* lexicon into *the* Bible." (p. 273)

My comments: Mrs. Riplinger has 'colored' her words again by assuming Liddell's work was *wine-washed*; in other words, he was full of alcohol as he developed his lexicon. Certainly, no one would approve of drinking while employed or at any time. But it is spin to claim Liddell was winebibbing while working in order to justify one's conclusions. Was she there when this occurred? Perhaps this is another false charge without justification as is common in her work(s). The words did not jump from his lexicon "into the Bible;" rather, the translators chose them.

Quote 84

"The manuscript diaries of John Addington Symonds contain a lurid depiction of sexual violence at Harrow in mid-century [under dorm supervisor B.F. Westcott, later of the *Revised Version*]. Far from preventing such activities, the headmaster, Dr. Charles Vaughan [another *Revised Version* committee member] was a party to them until his resignation [from Harrow] was demanded and obtained under threat of a criminal prosecution..." (p. 283) (The "..." is Mrs. Riplinger's not mine, KD).

My comments: Many authors have repeatedly proven the poor moral character and lack of Bible Christianity in the Revisers.

QUOTES AND COMMENTS

Quote 85

"Ask any Greek-spouting professor or pastor, ' What lexicon do you use?' Many use *Thayer's Greek-English Lexicon of the New Testament* because it is the least expensive. If he really does not know how to read Greek, he probably uses one of Thayer's stepchildren, *Vine's Expository Dictionary of New Testament Words* or Berry's *Interlinear Greek-English New Testament* by George Ricker Berry (lexicon in back)." (p. 330)

My comments: And why not? You have to start somewhere. Actually, my Greek teacher started with Arndt & Gingrich. I personally discovered Berry and Souter. And to complete my first collection of lexicons was the lexicon in the back of the UBS Greek New Testament 2nd Edition. Never did these lexicons unhinge my faith in the words of God because I never sought to correct the KJB. I sought to understand it! Since then, I have added many other lexicons.

Quote 86

"The naïve reader is then drawn down into this whirlpool, struggling to find the hidden 'meaning' of words, which are *already* self-evident in the context of each Bible usage." (p. 332)

My comments: Despite Mrs. Riplinger's claim, there are many passages in the King James Bible which are obscure or ambiguous. Whole denominations have been founded on bad doctrine arising out of these ambiguities. Context and KJB usage alone are not sufficient for consistent sound understanding of the King James Bible. In those cases either the student must refer to the Greek or Hebrew, or depend on the Greek and Hebrew skills of some trusted authority.

CLEANING-UP HAZARDOUS MATERIALS

Quote(s) 87

"Thayer was on the American translation committee for the corrupt Westcott and Hort Revised Version, as well as the American Standard Version." (p. 335)

"In the opening pages of *Thayer's Lexicon*, he lists the names of well over 300 pagans and philosophers whose writings he consulted to give hints as to 'meanings' and usages of Greek words. The Greeks' writings, of course, do not give meanings in Greek, let alone English. They can only exhibit the word *in use* and therefore only *hint* at its meaning in *that* context. The hint is still in Greek. Bringing it into English takes it miles from its origin. Pairing those Greek hints with words in our 500,000 word English vocabulary is a guessing game at best Thayer's final destination is miles further still from the mind of Christ." (p. 337-338)

My comments: No kidding! Unfortunately, the Greeks did not provide us with a Greek-English lexicon. How rude! Didn't they know we would need one? Why didn't Paul do it since he had the gift of tongues? Surely, God could have given him the ability to write a Greek-English lexicon through that gift. Surely God knew we would need one. After all, Paul was able to write his epistles in the 14 languages of Acts or the 70 languages of Genesis 10-11.

Can Mrs. Riplinger possibly be this naïve? Studying the word in its context in its original language is the only way that words can be brought from the dead language into a living language. Having skimmed *In Awe of Thy Word* I have the glimmer of an idea of how Mrs. Riplinger thinks that the translators of the King James Bible defined Greek words. Or for that matter, how they even translated. But then again, since she believes that they were reinspired, maybe they just sat there and it came in *Holy-Ghost-free-from-sinners* English. On the subsequent pages, Mrs. Riplinger lists many of the Greek authors with pejorative information about them.

QUOTES AND COMMENTS

Quote 88

"Thayer's use of pagan and "profane" Greeks led him to reluctantly list at the end of his edition those New Testament words for which he could find no pagan use, and therefore no 'definition.' Thayer will list words such as "collection" and say the word is "not found in profane authors" (1 Corinthians 16:1, 2). God said in 1 Tim. 4:7, "But refuse **profane**... fables." In 1 Tim. 6:20 he said, "avoiding **profane** and vain babblings." Aren't you glad the Holy Ghost gave us the words of God in a HOLY Bible in our own language? How convenient; how like God. "Every word of God is pure" (Proverbs 30:5)." (p. 342)

My comments: Thayer did not use the word *profane* the way that Mrs. Riplinger wants the reader to think. He did not use *profane* in the King James Bible sense to indicate something crude or risqué. In this context, it means non-spiritual or non-theological as used by Thayer. The same word used in the King James Bible means vulgar or crude. Again Mrs. Riplinger must know that. The quoted paragraph is purposely deceptive and defamatory. Her argument is irrelevant and absurd.

Quote 89

"Thayer's son-in-law, Casper Renee Gregory, wrote the Prologue for and re-issued, with fellow Unitarian, Ezra Abbot, the 8th edition of Tischendorf's corrupt Greek New Testament. Gregory also re-worked the numbering system for Greek manuscripts to make it seem more favorable to the corrupt text."... "So the final form of the American Revised Version (today called the *American Standard Version* and revised to be the *New American Standard Version*) was strikingly under Thayer's control, particularly since his "records of the earlier meetings" were the only ones remaining." (p. 345)

My comments: About the only place you can find the American Standard version of the Bible is on some dusty library shelf. It has been used as the basis for the *Amplified Bible*, The New American Standard Bible, and several other American produced editions of the Scriptures. There are some evangelical teachers and Christians who insist on using the New American Standard Version (NASV), especially in Bible colleges and seminaries. However, its day has come and is going. The new Scripture *de jour* is the English Standard Version (ESV). Almost every academic work I see lately comes from that version. And next year it will be something else. Those of us who believe the Bible literally, have nothing to fear from these new versions. They rarely last 10 years. In fact, it is the plethora of new Bibles which drove me back to the King James Bible. The thinking Christian knows that God did not give confusion.

Quote(s) 90

> "Schaff said he wanted to "disentangle the scriptures from traditional embarrassments, such as the theory of a liberal inspiration or dictation..." Many charged that his "teaching and writing did not meet biblical standards..." The ASV readings, seen today as definitions in *Strong's Concordance*, ame from Schaff and his Unitarian-led bandits, Thayer and Strong." (p. 349)

> "His [Thayer's][35] lecture begins and ends by charging the Bible with error. He consoles listeners saying, "No substantive part of the truth of Christianity is discredited, should we perchance discover that the collection and even the composition of its books are not free from traces of the **imperfection** which cleaves to all things human". He aligns his views with those of the Catholic Church. He says, "And in the second place allow me to remind you that the view of these writings in which we, as New England Puritans, have been reared has not been the prevalent view in the Christian church through the centuries. The church of Rome, as you know, recognizes ecclesiastical tradition as of coordinate authority with the written records..." (p. 350)

---

[35] The identification of Thayer is mine not Mrs. Riplinger's.

QUOTES AND COMMENTS

My comments: Let us concede once and for all that the revisers of 1881 and 1901 were apostates, pro-Roman Catholic, traditional church. Most of them had deep flaws in their theology and methodology. Several of them began with the specific purpose of undermining the Received Text and the King James Bible. It is not necessary to answer every one of Mrs. Riplinger's attacks on these men and their work. Their lexicons and other word study books reflect their prejudice. Unfortunately, they are the only comprehensive works with which we have to work. Not one of their Bible believing colleagues has taken in hand to do a complete comprehensive lexicon of the Greek New Testament which produced the King James Bible.

Quote(s) 91

"He [Thayer] hopes Christians will *stop* trusting in the Bible and —"running to it under every mental perplexity... proclaiming the same as the final and unerring answer of Infinite Wisdom... In looking upon it as primarily designed to give divinely authenticated information on all details of life and destiny, we are grievously overstraining its legitimate use. The view of the Scriptures here urged I have called a "change." But let me remind you again that it is such only in reference to current and local and comparatively recent views. Of the great mass of Christian believers down through the centuries it is doubtful whether more than a small fraction have held the hard and fast theory currently advocated among us today. **They may be said to have been unanimous and emphatic from the first in asserting the inspiration of the written word; but as to the degree and nature of this inspiration there has been great diversity, or at least indefiniteness among leading Christian thinkers all along**. It was not before the polemic spirit became rife in the controversies which followed the Reformation that the fundamental distinction between the "Word of God" and the record of that word became obliterated, and the **pestilent tenet gained currency that the Bible is absolutely free from every error of every sort**" (p. 352-353)

CLEANING-UP HAZARDOUS MATERIALS

My comments: At this point I choose to cease documenting her *ad hominem* and guilt by association attacks on the authors of the various Greek study aids. This author stipulates that the authors of these materials were not fundamentalist and may not in several circumstances have even been Christians. Were they the translators of the Scriptures and not the compilers of lexicons, I might agree to this criticism. The words of Scripture are defined by their usage. If the critic of a lexicon cannot demonstrate by the compilation of frequency and uses of words in both scriptural and non-scriptural contexts are faulty, the lexical discoveries of these stipulated heretics stand as valid. As noted earlier, the translator is not bound by the lexicon. The translator begins with the lexical definition and then observes how these are used in the particular work he is translating. At this point I skip to part three Greek New Testament Texts.

Quote 92

"Few know that Scrivener moved away from his original *Textus Receptus* (TR) position in his later book, *Six Lectures on the Text of the New Testament*, written *before* he created his TR Greek text. Scrivener did not recommend all of the readings in his TR and suggested *removing* numerous verses, as well as important words supporting the Incarnation, the sinlessness of Christ, and the Trinity." (p. 580)

My comments: What Scrivener did later in life it does not affect his work. The actual notes and text of the KJV translators were destroyed in the fire of London in the 1660s. The text that Scrivener published is the best printed approximation of the text of the KJB. Mrs. Riplinger's attack here is not on the substance of Scrivener's text, but an *ad hominem* attack attempting to remove the substance of his text as irrelevant.

QUOTES AND COMMENTS

Quote 93

"Scrivener worked with a motley crew of Unitarians, including Ezra Abbot, J. Henry Thayer, and G. Vance Smith, as well as New Ager Philip Schaff, and Blavatsky follower, C.D. Ginsburg (Old Testament). Also on Scrivener's RV committee was C.J. Vaughan, B.F. Westcott's pick and an old confederate during the Harrow scandal. Headmaster Vaughan was discharged from being Westcott's supervisor for encouraging homosexual behavior between adults and the children in the dorm directed by Westcott." (p. 582)

My comments: Yes he did. So what? We do not argue for the accuracy of the RV or the eclectic text constructed by heretics from inferior texts. Scrivener often opposed the substitution of an eclectic reading for an historic reading. He may not have been unanimous in his support of the TR, but he was at least honest with it. His text is an honest attempt to present the Greek text of the KJB New Testament. Mrs. Ripplinger will find a few minor details where, in her estimation, Scrivener does not perfectly match the KJB. But, it was his stated intention to provide the reader with the accurate Greek text underlying the KJB New Testament. His human frailties do not negate his work where it is accurate.

Quote 94

"In 1884, after Scrivener's *Revised Version* New Testament was published, he judged that the substitution of the RV for the KJB would be "on the whole, for the **better**." He boasts,
"If a judgment may be formed from previous experience in like cases, the revised [RV] and unrevised [KJB] Versions, when the former shall at length be completed [O.T.], are destined to run together a race of generous and friendly rivalry for the space of at least one generation, before the elder of the two [KJB] shall be superseded [dumped]..."
Scrivener is *not* an admirer of the King James Bible. (p. 583)

My comments: Again, it does not matter! What matters is, "Does the Scrivener's Greek New Testament accurately portray the

Greek text underlying the KJB New Testament?" It can't be found in Scrivener's character, associations, or philosophy. It is determined by translating Scrivener's text back into English and determining if it explains the KJB. That is the only measure of its value.

Quote 95

(Riplinger Quoting Scrivener, KD) "God **might**, beyond a doubt, have so guided the hand or fixed the devout attention of successive races of copyists, that no jot or tittle should have been changed in the Bible of all that was first written therein. **But** this result could have been brought about only in one way, so far as we can perceive, – by nothing short of a continuous, unceasing miracle: by making fallible men, nay, many such in every generation, for one purpose absolutely infallible. That the Supreme Being should have thus far interfered with the course of His Providential arrangements, seems, prior to experience, **very improbable**, not at all in accordance with the analogy of His ordinary dealings with mankind, while actual experience amply demonstrates that **He has not chosen thus to act**." (p. 590)

My comments: Ok, we get it. F.H.A. Scrivener did not believe that the actual manuscripts were infallible; neither does anyone else who knows anything about them. We do not argue for the perfection of the manuscripts. It is the perfection of the New Testament text that God providentially protected. And He did it by the plethora of resources He left us for comparison. He preserved the integrity of His revelation in a manner that allowed for man's imperfections without allowing those imperfections to alter His word.

Quote 96

"Scrivener came to see before he passed away that the **received text could not be supported** so unconditionally as he had once thought. But he expressed himself less distinctly in public..." (p.592)

QUOTES AND COMMENTS

My comments: So Scrivener was a hypocrite, saying one thing in private and another in public?

Quote 97

"... Or as one true believer, Dr. Kirk DiVietro, so aptly expressed in the title of his book, they trust *Anything But the King James Bible*." (p. 598)

"He [Scrivener, KD] paints up the botched Vaticanus with words such as "great" and "this treasure". He insists "codex Vaticanus" belongs in "its rightful place at the head of all our textual authorities." He covers up the fact that the Vaticanus is an upside-down manuscript. In Matt. 27:28 the true text says, "And they stripped him," but the Vaticanus says "And they clothed him." Why don't new versions tell you *that* in their margins?" (p. 599)

My comments: The entire generation which 'discovered' Vaticanus gave it accolades far above its value. Vaticanus has many flaws. These have been repeatedly pointed out by those of us who have studied the manuscript issue. Its text was held in reverential awe by those of a generation despite its many aberrations and inconsistencies.

Quote 98

"The so-called science of textual criticism was hatched by unbelievers, with Catholic priests at the helm. Scrivener adopted and adapted their methodology and waged his subtle war on the *Textus Receptus* with many of these "Canons" and "rules" of textual criticism." (p. 600)

My comments: I'm not sure what he was supposed to do. Scrivener was a consistent dissenter on Westcott's revision committee. I guess he could have boycotted the procedure and let the committee free to displace the words of God without opposition. Maybe he should have refused to provide the text of the King James Bible with the committee's changes noted?

Quote 99

"There are *well over* 5300 manuscripts of the Greek New Testament extant today. Scrivener on the other hand said that there were only "eighteen hundred to two thousand." This shows that Scrivener was dealing with much less than half of what is available today." (p. 603)

My comments: There are actually over 5500 manuscripts available. And what does that have to do with anything? Using the data he was aware of, Scrivener still felt many of the Westcott-Hort changes were unwarranted.

Quote 100

"Evil? – the main text of the majority of manuscripts? The KJB translators placed it in italics out of caution as they did many other words which have since been found to have Greek manuscript evidence." (p. 621)

My comments: Discussing I John 2:23, Mrs. Riplinger gives a new twist. Everyone everywhere has always taught, including the translators, that the italics in the King James Bible indicate words implied by the Greek which are not a part of the normal Greek grammar. These are not unnecessary words added capriciously by the translators. They are words which are implied by the Greek which uses several grammatical structures not found in English. I know nothing of words being in italics because the translators thought they should be there, but weren't quite sure.

Quote(s) 101

"Michael Maynard's *A History of the Debate Over I John 5:7-8* proves that the verse *does* belong in the text. He notes among other things that it is in the Syriac Bible and was quoted by Tertullian in the second century. Even the first Greek New Testament, the Complutensian Polyglot, contained I John 5:7-8. Scrivener errs saying that Erasmus only reluctantly put it into his Greek text. The world's leading authority on Erasmus, Henk de Jonge said, "The current view that Erasmus promised to insert the Comma Johanneum, if it could be shown to him in a single Greek manuscript has no foundation in Erasmus' work." (p. 622)

"Neither the KJB translators nor Erasmus were "Greek only." The Greek Orthodox church has never been God's sole repository of truth." (p. 626)

My comments: Mrs. Riplinger creates a straw man which she proceeds to shred for several chapters. Textual critics, good and bad, have appealed to the early translations of the New Testament, where they are available, to verify passages of the Greek New Testament. I am not aware of any textual critic that was "Greek only."

Just because the manuscripts were preserved in many cases by the Greek Orthodox Church doesn't mean that they were the originators of the manuscripts. Since their constituents used Greek as their primary language until the collapse of the Byzantine Empire, they had a pragmatic reason to continue copying Greek manuscripts.

Quote 102

"Scholars can only guess about the body of evidence which led Erasmus to frame his Greek text as he did. Erasmus had access to different copies from those of Scrivener. Scrivener believes that manuscripts and witnesses closer in time to the originals are more reliable. Scrivener reveres the uncial Vaticanus because it is 400 years older than many of the Greek cursives. By *his* criteria the witnesses available to Erasmus's should be more reliable than Scrivener's library (all other elements being equal e.g. orthography), as Erasmus lived 400 years closer to the time of the originals." (p. 627)

My comments: Can she be serious? It is not a question of when the critic lived but when the manuscripts he used were produced. Mrs. Riplinger has to know that. I have to believe that this statement was purposely provided to prejudice the thinking of the reader even though it has no basis in fact or logic.

Quote 103

Scrivener was chosen to do the "marginal" notes for the 1881 Revised Version's New Testament. It is there that *his own* personal prejudices are marked by his own signature.
"Soon after the beginning of their work in 1870 the New Testament Company of Revisers considered the question of providing **marginal** references for the **Revised Version**... Leave was granted, and in December, 1873, the Company passed a resolution requesting **Dr. Scrivener** and **Professor Moulton** to undertake the work of drawing up marginal references... [Later a] revision was undertaken by Dr. Moulton, but all his work was submitted to Dr. Scrivener for approval..." (p. 627-628)

My comments: Thank God he was. We have no better Greek text for the King James Bible. Scrivener took the published text of Beza and compared it to the King James Bible. Where that text did not seem consistent with the King James Bible, he sought readings from other contemporary published Greek New Testaments. As we have neither the actual text used by the King James Translators, nor their translational notes, this is the closest approximation of the text they used. I know Mrs. Riplinger protests that in several minutiae it is not perfect and I will concede that for this discussion though I do not know if it is true. But since Mrs. Riplinger's qualifications in Greek have not been established to be superior to Scrivener, her protestations have less credibility than Scrivener's work.

Quote 104

(In the USA it is available from AV Publications with the caveat that it *not* be used for study or translation, only for comparison.) (p. 631)

QUOTES AND COMMENTS

My comments: Mrs. Riplinger doesn't mind making a profit selling this horrible perversion of the Words of God. (Lest it not be clear, I am being sarcastic.)

Quote 105

"Unfortunately however, Scrivener's Greek *Textus Receptus* (TBS, Green, et al.) has become a holy grail in numerous conservative Christian pastor's libraries, college classrooms, translation centers, and publishing houses. Few are aware of its origin or its leaven (documented at the end of this chapter). This is hardly their fault since Scrivener entitled it falsely,
The New Testament in Greek According to the Text Followed in the Authorised Version Together with the Variations adopted in the Revised Version" (p. 632)

My comments: The convocation which authorized the Revised Version of 1881 required the translators to publish the Received Text and annotate any changes made by the translation committee. This is what Scrivener did. It was not his intention to produce a "new" Greek New Testament. Nor was it his intention, to in any way pervert the New Testament of the King James Bible. Whether he was convinced of the accuracy of the Received Text or not had nothing to do with his work. It was his job to produce the received text with all changes marked by bold face and included in the footnotes. This he did to the best of his ability. Assuming, as is reasonable, that the last published Greek New Testament would probably have been the base of their translation modified by personal notes and manuscripts, Scrivener chose Beza's 1598 text and introduced those changes reflected in the King James Bible. I personally studied the 120+ readings; the vast majority of them were incidental involving primarily the names of books and/or subscriptions. There were very few actual vocabulary differences. Scrivener also listed about 30 readings that he suspected might have come from the Latin. However, close examination indicated that these readings came either from an alternate Greek source, a secondary Greek rendering, or were retentions from former English Bibles as per the instructions of King James.

CLEANING-UP HAZARDOUS MATERIALS

Quote 106

(Quoting David Cloud:) "The **exact** Greek text underlying the King James Bible was reconstructed by Frederick Scrivener under the direction of the Cambridge University Press and published in **1891**." (p. 633)

My comments: I can only think that her purpose in bolding 1891 is to introduce a seeming error into David Cloud's statement. It is probably a typo or a reference to another later edition.

Quote 107

"Scrivener's *Textus Receptus* is included in many digital online and Bible software additions, including Logos Research Systems, Online Bible, BibleWorks,..." (p.633)

My comments: Since I was the person who provided Scrivener's text to both Logos Research Systems® and BibleWorks®, I am responsible for their inclusion. Since I am "one true Bible student" perhaps I should be the one and not Mrs. Riplinger to explain their inclusion.

Quote 108

"Some use Scrivener's Greek *Textus Receptus* in Jay P. Green's *Interlinear Bible, Greek-English*, with Green's faulty English below Scrivener's Greek. Green states on his copyright page that his Greek New Testament text is used by permission of the Trinitarian Bible Society. Green admits that Scrivener's Greek text was "reconstructed." Don Waite Jr. says Scrivener's method was to "backwards translate" from the KJB in the main. This was incompletely done due to Scrivener's dishonest methodology." (p. 634)

My comments: Mrs. Riplinger is distorting the record. She has fabricated information throughout her work pertaining to Don Waite, Jr. (see the Appendix, pp. 306ff, and pp. 204ff in this work for D.A.

Waite, Jr.'s statements concerning these matters). In addition, Scrivener took the most recently published Greek New Testament, Beza's 1598 edition, and where he could not find a reading in Beza's work, he identified them in other manuscripts. There were only 190 places out of approximately 160,000 words in the New Testament that were not found in Beza's text by Scrivener. He said:

> "**All variations from Beza's text of 1598, in number about 190, are set down in an Appendix at the end of the volume, together with the authorities on which they respectively rest.**" (*Scrivener's Annotated Greek New Testament*, p. ix, available from BibleForToday.org, $35 plus $5.00 S&H). [Editor's bolding]

Dr. Edward F. Hills, a **trained** textual critic at Yale, Westminster Theological Seminary, Columbia Theological Seminary, the University of Chicago, and Harvard said:

> "According to Scrivener (1884) [from Scrivener's *Authorized Edition of the English Bible,* Cambridge: University Press, 1884, pp. 296-297, KD], out of the 252 passages in which these sources differ [he is referring to Beza, Erasmus, Stephanus, and the Complutensian Polyglot, KD] sufficiently to affect the English rendering, the King James Version agrees with Beza against Stephanus 113 times, with Stephanus against Beza 59 times, and 80 times with Erasmus or the Complutensian, or the Latin Vulgate against Beza and Stephanus." [as quoted in Hill's *The King James Bible Defended,* Christian Research Press, Des Moines, Iowa, reprint 1993, *p. 220.]*

To infer as she does that Scrivener **purposely distorted** and twisted and falsified the Greek New Testament for some purpose is **dishonest** and removes integrity from her work.

I have a question for Mrs. Riplinger. How does she know that the Scrivener text is incorrect? Does she have an inspired original? Or, did SHE BACKWARDS TRANSLATE FROM THE KJB TO FIND ERRORS IN IT? [Editor's note: Mrs. Riplinger repeatedly makes mistakes, misquotes, and various distortions in her book, *Hazardous Materials*, about D.A. Waite, Jr. on pages 357, 634, 637-640, and 962.]

Quote 109

"This gives the impression that Green may not know that Scrivener's Greek text and Stevens (Stephanus) Text are *different*. Therefore his Greek may be a hybrid, and one should be cautious, looking for the unique errors of each individual text." (p. 634)

My comments: Does Mrs. Riplinger provide a list of the differences? No! Because the differences are so obscure that they would escape all but the most careful observation. They are not two different Greek New Testaments. They represent the consensus texts of the manuscripts available to each editor. And since they both come from Received Text manuscripts, the differences are minimal. **It infuriates me**, having collated both these manuscripts to each other, and knowing the insignificant variants between them, that Mrs. Riplinger wants the reader to believe that there is some cosmic conspiracy here.

Quote 110

"Those studying with the illusion that there is one English word, which is *the* "literal" translation of one Greek word, need to examine a copy of a Greek Concordance, such as Wigram's or Smith's." (p. 635)

My comments: I cannot imagine anyone except Mrs. Riplinger being so naïve as to believe there is only one English word for each one Greek word. She is introducing another strawman into the conversation.

QUOTES AND COMMENTS

Quote(s) 111

"[I]t has been necessary for us to adopt either a **different word** for translation, or a shortened form ... " *(The Interlinear Bible Hebrew-English,* Vol. 2, p. xiii).

"The cost of resetting the Hebrew **to fit** a fully literal translation into English would have been so great ..." *(The Interlinear Bible Hebrew-English,* Vol. 2, p. viii).

"In causative verb tenses a **shortened translation** was frequently required ... Due to **limitations of space**, we were not always able to translate the participle ... " *(The Interlinear Bible,* Preface).

"Green's English words are corrupt, taken from corrupt "lexicons" such as "Strong," "Vine," "Trench," "Thayer," "Brown-Driver-Briggs," (sic) and "Gesenius" *(The Interlinear Bible Greek-English,* Vol. 4, p. xv; *The Interlinear Hebrew-English,* vol. 2, pp. x, xiv). Such lexicons and their authors will be thoroughly discredited in this book. He says that, "Through the use of *The Interlinear Bible,* one can utilize the lexicons, word books, and other aids ..." *(The Interlinear Bible,* Preface). Therefore one is not reading Green, or any sort of literal English translation, but the nefarious lexical definitions of these corrupt lexicons.

"Green is a five-point Calvinist, carrying these heresies, like live viruses, on to everything he touches. (This heresy was also held by Theodore Beza, Edwin Palmer, NIV committee leader, Spiros Zodhiates, corrupt Greek reference book editor. It is exposed at the end of this chapter.) Such lack of spiritual discernment bites at Green's beliefs about the Bible, chomping the Trinitarian proof text (1 John 5:7) and other verses (Acts 9:5, 6 etc.) with these words,

"We have not deleted these from the Greek text supplied by the Trinitarian Bible Society, though **we do not accept them as part of the true** deposit of the Holy Scriptures" *(The Interlinear Bible Greek-English,* Volume 4, p. xi.)"

(Direct quotes from pp. 636-637 without alteration. All ellipses, and emphatic formatting are Mrs. Riplinger's work)

My comments: Mrs. Riplinger provides a series of quotations which she believes denigrate the interlinear Greek Hebrew of Jay Green. Only Mrs. Riplinger would assume the reader would be so foolish as to believe that an interlinear provides the one and only translation of the Hebrew original. The average reader realizes that the word chosen in an interlinear has to fit the space of the original language text. Certain compromises are always made in the interest of accommodating the original language. However the intelligent student takes the interlinear translation as a summary launching point to go and seek further knowledge about the reference.

Quote 112

"Scrivener's Greek *Textus Receptus*, magnified by some as if it were the original, was "constructed" **by** and **for** the Revised Version Committee of Westcott and Hort of 1881!" (p. 637)

My comments: Scrivener's work was not for the committee of 1881. If Mrs. Riplinger had done her homework, she would know the Scrivener's text was done in obedience to the instructions of the convocation which authorized the translation.

Quote 113

"As an RV committee member between 1873 and 1880, Scrivener was given the assignment of "backwards translating" the KJB into Greek to ascertain the KJB's Greek basis." (p. 637)

My comments: Unless Mrs. Riplinger can provide a direct instruction to Dr. Scrivener reflecting her comments, and I see no such documentation, one must totally discount this statement as fact manufactured out of thin air. The citation of D.A. Waite, Jr. at this point is totally absurd (see the next quote) (see the "Preface" and the "appendices" to this work). I know D.A. Waite, Jr. as well as his father. Neither of them believes what Mrs. Riplinger is putting into their pens.

QUOTES AND COMMENTS

Quote 114

"Those who use Scrivener's TBS edition (or Green's) thinking that they must go *back* to the Greek, have placed themselves in a foolish position. They are using a Greek text that was TRANSLATED FROM THE KING JAMES BIBLE! D.A. Waite Jr. notes in his English translation of Scrivener's original edition that Scrivener's assignment was to "backwards translate" the KJB..."When the fine details are examined it becomes clear that in the minutiae Scrivener did not always back-translate, as Waite also observes. What he did in fact was to create an entirely new entity, a Greek text that matches no other Greek text on earth and which matches no Holy Bible ever made, not even the KJB. It is not Beza's text, as some pretend; it certainly follows no other edition of the *Textus Receptus* in the minutiae...Although the text is titled, "the text followed in the Authorized Version," Scrivener takes an entire page admitting and delineating why and where it is *not*." (p. 637-638)

My comments: The distortions and outright lies in this passage totally destroy Mrs. Riplinger's credibility. She takes the statement that Scrivener's text was "constructed" and twists it into something that it was not intended to mean. Yes, Mr. Scrivener did in fact produce a PRINTED text that did not exist before. But that does not mean that he produced READINGS that did not exist before. Had Mr. Scrivener not told us that he began with Beza's printed text, we might in our wildest imaginations think that he reversed translated the entire King James Bible. **But he did tell us that he used Beza!** There were by my count 172 instances listed in this appendix in which the King James Bible did not match the readings of Beza's text. In those areas Mr. Scrivener scoured the printed texts available to him to find justification for those readings. Most of the time, it was a preference for the reading of Robert Stephanus that was chosen. Personally I wonder if Mr. Scrivener had begun with Stephanus would the results be the same? However, that's moot.

The world was quite aware that the King James Bible translators were not slaves to any one printed edition of the Greek New Testament. It might be equally said of them that they translated a Greek text not found anywhere else. They had at their fingertips multiple printed texts as well as access to a vast array of manuscript evidence. They did not slavishly follow Erasmus as many of their maligners assert. They did not slavishly follow Stephanus, Beza, Complutensian Polyglot, or any other.

Most people who have studied the issue, unlike Mrs. Riplinger, know that the notes on the discussions of the 1611 committee were lost in the fire of 1666 (see the "Appendices" for a description of the fire). Therefore, any explanation of their choice of variant is conjecture. What we have is the King James Bible and the knowledge that the 1611 committee produced it. **We know that they translated the New Testament from "the originall Greeke."**

If we know that the translation came from the Greek, and if we also know that at a given point the King James translators left Beza's text, then the only way to find what they did follow is to reverse translate that small passage and then search for that reading in one of the texts that were available to the translators. And that is what Scrivener did. He did not reverse translate the King James Bible *in toto* as Mrs. Riplinger would have us believe.

Don Waite, Jr's Comments About Riplinger's Charge

Furthermore, Don Waite, Jr. said:

> "I have attached a PDF copy of the first 39 pages (pages i-xxxix) of the *Doctored New Testament*. You can search in vain for the bogus statements attributed to me and to Dr. Scrivener. They simply don't exist.
>
> Nowhere in the *Doctored New Testament*—or in anything else I have ever written or said—can a **fair-minded person with even a rudimentary grasp of the English language** find support for this statement by Mrs. Riplinger: Dr. "Scrivener's assignment was to 'backwards translate the KJB.'"
>
> In footnote 2 from page xiv of *The Doctored New Testament*, one can find these words:

QUOTES AND COMMENTS

"In those KJV portions with no known Greek support, Scrivener let the readings of Beza's 1598 Greek NT stand (page 655, last paragraph). He did not backwards translate from Latin to Greek."

Please re-read these words VERY CAREFULLY and then answer the following questions:
(1) To whom does the *He* refer?
(2) What is the difference between saying He did NOT backwards translate and saying He DID backwards translate?
(3) What is the difference between *Latin* and *KJV English*?
(4) What is the difference between translating from *Latin to Greek* and translating from *KJV English to Greek*?
(5) What does it mean to *backwards translate*? The facts are clear. Dr. Scrivener REFUSED to backwards translate from KJV English—or from any other language—in preparing his Greek New Testament, originally designed for COMPARISON PURPOSES. A fair-minded person will read my words and those of Dr. Scrivener and make a good-faith effort to understand them properly."

More Comments About Riplinger's 'Backwards Translating' Charges

On p. 630, Riplinger directly claims that "Scrivener's Greek text... was translated *from* the English KJB originally." This statement is *not* supported by any of Scrivener's own comments in the original preface to his edition.

Riplinger also states on the same page that "Scrivener's anti-KJB prejudice...led him to mistranslate some of the KJB readings." Once again, Riplinger is claiming that Scrivener indeed *was* "back-translating" the KJB into Greek, which is *not* the case, and is *not* supported by any of Scrivener's own comments.

On p. 633, Riplinger claims that the Trinitarian Bible Society is "Today's copyright owner" of the Scrivener edition. Once more, this is *not* correct, since the entire Scrivener volume (including its text) is in the *public domain,* being well over 100 years old, and where copyright no longer applies. The Trinitarian Bible Society *freely* can publish this text, just as does the Dean Burgon Society in reprint form, and just as DiVietro and Robinson have done in electronic form for various Bible software programs. Yet, Riplinger falsely continues on this point:

> "[T]he word of God is not bound" (2 Tim. 2:9). The true Holy Bible will not be bound by special copyright restrictions which require permissions and restrict free unaltered use, because God is the author and owner. Therefore the Scrivener text cannot be the word of God."

On p. 634, the citation of Jay Green "on his copyright page that his Greek New Testament text is used by permission of the Trinitarian Bible Society" is correct. However, this does *not* relate to copyright of that *text* (which was clearly public domain even then), but to Green's direct cut-and-paste of the Trinitarian Bible Society's typographically reset *printed font* version of the Scrivener text which, without permission, would have been a pirating of their typesetting work.

On the same page, Riplinger states: "Green admits that Scrivener's method was 'reconstructed.'" Regardless of Green's language (which itself does not imply "backwards translation" but only editorial effort on Scrivener's part), Green is *not* Scrivener, and any claims regarding "reconstruction" or "backwards translation" should be established by Scrivener's own words, and not from what other people might say about him.

It is at this point that Riplinger quotes two words *well out of context* from Don Waite, Jr. She claims that Don Waite, Jr. "says Scrivener's method was to 'backwards translate' from the KJB in the main." Yet Don Waite, Jr. *nowhere* actually said or even suggested that Scrivener at *any* point "backwards translated" — whether "in the main" or otherwise. What Don Waite, Jr. *actually* said (in the same 2002 copy-machine page cited by Riplinger) was this:

> "In those KJV portions with no known Greek support [meaning from printed TR editions, as per Scrivener's preface], Scrivener (a man of great textual integrity) let the readings of Beza's 1598 Greek NT stand (p. 655). He refused to backwards translate from Latin to Greek!"

QUOTES AND COMMENTS

This statement is plain and clear: the point is that, when confronted with a KJB reading that did not have any support from existing Greek TR editions up to and including Beza 1598 (as per Scrivener's stated principles in his preface), Scrivener chose not to backwards translate those portions from Latin into Greek. One cannot take Don Waite, Jr.'s statement and use it to establish the opposite, i. e., to interpret his statement as suggesting that in all remaining places Scrivener supposedly did "backwards translate." Not only would this assumption be false, but it would be an extremely poor application of logic regarding the point of his original statement.

On p. 637, Riplinger once more misstates the case:

> "Scrivener was given the assignment of "backwards translating" the KJB into Greek to ascertain the KJB's Greek basis. Those who use Scrivener's TBS edition (or Green's) thinking that they must go back to the Greek, have placed themselves in a foolish position. They are using a Greek text that was TRANSLATED FROM THE KING JAMES BIBLE! D. A. Waite Jr. notes in his English translation of Scrivener's original edition that Scrivener's assignment was to "backwards translate" the KJB."

Once more, this claim of "backwards translating" as Scrivener's supposed "assignment" is *not* supported by Scrivener's own description of method given in his preface, and continues to *grossly distort* what Don Waite, Jr. said *in context* regarding "backwards translation" (as noted above). In addition, the blatant claim that Scrivener's Greek text "was TRANSLATED FROM THE KING JAMES BIBLE" is patently false, as Scrivener himself demonstrates throughout his preface discussion of method in preparing his edition.

Indeed, on p. 637, Riplinger *does* state "that in the minutiae Scrivener did not always back-translate, as Waite [Jr.] also observes." But once more, D. A. Waite, Jr.'s "observation" related *only* to those portions where there was *no* earlier Greek printed TR edition underlying the KJV, and where Scrivener *refused* to "backwards translate." Riplinger's statement, however, leaves the reader to *falsely* infer that in the *remainder* of his text—comprising by far the greater bulk—Scrivener supposedly *did* so "backwards translate." Again, this assumption by Riplinger is clearly refuted by Scrivener's own preface, and is *not* warranted by what D. A. Waite, Jr. wrote.

On p. 640, Riplinger once more falsely claims that "Scrivener admits that it [his Greek text] is generally a back-translation of the English KJB into Greek—a Greek text translated FROM the ENGLISH Bible." Again, appeal must be made to Scrivener's own preface, which *nowhere* states or suggests that his edition is a "back-translation" of any sort, and certainly *not* "of the English KJB into Greek."

On p. 642, Riplinger quotes extensively from Scrivener's own preface (which does *not* support her contention!) and then twice (!) concludes that Scrivener somehow created a "subjective and incomplete back-translation of the AV (KJB) into Greek." In reply to this, one need only examine Scrivener's *own* words as quoted by Riplinger, in which there is *no* mention or suggestion of "backwards translation" having occurred (e.g., "uniformly representative" does not translate into "backwards translation" by any means):

> The Cambridge Press has therefore judged it best to set the readings actually adopted by the Revisers at the foot of the page..., and to keep the continuous text consistent throughout by making it so far as was possible uniformly representative of the Authorized Version...The different elements that actually make up the Greek basis of the Authorized Version have an equal right to find a place.

On p. 643, Riplinger calls Scrivener's work an "imprecise reconstruction...based in places on 'presumed' words...[and] 'uncertainties.'" Again, these claims are *not* countenanced by Scrivener's own words in his preface: although he speaks of "the presumed Greek original of the Authorized Version," he does *not* claim to have made an "imprecise reconstruction." In addition, his comment regarding "uncertainties" is taken out of context. Mrs. Riplinger's perversion of his words is clearly contradicted by the full context by Scrivener's own statement that "These uncertainties do not however affect the present edition."

In summary, the claims made by Riplinger regarding "backwards translation" do not stand the test of open scrutiny, and are clearly seen to be a misapplication of what D. A. Waite, Jr. actually wrote.

Quote 115

"The telling RV notes and heavy type which reference RV changes have now disappeared from today's TBS and Green editions." (p. 639)

So what? If we use the Greek additions which accurately present the Greek that was translated into the King James Bible, why would we need the Westcott Hort perversions? If I want to know what Westcott and Hort did to the King James Greek, then I use an annotated version of Scrivener's. But if all I want to do is study a passage in Greek, I don't need to clutter it with heresy.

Scrivener begins his original RV committee's charge to him to create this volume for comparisons purposes for their project. In the original preface, Scrivener gives a seven-page description of the purpose of the work as related to his RV work. He adds an eight page appendix to the end of the volume listing the verses where he departs from the readings of Beza's Greek text. **He adds a final page to show *some* of the places where *he did not locate* the Greek text underlying the KJB in the printed source texts he used.**

Quote 116

"Observe four points, as you read the upcoming abstract from his original preface:
Scrivener admits that his Greek text was done *for the Revised Version Committee.*
Scrivener admits that it is generally **a back-translation of the English KJB** into Greek – a Greek text translated FROM the ENGLISH Bible.
Scrivener admits that his Greek text's paragraph divisions and punctuation are not from *any* Greek editions, but are taken from the English R*evised Version* (RV).
Scrivener created a false set of criteria for creating his text, perhaps due to his desire to downgrade the scholarship of the KJB translators, when compared to those of his RV committee. He used *only,*

CLEANING-UP HAZARDOUS MATERIALS

"Greek readings which might **naturally** be known through **printed editions** to the revisers of 1611 or their predecessors". (p. 639-640)

My comments: Distortion distortion distortion. Mrs. Riplinger accurately quotes Scrivener's "Preface." But her editorial notes are intended to twist Scriveners notes and rip Scriveners text from the hand of the King James Bible student.

What Mrs. Riplinger does not tell us is that Scrivener was following the directions of the convocation that authorized the translation. It was not an underhanded attempt to sell any faulty Greek New Testament. As part of the deliberations, Dr. Scrivener knew when the committee left the readings of the King James Bible. He was there when they discussed what readings were in the King James Bible and would be substituted with new readings from their committee conclusions. This is what he documented.

Quote 117

(Pages 641-643 in *Hazardous Materials*. All emphatic notations belong to Mrs. Riplinger not Dr. DiVietro)

"Scrivener's original Preface admits that his Greek text was only created because the RV's changes from the KJB (Authorised Version) burst the seams of the RV margin. His original Preface says, in part-
"The special design of this volume is to place clearly before the reader the variations from **the Greek text represented by the Authorised Version** of the New Testament which have been embodied in the **Revised Version**. One of the Rules laid down for the guidance of the **Revisers** by a Committee appointed by the Convocation of Canterbury was to the effect "that, when the Text adopted differs from **that from which the Authorised Version was made**, the alteration be indicated in the margin." As it was found that a literal observance of this direction would often crowd and obscure the margin of the Revised Version, the **Revisers** judged that its purpose might be better carried out in another manner. They therefore communicated to the Oxford and Cambridge University Presses a full and carefully corrected list of the readings adopted which are at variance with the readings **"presumed to underlie the Authorised Version,"** in order that they might be published independently in some shape or other. The University Presses have accordingly undertaken to

QUOTES AND COMMENTS

print them in connexion with complete Greek texts of the New Testament. The responsibility of the **Revisers** does not of course extend beyond the list which they have furnished.

"The form here chosen has been thought by the Syndics of the Cambridge University Press to be at once the most convenient in itself, and the best fitted for giving a true representation of the **Revisers'** work …. The Cambridge Press has therefore judged it best to set the readings actually adopted by the **Revisers at the foot of the page [omitted in TBS & Green editions]**, and to keep the continuous text consistent throughout by making it so far as was possible **uniformly representative of the Authorized Version**. The publication of an edition formed on this plan appeared to be all the more desirable, inasmuch as the **Authorised Version was not a translation of any one Greek text then in existence, and no Greek text intended to reproduce in any way the original of the Authorised Version has ever been printed.** [subjective and incomplete back-translation of the A V (KJB) into Greek]

"In considering what text had the best right to be regarded as **"the text presumed to underlie the Authorised Version,"** it was necessary to take into account **the composite nature of the Authorised Version** … Beza's fifth and last text of 1598 was more likely than any other to be in the hands of the King James's revisers … There are however **many places in which the Authorised Version is at variance with Beza's text**; chiefly because it retains language inherited from Tyndale or his successors, which had been **founded on the text of other Greek editions** … These uncertainties do not however affect the present edition, in which **the different elements that actually make up the Greek basis of the Authorised Version have an equal right to find a place** [subjective and incomplete back-translation of A V into Greek].

Wherever therefore the Authorised renderings agree with other Greek readings which **might naturally be known through printed editions to the revisers of 1611 or their predecessors, Beza's reading has been displaced from the text** in favour of the more truly representative reading, the variation from Beza being indicated by * [* is omitted in TBS and Green editions]. It was manifestly necessary to accept only Greek authority, though in some places the Authorised Version corresponds but loosely with any form of the Greek original, while it exactly follows the Latin Vulgate [This will be proven false]. **All variations from Beza's text of 1598, in number about 190,** are set down in an Appendix at the end of the volume, together with the authorities on which they respectively rest. Whenever a Greek reading adopted for the **Revised Version** differs from the **presumed Greek original of the Authorised Version,** the reading which it is intended to displace is printed in the text in a thicker type, with a numerical reference to the reading substituted by the **Revisers** … For such details the reader will naturally **turn to the Margin of the Revised Version** itself. ..

"It was moreover desirable to punctuate in a manner not inconsistent . **with the punctuation of the Revised Version**, wherever this could be done without inconvenience ...

"**The paragraphs** into which the body of the Greek text is here divided are those **of the Revised Version**, the numerals relating to chapters and verses being banished to the margin. The marks which indicate the beginning of paragraphs in the Authorised Version do not seem to have been inserted with much care ... (emphasis mine; *The New Testament in Greek According to the Text Followed in the Authorised Version Together with the Variations Adopted in the Revised Version,* F.H.A. Scrivener, ed., Cambridge: University Press, 1881; See preface, pp. v-xi).

"The punctuation and paragraphs of the RV are retained in the Greek TBS and Green editions. These are scarcely 'original' and are highly dubious, originating from this committee of arch-heretics. Scrivener adds that certain elements in Beza's Greek (e.g. some accents) are "discarded" or changed to what "appeared" correct to Scrivener (Scrivener, *The New,* p. xi).

"Scrivener admits his imprecise reconstruction of the Greek text is based in places on "presumed" words, "more likely" texts "uncertainties" and "precarious" ideas about what," appears to have been" the KJB' s sources (Scrivener, *The New,* pp. v, vii,viii, 655, 656). This hardly constitutes a final authority and Scrivener had no intention of creating an inspired edition. Maurice Robinson says that this edition does not even reflect "Scrivener's own textual preferences ..." as the previous chapter documented (Maurice Robinson, *Crossing Boundaries in New Testament Textual Criticism: Historical Revisionism and the Case of Frederick Henry Ambrose Scrivener,* http://rosetta.reitech.org/TC/vo 107 IRobinson2002 .html).

My comments: In this section from page 641 through 643, Mrs. Riplinger bows to a new low in documented distortions. She prints Mr. Scrivener's "Preface" in extremely small typeface except for the words which she wants to use to destroy and reverse what he said. By simply placing those words in regular font size and leaving unwanted words in small font size, she has avoided accusations that she used split quotations leveled at her previously. She has technically quoted the entire statement as is with full context. But the genius of this method is that it is so uncomfortable to read the small typeface that the reader naturally connects words that are separated by multiple words and attaches Mrs. Riplinger's intended meaning instead of author's intended meaning.

QUOTES AND COMMENTS

Quote 118

"Scrivener admits his imprecise reconstruction of the Greek text is based in places on "presumed" words, "more likely" texts, "uncertainties" and "precarious" ideas about what "appears to have been" the KJB's sources." (p. 643)

My comments: What else would she expect him to do? We do not have the notes or the text used by the 1611 translators. The best anybody, including Mrs. Riplinger, can do is to state their conclusions while they leave room for their own human error.

Quote 119

"Scrivener gives a list of 59 places in the KJB (a list he admits is "quite incomplete") which were "not countenanced by any **earlier edition** of the Greek" but which **'appear'** to follow "the Latin Vulgate". Notice that he does *not* say "any edition of the Greek." Notice that he does *not* say, "any Greek manuscript." He artificially limits his reconstructed text to "**printed editions**" "**earlier**" than the KJB. **Everyone misreads and misunderstands him**; perhaps that was his intent." (p. 644)

My comments: Mrs. Riplinger should know better. She seems to be the master of misquoting, misdirection, and misreading. I don't believe for one second the contention that Dr. Scrivener was purposely deceitful. At the beginning of his appendix he noted the printed editions of the Greek New Testament that were available to the translators. He NEVER said he did not access actual manuscripts. Mrs. Riplinger is arguing from silence. Unless she can provide the manuscripts and/or printed editions of the Greek New Testament which support the 59 readings she really has no leg to stand on. I examined each one of those readings and discovered that most of them can be explained by either a lesser preferred Greek rendering or compliance with the rules established by King James.

CLEANING-UP HAZARDOUS MATERIALS

Quote 120

"In these 59 plus places he follows Beza's Greek *Textus Receptus*. His text is wrong in these and the other undisclosed places for four reasons, the details of which will be thoroughly documented at the end of this chapter." (p. 644)

My comments: How does she know this? Has she collated the King James Bible to a Greek manuscript or printed edition that is more accurate? No. She has simply made a statement without any basis in fact or history. We will examine the four "facts," when we get to it.

Quote 121

"In other words, he assumed, as he admits, that he knows what Greek evidence the KJB translators had. He assumed they had only "printed editions," not old hand-written manuscripts (*manu* means 'hand'; *scripts* means 'written'). This is a bald assumption. **The KJB translators very obviously had Greek evidence because the readings, which he pretends came from the Latin, are in MANY Greek printed editions today.** Scrivener even had these Greek editions; he "assumed" that the KJB translators did not know of these readings, *since* they only appeared in "printed editions" since the KJB translation. Totally false is *the self-limiting criteria* he established to construct his Greek text (i.e. only *printed* editions *before* 1611, not Greek manuscripts pre-dating the KJB or Greek printed editions post-dating the KJB). The KJB translators had a wealth of hand-written manuscripts, compiled for 1500 years before the printing press was widely used. Perusal of the catalogues of the libraries in England before and during the KJB translation reveals many, many of these. The royal library and British Universities were storehouses of Bible manuscripts." (p. 644-645)

My comments: Several items in this paragraph drew my attention. First, it was interesting to see Mrs. Riplinger appealed to the meaning of manuscript. I wonder how she discovered its origins without using a lexicon. And if she didn't use the lexicon, is she sure that the writer of the dictionary which gave her this information didn't use a lexicon?

Even better, however, is her contention that the KJB translators should have used or might have used printed editions of the Greek New Testament published after 1611 (**Greek printed editions post-dating the KJB**). Only an ideologue of the first degree would expect a citation from a book that did not appear until after the publication of the book that cites it!

I do believe that the KJB translators did have access to other manuscripts of the Greek New Testament. I also believe that they had access to early translations. In that, I agree with Mrs. Riplinger. There was absolutely no reason for her to make her outlandish statement. However, to state that this is a fact when we do not have the notes of the translation committee is to assign certainty where there is only possibility.

Quote 122

> "**Fact 2:** Scrivener's text is based on human fallibility. He says his Greek choices in some places are only based on what "appears" to him. He gives what he admits to be a very "incomplete" list of places where he inserts non-KJB Greek ideas, abandoning the reader to wonder where his *other* mistranslations are located. He admits that his decisions are "precarious." He confesses,
> > "In the following [59] places the Latin Vulgate **APPEARS** to have been the authority adopted in preference to Beza. The present list is **probably QUITE INCOMPLETE**, and a few cases seem **PRECARIOUS**." (p. 645)

My comments: Once again Mrs. Riplinger conveniently misunderstands the intent of the author. Perhaps she forgets he was writing in the 1800s. This statement simply says, "I think these are places where the KJB resorted to the Vulgate but I can't be sure." That is a far more honest statement than what Mrs. Riplinger offers.

CLEANING-UP HAZARDOUS MATERIALS

Quote 123

"**Fact 3**: Scrivener's own text is peppered in these 59 places (and some others) with *faulty* vernacular-based texts. In the places where Scrivener does not follow the Greek text underlying the KJB, he follows Beza. Unknown to most TR advocates, Beza followed among other things, a Latin translation of the Syriac Bible, which makes it yet another Greek edition, in addition to Scrivener's, which was taken from a vernacular Bible. Complete documentation about Beza, including a quote from his own revealing Preface, is included at the end of this chapter. Scrivener's use of Beza's edition instead of the KJB's "Originall Greeke" does not represent the God-honored text." (p. 645-646)

My comments: Most students of manuscripts and printed editions of the Greek New Testament know that Mr. Beza did in fact make use of other translations in his text. And perhaps that is why 190 times the translators left the text of Beza. Nobody said Theodore Beza (Théodore de Bèze or de Besze) (June 24, 1519 – October 13, 1605) was infallible, anymore than Desiderius Erasmus Roterodamus (sometimes known as Desiderius Erasmus of Rotterdam) (October 28, 1466/1469, – July 12, 1536), Robert I Estienne (1503 – 1559), known as *Robertus Stephanus* in Latin and also referred to as *Robert Stephens* by 18th and 19th-century English writers, or Cardinal Ximénes de Cisneros) (1436 – November 8, 1517) who published the Complutensian Polyglot. **That's the reason that the KJB translators did not slavishly follow any printed edition.**

Quote 124

"**Fact 4**: Scrivener is unscholarly in assuming something that opposes everything that the KJB translators ever said in print. On the title page of their New Testament the KJB translators said they used the "Originall Greeke" not any Vulgate readings. Their detailed notes, taken by translator John Bois, never mention following the Latin Vulgate Bible. They list many other sources for reference, including one reference to the "Italian" Bible, and two to the "Old Latin," but

NEVER to the Latin Vulgate.... The Italian Diadoti and the Old Latin are pure editions. **Scrivener did not have access to these recently discovered notes of the translators.** Therefore what he "assumed" has been proven wrong and Scrivener's text along with it." (p. 646)

My comments: The notes of John Bois are helpful but they ARE NOT comprehensive! They do not explain every reading of the King James Bible. They do not provide the Greek text of the King James Bible. They did say that they had access to previous versions. Mrs. Riplinger is either ignorant of the content of Bois' notes OR she is willfully misleading the reader. Furthermore, the Old Latin texts demonstrate differences from the text of the King James Bible and the Italian Diadoti. Some differences can be attributed to TRANSLATION differences, but others cannot.

Quote 125

"Even the Latin Vulgate itself carried with it a large majority of readings from the pure Old Itala Bible. The Old Itala's origin goes back to the work of the "Holy Ghost" in Acts 2, when "out of every nation under heaven"... "every man heard them speak in his own language." The superscription above the cross was in Latin, as well as Greek and Hebrew (Luke 23:38). Many spoke Latin, especially those who lived in the countryside and provinces. The gift of tongues provided a way for the scriptures to be immediately put into Latin, as well as other extant languages." (p. 646-647)

My comments: Thus, we begin Mrs. Riplinger's most significant error. There is absolutely no hint in Scripture that God inspired his word separately and simultaneously in various languages. The gift of tongues on Pentecost was not given to provide the Scriptures in all known languages. Paul was very specific when he gave the purpose of tongues in I Corinthians 14. He appealed to Isaiah 28 where the specific purpose was a warning to Israel that they were about to miss a pronouncement of God and go into judgment. To try to make it any more than that is to add to Scripture and invoke the judgment of Revelation chapter 22.

Quote 126

"The *scriptural* viewpoint of vernacular scriptures shows them as "Holy Ghost" inspired and concurrent with Greek scriptures, via Acts chapter 2. Paul, the one who penned much of the New Testament said, "I speak with tongues more than ye all..." (I Cor. 14:18). As penman of much of the New Testament, the reason for his gift was obvious. His statement would lead to the conclusion that Paul's epistles would have been "inspired" in numerous languages and he, as well as others, would have had the gift to put the rest of the New Testament into all known languages of the day. The Bible never shows an exclusivity to the Greek language. This is made apparent by the kind of gift the Holy Ghost gave in Acts 2. Nor does it place Greek 'above' other languages, given the involvement of the "Holy Ghost" in the known languages of Acts 2." (p. 647)

My comments: Where does this come from? This is exactly the Roman Catholic teaching that the Bible was possibly originally inspired in Latin. Mrs. Riplinger has played right into the hands of a group that she considers her mortal enemies. Furthermore, the gift of tongues was given UNTIL the Scriptures were complete (1 Cor. 13:10). In addition, Paul's epistles were circulated among the various churches in Greek. There is no record or evidence of them being initially circulated in Latin, Gothic, Aramaic, or any other language until the second century or later.

Quote(s) 127

"God has preserved several original readings in the Old Itala, which were removed by unbelieving Jews from the Hebrew Old Testament and by the apostate Greek Orthodox church from the Greek New Testament (See elsewhere in this book for examples).

QUOTES AND COMMENTS

Again the KJB translators expressly stated that they did not follow the Latin Vulgate. A very *large* percentage of the KJB's translator's introductory "The Translators to the Reader" was taken up to express their utter contempt for the Catholic Church and its Latin Vulgate. In the KJB's preface the translators fearlessly said, "Now the Church of Rome" forces its members to –
"... first get a license in writing before they may use them; and to get that, they must approve themselves to their Confessor, that is, to be such as are, if not frozen in **the dregs**, yet **soured with the leaven of their superstition**. Howbeit, it seemed too much to Clement the eighth that there should be any license granted to have them in the vulgar tongue... So much are they **afraid** of the light of the Scripture, (*Lucifugae Scripturarum*, as Tertullian speaketh) that they will not trust the people with it...Yea, so unwilling they are to communicate the Scriptures to the people's understanding in any sort, that they are not ashamed to confess that we forced them to translate it into English against their wills. This seemeth to argue a **bad cause** or a **bad conscience**, or both. Sure we are, that it is not he that hath good gold, that is afraid to bring it to the touchstone, but he that hath the **counterfeit**; neither is it the true man that shunneth the light, but the **malefactor**, lest his deeds should be reproved; neither is it the plain-dealing merchant that is unwilling to have the weights or the meteyard,..." (p. 647-648)

"Has anyone else actually examined Scrivener's trumped-up list of so-called KJB Latin-derived words before? Scrivener's list requires knowledge of *both* Latin and Greek, as well as access to various Greek and Latin editions. I suspect God wanted to expose Scrivener, as almost fifty years ago he gave me a private Latin tutor; for the last 50 years he has kindly surrounded me in a world of wall-to-wall antique and modern reference books. Shockingly, when this list is actually examined the following is discovered:
Many, many of the instances cited on the Scrivener's so-called 'Latin list' **are countenanced by Greek texts.** In just one book at my fingertips I found **Greek support, representing the oldest Greek manuscripts, for 24 out of his 59 listed instances**. (Individually documented at the end of this chapter). (p. 650)

My comments: Yes, someone else has examined them. In October 1996 I submitted an examination of these verses to Dr. Waite. My paper, "Where the KJB leaves Beza's 1598 Greek Text," although based on fewer resources than Mrs. Riplinger claims to have had, nevertheless found that most of the readings could be explained by the Greek texts that I did have available to me. [Editor's note: Dr. DiVietro's paper, BFT# 2708, 48 pages, is available from Bible For Today.org for a gift of $5.00 plus $4.00 S&H]

Quote 128

"In all 24 instances Scrivener also had access to Greek editions which match the KJB.
 The KJB follows Tyndale or other earlier English Bibles in all of these 59 choices. This was done according to the rules laid down for their translation. Therefore the question is not entirely 'what Greek sources did the KJB translators have?' but 'what Greek manuscripts, pre-English and Old English Holy Bibles did Tyndale, the continental traveler, have access to over 350 years before Scrivener? ...That question neither Scrivener nor anyone else can answer. Documented elsewhere in this book is evidence proving that God has used editions other than the Greek and Hebrew to preserve certain readings." (p. 651-652)

My comments: Is this something hidden that Mrs. Riplinger has just brought to light? NO! It is a commonly known fact to anyone who has ever seriously studied the history of the Bible, especially its preservation and translation into English.

Quote 129

"In several cases, the KJB would have had to translate a nonsense sentence, not countenanced by the English language. Scrivener's RV, likewise adds words in these cases." (p. 652)

QUOTES AND COMMENTS

My comments: Big deal! Anyone with even a superficial knowledge of Greek knows that there are certain grammatical expressions in Greek that do not come easily into English. In places where words are clearly implied by the Greek or the Hebrew, they are supplied by translators. The KJB translators put those words in italics.

Quote 130

"In a few cases the reading of the KJB is merely one of the many English synonyms of the Greek word, which the KJB and all new versions use in either this or other places. He charges that in a few places the KJB "corresponds but **loosely** with any form of the Greek original..." Loosely or tightly, it still corresponds and he has no right to assume they had no Greek evidence just because the Latin Bible also says something similar. All Bibles are similar." (see pages 652-657, p. 670)

My comments: This can be continued later. Let us move on. What follows is another series of pages repeating the various verses in which Mrs. Riplinger asserts that some alternate Greek reading was used. She may or may not have been correct. Neither Scrivener nor Beza asserted that they were infallible. Those of us who wish to to view and study the Greek that underlies the New Testament have to start somewhere. The Scrivner's text appears to be closest to that which the translators translated. That is why it is used. That is why she attacks it so. Mrs. Riplinger **does not believe** that the King James Bible comes from a Greek text. But then, she appears to misunderstand the meaning of the word *text*.

Quote 131

"What will Greek-only followers do after seeing that Scrivener's Greek New Testament does not always represent *the* pure Greek text underlying the KJB, as so often stated? On what basis can they pretend Scrivener's Greek text is perfect? Will they become "early **printed** Greek texts only"? Which one of them? Or will they become

Scrivenerites, followers of their god-man who was given the final key to the *Textus Receptus* after nearly 2000 years without it (yet who himself did not even believe in the verbal plenary inspiration of even the originals)?" (p. 677)

My comments: This condescending, mean-spirited, willfully insulting verbiage here is unwarranted. No one that I know of makes any of the claims that she was making in this statement.

Quote 132

"The Greek text of Scrivener is not the Greek text of Theodore Beza (A.D. 1519-1605), though many assume that it is." (p. 681, see pages 678-681)

"Contrary to Beza's express statements, Scrivener likes to pretend that Beza *may* not have made "any great use" of "Tremellius' **Latin** version of the [Syriac] **Peshitta**," but must admit Beza had it "ready at hand"...In other words, Tremellius had translated the Syriac Bible into Latin. Beza used both the original Syriac and the Latin translation of the Syriac to help create his Greek edition." (p. 683)

My comments: What hypocrisy! This is exactly what Mrs. Riplinger claims that the 1611 King James committee did. She says they were not Greek only, but that they used other inspired originals in other languages to determine the text of their translation. Why then is it so wrong for Beza to have done the same (if he did)?

Quote 133

"Beza's Preface does mention his frequent access to the Latin and Syriac scripture readings, noting in part," (p. 684)
" ... *Graeco contextu, non mondo cum novem decim vetustissimis quam plurimis manuscriptis et multis passim impressis codicibus,* **sed etiam cum Syra interpretatione** *collato, et quam optima potui fide ac dilligentia, partim cum veterum Graecorum ac latinorum patrum scriptis, partim cum recentioribus, tum pietate, tum eruditione*

QUOTES AND COMMENTS

praestontissimorurm Theologorum versionibus, et variis enarrationibus comparato (Emphasis mine, KD)

My comments: Mrs. Riplinger's citation is completely in Latin without a translation. She knows that most of her readers don't read Latin. This is an old trick to document something you say with a foreign language leaving the reader with a dual impression: first, that you know what you're talking about, and second, that he doesn't.

Having run the paragraph through several Latin translators, the paragraph that she quotes in effect says that while he used the Greek, he did also consult the Latin Fathers and the Syrian when he needed to make a decision. This does not mean that his translation came from the Latin or the Syriac. It only says that when the Greek text had variants, he used those two sources to help him to determine what the original Greek readings should be. This was the exact same process the KJB translators used in their work. Mrs. Riplinger finds it wrong for determining the Greek text but perfectly legitimate for determining the English translation.

Quote 134

"Scrivener said that Beza used Stephanus's fourth edition as his basis, from which Beza departs in his 1565 edition–
"only twenty-five times, nine times to side with the Complutensian, four times with Erasmus, thrice with the two united; the other nine readings are new, whereof two (Acts xvii. 25; James v. 12) had been adopted by Colinaeus. The second edition of 1582 withdraws one of the peculiar readings of its predecessor, but adds fourteen more. The third edition (1588), so far as Reuss knows, departs from the second but five times, and the fourth (1598) from the third only twice, Matt. vi. 1...; Hebrews x. 17..." (p. 684)

My comments: If Beza's various editions were perfect, they would agree. Should it surprise the reader that as his experience and exposure to various source documents increased, his printed editions of the Greek text changed to accommodate them?

Quote 135

"Wetstein calculates that Beza's text differs from Stephen's in some fifty places." (p. 685)

My comments: Again this is an insignificant issue. What we are to deduce is that Scrivener's text is flawed because it is based on a flawed Beza text. BUT, by Mrs. Riplinger's admission the largest part of Scrivener's text (and therefore Beza) are the words that are translated into the King James Bible. This can have only one purpose: to indicate that the King James Bible did not come from the Greek text. But then we have a real problem since in their introduction to the King James Bible the translators wrote that they had translated from the "Originall Greeke." Were they liars or is Mrs. Riplinger leading the reader down a false trail?

My comments: What follows in her book is a description in detail of the five-points of Calvinism. Mrs. Riplinger launches an *ad hominem* attack on Beza along with a guilt by association attack. What she hopes to gain with this I don't know since many of the Puritan translators of the King James Bible were also five-point Calvinists. And the King James Bible came in large part directly from the Geneva Bible. These facts render this entire section moot, inflammatory, and totally irrelevant.

Quote 136

"Though Beza's Greek text was generally that which came down from the first century, evidently God saw at least 139 small errors in it, to which he alerted the KJB translators." (p. 689)

My comments: No Kidding! Nobody accuses Beza of being inspired of God. This entire chapter is relevant to the issues at hand. There can be no question that Scrivener's text is as close to the King James Bible as any Greek text we know. Mrs. Riplinger may complain about 25 or 30 readings in minutiae. She may complain that Scrivener did not believe in the Greek New Testament that he produced. She may believe that Scrivener was of the devil. None of that matters! A comparison of the King James Bible to the text of Scrivener shows that this text is the basis of the King James Bible. Did they have Scrivener's text at the table in 1611? **NO**!!! It was produced after-the-fact in 1881 as the best estimate of what the King James translators actually translated. It was based on Beza's text, because it is only reasonable that the translators would have started with a printed text and that was the last one printed before their work began. The translators were not slaves to Beza's texts, or Erasmus' texts, or Stephanus' texts, or any other texts. Nobody says they were! They brought all the evidence to the table. They carefully considered each passage using the evidence that they had. Then they chose the word, the Greek word, that the evidence pointed to and translated that word.

Quote 137

"The KJB translators never listed all of their Greek sources; they merely referred to them as "the Originall Greeke" on the title page to their New Testament." (p. 689)

My comments: I am getting sick of Mrs. Riplinger's "originall Greeke" as if the translators were trying to point to some mystical Greek text by their unusual spelling of their term. They were just spelling original Greek the way it was spelled in 1611.

Quote 138

"Their prime authority was the Bishops' Bible which carried forth the words of the English Bible since its genesis in Acts 2. The words of the 1611 English Bible (KJB) had their origin in languages and words which were given through the Holy Ghost's gift of tongues in Acts 2. The precursors of the English languages were the then extant languages of Gothic, early Anglo-Saxon, Celtic, and Latin. These were included among "every nation under heaven" which "heard them speak in their own language." (p. 690)

CLEANING-UP HAZARDOUS MATERIALS

My comments: I want to scream! The Bishops Bible is the words of the Holy Ghost on the day of Pentecost?!! If the Bishops Bible is the worthy inspired Words of God and the parent of the preserved Words of God, why are worthy translators tampering with it? Although King James told them to use the Bishops Bible as their source, it was in fact the Geneva Bible which was used as the base of the King James Bible. However, Anglo-Saxons were raving barbarians on the northern fringe of Europe. They were among the tribes of people what we now call Scandinavians. Their languages were not anticipated on the day of Pentecost. Mrs. Riplinger is doing exactly what she accuses her enemies of doing. She is **ADDING TO THE WORDS OF GOD**. There is absolutely nothing about the languages of Pentecost that is even remotely connected to the writings of the Scriptures.

Quote 139

"It was not hard for Jesus to change forms."Go tell my brethren..." (Matt. 28:10). (If all the vultures can do is light upon and chew on this metaphor until it is beyond recognition, they have proven themselves incapable of serious debate.) (p. 692)

My comments: The last sentence of that paragraph demonstrates another of Mrs. Riplinger's dishonesties. She has been placing her documentation at the end of the sentence in subscript separated from the text. Here she uses the same formatting to hurl a spear at her enemies. The statement on its face is absurd and incorrect. Mrs. Riplinger must know that in an actual discussion, her argument holds no factual water. And so she puts this small sentence into her text to summarily dismiss those who disagree with her fanciful interpretation. It is despicable. It is almost as empty as the Nazi's that offer a reward to anyone that can prove to them that there was a Holocaust. Mrs. Riplinger does not get to be judge and jury over her own comments.

QUOTES AND COMMENTS

Quote 140

"Scriveners (or Beza's) text is not the "exact" Received text or *Textus Receptus* God carried into Holy Bibles. These printed Greek one-man editions must be abandoned as *the final* authority or their followers must abandon all reason." (p. 692)

My comments: Talk about the pot calling the kettle black. In addition, does she realize or remember that there are differences in the vernacular texts over the centuries? Must we abandon them, also? Ridiculous!

Quote 141

"Readers who now find themselves confounded, can contritely ask God forgive them of any intellectual pride...Any one-man Greek text cannot be the sole repository of *the* 'truth,' because it produces rotten fruit by bruising the weak with doubt. The world of Greek texts and lexicons is a world of uncertainties and personal opinions. One might now ask, 'If Scrivener's, Green's, and Berry's Greek texts are not entirely reliable, *where* is the word of God? Wouldn't it be nice if God had sifted out all of the texts and lexicons and given us what he approved, in languages men could read? *He has*!...Isn't God good! Men can now stop wasting their short lives wading through Greek texts, looking for Scrivener's idea of "truth." The "babes" had it all along. Now let's "do it.""" (p. 693-694)

My comments: It must be nice to live in her dream world.

Quote(s) 142

(pp. 698-9)
"Although he did not write either the Greek or English texts of his *Interlinear Greek-English New Testament,* strangely George Ricker Berry (1865-1945) put his name alone on them. The Greek text is that of Stephens (Stephanus) third

edition, first published in 1550. The English so-called literal translation below the Greek is by Thomas Newberry. The critical footnotes are also those of Newberry. The Newberry family website says of George Ricker Berry's *Interlinear Greek-English New Testament,*

"This interlinear is simply an American reprint of the Bagster edition prepared by Thomas Newberry (1877) with a different Introduction and with G.R. Berry's Lexicon and Synonyms added to the end" (http://www.newblehome.co.uklnewberrylbible.html).

"The lexicon at the end contains mainly the corrupt definitions of Unitarian J. Henry Thayer and some by R.C. Trench. Generally speaking, Berry simply put his name on the cover and 'borrowed' the work of *others.* This was necessary because he was *not* a New Testament scholar, but was a professor of **Old** Testament and Semitic languages at Colgate University (1896-1928) and Colgate-Rochester Divinity School (1928-1934)!

"Berry's *Interlinear Greek-English New Testament* was actually published in its identical form (except for lexicon in the back) ...

"[George Ricker Berry] *The Interlinear literal Translation of the Greek New Testament with the Authorized Version conveniently presented in the margins for ready reference and with the various readings of the editions of Elzevir 1624, Griesbach, Lachmann, Tischendorf, Tregelles, Alford, and Wordsworth, to which has been added a new Greek-English New Testament Lexicon, supplemented by a chapter elucidating the synonyms of the New Testament, with a complete index to the synonyms,* New York: Hinds & Noble, 1897.

"Baker promotes it saying, "The Greek text in this volume is essentially identical with the one used by the translators of the King James Version" (back rover). Their "essentially identical" is qualified in Berry's back-limiter as he admits of his lexicon, " ... no mention has been made of the variant readings or the Textus Receptus itself'

QUOTES AND COMMENTS

My comments: Now it is the Berry Interlinear which comes under the crosshairs. The criticisms will be the same. It is not perfect. Berry used the Stephen's 1550 as his Greek text. We all know, including Berry, that it was not the exact text translated by the King James translators. Attacking this book adds nothing for Mrs. Riplinger's thesis.

Quote 143

"Would a Greek edition of the *Textus Receptus*, like Berry's *Interlinear Greek-English*, which omits **an entire verse, omits the Lord, and calls Jesus a sinner**, be a good Greek text to hand to Bible school students? Yet, some unknowingly do so. Would it be a help to easily molded Barbie dulls, who are too busy ' blogging' to bother with the 1200 verbal forms found in Greek? Yet these both claim to read 'the originals' in the *Textus Receptus*' using Berry's *English*." (p. 700)

"The *English* so-called literal translation of the Stephanus Greek text in Berry's *Interlinear Greek-English* was originally written by Thomas Newberry in 1893...Few take Berry's (Newberry's) *English* translation seriously, any more than a doctor would look in a pre-school reader for insights. It is simply a make-believe tool for those who feel compelled to pretend they are *reading* Greek words, when in fact they are simply reading *English* words." (p. 709)

My comments: Since I am according to Mrs. Riplinger "one true believer," I have standing to make the following comment. It is because of George Ricker Berry's *Interlinear Greek English* Bible that I am a "true believer." In my first Greek class, I was told that the United Bible Society second edition Greek New Testament was the authoritative Greek. I was told that any changes would be noted in the apparatus. That is a bold faced lie. I began a search for the Greek text of the King James Bible. The first one I was able to locate was George Ricker Berry's Interlinear. I created a grid so that I did not see the English. Knowing that the Greek text was the Stephanus 1550, I also realized that it was not always going to be the exact text of the King James

Bible. I knew that the translators had more materials at the table. I was not as naïve as Mrs. Riplinger assumes I was. Neither are other thinking students of the word of God.

Quote 144

"One **non-literal** example should give fair warning to the Greek neophyte. In Ephesians 1:5 Berry's Greek text says huiothesian (υἱοθέσιαν). Huios means "children" or "sons"; *thespian* from, *theo*, means "adoption of." Berry's English translates only "adoption," omitting any translation of the word "children" (or sons) – so much for a ' literal' translation. The KJB being literal says, "the adoption of children"; Berry's *English* which merely says, "adoption" is incorrect, not literal, or even remotely idiomatic. One could write a book about such errors. Berry himself admits elsewhere of the Holy Bible, the "... **Authorized Version** being in proximity, which **will make all plain...**" (p. 709-710)

My comments: At this point it becomes painfully obvious that Mrs. Riplinger either does not do her homework or is willfully deceptive. The word in question "υἱοθέσιαν" has nothing to do with the word *thespian*. A thespian is an actor in the theater. I am hoping desperately that this is a typo. Υἱοθέσιον is a compound word made up of the words for *son* and *to place or make*. No reputable lexicon connects it to thespian, an actor!

> **5206.** υἱοθεσία *huiothesía*; gen. *huiothesías*, fem. noun from *huiós* (5207), son, and *títhēmi* (5087), to place. Adoption, receiving into the relationship of a child. (Spiro Zodiates, The Complete Word Study Dictionary)
> HUIOTHESIA (υἱοθεσία , (5206)), from *huios,* a son, and *thesis,* a placing, akin to *tithēmi,* to place, signifies the place and condition of a son given to one to whom it does not naturally belong. The word is used by the Apostle Paul only. (Vines Expository Dictionary)

Υἱοθέσιαν [HUIOTHESIAN] is properly translated *adoption*. In this particular passage is the adoption of Roman custom, whereby a physical son is publicly recognized as a legal heir. In this adoption, we

QUOTES AND COMMENTS

have been placed as the formal heirs of God. There is nothing incorrect or incomplete in Berry's translation. The error is in Mrs. Riplinger's explanation.

Quote 145

"No Everlasting Punishment?

"And shall be tormented day and night **for ever and ever**" (KJB).
vs.

"... for the **ages of the ages**" (Rev. 20:10) (Berry, p. 664)

"The root for 'ever' seen in "for ever" or "everlasting life" (John 6:40) interestingly disappears when punishment is for "ever." Berry's 'age' is normally thought of as a period of time. What ' age' are you? Do you remember the Ice Age? Those who wrongly teach against everlasting punishment of the wicked pretend that when the 'ages of the ages' are over and there is "time no longer" (Rev.10:6) even the devil will be released from torment." (p. 710-711)

My comments: What Berry does is give to us the literal Greek, which is a literal translation of a Hebrew idiom. Whenever the Hebrew connects the absolute and the construct of the same noun, it implies the ultimate superlative. Hence, the King of Kings is the ultimate King. The Lord of Lords is the ultimate Lord. The Bible, the book of books, is the ultimate book. The Song of Songs, which is Solomon's, is the ultimate song. Thousands of thousands is the ultimate number. And the ages of the ages is the ultimate age, eternity.

Mrs. Riplinger exhibits the same simplistic understanding of the word *literal* as many liberals. When they want to disprove a literalist they over literalize to absurdity. Literal, in word by word translation, means what is the exact English equivalent of a Greek or Hebrew word as used in the passage. In interpretation, it means to receive the intended meaning of the word as used in the text. If it is part of an idiom, the idiom has to be recognized and interpreted not just the literal words used. The literal word is *aion* which has the meaning of age. It is only when it is part of the Hellenized Hebrew idiom described above that it means the *age of ages* or *eternity*. Even as a naïve first semester Greek student, I understood that. If she is the scholar she claims to be, she is aware of the same principle.

Quote 146

"He says that "I AM THAT I AM,", really means "I will be that I will be" or "**I continue to be, and will be, what I continue to be, and will be.**" This good side-splitting laugh is appreciated about now. No wonder God did not put Berry or Newberry on the KJB committee; the KJB is more succinct." (p. 712)

My comments: Too bad Mrs. Riplinger doesn't know enough Hebrew to understand that the divine name, as it first appears in the book of Exodus, is in the Hebrew imperfect tense which is normally translated as the future. In this work by Berry, it is not his desire to produce an easily readable English translation. Instead he is trying to bring out the full meaning of the word. Again there is nothing wrong with his translation in this context.

Quote 147

"Berry's Interlinear English is loaded with liberal watered-down words. The *very first line* of the *very first page* of Berry's *Interlinear* English translation begins diluting the unique Christian vocabulary of the Holy Bible. The title of the gospel of Matthew replaces the Christian word "gospel" with the secular "glad tidings"." (p. 713)

My comments: As before, Berry's intention in the interlinear is to elucidate on the English words of the King James Bible. The word *gospel* is an English derivative of the German *Gott spiel* or God speak. It is the translation of the Greek word εὐαγγέλλιαν which means literally *good news* or *good message*. While the Christian gospel is a particular good message, there is nothing wrong with understanding what the word *gospel* means.

Quote 148

"A master is in a ruling position and teaching may or may not be a part of that position; a teacher only instructs; they do not have the same meaning or connotation in English; a teacher is lower than the master. Condemnation is to be judged, found guilty and sentenced; a judgment is merely a decision; it tells nothing of the verdict or any consequences. The judgment may be 'not guilty.' In both cases the sword of the Spirit becomes a butter knife to butter-up and lather the liberal's conscience; it is no longer "powerful, and sharper...piercing," which causes men to 'tremble' at the "word" (Heb. 4:12; Isa. 66:2). (p. 714)

My comments: In this passage, I have to assume that she is attacking the comment on James 3:1 where the word διδάσκαλοι [DISDASKALOI] has a suggested definition of *teachers* in contrast to the KJB *masters*. Its literal meaning is *teachers*! It is the context of James 3:1 that makes it *masters*! Any person who actually understands language use would know the difference between a word in isolation and a word in context.

Quote 149

"Why do we need *his* English translation, when this book has shown that his English is not literal and he himself even admits that one must *look at the King James Bible* to "make all plain"?" (p. 714-715)

My comments: The first step of a journey is not the last one. No serious Bible student takes an interlinear translation as a final tool. It is a starting place, not the end. An interlinear's primary value is helping a fledgling student to find out which word they need to look up in other study tools. It is where as a first semester Greek student I started my journey.

We need Berry's English translation, or someone else's, if we are going to have an interlinear. If all we were going to do is assume that the King James Bible is totally self-explanatory and needs no other aids, then why do we need anything? Mrs. Riplinger's comments are intellectually disingenuous in this particular use of this quote. It is taken completely out of context from a small statement and she extended it to cover the entire Berry's interlinear New Testament. This cannot be justified by a serious scholarly effort.

Quote 150

"Berry follows Thayer's Greek *Grammar*. Thayer was a Unitarian who translated *German* grammars and lexicons into English." (p. 715)

My comments: So what! If there were no English lexicons and grammars, I would do the same thing if I wanted to learn Greek. I probably would have started with secular grammars—I have one or two in my collection. The dialect *Koine* used in the Middle East did not exactly match classical Greek, but at least I would have had a start. There is nothing wrong with building knowledge on previous knowledge. It is not necessary to reinvent the wheel every time you want to go for a ride.

Quote(s) 151

"In this vein Berry and Thayer refuse to translate the aorist verb tense contextually or with deference to the English idiom. They know that by doing so they can defuse the Holy Bible of its very life. The translators of the English Holy Bible (KJB) have always known that in these cases the context sometimes calls for a present, past, future, or perfect tense rendering. Yet to deaden the Bible, Berry and Thayer limit it often to the indefinite past, rarely translating it as the perfect. (The perfect tense implies the continuance of an act and its effects on the present). Berry's Interlinear often places the Bible and our life with Christ in the dead past; it becomes lifeless, just like J.H. Thayer wanted it to." (p. 715)

QUOTES AND COMMENTS

"The fact that Greek verb tenses do not match English tenses is well known among Greek ' scholars.' Berry admits of one case in particular saying, "If the learned were agreed as to a translation we should have kept to the same..." "If the learned" do not agree among themselves, on what authority should Berry's particular choice be accepted?...With his mishandling of the Subjunctive mood he admits, "we have deviated further from ordinary practice than in any other..." For example, in James 2:11 (aorist subjunctive) instead of the KJB's "Do not kill" (plain and to the point) he plays "Mother may I," saying, "Thou mayest not commit murder." He shatters three strong syllables into eight sissy syllables. As he admits, the KJB "will make all plain." (p. 716)

My comments: How many times will we repeat the same error? There is nothing wrong in a grammatical discussion of applying the grammatical convention in its literal intent and then modifying it back into its contextual sense. This is what was done all through the 1611 translation of the King James Bible in the margins. Often the marginal notes provide the strawy over-literal translation before they were smoothed by the translators into the text of the King James Bible.

Quote 152

"Why does the KJB render Eph.1:5 correctly, as demonstrated previously? Why is his Old Testament exactly 666 pages long?" (p. 722, see pages 718-722)

My comments: I just had to include this paragraph. To assign some sinister motive to Newberry just because his Old Testament translation is 666 pages long pushes me so far...

Quote 153

Dr. Gary LaMore of Canada cites these quotes from Burgon and concludes, "[A]nd yet his recognition that in "lesser details," the copies, **versions**, and Fathers **might yield** slight **corrections** if properly and soundly used". Therefore Burgon, with all of his hands on experience with Greek manuscripts, has concluded that versions, other than Greek, hold the original reading in some cases." (p. 733, see pages 729-733)

My comments: Knowing Dr. LaMore and having read Burgon, I know that Mrs. Riplinger has added her twist to this statement. Both Dr. LaMore and Dean Burgon believe in the general integrity of the received text. Both, however, hold out that there is a possibility of an error in any humanly produced printed text. BUT any change would require examination of the ENTIRE body of textual evidence. They would allow correction to that text with strongest support from the manuscript copies, early versions, lexicons and church fathers. However, neither one argued that those versions were directly inspired of God. Both would argue that early translations of the Greek text preserved the original readings in some certain areas. One example would be I John 5:7-8. To imply more than that is to invent "truth."

Quote(s) 154

Author Dr. Jack Moorman of Great Britain, one of today's most prolific collators and researchers, agrees with Burgon saying,

"Our extant MSS [manuscripts] <u>reflect</u> but do not <u>determine</u> the text of Scripture. The text was determined by God in the beginning (Psa. 119:89, Jude 3). After the advent of printing (A.D. 1450), the necessity of God preserving the MS witness to the text was diminished. Therefore, in some instances the majority of MSS extant today may not reflect at every point what the true, commonly accepted, and majority reading was..." (p. 733-734)

"And in those comparatively few places where it <u>seems</u> to depart from the majority reading, it would be far more honoring towards God's promises of preservation to believe that **the Greek and not the English had strayed from the original!**" (p. 734)

"Even Scrivener admits that versions make "known to us the content of manuscripts of the original older than any at present existing". The KJB translators would agree. The recently discovered notes of the King James translation committee by KJB translator John Bois notes in two places (Romans 12:10 and James 2:22) where the KJB translators said the Greek should be interpreted "as if it had been written" in Greek *another way.* There were originally Greek codices that were correct in James 2:22, for example, but many Greek codices are not...The *Encyclopedia Britannica* affirms, "The English of the New Testament actually turned out to be superior to its Greek original" because they accessed and confirmed the Received Text in Holy Bibles in other languages. The EB is of course referring to the edition of the *Textus Receptus* in hand, not the originals." (p. 734-735)

My comments: In these last several quotes, Mrs. Riplinger is again deceptive. Please note that she cites a few words from the author and then adds her own predicate to those words completely changing the intention of the original quote. If this is not the case, then why did she not quote the entire passage and allow the author to state this truth in his own words?

Quote(s) 155

"Evangelist Stephen Shutt reminds us, "Let it be clear, these languages were used by God at one time [ancient Hebrew and ancient Koine Greek]. Yet, interestingly enough, God did away with their authoritative solidarity at Pentecost" (letter on file). There are no verses in the Bible that indicate that the Greek Bible was to be the *only* Holy Ghost-built stepping stone to all other Bibles. "Search the scriptures," as Jesus said, such a directive is not found in the Bible. Surely if the Greek Bible were to have pre-eminence and be continually used as *the* tool to open up the scriptures there would be at least one verse stating this..." (p. 735)

"1ST: The Bible's explanation of the birth of "the scriptures" "to all nations" begins in Acts 2 with the "Holy Ghost" giving the gift of tongues so that "every man heard them speak in his **own language**" from "**every nation** under heaven" (Acts 2:4-12). The Holy Ghost could have given any gift imaginable, from flying for quick travel to walking through walls to escape prison. But he gave vernacular tongues because the Bible, not flying supermen, would be his vehicle to carry his words. The world was not *strictly* Greek-speaking, as we are sometimes told. The inscription on the cross was in Hebrew, Latin, and Greek. The word of God would have been needed immediately in Latin and Hebrew (Aramaic), as well as Gothic, Celtic, Arabic, and numerous other languages, some of which are listed in Acts 2:9-11." (p. 736)

"When "Samaria had received the word of God," it was not in Greek, but the Holy Ghost given Samaritan "word of God," from men who had received the gift of tongues."
(p. 737)

5TH: The Lord said to Peter, "What God has cleansed, that call not thou common" (Acts 11:9). Vernacular means common. In Acts 2 the Holy Ghost cleansed, for his use, what vernacular use had marred." (p. 737)

My comments: This is another "**What can I say!!!!**" This leap of pseudo-intellectual logic could cross the Grand Canyon of confusion. To equate the *word*, in this context with a vernacular translation of the Scriptures is such a *non sequitur* that it defies any serious consideration. There is no way that Acts 11 has any reference whatsoever to the Samaritan Pentateuch or the Aramaic targums. It referred specifically to the unclean animals in Peter's vision. It referred metaphorically to non-Jews. To even think that it referred to flawed Aramaic scriptures gives me a headache.

Quote 156

"Unscriptural beliefs abound about the transmission of the New Testament text. For example, Jay P. Green states in the Preface to his Greek New Testament text that God preserved the scriptures, "using the Greek Orthodox church" (p. 740, see page 738-740)

My comments: He did! Without the thousands of manuscripts, lectionaries, and preserved words of the church fathers preserved by the Greek church, we would have almost no evidence of the words of the New Testament—whether she likes it or not. The fall of Constantinople to Muslim forces produced a windfall of Greek manuscripts to Western Christianity. It enabled them to break free from the stifling grip of the Latin Vulgate.

Quote 157

"The Greek Orthodox Church is also called the Byzantine Church. The Greek text is also called the Byzantine text because most of the extant Greek manuscripts were produced in the regions of the Byzantine Empire and during that period. The thousands of Greek manuscripts that are used to validate readings in the New Testament were the product of, or were corrected and stored by, men in Greek monasteries. Frederick Scrivener, editor of an edition of the *Textus Receptus*, says that "...all or nearly, **all that we know,** not of the Bible only, but of those precious remains of profane literature," we owe to the "scribes" who were "members of religious orders, priests or **monks**" living in "convents." "More must still linger unknown in **monastic** libraries of the East" Even the Syriac Manuscript came from "the convent of S Mary the Mother of God."...Greek manuscripts are invariably described as being "found in some Eastern monastery." Would you go to a convent today to find the best version of the Bible? Would God give treasures to unsaved monks who have perennially had a distorted interpretation of the scriptures?" (p. 741)

"These unsaved monks have made alterations to the text many times over the course of centuries. Such alterations appear today in modern versions which say in their margins, "the oldest MSS say ..." (p. 742)

My comments: What Mrs. Riplinger fails to say is that the changes were often corrected by later monks when they saw errors in the text. It is these corrections in the manuscripts which are part of the confirmation process out of which came the New Testament text translated in the King James Bible. It is also the basis of rejecting those oldest manuscripts as faulty.

CLEANING-UP HAZARDOUS MATERIALS

Quote 158

"This [St. Catherine's monastery, **KD**] monastery today is the home of the second largest library of Greek and other language Bible manuscripts in the world, housing some 6000 manuscripts, 3000 being from the ancient period. It also houses 2000 idolatrous icons. When someone says, 'The Greek says...' he is likely referring to the Greek manuscripts which have been housed in this monastery. These manuscripts are not kept at St. Catherine's (or any other Greek monastery) because the Greek church and their monks love the word of God; they are kept because they are considered 'relics' and as such are superstitiously believed to have supernatural powers." (p. 742)

My comments: God works in mysterious ways. Using superstition, He preserved the most ancient copies of the Greek New Testament!

Quote 159

"Another source of manuscripts is the Greek Orthodox monastery Mt. Athos. 'Father' Harakas says,
"...going back at least to 962 A.D., is the Holy Mountain Athos, which consists of twenty monasteries..." "Another interesting note is that despite modern advances, **women are still not allowed on Mt. Athos**," known for its monasticism and thought to be a Holy Mountain." (p. 744-745)

My comments: What on earth does this have to do with Bible preservation? Mrs. Riplinger will stop at no limit to condemn by association, *ad hominem*, or any other literary device, even if she has to invent one.

What follows on the next few pages is a list of the heresies practices and other anomalies found in the Greek Orthodox Church which Mrs. Riplinger thinks are adequate to discredit any Greek manuscript coming therefrom.

QUOTES AND COMMENTS

Quote 160

"The Greek Bogamiles, Paulicians and others had the true Greek text which included the pure readings." (p. 759)

"Christians Must Reject Heretics & Their Writings" (p. 766)

My comments: There is a vast difference between the writings of heretics and those who copied the Scriptures. Even a flaming anti-God atheist can copy letters and get them right.

Quote(s) 161

"Ancient Greek Was for Ancient Greeks"

"...Like the now empty skulls of the men who made the manuscripts, thoughtless scholars mull over the lifeless hulls of manuscripts which no longer bear a living seed to living speakers. Jesus said, "the words that I speak unto you, they are spirit and they are life." Only living things can reproduce. The "life" and "spirit" did not die when Paul spake unto the Jews in the Hebrew tongue, when the Gothic and Latin Bibles burst forth into the English Bible, or when ancient Koine Greek became Modern Greek. Since when was Jesus Greek-only?" (p. 792)

(Quoting Harakas, KD) "...Did Jesus know Greek? We have no direct evidence that he did." (p. 792)

My comments: We don't? The Gospel writers attribute many sayings to Jesus and they do it IN GREEK! Are these the original words of Jesus? Can Mrs. Riplinger or anyone else prove they are not? I can argue from silence as well as she can.

Quote(s) 162

"Jesus' brother James probably spoke the same language Jesus spoke. In what language did he write the book of James? None of these facts are known *through the Bible*, because evidently God did not think 'original' *languages* were important to anyone who did not speak them. Jesus' words were translated into all the languages of the day via the gift of tongues. Even the Greek Bible would perhaps have been a translation of his words. Therefore translations can be inspired.

"When straining to find any indication in the Bible that the New Testament 'originals' were written *only* in Greek, some will cite Romans 1:16, which says, "the Jew first and also to the Greek." The context's previous parallelism in verses 13 and 14 had defined the "Greek" as the "Gentiles," "Greeks," and "Barbarians." This would include all extant languages (e.g. the Latins were Gentiles, the Goths and Celts were Barbarians etc.)...

"The ending letter 's' in Esaia**s**, used in the New Testament for the Old Testament name Isaia**h**, is similar not only to Greek, but to early inflected forms also seen in the Gothic, German, Spanish, and Latin Bibles...If all Bibles sprang forth from a solitary Greek original, instead of from Acts 2, the Italian and French Bibles (not the Latin, remember), which do not carry this Gothic-Greek-Germanic form forward, would also have this ending; they do not. English Bibles have not always carried the 's' forward. The Anglo-Saxon Bible says Esaiam, 'Isaiam,' or 'Ysia'; the post-Wycliffe period Bible says 'Ysaie', or 'Ysaye,' the Coverdale Bible of 1535 says 'Esay'...There are no proofs, either internal or external, that the ' originals' were written in Greek alone. (The Goths were living on the Black Sea during the time of Christ; it is not scriptural (Col. 1:5, 6, Rom. 16:26, etc.) to pretend that they had no scriptures until hundreds of years later when we were ' told' that Ulfilas translated them from Greek). Do we believe the scriptures or the writings of men? Our history of the Bible must come from the Bible, not from the writings and surmising of liberal non-regenerate British scholars.)" (p. 793-794)

My comments: It takes unmitigated gall to make such a statement when Mrs. Riplinger's assertions are found nowhere in the Scriptures. See the "Appendices" of this work for the meaning and intention of speaking in tongues according to the Scriptures. There is nothing in the scriptural doctrine of tongues to indicate that it was given for the production of the Scriptures in original languages. Furthermore, ask Dr. Stephen Zeinner if all dialects or all languages have a Bible in their "tongue." Even today, thousands of dialects do not have a Bible. Why should we **assume,** as Mrs. Riplinger does, that every language had a Bible immediately in their tongue? Ridiculous!

Quote 163

"If no **English** translation can express the original Greek, as he [Harakas, **KD**] and others claim, what about the *English* translation given when someone says, "That word in the Greek means ' such and such.'" That meaning given is someone's 'translation.' If no English translation can be correct, why give one to correct the KJB when studying the Bible? Or why not accumulate all of these corrections and more precise renderings and create a new bible? Voilà! Hundreds and hundreds of failed English translations of the Bible have attempted to do this with the very lexical words used to 'define' Greek words." (p. 795)

My comments: If Mrs. Riplinger were half the linguist she claims to be, she would know that it is almost always impossible for receptor language to perfectly provide an exact match to a donor language. There are implications and nuances that just do not attach to the verbal equivalents in the receptor language. Elucidating from the original Greek text is not the same as translating. Most often when done by a Bible-believing preacher, it is an attempt to infuse the King James word with all of its original force.

Quote 164

"James Strong's *Concordance* and its Greek Lexicon often use *Revised Version* words as definitions. The definitions in *Vine's Expository Dictionary* come quite often from this RV, as was demonstrated in chart form in the accompanying chapter which exposes W.E. Vine. Moulton and Milligan's *Vocabulary of the Greek New Testament* also uses the words from the RV as of 'definitions' for English Bible words. George Ricker Berry's *Greek-English Interlinear New Testament* uses RV words in its English Interlinear and Greek-English Lexicon. Lexicographer Frederick Danker says of the Brown, Driver, Briggs *Hebrew-English Lexicon,*

"BDB" "relies too much on word meanings of the RV...A large number of the words in new bible versions can be traced back to their original use in the *Revised Version*." (p. 826)

My comments: I am convinced that Mrs. Riplinger is playing which came first—the chicken or the egg? Her assertion that it was the egg flies in the face of the truth. Even if, and I don't concede the if, the RV was published before the original lexicon that Mrs. Riplinger is so opposed to, it did not come from the RV. The RV translators had already come to the conclusion that these were the meanings of the Greek words and use them as such in their work. The chicken always comes before the egg. What the books that she cited do is offer definitions for the words used in the RV and suggest they are superior. BUT they are all clearly marked and/or indicated.

Quote 165

(This reaction covers remarks made on pages 828-839. They are too numerous to cite here.)

My comments: The *ad hominem* **attacks continued** by Mrs. Riplinger on the pages above are too numerous to reproduce. What follows in her book is a detailed attack on the Freemasons and an attempt to link the translators of the Revised Version to the Freemasons and to assert that they were Jesuit plants. I am no friend of the Freemasons nor am I friend to homosexuals and child molesters. But even if Mrs. Riplinger's wildest charges are absolutely true, it does not have bearing on the accuracy of a lexicon.

Quote 166

(see pages 851-911)
"Lexicon authors Gesenius, Brown, Driver and Briggs were chief among those who gave cynical students what they wanted to hear. (Aren't most young people looking for an excuse to deny the Bible's authority?)" (p. 912)

QUOTES AND COMMENTS

My comments: No! I don't believe most young people are looking for an excuse to deny the Bible's authority. Most young Christians want to know what the Bible has to say. The problem is not in the students. It is in the teachers. Unfortunately, it seems to be the goal of many Bible college and seminary professors to destroy their faith in the Bible's authority.

Quote 167

(see pages 913-934)
(She is quoting Hatch, **KD**)
"Indeed, the theory that the Bible is inerrant is the ghost of modern evangelicalism to frighten children." (p. 932)

My comments: At this point, I am wondering if Mrs. Riplinger is willing to donate out of the millions of dollars received from sales of her materials enough money for a serious Bible-believing scholar to prepare a lexicon and grammar derived exactly as she would want, directly from the words of the King James Bible. I doubt very seriously that she would. She recommends *The King James Bible Built-In Dictionary* (Barry Goddard, AV Publications: Ararat, VA.), which she just happens to publish. She admits that only part of the book is done according to her proposed principles. The note on *propitiation* is a perfect example of the flaw in her system.

<u>1 John 2:2</u> And he is the **propitiation** for our sins:
  Romans 5:11 by whom we have now received the **atonement.**
  Hebrews 2:17 to make **reconciliation** for the sins of the people.
  Hebrews 10:12 But this man, after he had offered one **sacrifice** for sins
  Hebrews 10:14 For by one **offering** he hath perfected for ever them that are sanctified.

While these are aspects of the Atonement of Christ, there are distinctions between the words used in both Greek and English. Atonement means *covering* and is primarily used of the Old Testament temporary covering of sin until the cross would remove it. The propitiation was accomplished by the sacrifice and offering of Christ on the cross.

Propitiation and reconciliation are opposite sides of the same theological coin. The word behind reconciliation is καταλλάσσω [KATALLASSO]. The Analytical Lexicon of the Greek New Testament defines it:

> "καταλλάσσω   1aor. κατήλλαξα; 2aor. pass. κατηλλάγην; as restoring relationship between individuals or between God and man reconcile, change from enmity to friendship (2C 5.18); passive be or become reconciled (RO 5.10)"

The word propitiation is ἱλασμός [HILOSMOS]. The Vine's Expository Dictionary of New Testament Words defines it:

> "HILASKOMAI (ἱλάσκομαι, (2433)) was used amongst the Greeks with the significance to make the gods propitious, to appease . . . It is never used of any act whereby man brings God into a favourable attitude or gracious disposition. It is God who is propitiated by the vindication of His holy and righteous character, whereby, through the provision He has made in the vicarious and expiatory sacrifice of Christ, He has so dealt with sin that He can shew mercy to the believing sinner in the removal of his guilt and the remission of his sins."

Propitiation is the act by which God was appeased. On the cross, Jesus absorbed the wrath of God against sinful men, rendering God forgiving. At the same time, by his obedience, Jesus turned mankind back toward God and made him forgivable.

I also doubt very seriously that she learned Greek, Hebrew, and/or Latin without the aid of grammars and lexicons (if she really does know any of those three languages). If she says that she has learned them without any of the standard language aids, I may boldly conjecture that her integrity is gravely in danger of totally disintegrating.

With this, I believe attempting to document any further ridiculousness in the *ad hominem* attacks against Briggs Driver and Brown is to repeat the same things *ad nauseum* and gains no merit.

QUOTES AND COMMENTS

Quote 168

(see pages 964-1016)

"**The Truth:** Omitted Verses in ben Chayim
1.) The original ben Chayim Hebrew Bible wrongly omitted Joshua 21:36, 37.
"Jacob b. Chayim was the first who omitted these verses in the *editio princeps* of his Rabbinic Bible with the Massorah of 1524-1525.
"Of course these two verses *do* belong in the Bible and are exhibited in most of the Hebrew manuscripts. The King James Bible rightly includes these two verses. This proves that the KJB translators DID NOT follow the ben Chayim exclusively." (p. 1016)

My comments: This is an argument from silence. What she does not ask us is, "Did ben Chayim include these verses in subsequent editions?" If he did, then it is probable that the first omission was an oversight or typesetting error. Unless Mrs. Riplinger provides proof that no edition of ben Chayim's work includes these verses, her criticism of Ginsburg in this particular area is inaccurate and prejudicial.

The KJB translators had access to manuscripts and printed Bibles which included these verses. They were included in the earlier Bomberg presses of the Rabbinic Bible in four parts edited by Felix Pratensis, Venice, 1516-17, who "utilize the printed editions of his predecessors" for the text. They were in the second quarto edition of the Bible, Bomberg, Venice, 1521. They were in the Bible, Bomberg, 1525-1528 (quarto), which is a fusion of ben Chayim's and Pretensis' texts. This 1525 edition quickly reinstates the two verses taken out by ben Chayim. Ginsburg says of the 1525 edition that, "The text as a whole is substantially that of Felix Pratensis," a monk who dedicated his edition to the Pope. It was popular "at the time of the Reformation." One copy has "notes in the handwriting of Luther," who also use the Brescia edition of 1494.

Quote(s) 169

"Even Ginsburg admits that,
"...some of the model Codices and the Masoretic Annotators not infrequently differed in their readings, and that Jacob b. Chayim had to exercise his own judgment as to which was the better reading... " (p. 1017)

"In conclusion, none of the current editions of the Masoretic Text are the text of ben Chayim. The King James Translators did not follow ben Chayim exclusively... ".
"Although the KJB translators followed "the Originall sacred tongues, together with comparing of the labours, both of our own [previous English Bibles] and other foreign languages [Chaldee, Syriac, Spanish, French, Italian, Dutch] of many worthy men who went before us," they did not follow the 1524-25 edition of ben Chayim when it disagreed with earlier English Bibles or foreign editions. The "Originall sacred tongues" were not their 'final authority,' according to their own admission. Chayim's small errors were quickly fixed by Bomberg's next edition in 1525. It is no longer available

"The following are 8 examples of why the current printed and software *editions* of the Massoretic Hebrew Bible cannot be used to ' correct' the Holy Bible, to study the Holy Bible, or be used to translate Holy Bibles. **The examples are serious only in the sense that Hebrew editions which omit these words are not following the pure Massoretic Text and are therefore guilty of disobeying God's command to "diminish not a word"** (Jeremiah 26:2). [Emphasis mine KD] (p. 1019-1020)

My Comments: We are no more surprised that printed editions of the Hebrew text have some minor differences than we were that the printed editions of the Greek text have some differences. If one attempts to look up a word or verse from the King James Bible Old Testament and does not find it in a given Hebrew edition, he simply needs to keep looking. It will be in another edition. They did not make up the words.

QUOTES AND COMMENTS

Quote 170

"Eight strikes against Massoretic Hebrew *one-man* editions:
1. In Numbers 33:8 the KJB says, "and they departed from before Pi-hahiroth." The KJB does not follow the ben Chayim text, but adds **"the textual reading in many [Hebrew] MSS., in the Samaritan, the Chaldee, the Septuagint, the Syriac and the Vulgate"** (Ginsburg, *Introduction*, p. 192). He also reports that the KJB here exactly matches the 1545 German Luther, the 1531 Swiss German Zurcher, the 1532 French Olivetan, the 1855 French Martin, the 1641 Italian Diodati, the 1637 Dutch SV, the 1569 Spanish Reina, and the 1865 Spanish Valera.
2. In 2 Sam. 8:3 the King James Bible says "the river Euphrates." Ginsburg admits that "...this reading was exhibited in some MSS. As this is actually the textual reading in the parallel passage in 1 Chron. 18:3 "...In these manuscripts it is *in* **"the text"** in 2 Sam. 8:3 not in the margin. Wrongly, the Hebrew texts of Ginsburg (TBS) and Letteris (B&FBS, Hendrickson, Green) merely say, "the river." In this case the KJB is *not* following the Hebrew of ben Chayim (or the text-type of Ginsburg (TBS) or Lcttcris (B&FBS, Hendrickson, Green), but the "Originall," as noted on their title page, as well as all vernacular Bibles (Ginsburg *Introduction*, p. 310). Nico Verhoef reports that the KJB rcading matches exactly the 1545 German Luther, the 1531 Swiss German Zurcher, the 1532 French Olivetan, the 1855 French Martin, the 1641 Italian Diodati, the 1569 Spanish Reina, the 1865 Spanish Valera, and the 1637 Dutch SV. Nadine Stratford of France reports that the KJB also matches the 1669 French Geneva, the 1744 Martin, 1996 French Ostervald, the Darby 1988, the BFC Francais Courant, and a half-dozen more modern French Bibles.
3. In 2 Sam. 16:23 the King James Bible says "as if a man." Ginsburg admits, these words are "in the text after the verb" "in some [Hebrew] MSS., in several of the early editions and in the ancient Versions" (Ginsburg, *Introduction*, p. 310). **Critics of the KJB will pretend that the KJV got it from the margin, as they likewise pretend regarding 2 Sam. 8:3; however, as stated earlier, things which are in the margin in one manuscript (and in Ginsburg's ben Chayim), are IN THE TEXT in other manuscripts.** Ginsburg (TBS), Letteris's (B&FBS, Hendrickson, Green) and ben Chayim do not have the words "as if a man." Therefore the KJB did not follow the ben Chayim edition or a text like theirs here. Nico Verhoef reports that the KJB

matches exactly the 1545 German Luther, the 1531 Swiss German Zurcher, the 1532 French Olivetan, the 1855 French Martin, the 1641 Italian Diodati, the 1569 Spanish Reina, the 1865 Spanish Valera, and the 1637 Dutch SV (ita1.). Today's French King James Francaise also matches the KJB.

4. In Ruth 3:5 the King James Bible says, "all that thou sayest unto me I will do." Ginsburg (TBS), and Letteris (B&FBS, Green, Hendrickson, et al.), and ben Chayim omit "unto me." Ginsburg admits that "unto me" is **"in the text in many MSS.**, in several of the early editions, in the chaldee and in the Syriac ... " Again critics will tell you that the KJB follows the margin *(keri)*, not knowing that MOST HEBREW manuscripts have "unto me" **in** the TEXT, not in the margin. Ginsburg's "own Massorah" [marginal *keri]* hides the truth saying "unto me" is a marginal *keri* reading! (Ginsburg, Introduction, p. 312). His margin has many such distortions. Nico Verhoefreports that the KJB exactly matches the 1532 French Olivetan, the 1855 French Martin, the 1641 Italian Diodati, the 1865 Spanish Valera, and the 1637 Dutch SV (ital.). Nadine Stratford reports that the KJB reading is seen in all old French Bibles, such as the 1669 French Geneva and the 1744 Martin, as well as most modem French Bibles.

5. In Ruth 3:17 the King James Bible says, "to me." Ginsburg (TBS), Letteris (B&FBS, Hendrickson, Green), and ben Chayim omit these two words. Ginsburg admits, "As in the preceding passage the [his] *Keri* is exhibited **in the text in many MSS**., in several of the early editions, in the Chaldee, the Septuagint and the Syriac" (Ginsburg, *Introduction,* p. 312). Therefore when you are told that the KJB derived its reading from the *keri* margin, remind them that MOST manuscripts have it *in the text,* not in the margin. Ginsburg's marginal notes do not tell the truth, calling it a *keri* reading. Again the KJB did not follow ben Chayim or the erring Ginsburg, Green-type text. Nico Verhoef reports that the KJB matches exactly the 1545 German Luther, the 1531 Swiss German Zurcher, the 1641 Italian Diodati, and the 1637 Dutch SV (ital.) Nadine Stratford reports that the KJB reading is seen in all old French Bibles, such as the 1669 French Geneva and the 1744 Martin, as well as most modem French Bibles.

6. Judges 20:13 in the King James Bible says "children of Benjamin." Ginsburg (TBS) and l.cucris (B8.: FBS, Hendrickson, Green) and ben Chayim omit "children of' before "Benjamin." As always Ginsburg pretends the KJB has a marginal *keri* reading, but admits in the next breath that "other MSS. again have "sons of," ["children of'] **in the**

QUOTES AND COMMENTS

text which is also exhibited in the Chaldee, the Septuagint and the Syriac ... " (Ginsburg, *Introduction,* p. 313). Nico Verhoef reports that the KJB matches exactly the 1545 German Luther, the 1531 Swiss German Zurcher, the 1532 French 01ivetan, the 1855 French Martin, the 1641 Italian Diodati, the 1569 Spanish Reina, the 1865 Spanish Valera, and the 1637 Dutch SV. Verhoef observes that his Hebrew from the 1740s reads *in the text* here as the KJB. His is a Hebrew-Greek dig lot in right column, and the German Luther, old letter type, in the left column.

Items one through seven are in Verhoef s 1740 Hebrew edition, either in the text or in the margin.

Ginsburg's admissions that 'these words are in many manuscripts' cannot be *readily* found *in the notes* of his Hebrew edition for all to see, but are hidden away in tiny print in his huge 1,028 page *Introduction* which few have ever read." (p. 1023)

My comments: I included the entire text of this particular criticism here to demonstrate the absurdity of the argument. I'm not sure what happened to the other two instances since these are all Mrs. Riplinger included. If these eight verses are all that she can produce to compare against the volume of the Hebrew Scriptures, her argument is easily answered. The King James Translators were not slavishly bound to any particular printed text. They clearly leaned very heavily on the ben Chayyim text but did exercise the evidence at hand to make judgments.

Mrs. Riplinger criticizes Ginsburg for allegedly hiding documentation in obscurity in his large volume. What hypocrisy! Mrs. Riplinger is also guilty of obscuring quotations variously, i.e., using large extended quotes, placing unwanted words in tiny fonts in her 1200 page *Hazardous Materials* to make those she wants to cherry pick from the quote stand out even if they are not physically or syntactically connected. We have noted above that she also plays loose with some quotations.

Quote 171

"These two editions of the 'Massoretic Text,' Ginsburg and Letteris, do not even match *each other.*" (p. 1025)

My comments: I see a pattern developing that necessitates a response. We do not hold to the inerrancy of any printed edition of Greek or Hebrew text but that does not mean the King James Bible translators did not use the Greek and Hebrew texts as the source of their translation.

Quote 172

"Like all Bible doubters, he says he includes his view of the variants he 'scoured' up, "in fairness to the Biblical student to afford him an opportunity of judging for himself as to which is the preferable reading." (p. 1029)

My comments: Surprisingly, on this point I find some agreement with Mrs. Riplinger. It is the job of the translator to translate. Providing variant readings which have been rejected by the translator causes more confusion than help. Normally, it is not the serious student with a working knowledge of Hebrew or Greek who selects an alternate reading. It is the doubter looking for an excuse to change the Word of God, a doubter whose depth of knowledge is based on the lexicon at the end of Strong's concordance.

Quote 173

"In many manuscripts the words of the Hebrew Old Testament are often written continuously, that is, there are no spaces between words. This infrequently gives critics like Ginsburg an opportunity to change the meaning of the sentence. Ginsburg introduces in his margins the choices of what he calls "the best Biblical **critics**," with regard to *word divisions*. He boasts that "the Biblical critics are more or less unanimous in accepting them." Of these Bible criticisms he

says in the margin (in Hebrew) "it ought to be so" or "it appears to me."
"Word divisions do seriously affect the translation of a few readings and affect some less seriously." (p. 1029)

My comments: I have not read sufficient materials advocating the antiquity of the vowel points to be convinced. There does seem to be reasonable biblical indications that they are genuine and original. The vowel pointing does indicate the word breaks. The continuous text would only obscure word breaks if it is a consonantal text. Vowel shifts and other diacritical markings indicate word, sentence, and paragraph shifts.

However, it is my understanding that it is the task of the Temple cantor to preserve the word divisions of the original text. So that even if the vowel points were not from the beginning, the word divisions, and paragraphs are maintained and preserved by them.

On page 1034, as she did with certain of the despised New Testament scholars, Mrs. Riplinger connects Ginsburg with the Luciferian's and other occultists. It really gets boring. On page 1042, Riplinger summarizes Ginsburg's book on the Kabbalah.

Quote 174

"Ginsburg says that in the end, man will be God and rule the world under *En Soph*, **a woman!** He writes, "In that state the creature will not be distinguished from the Creator...Then the souls will rule the universe like God, and what **she** shall command he will execute." (p. 1045)

My comments: Riplinger wastes the next group of pages establishing the occultic credentials of Ginsburg. She then launches into the Dead Sea Scrolls, Ginsburg's theology etcetera, etcetera, etcetera; *ad hominem* attack after *ad hominem* attack. The sad part is I don't know any fundamentalist that puts any stock in Ginsburg's Kabbalah writings. So it's all wasted verbiage.

Quote(s) 175

"The Trinitarian *Bible* Society's current Old Testament is that of Ginsburg. Therefore it is *not* authoritative in the minutiae and cannot be used for Hebrew 'study' or by Old Testament translators as their *final* authority, as the TBS suggests. It is helpful, however in revealing errors in the *Biblia Hebraica Stuttgartensia.*" (p. 1059)

"TBS director E. W. Bullinger published his own study Bible called **The Companion Bible**. It purports to give insights into the Bible from *the* Greek and Hebrew. Bullinger recommends the critical text in his *Companion Bible*. Naïve readers may miss the fact that *all* of his references and comments are based on the corrupt Greek text of Westcott and Hort. His critical Hebrew notes are from Ginsburg." (p. 1060)

"Reliance on their defective Hebrew edition by Ginsburg leads the TBS to state: "The Trinitarian Bible Society does not believe the Authorised Version to be a perfect translation, only that it is the best available translation in the English language...The final appeal must always be to the original languages, in the original Greek and Hebrew texts"...Small wonder they think the KJB is not perfect; they are comparing it to their imperfect Ginsburg text (and no doubt reading Ginsberg's Hebrew with a corrupt Gesenius, Brown, Driver, and Briggs *Hebrew-English Lexicon.* (p. 1063)

My comments: The statement of the TBS is true. Mrs. Riplinger's spin is not. Her objection is to the statement that the King James Bible is not perfect. TBS is not saying that it is flawed! A translation can be 100% accurate and still not be perfect. What the statement means is what any other honest Bible student knows. No translation from one language to another can ever carry all the nuances and implications of the original language into the receptor language. Therefore, technically, NO TRANSLATION of any complex literary work IS PERFECT.

To read the fullness of the Scriptures without any chance of misunderstanding, one must read the words of the original autographs with full understanding in the language from which it came. This removes ambiguities and false impressions which can develop even in the most accurate translations.

This does not mean that the translation is inaccurate. Nor does it mean that a Bible student having only the English cannot understand the Bible. It does not mean that any given **printed edition** of the Greek or Hebrew is absolutely faithful to the autographs in every point of minutiae. BUT, there are things to be learned and elucidated in the original Hebrew and Greek texts of the Bible.

Since the translators of the King James Bible freely admitted that they had translated it from the original languages, it is legitimate and helpful to look at those same languages. When a printed text does not support what is written in the King James Bible, one never presupposes that the King James translators got it wrong. After all, they were eminently far more qualified to translate the Bible than a first year Bible college student or even the most qualified of modern scholars.

When the KJB does not seem to follow the known Greek or Hebrew text, the true Bible student assumes that in that place either the translators chose a secondary or tertiary meaning of the Greek or Hebrew or they translated a different Greek or Hebrew word(s). The true Bible student tries to discover why the translators translated as they did to gain a fuller understanding of the passage. He is not dependent on Ginsburg, Thayer, or any other given commentator.

Quote 176

"Unfortunately, even conservative translators of foreign editions are haplessly resting on every jot and tittle of Ginsburg's Hebrew or J.P. Green's Interlinear. Such translators have not done a thorough collation with historical texts to uncover the unsoundness of these currently available one-man Hebrew editions, nor do they know the history of their particulars." (p. 1063)

My comments: It would be wonderful if every translator of the Bible in every language had a perfect understanding of the language in which he is working. But not every translator is a professional translator. Some are blue-collar workmen missionaries trying to give the people to whom they minister the word of God in their own language. Yes, some are dependent on interlinears and lexicons. And no, that is not the ideal situation. Would she deny the recipients of those translations the words of God in their language, even if they are imperfectly presented? Was the very first translation into English perfect? Was not the KJB the capstone of three centuries of translations and refinements? Would Mrs. Riplinger deny those language groups the words of God until God decided they were worthy of a divinely inspired version in their language?

What solution would Mrs. Riplinger have? I am sure she thinks that a person this superficial would be more accurate if they superficially just translated the King James Bible into their language. But then if they are that superficial, and they come to a passage in the King James Bible that can be understood in more than one way (all but one being errant), what do they do? When the receptor language is ambiguous, what do they do? They are denied any help from study aids because they are all evil.

Quote 177

"Once Origen and Jerome had used Greek and Hebrew to birth their corrupt one man 'bible' editions, Greek and Hebrew Bible study was not attempted for well over one thousand years." (p. 1070)

My comments: This is simply not true. Biblical scholars did not suddenly erupt with the intuitive knowledge of Greek and Hebrew during the Renaissance. They learned it somewhere! And they learned it from those who kept the study alive in obscure monasteries (which only means places of being alone until perverted by the Roman Catholic and various Eastern Orthodox Churches). They were kept alive in Jewish communities. And when they burst back into the open air like a spring from deep below the surface, the Reformation burst out as well.

QUOTES AND COMMENTS

Quote 178

(see pages 1076-1095)

"Why is it that once the devil has a man, through occult involvement, such as Reuchlin or Ginsburg, he moves him into the 'Christian college,' teaching Greek or Hebrew, or has him begin editing and revising the Bible? Reuchlin was the "Father of Greek and Hebrew study," while Ginsburg's edited Hebrew text is today's holy grail. Let this be a warning as to what the devil's goal is –*questioning and redefining the word of God.*" (All emphases are Mrs. Riplinger's) (p. 1091)

My comments: The pages above are again *ad hominem* attacks on all the people who Mrs. Riplinger says are in the direct line of all Greek and Hebrew studies. This quote is representative of the section. She shows (at least to her satisfaction) that men like Ginsburg, Reuchlin, and others were both under the influence of the occult Kabbalah and agents of the Roman Catholic Church to undermine Biblical Christianity.

Quote(s) 179

(This begins part six of the book and probably the most important part. In this part, Riplinger discusses inspiration, preservation, translation, and inspiration.)

"God knew the Greeks, as a nation could not bear the responsibility of preserving the word of God. He immediately provided a safety net in Acts 2 and 1 Cor. 14:21 to catch the words they were apt to lose. The Acts 2 "Scriptures in tongues," as Wycliffe called them, were created directly by the Holy Ghost and were not man-made *translations* from 'the' Greek. These "Scriptures" would have quickly been available in Latin, Coptic, Gothic, Celtic, Ethiopic, Arabic, Hebrew and a myriad of other languages.
"Chrysostom [thought] that each had a special language assigned to him, and that this was the indication of the country which he was called to evangelize. (Hom. in Acts ii). Some thought that the number of languages spoken was

seventy or seventy-five, after the number of the sons of Noah (Gen. x) or the sons of Jacob (ch. xlvi) or one hundred and twenty, after that of the disciples."

Syria is very close to Judea, Galilee, and Jerusalem. With the growth of the church at Antioch and Damascus, there was no doubt an immediate need for Syriac gospels and epistles. The importance of the churches at Antioch and Damascus made an immediate Syriac translation mandatory. Matt. 4:24 notes of Christ, "and his fame with [sic] throughout all Syria."

In the **provinces**, especially at distance from the chief seats of commerce, **Latin was the only language generally spoken**, and in such places the necessity must have first arisen of rendering at least the New Testament into a tongue to be "understanded of the people'"

God closed the canon at the end of the book of Revelation with a warning not to "add onto these things." However he never said he would not *translate* the canon (Acts 2, 1 Cor. 14:21, Col. 1:6, Romans 16:26, Esther 8:9), *preserve* its inspiration (Ps. 119:160, 100:5, 105:8, Mat. 5:18, Isa. 40:8) or *purify* it as languages change (Ps. 12:6, 7, Prov. 30:5, Psalm 119:140). (He said the gift of tongues would cease, along with the sign gifts for Israel. But both Dr. James Sightler and Dr. Norris Belcher have suggested to me that he never made such a statement about the gift of "interpretation," a word which is always used in the New Testament to mean going from one language to another. It appears to be no stranger than the gift of helps.) Acts chapter 2 and 1 Cor. 14:21 assure us that it is God himself who "speaks" his word in "other tongues" and therefore must superintend the translation of his words. He is no respecter of persons. Would he not answer the prayers of translators who ask for wisdom and *his* very words? Could translators be in a safer place than to be stranded on God's omnipotence?

The Greek language has never been primary for other language groups (except of course for Greeks). Few Bibles ever were created from Greek, without recourse to other vernacular editions also, as will be evidenced by a bank of examples in this chapter." (p. 1095-1097)

My comments: No one ever said that God chose the Greeks as a nation to preserve His Word. This statement is totally irrelevant. It is not the Greek NATION that preserved God's word. It is the Greek LANGUAGE. Every responsible and accurate historian and linguist knows that the conquest of the Persian Empire by the Greek armies of Alexander created a vast Greek speaking empire. From the time of Alexander until the time of Jesus, about 300 years, the entire eastern world was ruled by Greek administrators and kings. Greek was the universal language of the first century, not Latin. Roman emperors all read and spoke Greek at that time. Latin was only the language of the government. Writing in Greek made the Scriptures immediately available to the entire eastern world. While Greek may not have been their first language, it was the common language.

Chrysostom is not God. While he was a great preacher of the early world, I am sure that Mrs. Riplinger knows that he was part of the "corrupt Greek Orthodox Church." Using Mrs. Riplinger's' philosophy of guilt and incompetence by association, he could not possibly speak with authority.

Syria, which included the land and population of Israel, was under the domination of the Greek Seleucid kings for over 300 years. Egypt was under the Ptolemies for the same period of time. Both were completely dominated by the Greek language. While Aramaic was the first language of Syria and Israel, literate people of either nation spoke Greek. Turkey, under the name of Asia, also was under Greek influence and spoke Greek. Greek was the language of literature, government, and commerce throughout the world.

Passages that Mrs. Riplinger uses on Page 1096 to prove **the inspiration** in translation are not relevant to that tenet. Also, at the bottom of page 1096, she makes the following absolutely false statement.

"The Greek language has never been primary for other language groups (except of course for Greeks).

Quote 180

"H. C. Hoskier, one of the rare scholars who has collated a large and wide range of actual ancient manuscripts, concluded that the originals were created immediately in multiple languages." (p. 1097)

My comments: This statement does not mean, as Mrs. Riplinger implies, that the New Testament was simultaneously inspired in multiple languages. It means that translations immediately followed the giving of the New Testament books. As the early Christians carried out the Great commission, they translated the Word into the languages of those to whom they ministered. I am presently attempting to acquire Mr. Hoskier's words because I am sure he has been quoted out of context. No man who believed that the New Testament manuscripts had no authority would have dedicated as much time as he did collating and commenting on various manuscripts.

Quote 181

"Hoskier makes three observations...
Originals: Some or all of the first originals they have been in languages other than Greek.
Concurrent: Multiple language editions were available immediately and were concurrent with Greek editions.
Continuity: The Greek manuscripts we now use to determine the text were often made from vernacular, not Greek, editions.
Conclusion: Greek manuscripts have historically been no more authoritative than vernacular editions." (p. 1097)

My comments: This is absurd! If the vernacular translations were made 30 minutes after God gave the originals, they would not be equal to the originals. I would have to see Hoskier's words in their context to trust Mrs. Riplinger's representation. Only if God supernaturally inspired versions in those other languages would they hold the same authority as the originals in Greek. And if they were inspired, they would not have been translations.

Quote 182

"Hoskier believes, like Wycliffe, that the original books of the Bible were written in the language to whom they were addressed (i.e. Hebrew, Latin, Greek, etc.). He refers to–

QUOTES AND COMMENTS

"...the original languages [plural] in which the "Ur-texts" [plural] of the different books of the New Testament were written" (p. 1097)

My comments: Even if Mrs. Riplinger is not misrepresenting Hoskier's position, a great scholar can be wrong. Absent any physical evidence, these statements are based on conjecture, not facts in evidence. To any normal reader's words, the original languages would immediately invoke Hebrew, Aramaic, and Greek. On the following page she continues to cherry-pick his writings.

Quote 183

"Now the point is that both the Latin and Syriac go back so far that they point almost to a **concurrent origin**, practically as old as the Greek..." (p. 1098)

My comments: Riplinger quotes Hoskier as having written "almost to a concurrent origin..." **Almost** indicates that even if it did exist, it was not original, but subsequently produced. He can only assume that very early the Gospels appeared in polyglot version in Greek, Syrian, and Latin. He admits that there is absolutely no manuscript evidence of such a polyglot.

Who knows what those three dots represent in the quote above. In *New Age Bible Versions,* Mrs. Riplinger was guilty of using ellipses (...) to put words into a single quote that were separated by dozens of pages and had no relationship to each other. She has demonstrated a propensity for cherry picking words within a given volume that bear no relationship to each other, but rather serve her purpose. Simply put, I do not trust her when she tries to make this say what it does not say. Hoskier says **almost to a** concurrent origin, not **to a** concurrent origin. It is Riplinger's bold print that causes the misconception. He is arguing for a Greek original, parallel with a Syriac and Latin translation, which circulated as an early exemplar. This in no wise is evidence for pure inspired originals in Syriac and Latin.

By the following quotes on page 1099, Mrs. Riplinger actually slips up. Hoskier is discussing the origin of Codex Aleph. He is not discussing the authority of various translations, only their existence and possibly use.

Quote 184

"Greek was not the sole language of the area, nor of the New Testament. The sign above the cross was written in Hebrew, Latin, and Greek because these were the predominant languages of the day." (p. 1099)

My comments: Nobody is arguing that Greek was the only language spoken in the world. But it was the most common language in the ancient world. Moreover, it was the lingua franca of the day just as English is today. Its use spanned from the Indus River to the Gates of Rome. Although it was not necessarily the first language of any given people, it was the common second language.

The quote which follows on page 1100, is used to argue for a lost source of the Gospels. She is arguing the argument of the Roman Catholic Church that underlies their demand for centuries that any translation of the New Testament must come from the Latin because according to them, it was the original language of the New Testament. The confraternity version of the Bible, a Roman Catholic contemporary to the Revised Standard Version, states clearly that it was compared to the Greek and Hebrew but at any given controversial passage, the Latin would prevail. It was not until the addition of Carlo Maria Martini to the United Bible Society Greek New Testament committee that they finally dropped the demand that the Latin be the final authority.

The fact that the Greek text gives the Hebrew and/or Aramaic original of a given word (i.e., Calvary = Golgotha) argues strenuously for Greek original. Were the Hebrew or Aramaic translations equal in inspiration to the Greek, there would be no need for such explanatory notes. Mrs. Riplinger says:

Quote(s) 185

"I would not suggest the liberal theory that the original gospel of Matthew was written *exclusively* in Aramaic, a theory which has been fomented by Catholics. However, it is important to see McClintock, Strong, and Hoskier's observations that the originals may not have been written *strictly* in Greek and vernacular editions born out of Acts 2 accompanied the originals immediately...

Hoskier demonstrates that "the texts were concurrent" of Greek, Latin, Aramaic, Coptic and others. Hoskier sees, "a **concurrent** Syriac or Aramaic version lying **alongside the Greek**." He said, "In other words, as regards the Gospels, Latin and Syriac were made at the same time, or Latin and Greek from a Syriac originals; or Latin from a Graeco-Syriac original." "The real facts stand out clear as light that **Syriac, Latin and Greek were concurrent ever so early**, and in the time of Justin and Irenaeus"

"We are driven to the conclusion that the Holy Scriptures of the New Testament existed in Syriac translations at an early date; a date at least as early as that of the oldest Latin translations, and practically **contemporary with the Greek originals**. When the antiquity of Latin and Syriac versions is fully recognized, the discussion concerning Aramaic originals of certain Books will become in some directions simplified but in turn raise other nice questions."

The Bible cannot clearly be made to give any other impression than that its books were made available immediately and concurrently in multiple languages. No primacy and exclusivity of the Greek language is afforded by Acts 2." (p. 1100-1101)

Hoskier gives hundreds of pages of examples demonstrating his conclusion that even Greek manuscripts, used to establish the current text, were taken from vernacular editions. He says:

"The point, therefore, is that it was not necessarily "through the medium of a Greek text" but through the medium of a Graeco-Syrian-Latin text existing A.D. 150." (p. 1101-1102)

My comments: (see my previous comment(s), KD) I feel like US forces in Korea at Pork Chop Hill; we have to fight the same battle over and over and over again. If the Syriac and the Latin translations of what Hoskier calls "**the Greek originals**" were perfect and equally inspired, there would be no need for a polyglot. The Syriac version would simply go to the Syrians. There would be no need for a parallel

Greek translation since it would add nothing. Mrs. Riplinger is doing what charismatics do with I Corinthians 12 to 14. She is using the very words that disprove her theory to prove it. She is making a one hundred and eighty degree reversal of the original intent of Hoskier's words. It is reprehensible!

Quote 186

(see pages 1102-1104)

My comments: The entire line of reasoning on the pages above is predicated on a purposeful distortion of the facts. While it is very true that Beza may have had the work of Tremellius available as he worked, it did not become the underpinning of his Greek text. Mrs. Riplinger knows that. If she doesn't, she has no business writing this book. However, since Beza's text is not among those commonly used today, her arguments are completely moot. Her real attack is against Scrivener and even here she falls flat.

The exact Greek text of the King James translators has been lost. Their notes were destroyed in the fire of London in 1660. While we do have some brief notes by John Boyce, they are far from complete.

Instead of letting Mrs. Riplinger tell us what Dr. Scrivener let slip, let Dr. Scrivener tell us:

> "In considering what text had the best right to be regarded as "the text presumed to underlie the "Authorized Version," it was necessary to take into account the composition nature of the Authorized Version, as due to successive revisions of Tyndale's translation. Tyndale himself followed the second and third editions of Erasmus's Greek text (1519, 1322). In the revisions of his translation previous to 1611 a partial use was made of other texts; of which ultimately the most influential where the various editions of Beza from 1562 to1598 , if indeed his Latin version of 1556 should not be included. Between 1598 and 1611 no important addition appeared; so that Beza's fifth and last the text of 1598 was more likely than any other to be in the hands of the King James revisers, and to be accepted by them as the best

standard within their reach. It is moreover found on comparison to agree more closely with the Authorized Version and any other Greek text; and accordingly it has been adopted by the Cambridge press as the primary authority. There are however many places in which the Authorized Version it is at variance with Beza's text; chiefly because it retains language inherited from Tyndale or his successors, which have been founded on the text of other Greek editions. In these cases it is often doubtful how far the revisers of 1611 deliberately preferred a different Greek reading; for their attention was not specifically directed to textual variations, and they may not have thought it necessary to weed out every rendering inconsistent with Beza's text, which might linger among the older and unchanged portions of the version. On the other hand some of the readings followed though discrepant from Beza's text, may have seemed to be in a manner sanctioned by them, as he had spoken favorably of them in his notes; and others may have been adopted on independent grounds. These uncertainties do not however affect the present edition, in which the different elements that actually make up the Greek basis of the Authorized Version have an equal right to find a place. Where ever therefore the authorized renderings agree with other Greek readings which might naturally be known through printed editions to the revisers of 1611 or their predecessors, Beza's reading has been displaced from the text in favor of the more truly representative breathing, the variation from Beza being indicated by *. It was manifestly necessary to accept only Greek authority, though in some places the Authorized Version corresponds but loosely with any form of the Greek original, while it follows the Latin Vulgate. All variations from Beza's text of 1598, in number about 190, are set down in an appendix at the end of the volume, together with the authorities on which they respectively rest."

Scrivener did not reverse translate his Greek text. He says very clearly that **he used Beza's text** as the basis of his text because of specific considerations. First, it was the last major printed edition of the Greek New Testament done prior to their translation work; and, second, in collating the known Greek texts of the day with the King

James Bible, Beza's text matches the King James Bible more closely than any other printed Greek text.

Quote 187

"The original Latin and Gothic Bibles from Acts 2 carried Christ to Europe. As languages continued to be confounded by divergent dialects, God gave each of these languages his words, "forever settled in heaven," which would judge people in the last day (John 12:48). As language changed, Holy Bibles were "given" and "purified" (2 Tim. 3:16, Psalm 12:6, 7) to fit the linguistic need. The Italic, Gallic, Celtic, and Old Saxon editions came forth. As will be demonstrated, *new New Testaments have usually been birthed from previous vernacular New Testaments.* For example, the pure Old Latin Bible became the Romaunt, Provençal, Vaudois, Toulouse, Piedmontese, and Romanese Bibles. It is unlikely that Greek was even accessed worldwide in most cases because of the lack of availability of Greek manuscripts, compounded by a lack of skill in that language. Scrivener admits,
"The fact that versions as a class go much further back than [Greek] MSS., constitutes one of the chiefest points of their importance...some are secondary versions, being derived not from Greek..." (p. 1105-1106)

My comments: Yes, it is true that there are versions which are older than some of the Greek manuscripts that we have. Mrs. Riplinger fails to note that **version** is a technical term reserved for a direct **translation.** A version (translation) may be earlier than a manuscript of the original language text, but it cannot be older or even contemporary to the text it translates. These translations help us to understand what was translated by the source of that translation. Sometimes, and I emphasize sometimes, it is possible to determine what was the source of the translation of the translation from which the version we are observing. And this can sometimes help us to verify the original Greek reading. Secondary and tertiary translations in their own right do not establish the words of God.

QUOTES AND COMMENTS

Quote 188

"The Koine Greek New Testament had but minor use as a medium of comparison and translation from the first century to the 15th century. Its use was local and somewhat metropolitan; it was limited to Greek-speaking people during the centuries and locales encompassed by the Roman and Byzantine Empires." (p. 1106)

My comments: Its use may have been confined to the Greek speaking people, but since the entire Eastern Roman Empire spoke Greek and existed continually until the 15th century, it was there and in constant use. I have a Greek New Testament which contains the formal blessing of the Greek Church. It contains all of the verses that we find in the King James Bible including Acts 8:37, Colossians 1:14, I Timothy 3:16, I John 5:13, *et al.* Just because translators did not take advantage of its existence does not mean that it ceased to be the words of God.

Quote(s) 189

1. "Its current craze, beginning with the German higher critics, later adopted by Unitarians, and promulgated recently by liberals, who see it as an avenue to sweep away the authority of the Holy Bible...
2. The use of Greek MSS as a medium of comparison slightly before and past the 16th century when Greek manuscripts were carried into Europe by the Greeks as they fled from the Turks...Their usage at this time simply brought attention to a Greek text which affirmed what European vernacular Bibles already said. It was a confirming witness, not a textual revolution of discovering lost readings. The pre-and post-Reformation era's new access to Greek or Hebrew editions only verified *already existing readings* the French Geneva, the Italian Diodati, the Spanish Reina-Valera, and the German Luther. Of the Gothic Scrivener concedes, "Its dialect is marvelously akin to that of modern Germany."" (p. 1106-1107)

My comments: You be the judge!

ULFILAS' GOTHIC	LUTHER'S GERMAN	ENGLISH
atta unsar þu in himinam,	Unser Vater in dem Himmel!	Our Father, which art in heaven.
weihnai namo þein.	Dein Name werde geheiligt.	Hallowed by thy name.
qimai þiudinassus þeins.	Dein Reich komme.	Thy kingdom come
wairþai wilja þeins, swe in himina jah ana airþai.	Dein Wille geschehe auf Erden wie im Himmel.	Thy will be done, on earth as it is in heaven.
hlaif unsarana þana sinteinan gif uns himma daga.	Unser täglich Brot gib uns heute.	Give us this day our daily bread
jah aflet uns þatei skulans sijaima,	Und vergib uns unsere Schuld,	And forgive us our debts
swaswe jah weis afletam þaim skulam unsaraim.	wie wir unseren Schuldigern vergeben.	As we forgive our debtors
jah ni briggais uns in fraistubnjai,	Und führe uns nicht in Versuchung,	And lead us not into temptation
ak lausei uns af þamma ubilin;	sondern erlöse uns von dem Übel.	But deliver us from evil
unte þeina ist þiudangardi jah mahts jah wulþus in aiwins. amen	Denn dein ist das Reich und die Kraft und die Herrlichkeit in Ewigkeit. Amen.	For thine is the kingdom, and the power, and the glory, for ever. Amen

Well there you have it; you can compare the Gothic to Luther's Bible. Don't they look almost identical? I think sometimes Mrs. Riplinger, who loves charts, has a tendency to forget them when the facts don't exactly match theories.

Quote 190

"A large percentage of the translations discussed in these books were made in the centuries immediately following the publication of the 1611 Authorized Version (King James Bible) and marked by the British missionary and colonization movement...it becomes quite clear that it is not an exaggeration to say that the majority of individual translation

QUOTES AND COMMENTS

projects since the first century have been taken up initially with a vernacular Bible, not a Greek text." (p. 1108)

My comments: Yes, that is true. Translations usually follow closely great missionary movements. When the missionary cannot work competently in Greek and Hebrew he/she will often translate the Bible of their native tongue.

And so it was with the English Bible. It began with Wycliffe's translation of the Latin Vulgate. This edition produced in the 1380's was the primary English translation of the Bible until over 100+ years later. At that time, Tyndale translated from the Greek and Hebrew, with comparison to the German of Luther. Many of Wycliffe's translations continue into the King James Bible not because they were in the Vulgate but because they were accurate. Those that were not were changed.

Tyndale's Bible was a one-man task. It had all the flaws of a single man's work. In addition, it was not finished. Tyndale was harried to death. His successors, Coverdale etc., did finish his work. It was further revised in the Bishops Bible and the Geneva Bible. Again, where Wycliffe and Tyndale offered correct translations, there was no need to change them. That does not mean that the translators did not compare the English to the Greek and bring the English into conformity with the Greek (or Hebrew) as necessary. It is wrong to say that Tyndale simply translated earlier English dialect Bibles into his contemporary English. He translated the Bible from Greek and Hebrew. So did the 1611 translators. Yes, the language of Wycliffe, Tyndale, Coverdale, and Geneva Bibles were often correct, but they translated.

What follows on pages 1008 through 1012 is a list of Bible **translations with** an attempt to show that they generated from vernacular versions in an attempt to justify Mrs. Riplinger's doctrine of inspiration by translation. If there is a single flaw in any of these translations, Mrs. Riplinger's theory is completely debunked.

Quote 191

"It was originally the standard practice of Bible Societies to translate only from vernacular Holy Bibles. The original

American Bible Society, founded in the early 1800s, insisted that all translations be made directly from the King James Bible. Use of lexicons or a Greek or Hebrew text was forbidden. The 1881 *Baptist Encyclopedia* says, **"The English translation had been made the standard to which all other translations should conform..."** not "the Greek and Hebrew texts." (my bolding, KD) (p. 1112)

My comments: The concluding sentence of the above paragraph has a critical ellipsis. It is clearly a cherry-picked, manipulated, disjointed quotation. The predicate, not "the Greek and Hebrew texts," is provided by Mrs. Riplinger. It is not part of the Encyclopedia article. Unless I see the entire quote and am able to discern that this was the intent of the editor, the reader is completely justified in ignoring it.

Quote 192

"Dr. Gutjahr of Stanford University reiterates that, "This emphasis on the common English version (the King James Version) as the root translation from which translators had to work" brought about a split and the formation of the liberal American and Foreign Bible Society, who wanted to use so-called "Originals" of Greek and Hebrew...Making all translations from the KJB was the foundational conviction of the American Bible Society. Their refusal to allow the use of 'Greek' came to a head in their ruling related to Adoniram Judson's translation, which they refused to print because it was not translated directly from the KJB but from Greek." (p. 1112)

My comments: Let me borrow from Mrs. Riplinger's playbook and argue from silence. It should have been very easy to document this statement if it is true. Mrs. Riplinger chose not to. This draws into question the veracity of her statement. Could this be just her interpretation of the facts and not the facts themselves?

QUOTES AND COMMENTS

Quote 193

"England's Prime Minister, Winston Churchill wrote the four volume classic, *The History of the English-Speaking Peoples*. In it he boasts that the King James Bible has been translated into 760 languages, which is no doubt more than have ever been translated from the Greek text." (p. 1113)

My comments: A translation, which uses as its guide a good translation of the original, will generally be reliable. Since the King James Bible is unusual in its English reproduction of the Greek and Hebrew texts from which it comes, it does become a reliable source for secondary translations. However, for those translations to be completely reliable preservation of the inspired Words of God into a given language, it is essential for those translations to be diligently compared to the very words which God spoke out.

Quote 194

"4. Since it would be a monumental task to translate directly from Greek, many new editions are translated from vernacular Bibles and only later checked or corrupted with the Greek text...Yet the title pages of many Bibles imply that *the entire volume* was ' translated from the original.' Many have taken the early existing translations and changed them to match the critical Greek text. Removing words to match the critical text can hardly be called 'translating.' Sadly when the corrupt critical Greek text of Griesbach was introduced, many vernacular translations were changed to match it. I purchased the rare Pashto (dialect from India) New Testament from the *mid*-1800s, assuming that it would not have been corrupted by the critical text and found it had already been tampered with." (p. 1114)

My comments: Why reinvent the wheel? There is no need to change what is accurate! That does not mean it has not been translated. What it means is that the translation already available is accurate, acceptable, and desirable to the translators.

When they use the critical text, it is a different story. Because we believe that the historic *Textus Receptus* is the original words of God, the inspired words of God, we believe that correction to the Textus Receptus is the only acceptable correction.

Quote(s) 195

""'A certain portion of the books of the Old Testament was allotted to each of the [Modern] Greek [Old Testament] translators, **who with the English authorized version**, the French of Martin, and the Italian of Diadoti, before them, consulting also the Septuagint, the Vulgate, and other versions and aids where necessary, **made as good a translation as they were able into the Modern Greek.**'"

"It was only *after* the Greek Old Testament was completely translated directly from the KJB and other versions that, "It was then the office of Mr. Leeves and Mr. Lowndes to compare this translation with the Hebrew, calling in the aid of other versions and critical commentaries, and to make their observations and proposed corrections in the margin of the manuscript...The marginal suggestions were discussed in a committee meeting and either accepted or rejected. But the KJB tightly wove the warp and woof for the Modern Greek Old Testament, which remains the purest available today." (pp. 1115-1116)

My comments: When the final result was brought into conformity with the Hebrew texts it was no longer translation of the King James Bible or any other vernacular text. It was a translation of the Hebrew text.

On pages 1116 through 1120, Mrs. Riplinger cites a book *The Bible of Every Land* and lists a number of translations of the Bible which come from the King James Bible or some other vernacular Bible.

Quote 196

"The following language groups at one time had Bibles translated from the vernacular Vulgate, which, while missing some things, is generally much less corrupt than a critical

QUOTES AND COMMENTS

Greek text: Russian, Arabic, Breton, Maltese, German, Flemish, Spanish Reyna, Polish." (p. 1120)

My comments: Mrs. Riplinger would rather see a translation from the Vulgate Bible than from the critical Greek and Hebrew texts! What happened to her insistence that a printed Hebrew or Greek text has to be perfectly consistent with the King James Bible or it is not a legitimate translational source? Suddenly she relaxes that rule so that an IMPERFECT, vernacular Vulgate is a legitimate translation source.

If that is legitimate, then English-speaking people should have been satisfied with the Douay Rheims version of the Bible, which is an English translation of the Latin Vulgate. Some say that Wycliffe used a vernacular Vulgate and not the official Clementine Vulgate for his translation. Perhaps the English speaking world should have been satisfied with his translation instead of progressively working toward the King James Bible. She must know that she is fishing at this point. It is disgusting!

Vernacular Bibles have proven to be a strong safety net when the Hebrews and Greek manuscripts are inconsistent. These vernacular manuscripts can restore to prominence minority readings that include Bible words and verses that were dropped from the majority of the evidence because they did not fit the bulging apostasy of the recording groups (i.e., 1 John 5:7-8).

Vernacular Bibles, especially those most ancient, do give testimony to the inspired words of God. There are times when the vernacular Bibles throw their support behind an unpopular yet extant reading in the Greek or Hebrew texts. They clarify the original text. They are important tools in preserving the original text. Contrary to Mrs. Riplinger's intention, there is no basis for saying that they are equal to the original text.

Quote 197

"Likewise God preserved his words in Bibles other than those of the corrupt Greek Orthodox church and Hebrew nation, when those language groups destroyed certain readings for sectarian reasons. Charges that the KJB

CLEANING-UP HAZARDOUS MATERIALS

wrongly followed the 'Latin' in a verse are only made by those who do not understand the history of Bible preservation; the Latin merely matches other preserved vernacular Bibles, as one would expect." (p. 1121)

My comments: I cannot believe how Mrs. Riplinger is double speaking in these places. Earlier (and I'm sure she wants us to forget), Mrs. Riplinger was outraged to think that the King James translators followed the Latin Vulgate. Now all of a sudden, the Latin Vulgate is just one of many vulgar translations. How hypocritical! She cannot have it both ways. I do not believe that the King James Bible in any place follows the Latin Vulgate. I have studied the supposed Vulgate-isms in the King James Bible. I did not find a single one that was not supported by the Greek. Sometimes the English reading followed a secondary tertiary, etc. or lower priority meaning, but it could always be justified by the Greek.

Quote 198

"Pure Bibles have existed in all countries, but a large percentage appear to be out of print, preserved by God on library shelves, waiting to be sought, found, collated, and reprinted. Many language groups are consequently left with only those widely proliferated tainted editions printed by liberal Bible Societies from the corrupt texts." (p. 1122)

My comments: So much for God giving every people a Holy Bible in their language. God must have given it and then taken it back. Again, she argues a point with no physical evidence to support it. She just knows there are pure Bibles out there somewhere that will back up her thesis. Maybe with the millions her books bring in she can finance an expedition around the world to find these important rare books.

Quote(s) 199

(The paragraph that follows is placed in very tiny font and made to appear as an insignificant footnote (KD), which says:

QUOTES AND COMMENTS

"(The word 'inspired' is derived from the verse, "All scripture is given by inspiration of God..." Grammatically, the Bible can be called 'inspired.' Consider this grammatically identical parallel: ' All pure water is produced by the distillation of Jones Bottled Water Company.' This water is therefore called 'distilled water,' just as the Bible is called 'inspired scripture.' As a word of personal testimony I might add that before I was saved I was determined to read the *entire* university library. But when I finally read the King James Bible in my late twenties, I knew it was not a book written by man. I got saved and have never gotten over the *difference* between it and other books. It is alive. Later as a professor, the Lord knew I would witness to students, so he spread me thin, teaching 17 *different* college courses, including upper division courses in over six *different* and highly divergent majors, several in which I had no academic experience. This necessitated *much* more reading. After sixty years in a world of books, I can say that the King James Bible stands *so far* above the books of even the best and brightest men, one could never attribute it to the brilliance of the translators.)" (p. 1134)

"What does "given by inspiration" mean? What is "All scripture"? These questions hopefully will be resolved for the reader in this section. I will begin with a discussion of the Greek text, only because that is where this discussion usually, and I might add, somewhat incorrectly begins. My analysis will be Biblical and will not come from the standard corrupt secularized lexicons and critical editions..." (p. 1135)
"In other words, the word of God is not just ink on paper, like other books; its words are "spirit." Since the spirit of God is alive, his words are also alive." (p. 1136)

"Breath is tangible; the spirit is not tangible. Those who are afraid to call the KJB "inspired" are wrongly focusing on the *physical* character of Strong's or Moulton's erring definition, "breathe"; they know that God did close the canon and stopped the physical sign gifts. But God's "Spirit" is still striving with man, comforting man, and leading man into all truth. God never said the Spirit;..." (p. 1136)

"A word's context is the determiner of usage and meaning. That is why the OED's definition ("**in**fluence of the **Spir**it of

God,") has taken directly from the words of 2 Tim. 3:16 ("**inspir**ation of **God**")." (p. 1140)

"God demands no knowledge of Greek or the methodology of lexicographers. The definition of "inspiration" is "plain to him that understandeth" (Prov. 8:9). The word "inspiration" is a compound word. Even a child can see the definition within the word ' in-spir-ation.'" (p. 1141)

My comments: It amazes me that such a brilliant educated woman as Mrs. Riplinger does not know what a compound word is. I would like to see Mrs. Riplinger's formal résumé so that I could verify the academic claims she makes in this quote. She is not demonstrating such vast education and experience, if it is indeed true.

An elementary school child is taught the definition of a compound word. They know that a compound word is a single word made up of two or more other words. Words such as farmhouse, jackhammer, etc., are compound words.

A word may be complex but not compound. The longest formal word in the English language for many years was *antidisestablishmarianism*. It is made of many meaningful morphemes but it is not a compound word. In the same way words like *incompetence* or *inspiration* are not compound words. The morpheme *in* is not the freestanding preposition *in*. No other part of this word is a complete word. No one of the three syllables is a complete word. Inspiration is not a compound word. The English word, *inspire* or *inspiration* comes from the Latin meaning TO BREATHE! Note the following definition from *Webster's Revised Unabridged Dictionary* (1913 + 1828):

Inspire (Page: **770**)
In*spire" (?), v.t. [OE. enspiren,   OF. enspirer, inspirer, F. inspirer, fr. L. inspirare; pref. in- in + spirare to breathe. See **Spirit**.]
1. To breathe into; to fill with the breath; to animate.
When Zephirus eek, with his sweete breath,
Inspir\'8ad hath in every holt and health The tender crops. *Chaucer.*
Descend, ye Nine, descend and sing, The breathing instruments **inspire**. *Pope.*

QUOTES AND COMMENTS

In these words a PREFIX is not an independent word. Mrs. Riplinger's whole discussion of this aspect of inspiration is devoid of any genuine grammatical or etymological basis. If this were a court of law, she would be guilty of bearing false or faulty witness. She is manufacturing facts.

Quote 200

"In plainer words, the verb "is" must be inserted with "given" and "profitable"; it cannot be "was," nor "is being," nor can the word "is" be used only once. Therefore, according to Greek grammar rules, inspired Scripture "is." (It is not merely settled in heaven, as scripture is described as "profitable" to man). Having taught English to Greek speaking adults, I can attest to the fact that the usage of "is given," in both English and Greek, is a "continuing action," to use the words of Polly Powell, a former instructor of English at Clemson University (phone conversation). In English, "is given" is a present tense verb; it is not time sensitive. In this context "is given" cannot be bound to the time of the writing of the Bible. It is an irregular verb and its passive voice indicates that the scripture receives the action of 'spirit' (spir) of God." (p. 1146)

My comments: I am not sure which words in the above paragraph belong to Gail Riplinger and which words belong to Polly Powell. But I do know that it's a bunch of grammatical nonsense. The word *is* does not appear in the Greek text neither does *given*. They were added because the context demanded them.

In the English construction of this verse, the supplied "is" becomes the auxiliary verb to "given" which comes from THEOPNEUSTOS (God-breathed). The Greeks words, "All Scripture God-breathed" is smoothed to all scripture *is* given by inspiration of God. The English verb of the sentence is "is given" is composed of the auxiliary verb *is* and the past participle of *give* which forms the English perfect tense. This tense indicates a past punctiliar event with continuing effect. The words exist today because they were given in the past. It does not mean they are constantly being given. The words of God were given to mankind at a time in the past, and as a result, we continue to have them. It does not mean that they are constantly being given. Not in Greek and not in English. And so, Mrs. Riplinger is so far into left field on this one, she cannot see home plate.

Quote 201

"Warfield Moves the Inspiration Bull's-Eye..." (p. 1149ff)

My comments: What follows is a list of liberal scholars who try to justify their disbelief in the Scriptures by limiting inspiration only to the original autographs. This is a total *non sequitur*. **Those of us who will not use the word inspiration with translations but reserve it only to the original Greek, Hebrew and Aramaic words which God's Spirit gave to men, do not believe that only the actual physical documents written by the writers of Scripture at the moment of inspiration are the inspired words of God.**

We believe that the words that were on those pages (whether vellum, papyrus, parchment, stone tablets, or clay tablets) are the inspired words of God and that God has preserved those words to us in their original forms of Greek, Hebrew, and Aramaic. Because we have the original words of God, we know that our English translation is an accurate, reliable translation of the originals.

God uses this wonderfully trustworthy translation to save souls and to direct them in the things of God. The English Bible is unlike any other English book. It truly breathes with the power of God. But we do not believe that God gave the actual words of the 1611 King James Bible directly to men. The Bible was not re-inspired in 1611 or in 1769.

Quote(s) 202

"Warfield sought to merge what he learned in Germany with his previous conservatism. On one hand Warfield wrote against the rank unbelief of Briggs, the German higher critic (and author with Brown and Driver of the corrupt English edition of Gesenius' *Hebrew Lexicon*, unwisely used today...However, Warfield could not defend the Bible in hand. He did not have a strong enough background in manuscript evidence or a humble enough faith in the scriptures to counter the barrage of textual variants and 'problems' thrust at him in the German classroom. He invented a plan whereby he could retain the creed, that stated that 'the Bible' was inspired. He redefined the word 'Bible' for seminary students. **He moved the locus of inspiration from the Holy Bible to the lost originals.**" (p. 1152)

"What this means is that as the originals have long since turned to dust, no inspired text exists today...Warfield's book on biblical inspiration is still hailed as a 'classic', but his viewpoint has done more to undermine confidence in Scripture than almost any other in the last 150 years or so." (p. 1157)

"Not just the immediate context of 2 Tim. 3:16, but every usage of the word "scripture[s]" in the New Testament refers to copies or translations, not the originals. Therefore the word "scripture" cannot refer to the originals alone." (p. 1160)

My comments: Once again, Mrs. Riplinger is guilty of twisting what is said. The Dean Burgon Society and other defenders of the King James Bible do not claim that inspiration lies only on the original physical pages with the original pen strokes of the original author. We believe without apology that inspiration is used of the very words which God breathed out, the original text of the original autographs, not the original media. Mrs. Riplinger has not in all 1200 pages of this tome addressed that issue except by disparagement.

Quote 203

"Therefore the term "All scripture" *cannot* refer to only the originals, 'from Genesis to Revelation.' It must include copies of the originals, as well as vernacular versions, as the following section will prove." (p. 1161-1162)

"Romans 16:26 refers to "the **scriptures** of the prophets... made **known to all nations**. One cannot *know* something that is in another language. What he does know is referred to as "scriptures," "All" of which are "given by inspiration of God" according to 2 Tim. 3:16. Many say that a Greek *translation* of the Hebrew Old Testament was used by Timothy, who knew the "**scriptures**" and whose father was a Greek. "Apollos, born at Alexandria," and "mighty in the **scriptures**" may also have had a Greek translation of the Old Testament (Acts 18:24-28). (Theirs was certainly not the Vaticanus sold today as the Septuagint, nor would Jews in Israel, including Jesus, have used a Greek Bible.)" (p. 1162)

My comments: You could not possibly pervert the meaning of Romans 16:26 more than Mrs. Riplinger has just done. Let's cite the WHOLE verse.

Romans 16:26 But now is made manifest, and by the scriptures of the prophets, according to the commandment of the everlasting God, made known to all nations for the obedience of faith:

First, she chops it in pieces to make it say what she wants it to say. Romans 16:26 does not say that the Scriptures are made known to all nations. The previous verse gives us the subject of this verse:

Romans 16:25 Now to him that is of power to stablish you according to my gospel, and the preaching of Jesus Christ, according to the revelation of the mystery, which was kept secret since the world began,

The passage is focused on the mystery of the ages. A Saviour, Jesus Christ, would come and make a provision for sins. Once he had made the provision for the forgiveness of sins, that forgiveness would be preached to all nations. This was a mystery, a truth not fully revealed before, hidden from the eyes of the world until the Apostle Paul received his revelation, and is the Gospel now preached. It is this mystery supported by the Scriptures, which was spread by the preaching of Paul and other Christians to the known world. It is the mystery that is now preached to all nations of the earth that is in view here. There is absolutely NOTHING about the translation of the Scriptures in these verses.

Secondly, there is no hard evidence to back up her contention that Timothy or Apollos were taught from a Greek translation of the Old Testament Scriptures. Whenever any Bible writer quoted the Hebrew Scriptures, the quote is correct to the Hebrew text. Even those who

QUOTES AND COMMENTS

believe in the pre-Christian existence of the Septuagint readily admit this.

Quote(s) 204

"The **script**ures are the written words of God. The Bible equates "scriptures" with the word of God." (p. 1163)

"The phrase "the word of God" summarizes and re-iterates the fact that the Holy Bible is still God's words, not man's words (i.e. not the words of the KJB translators, etc.). Some have tried to re-define the few simple words –"the word of God." In any other usage the phrase 'the word of John' means that they are John's words, not someone else's." (p. 1163)

"The vernacular versions continue to be God's living spirit communicating to each reader through his own culture, using Biblical language. For example, in the Greek Bible in the book of Acts the heathen were described as worshipping the *Greek* goddess *Artemis*. In the English Bible, she is called 'Diana' because that is the name by which she was known to "all Asia and the world" (Acts 19:27). Any witch today in America, France or Germany identifies Diana as her goddess, not the strictly Greek national goddess Artemis." (p. 1164)

My comments: We do believe the Scriptures are the words of God. We have no argument there. We believe any place we have an accurate translation of the true Hebrew and Greek words which God spoke out, we have the words of God in our vernacular language. Not because God spoke them out in the vernacular language but because the vernacular words carry the full impact and meaning of the words that He spoke out in the originals. It is not derived inspiration, but it is derived power and impact. They are the words of God.

What does Mrs. Riplinger's discussion of Diana-Artemis have to do with the discussion? The connection is not clear. Artemis and Diana were two names of the same goddess. If one name makes a clearer identification in the receptor language, then it is the right word. Bob Dylan and Robert Zimmerman are the same person with two names. Which one brings more universal recognition? John Wayne was born Marion Mitchell Morrison. Gerald Rudolph Ford, Jr. was born Leslie Lynch King, Jr. Marilyn Monroe was born Norma Jeane Mortenson. The list goes on of people with two or more names. If we wanted the general public to know who we are talking about, which name would we use? The same principle holds in translation. Either name would be accurate and are the words of God but one gives better recognition than the other.

The witches I have known (and I have known a few) most often prefer the ancient names of the various gods and goddesses. But I have not known all the witches in America, France, and Germany. I cannot speak for all of them. Neither can Mrs. Riplinger.

Quote 205

> "What is biblical language? The word 'holpen,' for example, is God's Biblical English word for 'helped.' The word was historically used only in the Bible. The word 'help" is much more archaic (800 A.D.) than 'holpen,'" (p. 1164)

My comments: She has to be kidding. No one in their right mind would make such an absurd statement. It is better to simply admit that 'holpen' is an obsolete form of the verb *to help*. Help may have been in constant use since 800 A.D., and holpen may have come into existence afterwards. (Which we would have to agree with since it is impossible to get a form of the verb unless the verb already exists). But *holpen* never caught on in common use.

Mrs. Riplinger does that which she claims no one else should do. She defines the word in the King James Bible! She tells us that it should be *helped!* The epitome of hypocrisy! On pages 1164-1180, the 'quotes' do not support Mrs. Riplinger's thesis. It is not uncommon for writers to use these words on these pages in hyperbolic recognition of the magnificence, power, beauty, and effect of the King James Bible. Without knowing their context, we just do not know the intention of the author.

QUOTES AND COMMENTS

The formal documentation Mrs. Riplinger provides is secondary. We don't know the context of the quotes within their contexts on these pages.

After using gematria, the assigning of mystical meanings to the letters of words, Mrs. Riplinger now proceeds to point out what she considers prideful responses to her book in a preemptive strike against anyone who might criticize it. Over several pages concluding her book, she condescendingly says many things. It is from these pages that the section "Challenges" in this book arises. For example, she says others will say,

> "I am a solid fundamental Christian, therefore I could not be wrong about *anything*; God wouldn't give *this* author this information *before* giving it to me.' [Maybe it was given to this disabled author, with a heart for 'helps,' because you were rightfully busy doing important things which this author cannot do.]
> 'I must quickly skim for some small error to prove this wrong. I couldn't have been wrong all these years. I must find something somewhere in the book to show that I know something that this author does not seem to know.' [This may be a test of your humility. "Humble yourselves therefore under the mighty hand of God..." (1 Peter 5:6),] (p. 1192)
>
> 'I don't believe that Greek and Hebrew study is wrong (although I have not read this book, documenting its problems, nor can I refute it).' ["He that answereth a matter before he heareth it, it is folly and shame unto him" (Proverbs 18:13)]." (p. 1193)

My comments: Mrs. Riplinger, I have read *Hazardous Materials* carefully three times. The first time your thesis shocked me. The second time I wanted to make sure I understood what you wrote. The third time I read it to let it sink in and generate reactions. I have tried to respond honestly and factually to what I consider your distortions. I have no more to say to you. It would not help.

Pastor Kirk DiVietro, M.Th., Ph.D.

CLEANING-UP HAZARDOUS MATERIALS

APPENDIX

[Editor's note: Mrs. Riplinger writes vary disparagingly of Dr. Maurice Robinson on pages 591, 640, 643, 659, 1013, 1014 in *Hazardous Materials*. In the testimony to follow, Dr. Robinson answers several of the attacks, which is sufficient to characterize Mrs. Riplinger's errors.]

TO WHOM IT MAY CONCERN:
Maurice A. Robinson — 5 January 2010

The comments that follow are intended to clarify certain claims made by Gail Riplinger concerning the present writer's (Maurice A. Robinson's) involvement with and contributions to various Greek New Testament projects in both printed and electronic form. The comments in question have been forwarded to me by D. A. Waite, Sr., and compared where possible to the cited sources.

It should be expressly noted that the present writer does not share the textual or translational views of either Gail Riplinger or D. A. Waite, Sr., and in this sense remains impartial to the entire matter under discussion

Item 1. Riplinger states:

> Vonnie Waite's BFT newsletter and radio program pretended that I lied when I wrote that Maurice Robinson was involved with an edition called The Interlinear Literal Translation of the Greek New Testament. She said, "Recently it was pointed out to me another gross error in the *Hazardous Materials* brochure...the part which mentioned Dr. Maurice A. Robinson's name. Somehow Riplinger makes Robinson the editor of the Interlinear Literal Translation of the Greek New Testament — which title refers to George Ricker Berry's 1897 Interlinear, and nothing else! The truth is that the only "interlinear Bible" that Dr. Robinson worked on was Jay Green's Interlinear Bible — and then, he worked "only" on the Old Testament portion!

The statement of Vonnie Waite is correct: my only work on any interlinear Bible was for Jay Green (in the 1970s), and then only as Associate General Editor of the Old Testament portion, and not of the Greek New Testament portion (which section was done solely by Green himself). I have not been and (by reason of timeframe) could never have been involved as an "editor" of George Ricker Berry's Interlinear published in 1897 (actually Thomas Newberry's work, to which Berry only added a lexicon and synonym studies; however, since Newberry's name appears nowhere within that volume, I will refer to it as the Berry Interlinear).

Item 2. Riplinger states:

> Robinson's name is listed as an editor for the said edition of the Textus Receptus. It is sold by Logos and can be seen at the following web site [URL follows] . . . . Robinson's name is listed as coeditor for his recent input on the morphology . . . . See the accompanying ad and cover for additional documentation.

The statement above is quite incorrect, and indicates a leap to a conclusion that is not warranted by the facts (which Riplinger could easily have learned had she bothered to inquire further rather than assuming conclusions drawn from ad-copy statements written by someone else).

The correct information is as follows:

I have freely supplied various electronic Greek text data, along with corrected Strong's number information and declension/parsing information to various electronic Bible software manufacturers. These include the Online Bible, Bibleworks, Logos, E-Sword, and others that I cannot recall, since permission is always freely granted and the Greek texts prepared have all been released into the public domain. The Greek texts I have prepared and supplied electronically (Byzantine Textform 1991/2005, Westcott-Hort 1881, Antoniades 1904, Elzevir 1624, Stephens 1550, and Scrivener 1894) were solely comprised of the

APPENDIX

Greek text alone, with no interlinear renderings provided nor English translations of any word within those Greek texts, nor were any specific value judgments passed on any of the Greek texts as supplied electronically (although I have clearly expressed preferences for the Byzantine Greek Textform in numerous other venues).

The manner in which a software publisher may choose to label any electronic text which I prepared is not my concern, and may well be inaccurate at points. For example, one software publisher some time ago had listed my Byzantine edition as a "representing the Western text," which it most certainly did not. I became aware of this misstatement only after several years of their advertising such in their literature, at which point I sent a clarifying email which (I hope) caused the error to be removed (I have not bothered to verify that this ever was done, however).

I nowhere see in the attached advertisements that Logos ever said I was one of the "editors" of the Berry Interlinear. Certainly, if Logos themselves decided to incorporate Berry's interlinear translation into their software module, that action had nothing whatever to do with me or my work, which was restricted solely to providing the Greek text of the Stephens 1550 Textus Receptus corresponding to that which is printed in Berry's volume — a text that is merely reproduced and not "edited" at all; this raw text as supplied was also accompanied by Strong's numbers and declension/parsing information equally supplied by me.

On the basis of the same logic, and following other portions of the Logos Research System's advertisement, I must suppose that Riplinger would also consider me to be an "editor" of the Westcott-Hort Greek text, the Elzevir Greek text, and the Scrivener Greek text — which assumption most certainly would be false. My work simply reproduced the unaccented, unpunctuated, electronic form of the Greek text as found in each of those editions in a manner similar to that for the Stephens text as printed in Berry. I claim no "originality" or "editing" for any supplied text beyond that of the Byzantine Textform, which William Pierpont and myself prepared and distributed in varying electronic forms in 1991 and 2005.

The Logos advertisement cited states that their version of "Thomas Newberry's Greek-English Interlinear provides a word-by-word interlinear presentation of the 1550 Textus Receptus"; this I had no part in whatever. This is followed by the correct statement in relation to my supplying of "morphology codes and Strongs [sic] numbers" taken from my own "edition" (their terminology, not mine!) "of the 1550 Textus Receptus."

To summarize: the claims stated by Riplinger are not correct, and are based on a misapprehension gleaned from some advertising blurb, without verification regarding the actual situation from either the present writer or other reliable sources.

Item 3. Although not included in the material cited above, there is a similar misuse and misrepresentation of my name in Riplinger's own advertising material at her website, under the entry "Riplinger Testimony with Questions & Answers," in which "Dr. Waite's wife interviews Gail after a presentation at a pastor's conference." Riplinger writes:

> Also includes a very lengthy and lively audience question and answer session with an audience of mainly pastors and a few others, including one feeble and sorely defeated new version editor (Maurice Robinson of the Pierpoint [sic] - Robinson so-called Majority Text).

Although I was present on that occasion in the early 1990s, along with a number of students from my Greek textual criticism class, we were there as observers only, and did not in any manner participate or ask questions (this includes the class members per my instructions). Riplinger's statement above leads the reader to infer that not only must I have asked questions (which I did not), but also that my questions supposedly were answered in such a manner that I appeared "feeble and sorely defeated." Again, a patently false impression. If this is not misrepresentation, I don't know what would constitute such. In addition, the statement clearly errs in claiming that I am somehow a "new version editor" — a phrase that Riplinger uses in relation to English translations and not to Greek text editions. For the record, I have never been a part of any translation team or advisory board for any "new version" in English or any other modern language. Both of these misleading and inaccurate statements by Riplinger should therefore be eliminated from her public advertisements, along with her misrepresentation of me as somehow an "editor" of the Berry interlinear.

—end statement—

A TESTIMONY

By

Mrs. D. A. Waite

A PHONE CALL TO GAIL RIPLINGER

In October 2007, I called GAIL RIPLINGER asking her about the rumors that were going around the e-mail world, along with three copies of three marriage licenses. WAS IT TRUE? The e-mail said she had been married three times and divorced twice. I had to know if it were true. So I called Mrs. Riplinger and asked her, *"Have you ever had any other husband than Mike Riplinger?"* My husband, Pastor D. A. Waite, got on the phone, too. She testified to us that day that she had had only one husband. I believed her. My husband believed her.

So if anyone asked us about Mrs. Riplinger's several alleged marriages, we could truthfully answer them, *"She only has had one husband!"* We believed this to be true. After all, we asked her personally and she denied the rumors.

GAIL & FRANK KALEDA LIVED IN A TRAILER

It was not until sometime in 2008, that I began to doubt Gail Riplinger's denial of more than one husband. For the following reasons her answer did not ring true : my husband and I had a friend who had a friend who knew her and her second husband very well. It was during the time when she and Frank, her second husband, lived near Kent University in Ohio. They lived in a house-trailer there. They attended a Pentecostal Church–then a Baptist one there. They were a part of some kind of campus Bible study. They appeared to be a happily wedded couple. (But I know one can't always tell by looking.)

In fact, Gail wrote six books while at Kent, writing under her married name Gail Kaleda. When I heard all this, I was greatly troubled!

A PICTURE IS WORTH A THOUSAND WORDS

So, in the early part of 2009, another friend of ours met, by way of e-mail and phone, a former relative of Mrs. Riplinger's second husband. WE HAVE A PICTURE OF HER AND FRANK ON THEIR WEDDING DAY. That picture proved beyond a shadow of doubt that Mrs. Riplinger had lied to us. IT WAS A SAD DAY FOR ME TO REALIZE WE HAD BEEN DELIBERATELY LIED TO BY GAIL!! Her first and third husbands are living. She has been married to Mike Riplinger for about twenty-five years. They have an adult daughter, and–according to the daughter–they are very happy together. (But once again "happiness" can't always be proven by looking. But I have no reason to believe they are not happy.)

RIPLINGER'S DAUGHTER DEFENDS HER MOTHER
TWO MARRIAGES NOT CONSUMMATED!

Because I don't search the internet much at all, I was not aware that Mrs. Riplinger's daughter was writing a book about her mother until someone sent me this information. From what I understand from the internet, a few paragraphs of that contemplated book are found under Mrs. Riplinger's pastor's explanation of the three marriages and two divorces. To my surprise, it was almost a verbatim copy of part of an e-mail letter (July 21, 2009) I received from the daughter. The daughter had responded to my July 9-14, 2009 letter which I sent to Mrs. Riplinger's daughter's house by mistake. (I thought it was her mother's house. I can explain all this mix-up of why the UPS two-day-letter was sent to the wrong house--but not at this time.) In that daughter's letter, she says that the two marriages were marriages only on paper ("*non-consummated*"). I know the second husband has died. According to the daughter, he left "unsaved" Gail to pursue his "homosexual lifestyle" but, the witness at Kent said the Kaledas lived together as a couple in their trailer-home, going to church and Bible studies and having friends. (I DON'T KNOW FOR SURE YET WHAT WAS WRONG WITH THE FIRST HUSBAND, BUT I AM TOLD THAT HE IS LIVING IN A HOUSE WITH A WOMAN.)

APPENDIX

So Mrs. Riplinger (according to the daughter who was not there, anymore than I was) does not consider herself to have been married before at all. This is difficult to jibe (as I said before) with the information received from my friend's friend that for several years the second-marriage couple lived by Kent University in a trailer, went to church together, and were active together in various activities, etc. (Once again I reiterate, one can't tell the happiness of a marriage by *looking*.)

(Just a personal comment: I know a few women who have been fooled by husbands who never consummated their marriages. This is VERY sad! But for a woman–if true--not to recognize the signs of such a man twice is beyond me.)

NOT THE MARRIAGE & DIVORCE ISSUE
NOT THE INSPIRATION OF THE KING JAMES ISSUE

I do not want to go into all this any more than I have to. It is rather sordid and very sad. I had no idea that the pastor in Hammond, Indiana (whom I have never met or spoken with) was investigating on his own some of this situation. (I DO NOT KNOW THE MAN.) I only gathered this from what was written on the HACAlumni.com web page written by the Riplingers' pastor in Virginia. He implored the Indiana pastor to call Gail personally. Well, I did–and she lied to me. I get no thrill over this news.

IT'S THE LYING ISSUE

This whole thing, FOR ME, has nothing to do with the *"MARRIAGE & DIVORCE"* issue or the *"INSPIRATION OF THE KING JAMES BIBLE ISSUE."* It has to do with the truth. Her three marriages and two divorces are a separate question. I just wanted to know the truth. It appears to me that she has made *"lies her refuge"* (Isaiah 28:15). It seems that *"hail"* has swept away her *"refuge of lies"* and *"the waters"* have overflowed her *"hiding place"* (Isaiah 28:17) How much better if Gail Riplinger had answered truthfully my question, *"Have you ever been married before?"* when I asked it when all the rumors first began to surface. It may have been difficult to answer. The truth and its explanation would have been received– understood or not understood. But it would have been the truth. You can ask to see the letter I sent her by e-mail and UPS mail. (BFT #3420 @ $3.00 + $2.00 S&H)

MORE ON GAIL RIPLINGER
RIPLINGER LIES ABOUT HER FORMER MARRIAGES
I CALLED GAIL PERSONALLY
"IS IT TRUE YOU HAVE BEEN MARRIED THREE TIMES?"

Before the Dean Burgon meeting–which was in Chicago the middle of July 2009–I decided it was time to expose Gail Riplinger's lies concerning her three marriages. PREVIOUSLY, MY HUSBAND AND I HAD CALLED HER ON THE PHONE IN 2007. I ASKED HER, MYSELF, IF SHE HAD BEEN MARRIED TWICE, BEFORE SHE MARRIED MIKE RIPLINGER. I ASKED HER IF SHE HAD BEEN DIVORCED TWICE BEFORE HER MARRIAGE TO HER PRESENT HUSBAND. You see, we had received copies of three marriage licenses from people. THEY SAID SHE HAD BEEN MARRIED THRICE AND DIVORCED TWICE BEFORE HER PRESENT MARRIAGE. Because Mrs. Riplinger said she was not married to ANYONE but Mike, in her defense, we believed her. So we always told people what she told us: *"She said she was never married before. She told us so in her own words!"*

ONLY ONE HUSBAND EVER!

THEN IN 2008, WE DISCOVERED SHE LIED TO US! Up until this time, we believed whatever she said to us, for we thought she was a woman of truth! In 2008, we learned THROUGH A FRIEND, who had a friend, that GAIL RIPLINGER was known as Mrs. FRANK KALEDA at OHIO'S KENT UNIVERSITY. (Frank was her second husband.) This surprised us greatly, as she had denied any other marriages except to MIKE RIPLINGER. So we made some investigations of our own in 2009; but I did not know how, when, or why to reveal it.

GAIL UPSET OVER AN ARTICLE SHE DID NOT WRITE

IT WAS ACTUALLY GAIL RIPLINGER, HERSELF, THAT PROVOKED ME TO EXPOSE HER MARRIAGE LIE! SHE WAS DISTRESSED THAT *"HER RIPLINGER NAME"* WAS ON AN ARTICLE IN THE *LANDMARK BAPTIST ANCHOR* WHICH SHE DID

APPENDIX

NOT WRITE! THE ANCHOR is published OUT OF LANDMARK BAPTIST COLLEGE IN HAINES CITY, FLORIDA!

IT STIRRED ME TO ACTION!! She did not want <u>any lie told about her</u> in regards to the authorship of the bogus article. It turned out that it was written by a man named HERB EVANS–a real RUCKMAN FOLLOWER. (She appears to be a PETER RUCKMAN runner-up, herself,–and even worse!)

GAIL WAS HORRIFIED THAT HER NAME WAS ON AN ARTICLE, AS THE AUTHOR, THAT SHE HAD NOT WRITTEN! <u>In truth, she did not write it</u>! MY COMMENT: It appears to me that Mrs. Riplinger does not care if she misquotes other people wrongly–just so no one misquotes her!

I WROTE A LETTER TO HER IN JULY '09

I SENT AN ORIGINAL WITH PICTURES BY PDF E-MAIL

All this information is in my <u>long letter</u>, written to her in July '09- -just prior to the July 22-23 DEAN BURGON SOCIETY ANNUAL MEETING. I had hoped she would answer me <u>before</u> the DBS WOMEN on July 22, 2009. I was in a personal quandary. I had already PREVIOUSLY called her on the telephone. It was then that she lied to me and to my husband! I saw no point in calling her again. I felt she would continue to lie to me. It took me much longer to write that July letter than I expected it to take. It was a letter of personal, emotional pain. (Perhaps she would call and explain.) Because I wanted her to receive it quickly and hear her response (if she had any), I sent the <u>first copy</u> of the letter to Mrs. Riplinger by a <u>PDF E-MAIL</u>. <u>It must have gotten there prior to the DBS meeting</u>. If she had her e-mail/computer with her--if she were out of town--she would have received my PDF. Then-- <u>I sent a paper copy of the letter BY NEXT DAY UPS to what I thought was her home address–according to the phone company</u>. (Our BFT shipper said the UPS letter would not be delivered to a box. All I had was a box number.) <u>The telephone company was called and we sent the UPS letter to the address the phone company gave us</u>. I did not realize that her home address was a rural route box number. I do not do the shipping in the BIBLE FOR TODAY. United Parcel does not usually ship to box numbers.

CLEANING-UP HAZARDOUS MATERIALS

PICTURES OF SECOND WEDDING DAY

I HAD PROOF POSITIVE THAT SHE WAS MARRIED TO A SECOND HUSBAND! I had TWO pictures of her on GAIL'S happy SECOND wedding day. (Ask us for a copy of this 21- page GAIL RIPLINGER LETTER BFT# 3420 @$4.00 +$2.00 S&H) I do not send the pictures in the letter (BFT #3420) as a courtesy to the man who gave them to a friend for me; but I did show them in Chicago to the women–and I think they are on the web for the DBS WOMEN '09. THOSE WEDDING PICTURES WERE THE FINAL PROOF OF HER LIE! People may lie, but pictures don't! I DID SHOW THEM TO THE DBS WOMEN. This exposure has not been easy for me! (And not for her either!)

DID MY UPS MAIL-LETTER GO TO THE WRONG HOUSE?

I sent the "UPS Mail letter" to what turned out to be her daughter's home (according to the daughter). I thought it was Gail's home. Since then, I have discovered that her daughter's home and GAIL's home are in the same place or property. So both the box number and the street address are to the same location. (For some reason, her married daughter still has her phone listed under her maiden name of "RIPLINGER" and not her married name--because the daughter said it was her house & not her mother's.)

Because her daughter interceded for her mother, Gail may not have received the UPS mail letter addressed to her, I SENT A THIRD PAPER COPY (ADDRESSED TO GAIL RIPLINGER to the box number that we have for her book deliveries. Her daughter had opened my letter THAT WAS ADDRESSED TO HER MOTHER, NOT HER, and answered it. I received the DAUGHTER'S LETTER by E-MAIL when we got home from Chicago. MRS. RIPLINGER HAS NEVER RESPONDED, HERSELF, TO MY LETTER! Evidently, my letter was not as important as having her name put on an article she did not write in the *LANDMARK BAPTIST ANCHOR*. That *ANCHOR* LIE WAS DREADFUL FOR HER--BUT THE FACT THAT SHE LIED ABOUT HER MARRIAGES WAS NOT! I guess!.

SINCE THE DAUGHTER TOLD ME THAT I SENT THE LETTER TO HER ADDRESS AND NOT HER MOTHER'S, I WAS BAFFLED. According to the phone company, this was the RIPLINGER ADDRESS;

yet, according to the *"never-tell-a-lie"* daughter, it was <u>not</u> her mother's address. It was her (Bryn's) address.

We recently saw some copies of legal papers from the AV PUBLICATION CORPORATION 2008 annual report, where the legal address of the corporation is 386 HAINTED ROCK LANE, ARARAT, VA. 24053. That is the very address where I sent the UPS letter to Mrs. Riplinger that her daughter said was sent to her address instead of her mother's. <u>I have been told on good authority that this Hainted Rock Lane address is the same place as the Route 1, Box 124; Ararat, Virginia address.</u> THE BIG FUSS THAT IS BEING MADE BY THE RIPLINGERS IS THAT I DIDN'T SEND MY LETTER TO THE ADDRESS I HAVE KNOWN FOR MANY YEARS. THIS IS JUST *"SMOKE."* <u>It may be another case of denying public records</u>! Or there may be more than one house on the property.

TWO UNCONSUMMATED MARRIAGES?
PAPER HUSBANDS

SO, <u>THROUGH HER DAUGHTER,</u> Bryn Shutt, <u>MRS. RIPLINGER IS SAYING THAT HER TWO FORMER "HUSBANDS" WERE ONLY "HUSBANDS ON PAPER!"</u> She reported that these *"paper husbands"* were *"losers."* According to the daughter, Gail is claiming that both husbands never consummated the marriages and at least one was a *"homosexual."* I do not know if this is true or false. No claim was made on the divorce papers that there was "homosexuality," or "no consummation" of either of the marriages. My husband called a brother of the second husband asking about the "homosexuality;" but, he would not talk to him.

All I do know is that Riplinger has gone around ministering in churches and colleges, receiving an honorary degree--without being forthcoming about her previous two marriages and two divorces. She has now come out with a new definition of *"marriage."* – It is called "a marriages on paper only."

"ANOMALY" OR "HOMOSEXUALITY"??
STRAINED FRIENDSHIPS

THE DAUGHTER WROTE AN ARTICLE IN THE SEPTEMBER '09 LANDMARK BAPTIST ANCHOR that said, concerning Riplinger's first two husbands the following: "These men's physical anomaly or homosexuality, neither of which she had anticipated, deferred anything but a strained friendship, wrought with their cruelty.

HER GRACIOUS PATIENCE

I looked up the word, "anomaly." In my computer dictionary it means "rare"–perhaps "irregular." The daughter goes on, "Many years before she met my father, her gracious patience had left her waiting many years for the return and repentance of the one, now dead, who had abandoned her almost from the start to pursue his homosexual lifestyle. . . ."

COMPLETE ABANDONMENT

I am trying to reconcile the fact that we were told in our own investigation that she and the second husband lived in a trailer near Kent University, and they attended church and Bible studies with our informant. Of course, this does not prove that the husbands did, or did not have "physical anomaly," or were "homosexual" but, it shows that they lived together with the appearance of "man and wife." (I know of a woman married to a man for thirteen years, and left the marriage a virgin.) I am not doubting the sexual conditions, though I question them. But I am doubting the complete abandonment. Also, after one "rare" marriage, why would a woman step into a second one?

FIVE YEARS & A HOUSE

A source has come to us which summarizes well GAIL'S first two marriages with legal papers to prove the words. The source says that on the first divorce papers, there is no claim that the first husband, Mr. Latessa, could not consummate their marriage, or that he was a homosexual. In fact they remained married for five years and bought a house together.

FOUR YEARS, A HOUSE, A CORPORATION

The divorce records and deed records show she and MR. KALEDA, the second husband (who is deceased), bought a house in Kent, Ohio, four years into their marriage. That shows he did not abandon her immediately, as her daughter falsely claims. Proof of this is a public record. Four years into their marriage, FRANK & GAIL KALEDA filed together, with the OHIO SECRETARY OF STATE, to start a corporation called *TRUTH AND LIFE*. They both signed legal papers, listing the address in a trailer––probably the one I referred to

APPENDIX

in another part of this UPDATE. Of interest, Gail married her present husband, Mike, two months after her divorce from Kaleda. By the way, Gail did not claim "abandonment" or "homosexuality" as the reason for the divorce, or any request for an annulment because of any "physical anomaly" for either man. I am not saying these personal complaints were not there, but I question them. They were not listed for reasons for divorcing. Nor was the humiliation severe enough, if it were true, for her to get out of the marriages immediately! How can I believe Gail or Bryn about anything??!!

WHY DID GAIL RIPLINGER LIE?
WHAT IS TRUTH?

I REALIZE THAT IN BIBLE-BELIEVING CAMPS THERE IS A CONTROVERSY OVER THE DEFINITION OF "INSPIRATION," AS WELL AS THE "MARRIAGE & DIVORCE QUESTION."--BUT MY "BEEF," IN ALL OF THIS SAD SITUATION, IS WITH TRUTH vs. LIES!

WHAT BOTHERS ME IS THAT GAIL LUDWIG LATESSA KALEDA RIPLINGER LIED TO ME WHEN MY HUSBAND AND I ASKED HER DIRECTLY IF SHE HAD ANY OTHER HUSBAND BUT HER PRESENT ONE, MIKE RIPLINGER. SHE SAID NO! No matter how I posed the question, she said, "NO!"

I know people who are divorced and remarried—some more than once—and they have never lied to me about it—or to others. They may not be proud of their past lives, but they are honest! Here is a woman who is featured as a *"self-taught-authority"* on the King James Bible teaching her own brand of false *"inspiration,"* influencing thousands of people to her way of thinking, and manifesting a marriage & divorce pattern to be followed by other unhappy women.. YET, SHE COULD NOT BE HONEST ABOUT HER PERSONAL MARRIAGE HISTORY TO ME! No wonder some of her statements in her books are not factual!

WHEN DID THE TRUTH COME OUT?

I really do not know WHEN the truth came out about Mrs. Riplinger's PREVIOUS marriages! Personally, I don't think it was before the LANDMARK BAPTIST ANCHOR attributed Herb Evan's article to her. (I DON'T KNOW.) If I remember, that FALSE

CLEANING-UP HAZARDOUS MATERIALS

AUTHORSHIP was revealed in July, 2009 or so. Perhaps her daughter's defense of her mother's marriages, that was published on the HYLES ANDERSON COLLEGE'S ALUMNI'S website (NOT SURE IT IS AN OFFICIAL WEBSITE), was posted before the DEAN BURGON SOCIETY MET IN MID-JULY '09. Maybe after??? (Someone mailed it to us after DBS was over and after DAUGHTER BRYN wrote to me defending her mother.) It is not my practice to search the internet very much at all. I have all I can do to take care of my own affairs.

Bryn RIPLINGER Shutt's words on that website, with some modification, were almost exactly the same words the daughter e-mailed me around July 21. Also, they are similar words (with some EDITORIAL facts ???) written in a recent LANDMARK BAPTIST ANCHOR out of Haines City, Florida.

I DO NOT CLAIM TO BE THE ONE WHO BROKE THIS STORY! I was not trying to be a news breaker. I felt compelled to tell it! It was one of the hardest things I had to do! I REALIZE that many people have been persuaded to defend the King James Bible because of GAIL RIPLINGER! I do not take any of that fact from her. To write about this was one of the most difficult things I have had to do. I felt it had to be told. I don't know what caused Mrs. Riplinger to *"fess up"*–but I am glad she finally has admitted her marriage/divorce history!

BUT AS I WRITE NOW, A THOUGHT HAS COME TO ME. The *"source"* who gave us the TWO KALEDA WEDDING PICTURES asked me for Gail Riplinger's phone number. I gave it to him from my personal file. If her former brother-in-law phoned her, then she would have been aware of my investigation. That would have caused the flurry of writing the "truth" (according to Gail Riplinger) by BRYN RIPLINGER SHUTT! I have no idea if this is true or not–just conjecture on my part!

MORE UNTRUTHS BY RIPLINGER

SHE HAS PREVARICATED IN OTHER AREAS BESIDES HER MARRIAGES. She lied that our oldest son said that SCRIVENER *"backwards translated"* his Greek New Testament from English to Greek. I covered that falsehood in *THE GAIL LETTER* (BFT #3420 @ $4.00 + $2.00 S&H). Our son, D. A. Waite, Jr., never said that. But

APPENDIX

she said he did. Does that make it true? Who will be the hundreds of preacher-men, who will sit at her feet and learn that wrong fact which is a serious lie ?

A WOMAN TOLD US RECENTLY THAT SHE WAS READING RIPLINGER'S *HAZARDOUS MATERIALS*, AND SAW OUR SON'S NAME IN THERE. She said to her husband, *"I didn't know that Dr. Waite's son believed Scrivener backward translated his Greek from the English!"* Well, he doesn't! That is one of Riplinger's lies! How many others are believing this Riplinger lie, I don't know!

RECENTLY IT WAS POINTED OUT TO ME ANOTHER GROSS ERROR IN THE *HAZARDOUS MATERIALS* BROCHURE. Riplinger's *HAZARDOUS MATERIALS* book, not only gives false information regarding D. A. Waite, Jr.'s *"supposedly"* claiming *"back translation"* by Scrivener, when he never said it; but, the part which mentioned DR. MAURICE A. ROBINSON'S name. Somehow Riplinger makes Robinson the editor of THE INTERLINEAR LITERAL TRANSLATION of THE GREEK NEW TESTAMENT–which title refers to George Ricker Berry's *1897* INTERLINEAR, and nothing else! The truth is that the only *"INTERLINEAR BIBLE"* that Dr. Robinson worked on was JAY GREEN'S *"INTERLINEAR BIBLE–*and then, he worked *"only"* on the OLD TESTAMENT portion! Where will her lies stop?

Then, this same person drew an astute conclusion: "Apparently Riplinger has a severe problem in getting her facts correct, and one must wonder whether to believe anything she says, particularly with what appears to be her massive 'conspiracy theory' denigrating any and all resources that deal with the original language texts, lexicons, and study materials!". I could not have said it better.

POSTMODERNIST LYING
TRUTH IS RELATIVE & SUBJECTIVE
THE END JUSTIFIES THE MEANS

I was re-listening to one of my past radio programs on THE EMERGENT CHURCH (JFWCD-11 7). I was quoting several men on the subject. One was Dr. Jeffery Koo from Singapore. HE WAS GIVING A DEFINITION OF WHO A POST MODERNIST was. My ears pricked up. It seemed to me that the definition fits Mrs. Riplinger to a

"T" in regards to her lying about never having been married before! Let me write it out for you today.

"The POST MODERNIST, in his pessimism, will conclude that TRUTH is relative and subjective. There is no such thing as an absolute or subjective truth. TRUTH CAN BE ANYTHING AND ANYWHERE. Whatever claims to be true or truth is met with scepticism. Pragmatism takes over. What ever works must be right and good! The end justifies the means, even if the means of getting there is morally wrong."

GAIL RIPLINGER IS A PRAGMATIC!

DR. WAITE AND I CAME TO GAIL AS A FRIEND, AND AS A FRIEND, SHE LIED TO US. I've come to the conclusion that she is a *"postmodernist"* person. Her truth is her truth. It may or may not be my truth! It may not be THE TRUTH! She was married three times and divorced twice. THAT IS A FACT! I asked her if she were ever married to anyone but Mike, and she said emphatically, "NO!" I did not ask her if she consummated the marriages. I asked if she were married. SHE IS A PRAGMATIST. She makes her truth to be her truth and not necessarily THE TRUTH!

GAIL RIPLINGER'S LIES

TO DR. AND MRS. D.A. WAITE

November 24, 2009 (David Cloud, Fundamental Baptist Information Service, P.O. Box 610368, Port Huron, MI 48061, 866-295-4143, fbns@wayoflife.org; for instructions about subscribing and unsubscribing or changing addresses, see the information paragraph at the end of the article)

INTRODUCTION

Since the early-1990s, Gail Riplinger has been a very bombastic voice for the King James Bible. Her shrill demeanor, mocking tone, and sensational approach have somehow proven popular.

Like Peter Ruckman, Riplinger has probably done more damage to the cause of the KJV than good. She has defied the Bible she claims to uphold by teaching men (1 Timothy 2:12), and, to make matters

APPENDIX

worse, she has smeared and belittled her opponents in a manner that is not befitting anyone with a Christian testimony.

Now she has now been proven beyond any reasonable doubt to be a liar.

She has maintained for years that she has only been married once, but in fact she was married three times.

Unlike Riplinger, Dr. D.A. Waite is widely known as a legitimate biblical scholar and even-tempered man who is honest and forthright. He has a good Christian testimony.

He has been very kind to Gail Riplinger and has done her many favors. She returned those kindnesses with dishonesty and double-dealing. If this is how she treats her friends, how much could she possibly be trusted in anything?

With his permission, we are reprinting Dr. Waite's testimony regarding Riplinger.

GAIL RIPLINGER'S LIES TO DR. AND MRS. D. A. WAITE

The following testimony about Gail Riplinger, author of The New Age Bible Version, is from Dr. D.A. Waite, director of Bible for Today, 900 Park Ave., Collingswood, NJ 08108, BFT@BibleForToday.org:

Here is a chronological accounting of our experiences with Gail Riplinger.

1. Sometime in 2007 - Mrs. Waite and I were informed by uncertified documents sent to us that Gail Riplinger had had three husbands and two divorces.

2. October 24, 2007 - Mrs. Waite and I phoned Gail Riplinger to find out her explanation of these certified documents. Since we thought we were friends of hers. We thought she would tell us the truth. When Mrs. Waite asked her pointedly, if she had only had Mike Riplinger as her one and only husband and her one and only "marriage," she said, "Yes." Mrs. Waite asked if Gail had ever had any other husband. She said, "No." She denied strongly that she had ever had any other "marriages" but the present one with Mike Riplinger.

3, January 10-11, 2008 - At the Princeton King James Bible Conference, during a question and answer period, I was asked about the allegation that Gail Riplinger had been married three times and divorced twice. I said I had heard that also, then I gave my questioner

Gail Riplinger's answer to me to the effect that she had had only one "marriage." Since Gail told Mrs. Waite and me this and since I thought we were friends and I thought she would never lie to us, I believed her. Because of my answer, one publication accused me of being part of a cover-up of Mrs. Riplinger's marriages and divorces. Nothing could be further from the truth. I simply repeated what I was told by Mrs. Riplinger.

4. June 2008 - Because of continuing information and doubts about Gail Riplinger's marriages and divorces, I requested and received certified copies of Gail Riplinger's three marriages and two divorces to be to be certain that they were genuine. I found them to be genuine and unquestionably true documentation. On June 26, 2008, June 30, 2008, and July 1, 2008, CERTIFIED COPIES of Gail Riplinger's three marriage licenses and two divorces were dated by Ohio officials and mailed to me. Among other things, here are what these CERTIFIED COPIES reveal:

(1) Terry Edward Latessa married Gail Anne Ludwig (now Riplinger). The marriage license was dated June 2, 1969 in Trumbull County, Ohio. The marriage was certified on June 7, 1969.

(2) Franklin Alex Kaleda married Gail Anne Ludwig (Latessa now Riplinger). The marriage license was dated November 1, 1976 in Portage County, Ohio. The marriage was certified on November 5, 1976. Gail Riplinger's first divorce was from Terry Edward Latessa on February 12, 1975.

(3) Michael Domnick Riplinger married Gail Anne Ludwig (Latessa Kaleda). The record shows that Gail had been "previously married" two times. The marriage license was dated September 4, 1984 in Summit County, Ohio. The marriage was certified on October 27, 1984. Gail Riplinger's second divorce was from Frank Alexander Kaleda on August 6, 1984.

5. January 2009 - We received two pictures of Gail Anne Ludwig (Latessa) Kaleda and Franklin Alex Kaleda. Rev. Richard Gordon who performed the marriage, was also in the picture. It appears that he had just solemnized the marriage and the groom was about to kiss the bride at her second marriage.

6. July 9-14, 2009 - Mrs. Waite wrote a 9-page letter with 12-pages of enclosures (a total of 21 pages in all) to Gail Riplinger in which

APPENDIX

she confronted her about her lies to her and me in our telephone call of October 24, 2007. The letter was sent by UPS to her address in Ararat, Virginia. A copy of the letter was also sent to her E-mail address so she could receive it and reply (if she wanted to) prior to the Dean Burgon Society's (DBS) Women's Meeting Wednesday, July 22, 2009. [Copies of this letter and enclosures are available in either of two ways: (1) by giving us your E-mail address so we can send you a PDF without charge; or (2) by sending a self-addressed envelope with 3 stamps on it.]

7. July 22, 2009 - Having heard nothing from Gail Riplinger by way of apology, correction, or some kind of excuse for her lies, Mrs. Waite gave a report on this situation to the DBS Women, and distributed her letter and attachments to the ladies present.

8. July 24, 2009 - Upon arriving home from the Dean Burgon Society (DBS) meetings in Chicago, Illinois, we found an E-mail letter (dated July 21, 2009) from Gail Riplinger's daughter, Bryn. Knowing that there was no more denying Gail's three marriages and two divorces, Bryn finally admitted that there were two other "marriages" but that they were "on paper only." In other words, Bryn (and her mother as well) was redefining the official Ohio State (and other States) what "marriage" is. Her letter (as the facts determine) contained many more lies in attempting to explain away her mother's lie about her three marriages and two divorces. Gail Riplinger has never replied to Mrs. Waite's letter.

9. Further Information. Many more details about this situation can be found in the following materials: (1) Mrs. Waite's 21-page letter to Gail Riplinger of October 24, 2009. (2) Mrs. Waite's BFTUPDATE of August, 2009; (3) Mrs. Waite's BFTUPDATE of September, October, November, 2009, and (4) further documents either from Mrs. Waite, or from me.

It is sad to us to have what we considered a "friend" to turn from the TRUTH to LIES to such an extent that we have had to separate from her and publicly expose her "unfruitful works of darkness" (Ephesians 5:11) as the Bible commands us.

Pastor D. A. Waite, Th.D., Ph.D.
Bible For Today

GAIL RIPLINGER'S LIES
TO THE WAITES - PART 2

December 21, 2009 (David Cloud, Fundamental Baptist Information Service, P.O. Box 610368, Port Huron, MI 48061, 866-295-4143, fbns@wayoflife.org; for instructions about subscribing and unsubscribing or changing addresses, see the information paragraph at the end of the article)

On November 24, 2009, we published a report from Dr. Donald Waite, founder of Bible For Today, about the lies that were told to him and his wife by Gail Riplinger, author of New Age Bible Versions. (The report is entitled "Gail Riplinger's Lies to Dr. and Mrs. D. A. Waite.")

In 2007, the Waites received uncertified reports that Riplinger had been divorced twice and married thrice. On October 24 of that year, they called her to inquire about the matter, and Mrs. Riplinger expressly told them that she had been married only once, to her current husband Mike Riplinger. Wanting to be certain that she wasn't misunderstood and wanting to be absolutely sure of the matter, Mrs. Waite posed the question in a variety of ways, but Gail strongly denied that she had ever had any other marriages. As a result, Dr. Waite defended her at the Princeton King James Bible Conference in January 2008. When someone inquired at a question-answer session if Riplinger was divorced, Waite said that he had confirmed directly from her that this was not true. In June 2008, the Waites, having decided to pursue the matter further, obtained certified copies of Gail Riplinger's three marriage licenses and two divorce papers.

Gail was married to Terry Latessa in June 1969, and that marriage ended in divorce five and a half years later, in February 1975. In November 1976, Gail married Franklin Kaleda. That marriage ended in divorce eight years later, in August 1984. Less than two months after her second divorce, Gail married Michael Riplinger.

In July 2009, Mrs. Waite wrote to Gail Riplinger to confront her with the evidence and to challenge her about the lies. As of this writing, five months have passed, and the Waites have not received a personal reply or apology from Riplinger.

APPENDIX

They did receive an e-mail, though, from Bryn Riplinger Shutt, Gail Riplinger's daughter. This was sent on July 21, 2009. She claims that Gail's first two marriages were not "consummated" and that at least one of her former husbands was a homosexual. Shutt says, "These men's physical anomaly or homosexuality, neither of which she had anticipated, deferred anything but a strained friendship, wrought with their cruelty." Shutt also says that Riplinger's first husband "abandoned her almost from the start to pursue his homosexual lifestyle."

This "explanation," which has been published in various places, only increases the problem.

First, even if Riplinger's first two marriages ended because of an "anomaly," they were still marriages and the divorces were real divorces, so Gail Riplinger was lying to the Waites no matter how you cut it. There is a legal process for annulling a marriage, but Gail did not pursue such a course on the basis of a "physical anomaly" in either case.

Second, as we have seen, the first marriage lasted over five years and the second marriage lasted eight years. That is a long time for a woman to stay with men who have "anomalies"! These were not marriages that lasted a few weeks or months.

Third, in the divorce filings, there was no mention of "homosexuality" or "no consummation" or an "anomaly."

Fourth, the Waite's investigation into the matter uncovered the fact that Gail lived with her second husband in a trailer near Kent State University; they attended church and Bible studies together there and bought a house together four years into the marriage. They also started a corporation called Truth and Life. Both signed the legal papers.

In the September-November 2009 edition of their paper, BFT Update, the Waites published the following observation:

"Apparently Riplinger has a severe problem in getting her facts correct, and one must wonder whether to believe anything she says, particularly with what appears to be her massive 'conspiracy theory' denigrating any and all resources that deal with the original language texts, lexicons, and study materials."

The Waites also say, "It is sad to us to have what we considered a 'friend' to turn from the TRUTH to LIES to such an extent that we have had to separate from her and publicly expose her 'unfruitful works of darkness' (Ephesians 5:11) as the Bible commands us."

More details about this situation can be found in the following materials from Bible For Today -- BFT UPDATE of August 2009 and BFT UPDATE of September-November, 2009. Bible For Today's contact information is 900 Park Ave., Collingswood, NJ 08108, BFT@BibleForToday.org, 856-854-4747.

[Distributed by Way of Life Literature's Fundamental Baptist Information Service, an e-mail listing for Fundamental Baptists and other fundamentalist, Bible-believing Christians.] http://www.wayoflife.org/publications/index.html. Way of Life Literature, P.O. Box 610368, Port Huron, MI 48061. 866-295-4143, fbns@wayoflife.org.

Setting the Record Straight

By
Mr. Donald Waite, Jr., M.A., M.L.A.

I have attached a PDF copy of the first 39 pages (pages i-xxxix) of the *Doctored New Testament*. You can search in vain for the bogus statements attributed to me and to Dr. Scrivener. They simply don't exist.

Nowhere in the *Doctored New Testament*—or in anything else I have ever written or said—can a **fair-minded person with even a rudimentary grasp of the English language** find support for this statement: Dr. "Scrivener's assignment was to 'backwards translate the KJB.'"

In footnote 2 from page xiv of *The Doctored New Testament*, one can find these words:

> **"In those KJV portions with no known Greek support, Scrivener let the readings of Beza's 1598 Greek NT stand (page 655, last paragraph). He did not backwards translate from Latin to Greek."**

APPENDIX

Please re-read these words VERY CAREFULLY and then answer the following questions:

(1) To whom does the *He* refer?

(2) What is the difference between saying He did NOT backwards translate and saying He DID backwards translate?

(3) What is the difference between **Latin** and **KJV English**?

(4) What is the difference between translating from **Latin to Greek** and translating from **KJV English to Greek**?

(5) What does it mean to **backwards translate**? The facts are clear. Dr. Scrivener REFUSED to backwards translate from KJV English—or from any other language—in preparing his Greek New Testament, originally designed for COMPARISON PURPOSES. A fair-minded person will read my words and those of Dr. Scrivener and make a good-faith effort to understand them properly.

DEFINED KING JAMES BIBLE
Footnote Author and Editor's Introduction
by
Mr. D. A. Waite, Jr., M. A., M. L. A.

The King James Version has long been recognized as one of the greatest literary works in the English language. For over three centuries, it did more to influence the English-speaking people than any other single book. It influenced the way they acted, the way they thought, the way they wrote, and the way they spoke. Even in the Twentieth Century, English-speaking people around the world continue to be affected by the rhythm, cadence, beauty, and power of this venerable version. But how do we preserve--for the Twenty-first Century--the accuracy, beauty, and dependability of the classic King James Version without sacrificing clarity of understanding in a day of rapidly diminishing literacy? One answer may be the *Defined King James Bible*.

As its title suggests, the *Defined King James Bible* attempts to define archaic, obsolete, or uncommon English words that occur in the text of the King James Version. Since these definitions appear in the footnotes at the bottom of each page, the text of the King James Version (KJV) remains unchanged. Bold-faced type [**like this**] is used to highlight every word (or phrase) that is defined in the footnotes. If a dictionary classified a word definition as archaic (*Arc*) or obsolete (*Obs*) or rare (*Rare*), I listed the appropriate abbreviation *before* that definition. As you will soon notice, most of the uncommon words defined do not have definitions labeled archaic, obsolete, or rare.

But how did I determine which words to define? I began the *Defined King James Bible* project by collecting and then collating several lists of KJV words that others consider difficult today. These lists included the ones drawn up by the American Bible Society, the Trinitarian Bible Society (*Bible Word List*), O. Ray Smith (*King James Bible Dictionary*), and Dr. Laurence Vance (*Archaic Words and the Authorized Version*). I did not knowingly take my definitions from any of these sources, but I tried to include each unique word on these lists. Once I had collated these four lists, I began to locate, footnote, and define each word through a long series of complicated computerized searches and replacements. I used superscript numbers [1, 2, 9] for these primary footnotes.

After I had finished locating, footnoting, and defining these words on my collated list, I "locked in" each page and printed a final proof-reading draft. I then read through this entire draft of the *Defined King James Bible* looking for additional words or phrases that might be confusing. I marked these words and then made as many of these changes as a page would permit. I used superscript numbers and letters [1b, 1c, 2b, 8b] for these <u>secondary</u> footnotes and separated these footnotes from the original ones using double slash marks [//].

My main purpose in these footnotes (primary or secondary) was not to criticize the translators or the translation. It was instead to communicate (as clearly as possible) the meaning intended by the English words the translators chose to use. This was not always easy to do. Although my main purpose required the use of standard English dictionaries, occasionally I had to consult Greek and Hebrew Lexicons to determine which of the English definitions was best for the given word or context. Sometimes I could not decide on a suitable English definition for a given word and therefore gave an appropriate Hebrew (*Heb*) or Greek (*Gk*) meaning.

APPENDIX

Occasionally I gave both an English and a Hebrew/Greek definition. In almost every case, the KJV translators selected the best or one of the best English words possible at that time to convey the meaning of the Hebrew or Greek that they were translating. Notice that in almost every case, the definitions or synonyms are <u>longer</u> (usually considerably longer) than the KJV word being defined.

For those <u>primary</u> words on my original collated list, I tried to give several definitions that would suit most contexts. The reader will have to determine for himself which definition best fits a particular context. I tried not to inject my personal interpretation into these definitions. As a rule, I tried to be as concise as possible in defining a word. Often I tried to give several different definitions to give the reader a wider view of the word's scope.

In the case of those <u>secondary</u> footnotes (with the letter added to the number [1b]), I often had to shorten the full definition or give only one synonym where more would have been warranted. Occasionally I had no room to footnote every example of a few frequently-footnoted or marginally-necessary secondary words.

The reader will notice that I (usually) put a footnoted word in bold-faced type every time that it occurred. The definition occurs only once a page, however. In other words **tabernacle**5 may occur <u>seven</u> times on a page, but there will be only <u>one</u> {5 *Arc* temporary shelter} at the bottom of the page.

For definitions, I consulted several English dictionaries (usually in this order): *Webster's New World Dictionary* (Third College edition, 1994), *American Heritage Dictionary of the English Language* (Third Edition, 1992), *Mirriam-Webster's Collegiate Dictionary* (Tenth Edition, 1994), and the *Oxford English Dictionary* (1933). Almost all of the uncommon words in the King James Version were suitably defined in one or more of these modern dictionaries. For some definitions, however, I was driven to my (1971) micro-copied version of the historically-authoritative, multi-volumed *Oxford English Dictionary*. Virtually all of the definitions that I used were selected from one or more of these dictionaries. In many cases I had to shorten or modify the given definitions to fit available space. Those definitions preceded by <u>i.e.</u> were not precisely found in any dictionary but seem to fit the context by interpolation or extension from a given definition.

CLEANING-UP HAZARDOUS MATERIALS

The most commonly used KJV words that are classified as archaic include the second person pronouns (like *thee*, *thou*, *ye*) and the various archaic verb forms (like *know-**eth***, *did-d**est***, *had-**st***). A footnote at the beginning of each Bible book deals with this second person pronoun problem: "In the KJV *thou*, *thee*, *thy*, *thine*, and *thyself* always refer to <u>only one person</u>. *Ye*, *you*, *your*, *yours*, and *yourself* always refer to <u>more than one</u> person." The archaic verb problem is handled in an appendix at the end of the *Defined King James Bible*. This appendix lists each archaic verb form with its modern counterpart. In addition, several explanatory examples of typical archaic verb usage appear at the end of each Bible book as space permits: look-**eth** =look**s**, loved-**st** =loved.

It is my hope and prayer that the Lord will use my feeble efforts to help (as the KJV translators wrote) "make a good version better." In the words of Bunyan, "Keep the wheat; let the chaff fall to the ground" (introduction to <u>Pilgrim's Progress</u>).

In almost every case, the KJV translators selected the best or one of the best English words possible at that time to convey the meaning of the Hebrew or Greek that they were translating. Some may quibble with a few transitional choices that the translators made, but on balance they must admit that the translation decided upon for a given passage is one of the best if not the best way to translate it.

The *Defined King James Bible* begins with every word of the final revision of the King James Bible (KJV). [I used the public domain computerized edition of the 1789 Cambridge Press text. This computerized version has been extensively checked by others for its accuracy and authenticity. Since this computerized version bracketed each word italicized by the KJV, I constructed a mini-computer program to convert these bracketed words to the more familiar italics. (As most readers of the KJV know, italic type in the KJV indicates words logically supplied by the translators.)]

When studying masterpieces like *Macbeth* (by William Shakespeare), the *Federalist Papers*, (by James Madison, Alexander Hamilton, and John Jay) *Pilgrim's Progress* (by John Bunyan), The Defined King James Bible is my humble attempt to define the more archaic, obsolete, or uncommon words in the King James Bible.

Each page is divided by a center line into two columns. At the bottom of each center line is a page number (from 1-1651). At the top of each page's center line (and above the horizontal header line) is the name of the Bible book from which that page's text comes. The chapter and verse number that begins each page is located in the upper left hand corner

Since 1611, the King James Bible has been corrected for spelling and typographical errors. Its Gothic typeface has been replaced with the more readable Roman typeface.

For over a century after the English Reformation, the English people were described as a people of one book. And that book was the Bible. (as translated into English)

WHAT ABOUT GAIL RIPLINGER'S NEW BOOK?

August 29, 2005 (David Cloud, Fundamental Baptist Information Service, P.O. Box 610368, Port Huron, MI 48061, 866-295-4143, fbns@wayoflife.org; for instructions about subscribing and unsubscribing or changing addresses, see the information paragraph at the end of the article) -

I have been receiving requests from readers to review Gail Riplinger's new book "In Awe of Thy Word: Understanding the King James Bible, Its Mystery & History Letter by Letter." I have seen enough of Riplinger's writings to know what she is all about and this book is more of the same.

When I reviewed her first book (New Age Bible Versions) I saw that while she had many good things to say, she also mishandled the words of men and that her conspiratorial mindset colored everything she touches. I also suspected that she had what one Australian pastor friend calls "an attitude problem." When I wrote to her in those days to express my concerns, she didn't reply. To this day she has never replied to me personally, but she did include me in her next book (Blind Guides) and treated me like some sort of fool, mocked me, took my words out of context and twisted them to make me say things I do not believe, and slanderously lumped me in with modern version defenders such as James White. (For more about this see "Gail Riplinger's Slanders" at http://www.wayoflife.org/fbns/riplinger3.htm.)

Her newest book again contains many good things in defense of the KJV but it is interspersed with serious mistakes so that it is impossible to have confidence in her research or conclusions at any point.

For example, in chapter 22 she claims that John Wycliffe did not use the Latin Vulgate as the basis for his translation but that he used Hebrew, Greek, and Old Latin sources. She says it is a "myth" to say that Wycliffe used the Latin Vulgate. As a matter of fact, a careful comparison of the Wycliffe Bible with the Latin Vulgate and the Old Latin demonstrates that Wycliffe consistently used the Vulgate, with only a very few exceptions. I have done extensive research into the textual basis of the Wycliffe New Testament and it contains most of the textual corruptions found in the Vulgate. For example, the Wycliffe Bible omits "for thine is the kingdom, and the power, and the glory, for ever" in Mat. 6:13, "to repentance" in Mat. 9:13 and Mk. 2:17, "spoken by Daniel the prophet" in Mk. 13:14, "get thee behind me Satan" in Lk. 4:8, "the Lord" from 1 Cor. 15:47, "in Christ" in Gal. 3:17, and "God" in 1 Timothy 3:16, to mention only a few of its textual errors. In most of these instances, these things are omitted in the Wycliffe and the Latin Vulgate but are NOT omitted in the Old Latin, so that it is obvious that Wycliffe was indeed following the Vulgate rather than the Traditional Greek Text or the Old Latin.

Mrs. Riplinger gives so much seeming documentation that the average reader is convinced that her scholarship is sound, not being in a position to see that she frequently misuses her quotes and reaches conclusions not supported by the facts given in the documents that she cites as her authority.

Further, Mrs. Riplinger is completely out of place in teaching men as she does. Two things are forbidden in 1 Timothy 2:12, "But I suffer not a woman to teach, nor to usurp authority over the man, but to be in silence." The woman is not allowed to teach men and she is not allowed to usurp authority over them. Mrs. Riplinger is living in open defiance of this divine commandment.

She also is a true Ruckmanite, teaching that the English KJV is better than and has replaced the Greek and Hebrew, that there is no need today for learning or using Greek and Hebrew, and other such things. If her position were true we would not even have an English Bible because it was laboriously translated by men who learned Greek and Hebrew and diligently studied the Scriptures in those languages!

There is a strange, almost cultic element within the Independent Baptist movement, and Mrs. Riplinger is right in the middle of it.

The Fire of London

"Many of the records and other sources used for the translation of the KJB were lost in the Great Fire of London.

The Great Fire of London began on the night of September 2, 1666, as a small fire on Pudding Lane, in the bakeshop of Thomas Farynor, baker to King Charles II. At one o'clock in the morning, a servant woke to find the house aflame, and the baker and his family escaped, but a fear-struck maid perished in the blaze.

At this time, most London houses were of wood and pitch construction, dangerously flammable, and it did not take long for the fire to expand. The fire leapt to the hay and feed piles on the yard of the Star Inn at Fish Street Hill, and spread to the Inn. The strong wind that blew that night sent sparks that next ignited the Church of St. Margaret, and then spread to Thames Street, with its riverside warehouses and wharves filled with food for the flames: hemp, oil, tallow, hay, timber, coal and spirits along with other combustibles. The citizen firefighting brigades had little success in containing the fire with their buckets of water from the river. By eight o'clock in the morning, the fire had spread halfway across London Bridge. The only thing that stopped the fire from spreading to Southwark, on the other side of the river, was the gap that had been caused by the fire of 1633.

The standard procedure to stop a fire from spreading had always been to destroy the houses on the path of the flames, creating "fire-breaks", to deprive a fire from fuel. Lord Mayor Bludworth, however, was hesitant, worrying about the cost of rebuilding. By the time a Royal command came down, carried by Samuel Pepys, the fire was too out of control to stop. The Trained Bands of London were called in to demolish houses by gunpowder, but often the rubble was too much to be cleared before the fire was at hand, and only eased the fire's way onward. The fire blazed unchecked for another three days, until it halted near Temple Church. Then, it suddenly sprang to life again, continuing towards Westminster. The Duke of York (later King James II) had the presence of mind to order the Paper House demolished to create a fire break, and the fire finally died down.

Although the loss of life was minimal, some sources say only sixteen perished, the magnitude of the property loss was staggering. Some 430 acres, as much as 80% of the city proper was destroyed, including 13,000 houses, 89 churches, and 52 Guild Halls. Thousands of citizens found themselves homeless and financially ruined.The Great Fire, and the fire of 1676, which destroyed over 600 houses south of the river, changed the face of London forever. The one positive effect of the Great Fire was that the plague, which had ravished London since 1665, diminished greatly, due to the mass death of the plague-carrying rats in the blaze.

Charles II appointed six Commissioners to redesign the city. The plan provided for wider streets and buildings of brick, rather than timber. By 1671, 9000 houses and public buildings had been completed. Sir Christopher Wren was commissioned to design and oversee the construction of nearly 50 churches, not least of them a new St. Paul's Cathedral, construction of which began in 1675. The King also had Wren design a monument to the Great Fire, which stands still today at the site of the bakery which started it all, on a street now named Monument Street."

From: (http://www.luminarium.org/encyclopedia/greatfire.htm)

THE GIFT OF TONGUES

By
Pastor Kirk DiVietro

Tongues speaking is not new nor is it uniquely Christian. It was a part of the religious life of Canaan as recorded by Wen-Amon the Egyptian in 1100 B.C. Plato the Greek philosopher and Virgil the

APPENDIX

Roman poet both speak of the religious use of tongues. Both of these men were pagans.

The Old Testament also records the phenomena of tongues. King Saul in his jealous insanity spoke in tongues just before his attempt to murder David. The prophets of Baal on Mt. Carmel also spoke in tongues.

> I Samuel 10:6 And the Spirit of the Lord will come upon thee, and thou **shalt prophesy** with them, and shalt be turned into another man.
> I Samuel 18:10-11 And it came to pass on the morrow, that the evil spirit from God came upon Saul, and **he prophesied** in the midst of the house: and David played with his hand, as at other times: and *there was* a javelin in Saul's hand. And Saul cast the javelin; for he said, I will smite David even to the wall *with it*. And David avoided out of his presence twice.
> I Samuel 19:24 And **he stripped off his clothes also, and prophesied** before Samuel in like manner, and lay down naked all that day and all that night. Wherefore they say, *Is* Saul also among the prophets?
> I Kings 18:29 And it came to pass, when midday was past, and **they prophesied** until the *time* of the offering of the *evening* sacrifice, that *there was* neither voice, nor any to answer, nor any that regarded.

The word translated "prophecy" in these passages is a word which indicates more than just a supernatural message. It is a word which indicates the making of unintelligible sounds, speaking in tongues.

There are primarily five New Testament passages which deal with the doctrine of tongues.

> Mark 16:17 And these signs shall follow them that believe; In my name shall they cast out devils; they shall speak with new tongues;

One of the confirming signs of the apostles was to be the phenomena of speaking with "new tongues." This was fulfilled at Pentecost where we read:

> Acts 2:4 "And they were all filled with the Holy Ghost, and began to speak with other tongues, as the Spirit gave them utterance."
> Acts 2:5 "And there were dwelling at Jerusalem Jews, devout men, out of every nation under heaven."

CLEANING-UP HAZARDOUS MATERIALS

> Acts 2:6 "Now when this was noised abroad, the multitude came together, and were confounded, because that every man heard them speak in his own language."

This is the only definite recorded instance of speaking with tongues in the book of Acts. There are a few others which are ambiguous, but, which seem to be describing the phenomena. For the sake of this discussion, the author will consider them to be the manifestation of tongues. In Acts 2, there are fourteen specific, known, human tongues which were spoken, heard, and understood.

> Acts 10:46 "For they heard them speak with tongues, and magnify God. Then answered Peter,"

When Cornelius and his family got saved, Peter and his companions heard them speak with other tongues. Since Cornelius was a Roman Soldier, it would not be unexpected that in his excitement he may have begun to chatter off in his native tongue. Context and Peter's reaction would seem to indicate, however, that they were speaking with the supernatural gift of tongues.

> Acts 19:6 "And when Paul had laid *his* hands upon them, the Holy Ghost came on them; and they spake with tongues, and prophesied."

Again, the context almost demands that the tongues here are the supernatural gift of tongues.

The definitive passage on tongues is found in I Corinthians 12-14. The Corinthian church which was confused on almost every aspect of Christianity was confused on the gifts of the Holy Ghost. Paul prefaced his teaching on these gifts with I Corinthians 11:18-19.

> "For first of all, when ye come together in the church, I hear that there be divisions among you; and I partly believe it. For there must be also heresies among you, that they which are approved may be made manifest among you."

Heretics forced the clarification of many important doctrines. It was heretics like Tatian and Marcion which forced the early Christians to define the canon. It was heretics like Arius which forced early churches to wrestle with the true nature of Jesus Christ. The process continued through the ages. The heretical use of tongues in Corinth forced Paul to clarify the gift of tongues.

APPENDIX

From the close of the apostolic age until the reformation, only one group of Christian churches practiced speaking in tongues. These churches followed the man Montanus, who according to his critics claimed to be the Holy Spirit. The next recorded manifestation took place in 1685 when a small community of French protestants spoke in tongues. It is recorded that in 1731, the Jansenists, a Catholic counter-reformation group, met at their dead leader's grave and spoke in tongues.

The first American experience with tongues came in 1776 through the group founded by Ann Lee,—the Shakers. Shakers also forbid marriage and practiced mixed line dancing in the nude and made ecstatic utterances. Across the ocean in 1830, Edward Irving, a Scotch Presbyterian, started a tongues group in London.

The Mormons spoke in tongues from their earliest history. From the pages of a rare history book written in 1876 we read,

> "The Mormon theology teaches that there is one God, the Eternal Father, his Son, Jesus Christ, and the Holy Ghost; and that men will be punished for his own sins, and not for Adam's transgression; and that through the atonement of Christ all mankind may be saved by obedience to the law and ordinances of the Gospel, these ordinances being faith in the Lord Jesus, repentance, baptism for the remission of sins, laying on of hands by the gift of the Holy Ghost, and the Lord's supper; that man must be called of God by inspiration and of laying on of hands by those who are duly commissioned to preach the gospel and administer the ordinances thereof; that the same organization that existed in the primitive church viz., apostles, pastors, prophets, evangelists, etc., should be maintained now, that the powers and gifts of faith, discerning of spirits, prophecy, revelations, visions, healing, tongues and the interpretation of tongues still exist."[36]

In 1833 the gift of tongues was conferred; the re-translation of the Bible finished;[37]

---

[36] Devons, R.M., *Our First Century: One Hundred Great and Memorable Events:* C.A. Nichols & Co. Springfield, MA.: 1876. P 308
[37] Ibid. P. 310

"In 1835 a quorum of twelve apostles was organized among whom were Brigham Young and H. C. Kimball the former being then thirty-four years old , assuming the headship of the apostolic college and receiving the gift of tongues was sent on a missionary tour toward the east."[38]

In 1847, at the dedication of the Mormon Temple in Salt Lake City, Utah, Brigham Young and hundreds of Mormon elders and officials spoke in tongues.

The modern tongues movement began at the turn of the present century (the Christmas break of 1900-1901). A Charles F. Parham, founder and professor, at the Bethel Bible College in Topeka, Kansas, sent his students home for Christmas with an assignment. They were to search their Bibles and deduce the evidence of being filled with the Holy Spirit. When the students returned after the holidays, they reached a consensus. The filling of the Holy Spirit was evidenced by the speaking an unlearned tongue or language. A few days later, one of the female students, Agnes Ozman, actually spoke in tongues and the modern "Charismatic movement" was born.

The movement spread. In 1903, the Church of God, the first Pentecostal denomination, was founded. In 1906, Azuza Street Assembly was opened in Los Angeles. The meetings lasted three years and gave birth to many of the modern Pentecostal groups: the Assemblies of God, Foursquare Gospel Churches, Church of God in Christ, United Pentecostal, etc.

In the 1960, the tongues phenomena jumped to the mainline denominations. Father Dennis Bennet rector of an Episcopal Church in VanNuys, California, publicly announced that he had spoken in tongues. From that time until the present the tongues phenomena has grown geometrically until it now permeates almost every denomination and fellowship

The Greek word γλώσσας [GLOSSAS] is the word translated "tongues." The tongues movement is described theologically as "glossalalia." Γλώσσας indicates either the physical organ called the tongue or a language. Acts 2 is the only place in the Bible where the

---

[38] Ibid. p. 310.

APPENDIX

phenomena of tongues is described. As noted above, the apostles, filled with the Holy Spirit, began to spontaneously speak in 14 identifiable, human languages to an audience which understood that speaking naturally. On the basis of a misinterpretation of I Corinthians 13:1, modern tongues speakers describe their unintelligible utterings as the language of angels or a special prayer language.

> "Though I speak with the tongues of men and of angels, and have not charity, I am become *as* sounding brass, or a tinkling cymbal.) many charismatics have tried to define their unintelligible articulations as the language of angels. Paul used the subjunctive mood in this verse."

"Though I speak" is used in the sense of "If I could speak". Paul did not say that he could nor that anyone else should try to speak in the language of angels. He was using hyperbole for the sake of emphasis. In the Bible, ALL tongues are human languages spoken by men who have never learned them and are directed to an audience of those who, without supernatural intervention, understand what is being said. Angels, being spirit beings, not physical, have no reason to have a separate spoken language. When they speak, they always speak in the language of the person they are addressing.

Of the gifts, tongues was and is the easiest to generate and/or fake. The gibberish that is passed off as tongues today is a completely normal human phenomena and does not need supernatural explanation. The human vocal system is capable of generating every sound which is a part of every language known to man. If a person simply starts to utter noises that are not part of any language known to them, their brain will begin to organize those sounds into a language which is reproducible at will. They may not realize they are doing it.[39] Tongues, speaking an unlearned unknown language, can also be the result of demonic influence. They can also result from emotional

---

[39] Poythress, Vern S.: "Linguistic and Sociological Analyses of Modern Tongues-Speaking: Their Contributions and Limitations", Westminster Theological Journal. 1998 (electronic edition.). Philadelphia: Westminster Theological Seminary., Libronix Digital Library System

overload, which is why pro-charismatic services usually include long emotional "praise and worship" sessions.

What are genuine Bible tongues and what were their purposes? Let us let the Bible speak. I Corinthians 12-14 was written because of the abuse of tongues by the Corinthian church. It is very possible that the tongues being spoken there were normal human languages being passed off as a supernatural manifestation. Because of its position on the Greek isthmus, Corinth was a cosmopolitan city made up of many ethnic and language groups. It was a major trade crossroads. Not only did it open the market into the Greek peninsula, it was also an overland shortcut for trade. Traders could cut miles of sea travel and avoid the dangers of the Mediterranean Euroclydon by crossing the isthmus.

As a result the Corinthian church had members of many language groups. It would be easy for someone to stand and pretend to be speaking in tongues when all they were doing was speaking in the obscure language of their birthplace. If that is the case, then the admonition to speak in the commonly understood tongue (Greek) was to be preferred. If it were necessary for a speaker to use his native tongue, then his message to the church was only to be delivered if there were others who spoke his language and could interpret for the rest. Even this was to be kept to a minimum (two or three speakers).

The tongues of Acts, Mark, and I Corinthians were the actual speaking of words in non-Hebrew languages in the presence of Jews. Paul made that very clear. Every reference in I Corinthians to tongues is to speaking in a church service. Paul declared that the purpose of tongues was given in Isaiah 28:11-12.

> "For with stammering lips and another tongue will he speak to this people. To whom he said, This is the rest wherewith ye may cause the weary to rest; and this is the refreshing: yet they would not hear."

The times of *refreshing* was used in Peter's sermon of Acts 3. It is a reference to the kingdom of Christ. The implication of Isaiah is that when Israel hears and is dominated by Gentile languages, she should know that she has missed the kingdom. Peter said, if we repent and

APPENDIX

identify with Christ by baptism, perhaps God will send Jesus and the time of refreshing would come.

> Acts 3:19-20 "Repent ye therefore, and be converted, that your sins may be blotted out, when the times of refreshing shall come from the presence of the Lord; And he shall send Jesus Christ, which before was preached unto you:"

When Israel hears the Gospel of their God in Gentile languages, she should realize that God is telling them they are in danger of losing the kingdom and going into judgment. Tongues have nothing to do with *revelation* or *prayer*. They are simply a sign gift. Once the churches became primarily Gentile, the supernatural gift was no longer needed and paused by itself (I Corinthians 13:8).

There is absolutely nothing biblical to justify Mrs. Riplinger's contention that God gave tongues to produce separately inspired versions of the Bible in various languages, either the fourteen of Acts 2, or the seventy of Genesis 10-11, or to all the languages of the then known world. Neither is there any basis in history for such a claim.

KJB TRANSLATOR RULES

The translators of the King James Bible were bound by fourteen rules. A fifteenth rule was added to guarantee that the 14 would be obeyed. The translation of the KJV was not done exclusively by the official committees. Note rule 12. Virtually every preacher and scholar who knew Greek and Hebrew throughout the realm of Great Britain was given the opportunity to provide input on the translation. No translation was adopted which did not find consensus support.

1. The ordinary Bible read in church, commonly called the Bishops' Bible, to be followed and as little altered as the truth of the original will permit.

The first instructed them to make the "Bishop's Bible," so called, the basis of their work, altering It no further than fidelity to the originals required. In the result, however, the new version agreed much more with the Geneva than with any other; though the huffing king, at the Hampton Court Conference, reproached it as "the worst of all."

2. The names of the prophets and the holy writers with the other names of the text to be retained as nigh as may be, accordingly as they were vulgarly used.

CLEANING-UP HAZARDOUS MATERIALS

The second rule requires that the mode then used of spelling the proper names should be retained as far as might be.

3. The old ecclesiastical words to be kept, viz. the word "church" not to be translated "congregation." (The Greek word can be translated either way.)

The third rule requires "the old ecclesiastical words to be kept," such as "church" instead of "congregation."

4. When a word hath divers significations, that to be kept which hath been most commonly used by most of the ancient fathers.

The fourth rule prescribes, that where a word has different meanings, that is to be preferred which has the general sanction of the most ancient Fathers, regard being had to "the propriety of the place, and the analogy of faith."

5. The division of the chapters to be altered either not at all or as little as may be.

The fifth rule directs that the divisions into chapters be altered as little as may be.

6. No marginal notes at all to be affixed, but only for the explanation of the Hebrew or Greek words which cannot without some circumlocution be so briefly and fitly expressed in the text.

The sixth rule, agreeably to Dr. Reynolds's wise suggestion at Hampton Court, prohibits all notes or comments, thus obliging the translators to make their version intelligible without those dangerous helps.

7. Such quotations of places to be marginally set down as shall serve for the fit reference of one scripture to another.

The seventh rule provides for marginal references to parallel or explanatory passages.

8. Every particular man of each company to take the same chapter or chapters, and having translated or amended them severally by himself, where he thinketh good, all to meet together to confer when they have done, and agree for their parts what shall stand.

The eighth rule enjoins that each man in each company shall separately examine the same chapter or chapters, and put the translation into the best shape he can. The whole company must then come together, and compare what they have done, and agree on what shall stand. Thus in each company according to the number of members, there would be from seven to ten distinct and carefully labored revisions, the whole to be compared, and digested into one copy of the portion of the Bible assigned to each particular company.

9. As any one company hath dispatched any one book in this manner they shall send it to the rest, to be considered of seriously and judiciously, for His Majesty is very careful in this point.

The ninth rule directs, that as fast as any company shall, In this manner, complete any one of the sacred books, It is to be sent to each of the other companies, to be critically reviewed by them all.

10. If any company upon the review of the book so sent doubt or differ upon any place, to send them word thereof with the place and withal send the

APPENDIX

reasons; to which if they consent not, the difference to be compounded at the general meeting which is to be of the chief persons of each company at the end of the work. (Thus in the end they all had to agree enough to let all readings pass.)

The tenth rule prescribes, that If any company, upon reviewing a book so sent to them, find any thing doubtful or unsatisfactory, they are to note the places, and their reasons for objecting thereto, and send it back to the company from whence it came. If that company should not concur in the suggestions thus made, the matter was to be finally arranged at a general meeting of the chief persons of all the companies at the end of the work. Thus every Part of the Bible would be fully considered, first, separately, by each member of the company to which it was originally assigned; secondly, by that whole company in concert; thirdly, by the other five companies severally; and fourthly, by the general committee of revision. By this judicious plan, each part must have been closely scrutinized at least fourteen times.

11. When any place of special obscurity be doubted of, letters to be directed by authority to send to any learned man in the land for his judgment of such a place.

The eleventh rule provides, that in case of any special difficulty or obscurity, letters shall be issued by authority to any learned man in the land, calling for his judgment thereon.

12. Letters to be sent from every bishop to the rest of his clergy, admonishing them of his translation in hand, and to move and charge as many as being skillful in the tongues and having taken pains in that way, to send his particular observations to the company, either at Westminster, Cambridge, or Oxford. (This indicates that many must have aided in the work.)

The twelfth rule requires every bishop to notify the clergy of his diocese as to the work in hand, and to "move and charge as many as, being skillful in the tongues, have taken pains in that kind, to send his particular observations" to some one of the companies.

13. The directors of each company to be the deans of Westminster and Chester for that place, and the King's professors in the Hebrew or Greek in either university.

The thirteenth rule appoints the directors of the different companies.

14. These translations to be used when they agree better with the text than the Bishops' Bible Tyndale's, Coverdale's, Whitchurch's (Great Bible), Geneva.

The fourteenth rule names five other translations to be used, "when they agree better with text than the Bishop's Bible." These are Tyndale's; - Matthew's, which is by Tyndale and John Rogers; - Coverdale's; - Whitchurch's, which is "Cranmer's," or the "Great Bible," and was printed by Whitchurch; - and the Geneva Bible. The object of this regulation was to avoid, as far as possible, the suspicious stamp of novelty. To the careful observance of these injunctions, which, with the exception of the first five, are highly judicious, is to be ascribed much of the excellence of the completed translation.

15. Besides the said directors before mentioned, three or four of the most ancient and grave divines in either of the universities, not employed in translating, to be assigned by the vice-chancellor, upon conference with the rest of the heads, to be overseers of the translation, as well Hebrew as Greek, for the better observation of the fourth rule above specified.

To these rules, which were delivered to the Translators, there appears to have been added another, providing that, besides the directors of the six companies, "three or four of the most ancient and grave divines in either of the Universities, not employed in translating," be designed by the Vice-Chancellors and Head: of Colleges, "to be overseers of the Translation, as well Hebrew as Greek, for the better observation of the fourth rule.[40]

---

[40] The rules were provided by: Paine, Gustavus S., *The Men Behind the KJV King James Version*, Baker Book House, Grand Rapids, MI., pp 70-71 The commentary came from: McClure, Alexander W., *The Translators Revived: A Biographical Memoir of the Authors of the English Version of the Holy Bible*, Reprint by Baptist International Seminary, Oxon Hill, MD., pp41-44

APPENDIX

MARRIAGE RECORDS OF MRS. RIPLINGER

CLEANING-UP HAZARDOUS MATERIALS

MARRIAGE CERTIFICATE

1989

The State of Ohio, Trumbull County, ss.

I hereby Certify that on the 7 day of June, 1969, I solemnized the Marriage of Mr. Jerry Edward Latessa with M... Jaul Anne Lisalury

Filed and Recorded June 9, 1969.

Reed J. Bethon ...... Probate Judge   Rev. Richard Marciangelo
.... Ferrara ...... Deputy Clerk   Asst. Pastor Mt. Carmel - Niles O

APPENDIX

MARRIAGE RECORD

Probate Court, Portage County, Ohio

IN THE MATTER OF

    Franklin Alex Kaleda

AND

    Gail Anne Ludwig

MARRIAGE LICENSE APPLICATION

To the Honorable Judge of the Probate Court of said County

The undersigned respectfully make application for a Marriage License for said parties and upon oath states:

MALE

that said __Franklin Alex Kaleda__ is __27__ years of age on the __2nd__ day of __December__, __75__; his residence is __Apt. 415, 1800 Rhodes Rd., Kent, Ohio__ his place of birth is __Appollo, Pa.__, his occupation is __retail manager__, his father's name is __Frank John Kaleda__, his mother's maiden name was __Eva Rose Petroskaus__, that he was __never__ previously married _____ and that he has no wife living.

FEMALE

that said __Gail Anne Ludwig__ is __29__ years of age on the __10th__ day of __October__, __76__; her residence is __212 Sayers Ave., Niles, Ohio__ (Trumbull) her place of birth is __Columbus, Ohio__, her occupation is __student__, her father's name is __Wilson Ludwig__, her mother's maiden name was __Helen Frech__, that she was __once__ previously married _____ and that she has no husband living.

Medical and Laboratory Statement of Male Applicant filed __11-1__ 19 __76__
Affidavit of his Physician __Dr. Owen__
Medical and Laboratory Statement of Female Applicant filed __11-1__ 19 __76__
Affidavit of her Physician __Dr. Owen__

That the following is a statement of facts concerning his and her previous marriages and divorces.

Names of Parties	Names of Minor Children By this Marriage	Jurisdiction, Date, and No. of Divorce Decree
Terry Edward Latessa	none	# 74-DR-1543 Mahoning County Feb. 12, 1975

NUMBER 45789   DOCKET 84   PAGE 89

CLEANING-UP HAZARDOUS MATERIALS

That neither of said parties is an habitual drunkard, imbecile, or insane, and is not under the influence of any intoxicating liquor or narcotic drug, that neither has syphillis which is communicable or likely to become so and they have complied with the Ohio Serological Test.

Said parties are not nearer of kin than second cousins, and there is no legal impediment to their marriage.

It is expected that _____ is to solemnize the marriage of said parties.

x *Franklin Alex Kaleda*
x *Gail Anne Ludwig*

Sworn to before me by both applicants and signed by them in my presence this **1st** day of **November** 19 **76**.

S. L. Summers
Probate Judge

By *Margie A. Weaver*
Deputy Clerk

ENTRY

Probate Court, Portage County, O.,   November 1, 19 76.
Marriage License was this day granted to **Franklin Alan Kaleda** and **Miss Gail Anne Ludwig**

S. L. Summers
Probate Judge

MARRIAGE CERTIFICATE

The State of Ohio, Portage County.

I DO HEREBY CERTIFY, that on the **5th** day of **November** A.D. 19 **76** I solemnized the Marriage of Mr. **Franklin Alex Kaleda** with M **iss Gail Anne Ludwig**

Rev. Richard Gordon
Warren, Ohio

Filed and recorded **November 9,** 19 **76**

S. L. Summers
Probate Judge

CERTIFICATE TO COPY

The State of Ohio, Portage County.

I, the undersigned Probate Judge within and for said County, hereby certify the within to be a full and complete transcript from the record of Marriages, Vol. _____ Page _____, required by the laws of Ohio to be kept in the Probate Court of said County.

WITNESS my signature and the seal of said Court at _____ Ohio, this _____ day of _____, 19 _____.

_____
Probate Judge and Ex-officio Clerk
of the Probate Court of said County

_____
Deputy Clerk

PC-105

STATE OF OHIO } SS COURT OF COMMON PLEAS
PORTAGE COUNTY } SS PROBATE DIVISION
I HEREBY CERTIFY THIS TO BE A TRUE AND EXACT COPY OF THE *Marriage Record* FILED IN THE FOREGOING CASE
THOMAS J. CARNES - PROBATE JUDGE AND CLERK OF PROBATE COURT
DATE _____ BY _____
DEPUTY CLERK

APPENDIX

PRE-MARITAL CERTIFICATE No. 59311   PROBATE COURT, SUMMIT COUNTY, OHIO
Michael Demick Riplinger
Gail Anne Ludwig   and   MARRIAGE LICENSE APPLICATION

To the Honorable Judge of the Probate Court of said County.
The undersigned respectively make their application for a Marriage License for, said parties, and state:

SUMMIT COUNTY PROBATE COURT

OHIO DEPARTMENT OF HEALTH
DIVISION OF VITAL STATISTICS
COLUMBUS

Vol. 326   Page 59311   STATE FILE

CERTIFIED ABSTRACT OF MARRIAGE

GROOM	BRIDE
1. Full Name: Michael Domnick Riplinger	10. Full Name: Gail Anne Ludwig
2. Birth Number:	11. Birth Number:
3. Age last birthday: 34	12. Age last birthday: 36
Mo. April Day 28 Year 1984	Mo. October Day 10 Year 1983
4. Residence: 1526 8th Street 44221, Cuyahoga Falls, Summit Co, Ohio	13. Residence: 841 Fairchild, Kent, Trumbull County, Ohio 44240
5. Birthplace: Akron, Ohio	14. Birthplace: Columbus, Ohio
6. Occupation: Serviceman	15. Occupation: Professor
7. Name of Father: Carl John Riplinger	16. Name of Father: Wilson Ludwig
8. Maiden Name of Mother: Catherine Fugarino	17. Maiden Name of Mother: Helen Geraldine Frech
9. Previously Married (Number of Times): 0	18. Previously Married (Number of Times): 2

CONSENT OF PARENTS ....   CONSENT OF PARENTS ....

RECORD OF DIVORCE

that he was .... previously married   that she was twice previously married now Div
and that he has no wife living.   and that she has no husband living.
STATE   COUNTY   STATE Ohio   COUNTY Portage
Date of Decree   No. of Decree   Date of Decree 8-6-84 No. of Decree 84 CV065
Name of former wife   Name of former husband Frank Alexander Kaleda
Name of minor children   Name of minor children 0

That neither of said parties is an habitual drunkard, imbecile, or insane, or infected with syphillis and is not under the influence of any intoxicating liquor or controlled substances. Said parties are not nearer of kin than second cousins and there is no legal impediment to their marriage.

It is expected that   Judge Pike   is to solemnize the marriage of said parties.

The undersigned, say that their respective statements in the foregoing application, dated this   4th
Day of   September   19 84, are true

Michael D. Riplinger   Gail A. Ludwig

                                                   W. F. SPICER, Probate Judge

Counseling Service Proof on File Yes [] No []

CLEANING-UP HAZARDOUS MATERIALS

PROBATE COURT, SUMMIT COUNTY, September 7, 19 84   WAIVER
age license was this day issued to: For good cause shown, such license granted immediately "after the application therefore"
chael Domnick Riplinger and Gail Anne Ludwig
W. F. SPICER, Probate Judge
Phyllis Mauer, Deputy Clerk   W. F. SPICER, Probate Judge

MARRIAGE CERTIFICATE NO. 59311

I DO HEREBY CERTIFY, That on the 27th day of October A.D. 19 84, I solemnized the Marriage of Mr. Michael Domnick Riplinger with Miss Gail Anne Ludwig

Filed and Recorded October 30, 19 84

William B. Pike .... Name
Judge .... Title
Cuyahoga Falls, Ohio .... Mailing Address

W. F. SPICER,
Probate Judge

MARRIAGE RECORD NO. 326 SUMMIT COUNTY, OHIO

CERTIFICATION OF COPY

I certify this to be a true copy of the original *
V.326,pg.19.11 now on file in the Summit County Probate Court, State of Ohio.
This 30th day of June 2005

BILL SPICER
Judge and Ex-Officio Clerk

By Anthony Artin
Deputy Clerk
* except for redacted information

The Received Text: What is it?

A BRIEF EXPLANATION OF WHAT WE MEAN BY THE RECEIVED TEXT

The definition or explanation of the Greek Received Text (*Textus Receptus*, TR) of the New Testament has been confused, diluted, and twisted by the modern discipline of textual criticism. The definition is really quite simple (q.v.).

Dean John William Burgon (1813-1888) clearly presents the facts necessary for understanding the origin of the TR and 'what it is.' He preferred to call the Greek inspired text, which originated with the apostles and prophets, the Traditional Text, but he quickly explains that the same text is called by many different names. He said:

> "The one great Fact, which especially troubles him [HORT] and his joint Editor [WESTCOTT],—(as well it may)—is *The Traditional Greek Text* of the New Testament Scriptures. Call this Text Erasmian or Complutensian,—the Text of Stephens, or of Beza, or of the Elzevirs,—call it the 'Received,' or *Traditional Greek Text*, or whatever other name you please;—the fact remains, that **a Text *has* come down to us which is attested by a general consensus of ancient Copies, ancient Fathers, ancient Versions.**"[41]

And he said:

> "**The Traditional Text,...has been traced back to the earliest ages** in the existence of those sacred writings...It is evident that the turning-point of the controversy between ourselves and the Neologian[42] school must lie in the

---

[41] Dean John William Burgon, *The Revision Revised* (The Dean Burgon Society Press, Collingswood, NJ, originally published, 1883, reprinted 2000) 269.

[42] Neologian is the term coined by Dean Burgon and Edward Miller for the Alexandrian or 'new' Greek text constructed by textual critics that culminated with Westcott and Hort who were Burgon's contemporaries.

centuries before St. Chrysostom. If, as Dr. Hort maintains, the Traditional Text not only gained supremacy at that era but did not exist in the early ages, then our contention is vain. That Text can be Traditional only if it goes back **without break or intermission to the original autographs**, because if through break or intermission it ceased or failed to exist, it loses the essential feature of genuine tradition...I claim to have **proved Dr. Hort to have been conspicuously wrong, and our maintenance of the Traditional Text in unbroken succession to be eminently right.**"[43] [HDW, my emphasis]

Dean Burgon also said the following about the Traditional Text (TR):

"Variety distinguishing witness massed together must needs constitute a most powerful argument for believing such Evidence to be true. Witnesses of different kinds; from different countries; speaking different tongues:--witnesses who can never have met, and between whom it is incredible that there should exist collusion of any kind:--such witnesses deserve to be listened to most respectfully. Indeed, when witnesses of so varied a sort agree in large numbers, they must needs be accounted worthy of even implicit confidence... Variety it is which imparts virtue to mere Number, prevents the witness-box from being filled with packed deponents, ensures genuine testimony. False witness is thus detected and condemned, because it agrees not with the rest. Variety is the consent of independent witnesses...It is precisely this consideration which constrains us to pay supreme attention to the combined testimony of the Uncials and of the whole body of the Cursive Copies. They are (a) dotted over at least 1000 years: (b) they evidently [Burgon means by evidence, there is no doubt here, HDW] belong to so many divers countries,—Greece, Constantinople, Asia Minor, Palestine, Syria, Alexandria, and other part of Africa, not to say Sicily, Southern Italy, Gaul, England and Ireland: (c) they exhibit so many strange

---

[43] Dean John William Burgon, *The Causes of Corruption of the Traditional Text of the Holy Gospels Being the Sequel to the Traditional Text of the Holy Gospels, Vol. II* (Dean Burgon Society Press, Collingswood, NJ, 1896, reprinted 1998) 1-3.

APPENDIX

characteristics and peculiar sympathies: (d) they so clearly represent countless families of MSS., being in no single instance absolutely identical in their text, and certainly not being copies of any other Codex in existence,--that their unanimous decision I hold to be an absolutely irrefragable evidence of the Truth."[44] [my addition, HDW]

In conclusion, Dean Burgon said:

"...it will be perceived that a three-fold security has been provided for the integrity of the Deposit:—Copies,—Versions,—Fathers."[45]

A few additional comments should be made concerning the origin of **the term** "Textus Receptus" (Received Text), not the **text**.

"The origin of the term "Textus Receptus" comes from the publisher's preface to the 1633 edition produced by Bonaventure and Abraham Elzevir, two brothers and printers at Leiden: *textum ergo habes, nunc ab omnibus receptum, in quo nihil immulatum aut corruptum damus*, translated "so you hold the text, now received by all, in which nothing corrupt." The two words, *textum* and *receptum*, were modified from the accusative to the nominative case to render *textus receptus*."[46]

It should be pointed out that the Elzevir brothers were most likely influenced by the following Scripture:

John 17:8 (KJV) [8] "For I have given unto them the words which thou gavest me; and they have received them, and

---

[44] Dean John William Burgon, *The Traditional Text of the Holy Gospels, Vol 1* (The Dean Burgon Society Press, Collingswood, NJ, 1998) 50-51.

[45] Dean John William Burgon, *The Traditional Text of the Holy Gospels* (Dean Burgon Society Press, Collingswood, NJ, Originally published 1896, republished 1998 by the DBS) 23.

[46] Bruce M. Metzger, Bart D. Ehrman, "The Text Of The New Testament: Its Transmission, Corruption and Restoration", *Oxford University Press*, 2005, p. 152.

have known surely that I came out from thee, and they have believed that thou didst send me."
John 12:48 (KJV) [48] "He that rejecteth me, and receiveth not my words, hath one that judgeth him: the word that I have spoken, the same shall judge him in the last day."

Lastly, many modernistic textual critics will invariably try to claim that the TR began with Desiderius Erasmus. The TR began with the apostles and prophets. Erasmus formatted the first printing of the TR from many MSS that he examined. Furthermore, there are numerous false claims concerning the MSS Erasmus used to format the first printed TR. Contrary to many modern authors, he did **not** use "only four or five" MSS. He used MSS from every country and many libraries, including the Vatican. He refused to use the variants found in the corrupted MSS favored by modern textual critics.

H. D. Williams, M.D., Ph.D.

SCRIVENER'S APPENDIX A
"WRONG READINGS OF THE BIBLE OF 1611 AMENDED IN LATER EDITIONS"

The Authorized Edition of the English Bible (1611): Its Subsequent Reprints and Modern Representatives, F.H.A. Scrivener, Cambridge, 1884, pp. 147-202. Appendix A., "Wrong readings of the Bible of 1611 amended in later editions."

Catalogue of the variations from the original edition of the Authorized Version of the Holy Bible (1611), which, being found in all modern editions, have been retained in the Cambridge Paragraph Bible. Obvious misprints and the peculiar orthography of the original are excluded, and the dates annexed are those of the editions in which the several variations originated, so far as these can be ascertained.

APPENDIX

Genesis	Reading of the Authorized Bible	Variation of later editions
v. 32; vi. 10; vii. 13	Sem	Shem, 1619
vi. 5	God	GOD[1], 1629
viii. 13	six hundredth and **one**	six hundredth and **first**[2], 1629
ix. 18, 23, 27; x. 1, 2, 21	Japhet	Japheth, 1629
x. 14	Philistiim	Philistim, 1612 (not 1613), 1629
x. 19	Sodoma and Gomorrah (Gomorrah, 1612)	Sodom and Gomorrah, 1629
xiv. 15	Hoba	Hobah, 1638
xv. 7	Caldees (Chaldees, ch. xi. 31)	Chaldees, 1629
xv. 19	Kenizites	Kenizzites, 1629
xvi. 14; xx. 1	Cadesh (Kadesh, ch. xiv. 7)	Kadesh, 1638
xix. 21	this thing	this thing **also**, 1638
xli. 7	and wood	and **the** wood, 1616 (not 1617)
xxiii. 10	gates	gate, 1762
xxxiv. 3 *marg.*	to her heart	to the heart of the damsel, 1744
xxxvi. 33	Bozra	Bozrah, 1613
xxxix. 16	**her lord**	**his** lord, 1638
xii. 40 *marg.*	armed	be armed, 1629

[1] Heb. JEHOVAH. The words —Lord‖ and —God‖ are always intended to be printed in small capitals in the Authorized Version, when they are employed to translate that Holy Name. Adonai Jehovah is represented by —LORD GOD‖ about a hundred times in Ezekiel alone, and Jehovah Adonai by —LORD God‖ only in Hab. Iii. 19, itself corrected (perhaps wrongly) in the Cambridge folio of 1629. See Appendix B II. on Ps. xliv. 23.

[2] In some places this bold archaism (see above, p. 111) is retained in the text of the Cambridge Paragraph bible, e.g. Ezek. xliii. 27; 2 Esdr. vii. 68; I Macc. xiii. 51; 2 Macc. xi. 21; but not in I Kin. vi. 1; xvi. 8, 23.

Exodus	Reading of the Authorized Bible	Variation of later editions
xiv. 25 *marg* xv. 25	made a statute	made **for them** a statute, **1638**
xxi. 19 *marg.*	*ceasing*	*his ceasing*, 1638
xxi. 32	shekels	shekels **of silver,** 1638
xxiii. 13	**names**	name, 1769
xxiii. 27 *marg.*	*neck*s (so all in Josh. vii. 8)	*neck,* 1629
xxvi. 8	and the eleven	and the eleven **curtains,** 1629
xxx. 3 *marg.*	† Hebr. *the roof...and the walls*	† Heb. *roof,* 1629
xxxiv. 25	of Passover	of **the** passover, 1762
xxxv. 11	and his bars	and **his boards,** his bars, 1638
xxxv.29	**hands** of Moses	**hand** of Moses, 1629
xxxvii. 19	Three bowls made **he** after	Three bowls made after, 1629

Leviticus	Reading of the Authorized Bible	Variation of later editions
i. 8	in the fire	**on** the fire, **1638**
i. 9	the inwards	**his** inwards, **1638**
ii. 4	an unleavened **cake**	unleavened **cakes,** 1638
vi. 2	in ‖ fellowship...† violence	‖ in †fellowship ... violence, 1629 (nearly)
vi. 5 *marg.*	† Heb. *the day*	† Heb. *in the day,* 1629
x. 14	the **sacrifice**	the **sacrifices,** 1629
xviii. 21 *marg.*	*Moloc*	*Moloch,* 1629
xix. 34	shall be	shall be **unto you,** 1638
xx. 11	be put	**surely** be put, 1638
xxiii, 10 *marg.*	an Omer	*omer,* 1638
xxiii. 20	for the **priests**	for the **priest,** 1638
xxiii. 22	**the** field	**thy** field, 1638
xxv. 5 marg	*separations*	*separation,* 1629 C.[1], 1630
xxv. 6	**the** stranger	**thy** stranger, 1638
xxv. 31	**walls**	**wall,** 1769
xxvi. 23	reformed	reformed **by me,** 1638

APPENDIX

| xxvi. 40 | **the** iniquity (the iniquities, 1613) | **their** iniquity and the iniquity,1616 |

[1]By 1629, with or without C. annexed, we indicate the Cambridge folio of that year (see above, pp. 19-21), but by 1629 L., the London quarto

Numbers	Reading of the Authorized Bible	Variation of later editions
i. 2, 18, 20	poll	polls, 1769 (so all in ver. 22)
iv. 40	houses	house, 1769 (so all in ver. 42)
vi. 2	ÇÇ prefixed to first .separate.	ÇÇ prefixed to second .separate,. 1744 (not 1762), 1769
vii. 31, 55	charger	charger of the weight, 1762 (so all in ver. 43)
vii. 48, 53 & x. 22	Ammiud	Ammihud, 1638 (so all in ch. 1. 10)
vii. 54, 59 & x. 23	Pedazur	Pedahzur, 1638 (so all in ch. 1. 10)
vii. 61	a silver bowl	one silver bowl, 1638 (so all in ver 55, &c.
xix. 11 marg.	soul	soul of man, 1638
xxi. 20 marg.	hill	the hill, 1638 (Cf. Deut. xxxiv. 1)
xxi. 24	Jabok	Jabbok, 1629, C. and L1 (so all in Gen. xxxii. 22, &c.
xxii. 31 marg.	ÇÇ Bowed	ÇÇ Or bowed, 1629
xxiv. 3 marg.	open	opened
xxvi. 6	Hesron ... Hesronites	Hezron ... Hezronites, Bagster1846
xxvi. 21	Hesron ... Hesronites[2]	Hezron ... Hezronites, 1769

[2] Cambr. Synd. A.3.14 (see above, p. 14), Brit. Mus. 1276. 1.4 (not 3050. g. 2 or g. 3) have "Hezronites" in ver. 21, but "Hesron" in the same verse. Comp. also 1 Chr. v. 3.

Deuteronomy	Reading of the Authorized Bible	Variation of later editions
iv. 25	**shalt** have remained	**ye shall** have remained, 1762
iv. 32	upon earth	upon **the** earth, 1629
iv. 49	**of this side**	**on** this side, 1617 (not 1629 L., 1630), 1629 C.
v. 29	my commandments	**all** my commandments, 1629
ix. 10	of fire	of **the** fire, 1762
x. 10 *marg.*	*fortie*	*former*, 1629
xv. 11 fin.	**the** land	**thy** land, 1629
xvi. 4	**coasts**	**coast**, 1762
xvi. 5	**the** gates	**thy** gates, 1616 (not 1617, 1629 L., 1630), 1629 C.
xix. 6 *marg.*	*third day*	*the third day*, 1612, 1613 (not 1629 C. and L., 1630), 1638. Cf. ver. 4, &c.
xx. 7	in battle	in **the** battle, 1769. Cf. vers. 5, 6
xxvi. 1	the LORD	the LORD **thy God**, 1629, 1637.
xxviii. 5 *marg.*	*kneading troughs*	*kneading trough*, 1762. Cf. Ex. Viii. 3.
xxviii. 23	**the** heaven	**thy** heaven, 1638
xxviii. 42	**locusts**	**locust**, 1612 (not 1613 &c.), 1629
xxix. 26 text *marg.*	† **whom** he had not given † *Hebr. divided*: Or, *who had not given to them any* portion. †	‖ **who he had not** † **given** ‖ Or, who had not given to them any portion. † Heb. *divided*, 1629
xxxii. 15 & xxxiii. 5, 26	Jesurun	Jeshurun, 1638[1]
xxxiv. 1 *marg.*	Hill	*the hill*, 1638. Cf. Num. xxi. 20

[1] In Deut. xxxiii. 5 alone "Jeshurun" is read also in 1629 C and L, 1630. In Isaiah xliv. 2 the same form is found in 1616 alone of all our editions.

APPENDIX

Joshua	Reading of the Authorized Bible	Variation of later editions
iii. 10	Girgashites	the Girgashites, 1612 (not 1613),1629
iii. 15	at the time	all the time, 1638
vii. 14	and the households	and the household, 1616, 1617, 1629 C. (not 1629 L., 1630)
vii. 26	the place	that place, 1629
x. 10 & xvi.	Bethoron	Beth-horon, 1629. Cf. ch. xviii. 13, &c
xi. 8 marg.	burning of waters	burnings of waters, 1629[1]
xi. 17	unto Baal-Gad	even unto Baal-Gad, 1638
xii. 6	and Gadites	and the Gadites, 1762
xii. 11	Lachis	Lachish, 1613 (not 1616, 1617), 1629 C. and L.
xii. 18 marg.	Saron	Sharon, 1629
xiii. 27	Cinneroth	Cinnereth, 1629 – 1762 (Chinnereth, 1769 mod.) Cf. ch. xix. 35
xiii. 29	Manasseh, by	the children of Manasseh, by, 1638
xv. 33	Esthaol	Eshtaol, 1629 (Esthahol, 1630)
xv. 38	Dileam (Diieam 1612, Diliam 1617)	Dilean, 1629
xv. 42	Lebnah (Lebanah, 1630)	Libnah, 1638
xv. 43	Jiphta	Jiphtah, 1638
xv. 49	Kirjath-Sannath	Kirjath-sannah, 1629
xv. 50	Ashtemoth, Camb. Synd. A. 3. 14, but Ashtemoh, Oxf. 1611, 1612, 1613, &c	Eshtemoh, 1638
xv. 57	Gibbeah	Gibeah, 1629 C. and L., 1630
xv. 59	Maarah	Maarath, 1629

xix. 18	Isreel	Jezreel, 1629. Cf. ch. xvii. 16, &c
xix. 22	Shahazimath	Shahazimah, 1617
xix. 35	Cinnereth	Chinnereth, 1769
xix. 38	Bethanah	Beth-anath, 1629
xix. 44	Baalah	Baalath, 1629
xxi. 23	Gibethon	Gibbethon, 1629
xxi. 31	Helkah	Helkath, 1629

¹ Modern editions follow 1672, 1769 in omitting —of waters.||

Judges	Reading of the Authorized Bible	Variation of later editions
i. 31	Achzib, nor Helbath, nor Aphik	of Achzib, nor of Helbah, nor of Aphik, 1762 (Helbah, 1629, &c)
i. 36	*Maale-*	*Maalth-*, 1629
iv. 21	† took (first)	† took (second), 1629
v, 26 text	† smote (first)	† with the hammer
marg.	† Heb. hammered	† Heb. *she hammered*, 1629
v. 29 *marg.*	*words*	*her words*, 1638
v, 30 *marg.*	† Heb. *for the necks of the spoil*	Delet 1638
xi. 1 *marg.*	*Jephte* (Jephthah Heb. xi. 32)	*Jephthae*, 1629
xi. 2	his **wives** sons	his **wife's** sons, 1762¹ (wifes, 1744)
xi. 31 *marg.*	*shall come forth*	*which shall come forth*, 1629
ibid.	Or, *I will offer*	Or, *or I will offer*, 1638
xiv. 17	while **the** feast	while **their** feast, 1638
xxi. 19	Lebanon	Lebonah, 1629

¹ The apostrophe does not appear in our Bibles (see, however, below, p. 235 note 1) before 1762, nor constantly before 1769 (e.g. not in 1762, Ezra ii. 59. Neh. vii. 61, Ps. vi.4; xxxi. 16; xliv. 26; lxxxi. 12; cvii.27; cxl.3, &c). Through the errors of these books, it is sometimes

APPENDIX

misplaced, as is noted in this list within brackets. Cf. 1 Sam. ii. 13. I Chr. vii. 2, 40. Ezra ii. 59. Ps. Lxxxi. 12. Matt. xiv. 9. Mark vi. 26, in which places, unless the contrary be stated, the apostrophe is placed right for the first time in the Cambridge Paragraph Bible.

Ruth	Reading of the Authorized Bible	Variation of later editions
ii. 3 marg.	‖ Called Math. i. 5, Booz	Brought up to ver. 1 marg. in 1762

1 Samuel	Reading of the Authorized Bible	Variation of later editions
i. 20 text	† time	† when, 1638
marg.	*revelation* (so 1612, 1613, 1629 L)	revolution, 1616, 1617, 1629, 1630: *in revolution*, 1638
[ii. 13	**priest's** custom, 1762, 1769	**priests' custom]**, See **p. 152 note.**
iv. 21 marg.	‖ Ichabod, saying, ‖ The glory ‖ *That is, where is the glory,?*‖ *Or, there is the glory*	‖ Ichabod, saying, The glory, ‖ *That is, where is the glory? Or, there is no glory*, 1629
v. 4 marg.	the filthy part[1]	the filthy part, 1616, 1617
vi. 7	**the** calves	**their** calves, 1629
x. 10	a company of **the** prophets	a company of prophets, 1629
x. 23	**the** shoulders	**his** shoulders, 1638
xiii. 18	Bethoron	Beth-horon, 1629
xvii. 38 *marg.*	*clothed*	*clothed David*, 1638
xviii. 27	David arose	David arose **and went**, 1629
xxv. 16	keeping sheep	keeping **his** sheep, 1629
xxviii. 7	And his **servant** said	And his **servants** said, 1629

[1] That this marginal rendering of 1611, 1612, 1613 cannot be designed appears from the version of Temellius and Junius, which,

CLEANING-UP HAZARDOUS MATERIALS

especially in the margin (see above, p. 44), our Translators closely follow;—*quod referebat piscem.* See Cardwell, *Oxford Bibles*, p. 16.

2 Samuel	Reading of the Authorized Bible	Variation of later editions
iii. 26	Shiriah	Sirah, 1629
vi. 12	pertained	pertaineth, 1638
viii. 11	he had dedicate[1]	he had dedicated, 1612 (not 1613)
xi. 1	that after the year (that 1613)	after this year, 1762
xi. 3 [marg.]	Bath-Shuah, 1762, 1769	Bath-shua, Bagster 1846, American 1867. Cf. 1 Ch. iii. 5
xi. 21	Jerubesheth	Jerubbesheth, 1629
xiii. 20 marg.	set not thine heart	set not thine heart upon, So Bagster 1846, Cf. ch. xviii. 3 marg.
xv. 3 marg.	none will hear you	none will hear thee, 1638
xvi. 12	requite good	requite me good, 1629
xix. 34 marg.	† How many	† Heb. How many, 1616, 1617
xxi. 4 marg.	silver or gold	silver nor gold, 1616, 1617
xxiii. 32	Eliahaba	Eliahba, 1629
xxiii. 37	Berothite	Beerothite, 1629

[1] But these archaisms we have elsewhere retained: e.g. 2 Kin. xii. 18. See above, p. 102. Compare I Chr. xxvi.20, Appendix C pp. 220, 221.

1 Kings	Reading of the Authorized Bible	Variation of later editions
iv. 10	Heseb, marg. Ben-Heseb	Hesed, marg. Ben-Hesed, 1629
vi. 1	fourscore1 ... Cf., ch. xvi. 8, 23	eightieth, 1762
vii. 42 marg.	upon the face Cf. 2 Chr. Iv. 13 marg.	upon the face of the pillars, 1638
vii. 51 marg.	things of David	holy things of David, 1629
viii. 61	the LORD your God	the LORD our God, 1629
ix. 11	that then Solomon	that then king Solomon, 1638

APPENDIX

ibid.	Galile (Tobit i. 2)	Galilee, 1629. Cf. C. and L., 1630
xi. 1	Sydonians Camb. Synd. A 3.14 but Sidonians Oxf. 1611, 1612-1638	Zidonians, 1629. Cf. vers. 5. 33
xi. 5	Amorites (Ammorites 1612)	Ammonites, 1629
xi. 33	Ashtaroth (pl. Cf. Judg. X. 6)	Ashtoreth, 1629. Cf. ver. 5
xiii. 6	was restored again	was restored him again, 1638
xiv. 4 marg.	stood for hoariness	stood for his hoariness, 1638
xv. 2 [marg.]	Michaia, 1769	Michaiah, Bagster 1846, Camb. 1858, American 1867. Cf. 2 Chr. xiii. 2
xv. 10 marg.	grandmother	grandmothers, 1638, 's, 1762
xv. 14	Asa his heart[1]	Asa's heart, 1762
xv. 19	break the league	break thy league, 1629 C. and L., 1630
xvi. 8	twentieth and sixt (sixth 1613)	twenty and sixth, 1629. Cf. vers. 10, 15
xvi. 23	the thirty and one year[1]	the thirty and first year, 1769

[1] For these archaisms see above, p. 111.

2 Kings	Reading of the Authorized Bible	Variation of later editions
v. 11 *marg.*	† Heb. *said*	† *I said*, 1617 (not 1629 C. and L., 1630), 1638
viii., 19	promised	promised **him**, 1629
ix. 23	turned his **hand (Vulgate)**	turned his **hands**, (Heb., LXX.) 1629
xi. 10	the Temple	the temple **of the Lord**, 1638
xii. 19, 20	Jehoash	Joash, 1629
xiii. 24	Hazael **the** king of Syria	Hazael king of Syria, (not 1613), 1629
xv. 15	**the** conspiracy	**his conspiracy, 1638**
xviii. 8	fenced **cities**	fenced **city**, 1629
xviii. 18	Helkiah (so ver. 37 Camb. Synd. A. 3.14 alone, not being a reprint; see above, p. 6).	Hilkiah, 1629
xix. 37	Adramelech	Adrammelech, 1638. Cf. ch.

CLEANING-UP HAZARDOUS MATERIALS

		xvii.31.
xx. 1	Amos	Amoz, 1629. Cf. ch. xix. 2, 20
xx. 13	shewed them the house	shewed them **all** the house, 1638
xxi. 21 & xxii, 2	all the **ways**	all the **way**, 1629
xxiii. 13	Milchom	Milcom, 1638
xxiii. 21	this book of **the** Covenant	this book of **this** covenant, 1629[1]
xxiii. 31	Hamital	Hamutal, 1629
xxiv. 13	and the **treasure**	and the **treasures**, 1629
xxiv. 19	Jehoiachin (Cf. LXX.)	Jehoiakim, 1629
xxv. 4, 5, 10, 13, 24, 25, 26	Caldees	Chaldees, 1744

[1] This rendering of 1611 is quite justifiable, but the LXX, and Vulgate translate as in 1629.

1 Chronicles	Reading of the Authorized Bible	Variation of later editions
i. 9	Siba	Seba, 1629
i. 20	Hazermaveth	Hazarmaveth, 1634, 1638
i. 33	Ephar	Epher, 1638
i. 39 *marg.*	*Heman* 1611-1769$_2$ (Hemah 1617)	*Hemam*, Bagster 1846, Camb. 1858, American, 1867
i. 40 *marg.*	*Sepho*	*Shepho*, 1629. Cf. Gen. xxxvi. 23
i. 42	Bilham…Dishon	Bilhan, 1629 … Dishan, 1638
i. 44	Bosrah	Bozrah, 1629. Cf. Isai. Lxiii. 1, &c.
ii. 10	Aminadab *bis*	Amminadab *bis*, 1629
ii. 13 *marg.*	*Shamma*	*Shammah*, 1629
ii. 14	Nathanael	Nethaneel, 1638
ii. 18	Shobab	**and** Shobab, 1629
ii. 25	Ozen	Ozem, 1629
ii. 27	Ekar	Eker, 1638
ii. 42	Maresha	Mareshah, 1638. Cf. ch. iv. 21
ii. 48	Maacha. Cf. ch. ix. 35	Maachah, 1638
ii. 52 & iv. 1 *marg.*	Haroe	Haroeh, 1638
ii. 54	Salmah	Salma, 1638. Cf. ver. 51

APPENDIX

iii. 2	Maacha ... Adoniah	Maacha, 1638 ... Adonijah, 1629. Cf. 1 Kings. 5, &c.
iii. 3	Shaphatia	Shaphatia, 1629
iii. 5 *marg.*	*Bethsabe*	*Bath-sheba*, 1629
iii. 7	Noga	Nogah, 1638
iii. 8 *marg.*	*Beliada*	*Beeliada*, 1769 (*Becliada*, 1762)
iii. 10 *marg.*	*Abiam*	*Abijam*, 1629
iii. 11 *marg.*	*and*	*or, Jehoahaz*, 2 Chr., 1762
iii. 15, 16	Joakim	Jehoiakim, 1619
iii. 15 *marg.*	*Joachaz*	*Jehoahaz*, 1629
ibid.	Mathania	Mattaniah, 1638 (*Mattonia*, 1629)
iii. 15	Sallum	Shallum, 1629
iii. 16	‖ Zedekiah his son	Zedekiah* his son₁
iii. 18	Hosanna, Camb. Synd. A. 3. 14, B. M. 1276. 1.4 only. Hosama, Oxf. 1611, 1612-1630.	Hoshama, 1638
iii. 20	Hazubah	Hashubah, 1629
iii. 22	Semaiah, *bis*	Shemaiah, *bis*, 1629
iv. 6	Ahusam ... Ahashtari	Ahuzam, 1629 ... Haahashtari, 1638
iv. 7	Zoar	Jezoar, 1638
iv. 13	Saraia (Saraiah, 1616)	Seraiah, 1629. Cf. ver. 14
iv. 14	Charasim	Charashim, 1629
iv. 20	Simeon	Shimon, 1629. Cf. ver. 24
iv. 29	Bilha, *marg. Bela*	Bilhah, 1638, *marg. Balah*, 1629
iv. 31 *marg.*	*Hazar-Susa*	*Hazar-susah*, 1629
iv. 34	Amashiah	Amaziah, 1629
iv. 35	Josibia ... Seraia	Josibiah, 1629 ... Seraiah, 1638
iv. 36.	Jehohaiah, Camb. Synd. A. 4. 14 alone, but Jesohaiah, Oxf. 1611, 1612-1630	Jeshohaiah, 1638
iv. 37	Jedaia	Jedaiah, 1638
v. 2	chief ‖ **rulers**	‖ chief **ruler**, 1629 (place of changed by Bagster 1846)
v. 3	Ezron	Hezron, 1629
v. 6 *marg.*	*Tiglath-pilneser*	*Tiglath-pileser*, 1629

v. 8	Asah (Aza, 1630)	Azaz, 1629
vi. 2, 22 *marg*	Izahar	Izhar, 1629 Cf. vers. 18, 38
vi. 21 *marg.*	*Adaia*	*Adaiah*, 1629. Cf. ver. 41
vi. 40	Baasiah ... Melchiah	Baaseiah ... Malchiah, 1638
vi. 57	Libna	Libnah, 1638₁
vi. 60	Anathoth (Anathoch, 1617)	and Anathoth, 1629
vi. 69 & viii. 13	Aialon	Aijalon, 1629
vi. 78 *marg.*	‖ Or, *Bozor, Josh.* Xxi. 35	Delet 1629
[vii. 2, 40	**father's** house, 1762, 1869	**fathers'** house], see p. 152 note
vii. 18	Ishad	Ishod, 1638
vii. 18 [*marg.*]	*Jezer*, 1762, 1769	*Jeezer*, Bagster 1846, Camb. 1858, Amer. 1867. Cf. Num. xxvi. 30
vii. 24	Bethoron	Beth-horon, 1629
vii. 25	Reseph	Resheph, 1638
vii. 26 & ix. 4	Amihud	Ammihud, 1629
vii. 32	Shuah	Shua, 1638
viii. 11	Ahitub	Abitub, 1629
viii. 14	Jerimoth	Jeremoth, 1638
viii. 31	Gidor	Gedor, 1638. Cf. ch. ix. 37
viii. 31 *marg.*	*Zachariah*	*Zechariah*, 1629
viii. 36	Asmaveth	Azmaveth, 1638. Cf. ch. ix. 42
viii. 37	Elasa	Elessah, 1638. Cf. ch. ix. 43
ix. 12	Maasia	Maasiai, 1629
ix. 35	Maacha. Cf. ch. 11. 48	Maachah, 1629
ix. 44	Ismael	Ishmael, 1638. Cf. ch. viii. 38
x. 2 *marg.*	*Ieshui*	*Ishui*, 1629. Cf. 1 Sam. xiv. 49
xi. 15	to the rock **of** David	to the rock **to** David, 1629
xi. 33	Elihaba	Eliahba, 1629
xi. 34	Shageh	Shage, 1629
xi. 43	Maacah	Maachah, 1638
xi. 45	Zimri, *marg. Zimrite*	Shimri, *marg. Shimrite*, 1629
xi. 46	Elnaan	Elnaam, 1629
xii. 3 *marg.*	*Hasmaa*	*Hasmaah*, 1629
xii. 5	Bealiath	Bealiah, 1638
xii. 6	Azariel	Azareel, 1638
xii. 7	Jeroam	Jeroham, 1613 (not 1612, 1616, 1617, 1629 L., 1630), 1629 C.

APPENDIX

xii. 10	Mashmannah	Mishmannah, 1638
xii. 11	Atthai	Attai, 1629
xii. 20	Jediel	Jediael, 1638
xiii. 11 *marg.*	Heb.	That is, 1629
xiv. 6	Noga	Nogah, 1638
xiv. 7	Elpalet	Eliphalet, 1629
xv. 18, 20	**Zachariah**	Zechariah, 1638
xv. 18	Jaziel	Jaaziel, 1638
xv. 18, 20	Maasiah	Maaseiah, 1638. See 2 Chr. xxiii. 1
xv. 18, 21	Eliphaleh (Eliphaleb, 1612, ver. 18) ... Mikniah	Elipheleh ... Mikneiah, 1638
xv. 18	Jehiel (*second*)	Jeiel, 1629$_1$
xv. 21	Azzaziah	Azzaziah, 1638
xv. 24	Nathaneel ... Zachariah (so ch. xvi. 5)	Nethaneel ... Zechariah (so ch. xvi. 5), 1636
xviii. 8 *marg.*	Beta	*Betah*, 1769. Cf. 2 Sam. viii. 8
viii. 16 *marg.*	*Saraiah ··· Sisa*	*Seraiah ··· Shisha*, 1629. Cf. 2 Sam. viii. 17; 1 Kin. iv. 3
xxi. 7 *marg.*	† *And it was*	† Heb. *And it was*, 1616, 1615
xxiii. 10 *marg.* & ver. 11	Zisa	Zizah, 1638
xxiii. 19	Jekamiam	Jekameam, 1629
xxiii. 22	Jerimoth$_1$	Jeremoth, 1629
xxiii. 6	Nathanael	Nethaneel, 1638. Cf. ch. xxvi. 4.
xxiv 20	Jedeiah	Jehdeiah, 1629
xxv. 2 *marg.*	*by the hand*	*by the hands*, 1629. Cf. ver 6
xxv. 4	Eliatha	Eliathah, 1638. Cf. ver 27
xxv. 22	Jerimoth	Jeremoth
xxvi. 1 *marg.*	*Abiasaph*	*Ebiasaph*, 1629
xxvi. 16	Hosa	Hosah, 1629. Cf. ver. 10, ch. xvi. 38.
xxvi. 18 init.	**And** Parbar	**At** Parbar, 1638
xxvii. 6	Amizabad	Ammizabad, 1638
xxvii. 20	Azazziah	Azaziah, 1629
xxvii. 22	Azariel	Azareel, 1629
xvii. 27	Sabdi (Zabdi 1612) the Ziphmite	Zabdi the Shiphmite, 1629
xxvii. 29	Shetrai	Shitrai, 1638.
xvii. 33, 34	Ahitophel	Ahithophel, 1638. Cf. 2 Sam.

		xv. 12, 31, &c.
xxix. 2	the silver for *things*	**and** the silver for *things*, 1629
xxix. 29	‖ book of Samuel ... †book of Nathan	‖ book of Samuel... book of Nathan, 1629

[1] In ver. 4 the vowel points are different, and —Jerimoth‖ correct.

2 Chronicles	Reading of the Authorized Bible	Variation of later editions
iii. 10	most holy **place**	most holy **house**, 1629,
iv. 13 *marg.*	*upon the face*	add *of the pillars*. So Bagster 1846, also 1638 mod. In I Kin. vii. 42
vi. 27	**the** land	**thy** land, 1638
xi. 8	Maresha	Mareshah, 1638
xi. 10	Aialon	Aijalon, 1629. See p. 138 note 2
xi. 20	Atthai	Attai
xi. 20-22	Maacah	Maachah, 1629
xiii. 2	Gibea	Gibeah, 1629
xiii. 6	his **LORD**[1]	his **lord**
xviii. 7,8	Jimla (Jimlah, 1630)	Imla, 1612, 1638. But cf. I Kin. xxii.8, 9.
xx. 14 & xxix. 13	Jehiel	Jeiel, 1638[2]
xxiii. 1 & xxvi. 11 & xxxiv. 8	Maasiah	Maaseiah, 1638. Cf. ch xxvii. 7. See also 1 Chr. xv. 18, 20; Ezra x. 18
xxiv. 26	Shimeah	Shimeath, 1629
xxvi. 1	Jehoadan (Jehoiadan 1612)	Jehoaddan, 1638
xxv, 23	Joahaz	Jehoahaz
xxvii. 5 *marg.*	† *Heb. much*	† *Heb. this,* 1629
xxviii. 11	wrath of **God**	wrath of **the LORD**
xxviii. 22	**this** distress	**his** distress, 1638
xxix. 12	Amashai ... Jahalelel	Amasai, 1629, Jehalelel
xxix. 15 *marg.*	*of the Lord*₁	*of the LORD*, 1629
xxix. 27	with the †instruments	with † the instruments, Bagster 1846
xxxi. 5 *marg.*	*brought forth*	*brake forth,* 1629
xxxi. 6	**tithes** of oxen	**tithe** of oxen, 1638

APPENDIX

xxxi. 14	Immah (Immath 1612)	Imnah, 1629
xxxii. 5	**prepared** Millo	**repaired** Millo, 1616, 1617
xxxii. 10	For this *cause*	And for this *cause*, 1638
xxxiv. 12	Sechariah	Zechariah, 1612 (not 1613), 1629
xxxv. 8	Zachariah	Zechariah, 1638
xxxv. 9	Jehiel ... Joshabad	Jeiel[1]
xxxvi. 17	Caldees	Chaldees, 1638

[1] A strange oversight (retained up to 1630) in a matter about which our Translators are usually more careful than later editors, viz. in representing יהוה by LORD (or GOD, see p. 147 note 1) but יצדא by "Lord" or "lord." In ch. xxix. 15 marg. "Lord" is a misprint, the text being correct. Compare also Neh. i. 11; iii. 5; viii. 10. Ps. Ii. 4, and Append. C. p. 233 note 3.

[2] See above, p. 159 note.

Ezra	Reading of the Authorized Bible	Variation of later editions
ii. 2	Saraiah (Saraioh, 1617)	Seraiah, 1629. Cf. Neh. vii. 7 *marg*
ii. 22	The **children** of Netophah	The **men** of Netophah, 1638
ii. 24, *marg.*	Beth-Asmaveth	*Beth-asmaveth*, 1629, Cf. Neh. vii. 28
ii. 40	Hodavia, marg. Juda	Hodaviah, marg. Judah, 1629. Cf.Neh. vii. 43 marg.
ii. 50	Nephushim	Nephusim, 1629
[ii. 59	**father's**, 1769	**fathers'**]. See above, p. 152 note
iii. 2 marg.	Josua (but Josuah, Hagg. i. 1)	Joshua, 1613 (but Josuah, Hagg. i. 1)
iii. 5	that willingly offered, **offered** / add word?	that willingly offered, 1613
iv. 9	Apharsathkites	Apharsathchites. 1629
v. 12	Caldean	Chaldean, 1638
vii. 4	Zeraiah	Zerahiah, 1638. Cf. ch. viii. 4
vii. 9 *marg*	† *He* (*Hee*, 1616) *was the foundation*, 1611, 1612, 1613, 1616, 1617	† Heb. was *the foundation*, 1629 C.: was the f., 1629 L., 1630

vii. 23 *marg.*	† Heb. *Whatsoever*	† Chald. *Whatsoever*, Bagster, 1846
viii. 13 & x. 43	Jehiel	Jeiel[1], 1638
viii. 16	and for Jarib	also for Joiarib, 1638
x. 18, 21, 22, 30	Maasiah	Maaseiah, 1638. So Neh. iii. 23; viii. 4, 7; x. 25; xi. 5, 7; xii. 41, 42 in 1611. See 2 Chr. xxiii. 1.
x. 23	Kelitah	Kelita (″ א), 1638
x. 25	Jesiah	Jeziah, 1638
x. 33	Mattatha	Mattathah (″ ה), 1638
x. 35	Bedaiah	Bedeiah, 1638
x. 38	Bennui (Benui, 1612)	Binnui, 1638

Nehemiah	Reading of Authorized Bible	Variations of later editions
i. 11	O LORD (1611-1769)	O Lord, Oxf. 1835, Camb 1858, Amer. 1867. See above. P. 147 note.
ii. 12	what God hath put	what my God hath put, 1638
iii. 4, 21 & x. 5 & xii. 3	Merimoth	Meremoth
iii. 5, & viii. 10 prim.	LORD	Lord, 1629. See above, p. 147 note 1.
iii. 6	Besodiah	Besodeiah, 1628
iii. 15	Shallum	Shallun, 1629
vi. 10	Mehetable, Camb. Synd. A. 3. 14, B.M. 1276. l. 4 only, but Mehetabl, Oxf. 1611-1630	Mehetabeel, 1638
vi. 17 marg.	multiplied letters	multiplied their letters, 1629
vii. 7	Nahum	Nehum, 1638
vii. 24 marg.	Jora	Jorah. Bagster 1846. Cf. Ezra ii. 18
vii. 31	Michmash	Michmas, 1638
vi. 38	Senaa	Senaah, 1629. Cf. Ezra ii. 35
vii. 39	Jedaia	Jedaiah, 1629. Cf. Ezra ii. 36
vii. 46	Tabaoth	Tabbaoth, 1638. Cf. Ezra ii. 43

APPENDIX

vii. 54	Baslith	Bazlith, 1629
[vii. 61	father's, 1869	fathers']. See above, p. 152 note
ix. 7	Caldees	Chaldees, 1638
ix. 17	the wonders	thy wonders, 1638
x. 11	Micah	Micha, 1629. Cf. ch. xi. 17, 22
x. 18	Hodiah (Hodaiah, 1616)	Hodijah, 1638. Cf. ver. 13
xi. 8	Gabai	Gabbai, 1638
xi. 13	Meshilemoth	Meshillemoth, 1638
xi. 24	Meshezabel	Meshezabeel, 1612 (not 1613, &c), 1638
xi. 27	Hazer-Shual	Hazar-shual, 1638
xi. 28	Ziglag	Ziklag, 1612, 1613 (not 1629 L., 1630)
xii. 3 marg.	Sebaniah	Shebaniah, 1629 (not 1638), 1744. Cf. ver. 14
xii. 5	Madiah	Maadiah, 1638
xii. 21, 36	Nethanael	Nethaneel, 1629
xii. 36	Asarael	Azarael, 1629
xii. 41	Zachariah	Zechariah, 1638

Esther	Reading of the Authorized Bible	Variation of later editions
i. 8	for the king had appointed	for so the king had appointed, 1629
i. 9, 11, 12, 15-17, 19; ii. 1, 4, 17	Vasthi (Vulg.)	Vashti, 1629
i. 14	Tarshis	Tarshish, 1629
iii. 1	Amedath (Amm. 1629 C.)	Hammedatha, 1638. Cf. ch. viii.5; ix. 10, 24
iii. 4	Mordecai his matters	Mordecai's matters
iv. 4	the sackcloth	his sackcloth, 1629

Job	Reading of the Authorized Bible	Variation of later editions

i. 17	Caldeans	Chaldeans, 1638
iv. 6	; the uprightness of thy ways (, 1616, 1617) and thy hope?	, thy hope, and the uprightness of thy ways?[1] 1638
iv. 19	on them that	in them that, 1762. Cf. ver. 18
xx. 21 marg.	meats	meat, 1629
xxiv. 19 marg.	take it	take, 1629
xxiv. 22	// and no man	and // no man, Bagster 1846
xxxiii. 22	His soul draweth	Yea, his soul draweth, 1638
xxxix. 30	there is he	there is she
xli. 5	wilt thou bind	or wilt thou bind, 1638
xlii. 10 marg.	added to Job	added all that had been to Job, 1638

[1] In 1629, 1637 we find "; and the uprightness of thy ways, thy hope?" Though this has been noted as a mere error, the changes both of 1629 and 1638 (which all later editions have followed) are plainly unintentional and unique for their boldness. In the Paragraph Bible we have changed the comma after "hope" into a semicolon, although the Hebrew has only *Rebia* and *Athnakh* in the word before. Cf. Grote MS. Pp. 130, 131.

Psalms	Reading of the Authorized Bible	Variation of later editions
ii. 6 & marg.	Sion	Zion, 1638[2]. Cf. Ps. lxix. 35
xxix. 8, 9	ÇÇ shaketh ... to calve	shaketh ... ÇÇ to calve, 1629
xxxiv. 5	ÇÇ They looked ... were lightened	They looked ... ÇÇ were lightened,1629, 1638
xxxvii. 3 marg.	in truth and stableness	in truth, or stableness (1629), 1638
xxxix. 6 marg.	image	an image, 1629
xlii. 6	Missar	Mizar, 1629
xlii. 9	God, My (my 1612, 1630) rock, why	God my rock, Why (1629), 1638
xliv. title	of Korah	of Korah, Maschill, 1629
liii. 6	Jaakob (Jakob, 1630)	Jacob, 1619, 1638

APPENDIX

lix. title marg.	ÇÇ Or, to the chief Musician, destroy	ÇÇ Destroy, 1638. Cf. Ps. lviii. & lxxv. titles marg.
lxii. 10	become not vain	and become not vain, 1629
lxv. 1	Sion	Zion, Amer. 1867 only. See below, note 2
lxv. 9	and ÇÇ waterest it	ÇÇ and waterest it. Bagster 1846
lxix. 32	seek good	seek God, 1617
lxix. 35	Sion	Zion, 1761.Cf. p. 165 note 2
lxxv. title marg.	ÇÇ Or, to the chief musician destroy not (Altaschith, 1616, 1617 for [destroy not]) a psalm or song for Asaph.	ÇÇ Or, Destroy not, ÇÇ Or, for Asaph, 1638
[lxxxi. 12	hearts¹, 1769	heart's]. See p. 152 note.
lxxxix. 4 marg.	to generation and generation	Deest (ver. 4 being cited in ver. 1marg.) 1762.
xcix. 1	all people	all the people, 1612 (not 1613, &c.), 1769
cv. 30	The land	Their land, 1638.
cvii. 43	those things	these things, 1762
cxix. 101	that I may keep	that I might keep, 1638
cxxvii. 1 text *marg.*	that† (// Camb. Synd. A.3. 14; B.M. 1276.1.4 only; 1613) build † Heb. are builders	† that build † *that are builders*, 1638.
cxxii. 6	Ephrata	Ephratah, 1629. Cf. Ruth iv. 11; Mic. v.2.
cxxxix. 7	**fly**, Camb Synd. A.3. 14, & B.M. 1276, l.4 only, 1612, 1630; flie, Oxf. 1611, 1613-1629 L.	**flee**, 1629 C. Cf. Prov. xxviii. 17. See 2 Esdr. xiv. 15
[xzl. 3	**adders'**, 1769	**adder's**]. Cf. Isai. lix. 3 *marg.*
cxliii. 9	**flie**	**flee**, 1616 (not 1617), 1629

¹ The "eagle" should have been masculine throughout vers. 27-30, but after having regarded it as feminine thus far, it is too late to change here.

[2] So Ps. ix. 11, 14; xiv. 7; xx. 2; xlviii. 2, 11, 12; l. 2; li. 18; liii. 6; lxxiv. 2; lxxvi. 2; lxxviii. 68; xcvii. 8. Elsewhere 1611 has "Zion" except in Ps. lxv. 1, where all have "Sion" except Amer. 1867. Cf. Ps. lxix. 35

Proverbs	Reading of the Authorized Bible	Variation of later editions
vi. 19	and him that soweth	and he that soweth, 1769
vii. 21	With much fair speech	With her much fair speech, 1938
x. 23	as a sport (a sport, 1629 C.)	as sport, 1638
xi. 1	A † false	† A false, Bagster 1846 (So read.)
xx. 14	nought bis	naught bis, 1638
[xxvi. 3	the fool's, 1761	the fools']/ See [/ 152
xxvii. 26	thy field	the field, 1638
xxvii. 17	flie	flee, 1617 (not 1629L., 1630), 1629. Cf. Ps. cxxxix. 7
[xxxi. 14	merchants', 1769 (merchant, 1762)	merchant's], Cf. ch. xxx. 28. See p. 152 note.
Eccles.	Reading of the Authorized Bible	Variation of later editions
i. 5	**the** place	**his** place, 1628
ii. 16	shall be forgotten	shall **all** be forgotten, 1629
vii. 26 *marg.*	† *He* [*Hee.* 1613) that is (†Heb. *that is*, 1612 L., 1630)	† Heb. *he that is*, 1616 (not 1617), 1629
viii. 17	seek it out	seek it out, **yet he shall not find**

Canticles	Reading of the Authorized Bible	Variation of later editions
iv. 6	**mountains** of myrrh	**mountain** of myrrh, 1629
v. 12	rivers of **water**	rivers of **waters**, 1616 (not 1617, 1629 L., 1630), 1629

APPENDIX

vi. 5	is a flock	is **as** a flock, 1616, 1617, Cf. ch. iv. 1.
vi. 12 *marg.*	*the chariot*	*the chariots*, 1629

Isaiah	Reading of the Authorized Bible	Variation of later editions
viii. 8 *marg.*	*stretching*	*stretchings*, 1629
ix. 1	Galile. See Tobit i. 2	Galilee, 1629
xxiii. 13 & xlii. 14 & xlvii. 1, 5 & xlviii. 14, 20	Caldeans	Chaldeans, 1638 (1630, ch. Xivii. 5).
xxviii. 4	seeth **it** (it. 1638, 1744)	seeth, 1683 (Grote MS. P. 93), 1762
xxviii. 26 *marg.*	*as God*	*as his God*, 1629
xxix. 1 text	Woe…‖ the city	.ytic eht ‖…eoW ‖
marg.	*God*: Or, *of the city*	*God*. ,rO ‖*of the city*, 1629
xxxi. 9 text *marg.*	he shall … ‖ his strong (‖†his strong, 1629) ,rO ‖*his strength*: Heb. *rocke*	† he shall… ‖ his strong † Heb. *his rock*, &c. Or, *his strength*, 1638.
xxxiv. 11	The cormorant	**But** the cormorant, 1629
xxxvii. 17 *marg.*	*me*	*my soul*, 1638
xliv. 2	Jesurun	Jeshurun, 1616, Amer. 1867, only. See p. 150 note
xliv. 20	feedeth **of** ashes	feedeth **on** ashes, 1762
xlvii. 6	**the** yoke	**thy** yoke, 1629
xlix. 13	**heaven…God**	**heavens**, 1629 … **the LORD**, 1638
liii. 6 marg	**he** hath made	hath made, 1629
lvii. 8	made a covenant	made **thee** a covenant, 1638[1].
[lix. 5 marg.	**adders'**, 1769	**adder's**, Bagster 1846, Amer. 1867]. Cf. Ps. cxl. 3
lxii. 8 marg	if **he** give	if **I** give, 1629
lxiv. 1	**rent** the heavens (see p. 102)	**rend** the heavens, 1762
lxvi. 9	gnirb ot esuac … gnirb ‖	bring … ‖ cause to bring, 1629

355

[1] Cardwell (Oxford Bibles, pl 16) imputes this change to Bp. Lloyd in 1701. But he knew no more of Camb. 1638 than Bp. Turton did of Camb. 1629. See above, p. 41 note.

[2] So ch. xxii. 25; xxiv. 5; xxv. 12; xxxii. 4, 5, 24, 25, 28, 29, 43; xxxiii. 5; xxxv. 11; xxxvii. 5, 8-11, 13, 14l\; xxxviii. 2, 18, 19, 23; xl. 9, 10; xli. 3, 18; xliii. 3; l. 1, 8, 25, 35, 45; li. 4, 54; lii. 7, 8, 14, 17.

Jeremiah	Reading of the Authorized Bible	Variation of later editions
i. 13	the face thereof **was**	the face thereof **is**, 1762
iv. 6	**standards**	standard, 1629
xii. 15	will bring again	will bring **them** again, 1629
xv. 4 *marg*	*a moving*	*a removing*, 1629
xix. 11	no place **else** to bury	no place to bury, 1629 C., 1638
xxi. 4, 9	Caldeans	Chaldeans, 1638[2]
xxiii. 30	my **word**	my **words**, 1638
xxiv. 5 *marg.*	*captivity*	*the captivity*, 1629
xxvi. 18	Morashite	Morashite, 1629 Cf. Micah i.1.
ibid.	the high places	**as** the high places, 1629 Cf. Micah iii. 12
xxvii. 6	**the** words	**thy** words, 1629
xxxi. 14	goodness	**my** goodness, 1629
xxxi. 18	thou art the Lord	**for** thou art the Lord, 1629
xxxiii. 16 *marg.*	*Jehova [Iehova]*	*Jehovah*, 1629
xxxv. 13	and inhabitants	and **the** inhabitants, 1616 (not 1617), 1629
xxxv. 19 text	Jonadab...†Heb.**want** (†**shall not want**, 1629)	Jonadab...want.
marg.	† Heb. *there shall not a man be cut off from*, &c.	†Heb. *There shall not be cut off from Jonadab the son of Rechab*
xxvii. 24 *marg.*	or, lie	, or *a lie*, 1638.
xxxvii. 16	So the king	So **Zedekiah** the king, 1638
xl. 1	Ramath	Ramah, 1629 C. and L. (not 1630), 1638
xl. 5 9, 10 text *marg.*	all **the** cities ver. 9 † to	the cities, 1638 ver. 10.

APPENDIX

	serve †Heb. *to stand before. And so* verse 10¹	† *to serve.* † Heb. *to stand before*, 1629-1769, Bagster 1846, American 1867
xli. 1	Elishamah	Elishama, 1638.
xlii. 16	after you in Egypt	after you **there** in Egypt, 1629
xlviii. 36	**is** perished	**are** perished, 1762
xlix. 1	inherit **God** (so 1612, 1623)	inherit **Gad**, 1616, 1617... 1629 C. and L.
l. 10 & li. 24, 35	Caldea	Chaldea, 1638
li. 12	**watchman**	**watchmen**, 1629
li. 27	**her** horses	**the** horses, 1638
li. 30	**their** dwelling places	**her** dwelling places, 1629
lii. 31	Jehoiakim *bis*	Jehoiachin *bis* (Jehoiakin 1616), 1629

¹ This gross error of 1611-1630, though corrected long ago, is revived in most modern Bibles, e.g. D'Oyly & Mant 1817, Oxford 1835, Camb. 1858.

Lamentations	Reading of the Authorized Bible	Variation of later editions
ii. 2 *marg.*	*made to couch*₁	*made to touch*, 1629

₁ This rendering might possibly stand, but that Tremellius, from whose version our Translators mostly derived their margin in the Old Testament (see above, p. 44), has Heb. *facit ut pertineat*. Hence −*couch*‖ is a mere misprint.

Ezekiel	Reading of the Authorized Bible	Variation of later editions
i. 1	Jehoiakins	Jehoiachins, 1629 C. and L. (Jehoiakims 1617, 1630), 1638.
i. 3 & xii. 14 & xxiii. 14, 23	Caldeans	Chaldeans, 1638 (1612, ch. i. 3).
i. 17	**returned**	**turned**, 1769. Cf. vers. 9, 12
iii. 5 *marg.*	*deep of lips*	*deep of lip*, 1629

CLEANING-UP HAZARDOUS MATERIALS

iii. 6 *marg.*	*heavy language*	*heavy of language*, 1629
iii. 11	thy people	**the children of** thy people, 1638
iii. 26 marg.	nam A ||	† Heb. a man, 1629
v. i.	take **the** balances	take **thee** balances, 1638
vi. 8	that **he** may have	that **ye** may have, 1613
xi. 24 & xvi. 29 & xxiii. 15, 16	Caldea	Chaldea, 1638 (1630 ch. xvi. 29)
xii. 19	of them that dwell	of **all** them that dwell, 1629
xxi. 30 marg.	cause **to** it to return	cause it to return, 1629 C. and L.
[xxii. 10	**fathers'**, 1769	**father's**]. See above, p. 152 note.
xxiii. 23	Shoah	Shoa, 1629
xxiii. 43 marg.	smoderohw reH || ||	†† Heb. her whoredoms, 1629 C. & L. († † Heb. whordoms, 1617)
xxiv. 5	let **him** seethe	let **them** seethe, 1638
xxiv. 7	poured it	poured it **not**, 1613
xxiv. 25 marg	of **the** soul	of **their** soul, 1638
xxvi. 14	**they shall** be a place	**thou shalt** be a place, 1638
xxvii. 6 marg.	made hatches	made **thy** hatches, 1629
xxvii. 16 marg.	works	**thy** works, 1638
xxvii. 22, 23	Shebah	Sheba, 1638
xxvii. 27 marg.	**withal**, 1611-1630 (withal, 1744)	**with all**, 1629, 1638, 1762
xxxi. 4	† Heb. conduits	boJ .fC .8361 ,stiudnoc ,rO || xxxviii. 25.
xxxii. 22	Ashur	Asshur, 1638
xxxii. 25	all her **multitudes**	all her **multitude**, 1629
xxxiv. 28	**beasts** of the land	**beast** of the land, 1762
xxxiv. 31	my flock of my pasture	my flock **the flock** of my pasture, 1629
xxxvi. 2	the enemy **had** said	the enemy **hath** said, 1630 (not 1629 C. & L., 1638, 1744), 1771

APPENDIX

xxxvi. 15	the nations	thy nations, 1629
xxxix. 11	at that day	in that day, 1638
xlii. 17	a measuring reed	the measuring reed, 1638 Cf. vers. 16, 18, 19
xliii. 3 marg	See chap. 9. 2, 5	See ch. 9. 1, 5, 1769
xliv. 23	cause **men**	cause **them**, 1629
[xliv. 30	the **priest's**, 1769	the **priests'**], Gorle. See above, p. 79 note 2, and p. 152 note.
xlvi. 13 marg	of his year	a **son** of his year, 1638
xlvi. 23	a **new** building	a **row of** building, 1638
xlviii. 8	**they** shall offer	**ye** shall offer, 1638

Daniel	Reading of the Authorized Bible	Variation of later editions
i. 4	Caldeans	Chaldeans, 1638[1].
i.. 12	give † pulse	give us † pulse 1629
ii. 5 *marg.*	Cal. (2Camb. Synd. A.3.14)	Chald., 1638 (Chal. ch. ii. 14, in Camb. Synd. A.3.14: so 1616 in ch. v.).
ii. 8 *marg.* also v. 7, 9, 12, 16 *marg.*	Cald.2 Calde.2	Chald., 1638 Chaldee, 1638
[ii. 41	**potters'**, 1769	**potter's**]. See p. 152 note.
ii. 45 *marg.*	in hand, 1611-01769, Oxf. 1835, 1857, Lond. 1859	in hands, Bagster 1846, Camb. 1858, Amer. 1867. Cf. ver. 34 *marg.*
iii. 15	a fiery furnace	a **burning** fiery furnace, 1638
iii. 18	**thy** golden image	**the** golden image, 1629
iii. 21 marg	mantle…turbant	mantles…turbants, 1629
v. 17 marg.	fee, **as**	fee, Bagster 1846
vi. 13	the captivity of the children	the **children** of the captivity, 1629 C. (not L., 1630)
vi. 27 *marg.*	Heb.	Chald, Bagster 1846 only
vii. 18 *marg.*	*i. things* (*in things*, 1630)	that is, *things* 1613 (not 1629 L.), 1629 C.

CLEANING-UP HAZARDOUS MATERIALS

viii. 13 marg.	‖*The numberer*	,rO ‖*the numberer,* 1744
ix. 13 marg.	† *Heb. intreated the face*	† *Heb. intreated we not the face of the,* &c., 1638
ix. 26 marg. ix. 27 marg.	,rO ‖*shall have nothing* ,rO ‖*with the abominable armies*	Or, *and shall have nothing,* 1629 ,rO ‖*and upon the battlements hsall be the idols off the desolator,* 1762
xi. 13 marg.	*of times* [, 1744] *of years*	*of times* [, 1769] *even years,* 1762
xi. 24 marg. ibid.	*peaceable or fat think thoughts*	*peaceable and fat,* 1629 *think his thoughts,* 1629
xi. 38 text marg.	But in his estate… ‖ forces ,rO ‖*munitions.* Heb. *Maussin, or, as for the Almighty* (*Almightie* 1617) *God*	But † in his estate… ‖ † forces † Heb. (*potius,* ‖ Or) as for the Almighty God… ‖ Or, *munitions.* † Heb. *Mauzzim,* 1638 (so 1744, but in the same order as 1611), To *Mauzzim* 1744, 1762, 1769 add —or, Gods (*God's* 1744, 1762) protectors
xii. 8	O my **Lord** (so all before 1629 in ch. x. 16, 17, 19. Zech. iv. 4, 5, 13; vi. 4)	O my **lord** (אדוני), 1744 only here.
xii. 13	in the lot	in thy lot, 1638

[1] This rendering of the margin in 1611 comes, as usual, from Tremellius (above, p. 44), "*legiones detestationum desolantes.* Heb. *Alam detestationum desolantem: ala pro copiis metaphoricè, ut Isai.* viii. 8." Whatever may be its value, it ought not to have been displaced by 1762 (which 1769 and the moderns have servilely followed) for something not so very good of its own. In the Paragraph Bible, we have retained both. See above, p. 46.

Hosea	Reading of the	Variation of later

APPENDIX

	Authorized Bible	editions
iv. 4	**this** people	**thy** people, 1629
vi. 9 marg.	*Sichem* (*Sychem*, 1630)	*Shechem*, 1629, C. (not L.)
ix. 11	**flee** away	**fly** (flie 1629, 1638) away, 1744.
x. 5 marg.	‖*Chemarims*	,rO ‖*Chemarim* (*Chemarims*, 1629 C. and L., 1630), 1629, 1638
xiii. 3	dew **it** passeth	dew **that** passeth, 1638 (but not in ch. vi. 4)
10 [*marg.*]	Hosea ,1762, 1769	Hoshea, Oxf. 1835, &c.

Joel	Reading of the Authorized Bible	Variation of later editions
i. 16	**your** eyes	**our** eyes, 1629
iii. 13	**the** wickedness	**their** wickedness, 1629

Amoz	Reading of the Authorized Bible	Variation of later editions
i. 3 *marg.*	he, (*hee* 1616, 1617) *for four*	*yea for four*, 1629
i. 11	and kept	and **he** kept, 1762
viii. 3	songs of the **Temples** (temples, 1629)	songs of the **temple**, 1638
ix. 5	all that dwelleth[1]	all that dwell, 1629

[1] So in Amos vi. 7 Camb. Synd. A.3.14 alone has —first that goeth‖ for —first that go‖ of Oxf. 1611, 1612, 1613, 1616, 1617, &c. See Apppendix B, p. 212.

Jonah	Reading of the Authorized Bible	Variation of later editions
i. 16 *marg.*	a sacrifice	a sacrifice unto the LORD, 1638

Micah	Reading of the Authorized Bible	Variation of later editions
v. 2	Beth-leem	Beth-lehem, 1629 C. and L.

CLEANING-UP HAZARDOUS MATERIALS

| vii. 3 *marg.* | *the soul* | *his soul*, 1629 |

Nahum	Reading of the Authorized Bible	Variation of later editions
i. 1 *marg.*	*Lord*	LORD, 1638. See above. p. 147 note 1
i. 4	floure	flower, 1629. See 2 Estr. xv. 50
ii. 2 *marg.*	*and the pride*	*as the pride*, 1629
ii. 3 *marg.*	†† Heb. *fiery*	.rO ‖ ‖*fiery*, 1629
iii. 17	**The** crowned	**Thy** crowned, 1629

Habakkuk	Reading of the Authorized Bible	Variation of later editions
i. 9 *marg.*	*init.* † Heb.	) ,rO ‖† *before the following* Heb.), 1638
iii. 1 text *marg.*	Sigionoth *Shigianoth*	Shigionoth, 1762 *Shigionoth*, 1629
iii. 13	† by discovering	by † discovering, 1629-1762, Bagster 1846 (not 1769, mod.)
iii. 19	LORD God 1611-1630, 1762, 1769, moderns	Lord GOD, 1629 C., 1638, 1744. Cf. Zeph. i. 7. See p. 147 note 1.

Zephaniah	Reading of the Authorized Bible	Variation of later editions
iii. 11	**mine** holy	**my** holy, 1629 C. & L., 1630. Cf. *marg.*

Haggai	Reading of the Authorized Bible	Variation of later editions
i. 1, 12, 14 & ii. 2	Josuah Cf. Ezra iii. 2 *marg.*	Joshua, 1629 (ver. 12, 1629 L.)

Zechariah	Reading of the Authorized Bible	Variation of later editions
i. 1, 7	Barachiah	Berechiah, 1762[1]
iv. 12 *marg.*	*by the hand*	*by the hand of*, Bagster 1746; cf. ch. vii. 7, 12 *marg.*

APPENDIX

vii. 7	**or** the plain	**and** the plain, 1638
viii. 19 marg.	†† Heb. *solemn*	‖ ‖ Or, *solemn*, 1762
viii. 21 marg.	*the face*	*the face of the LORD*, 1638
xi. 2	**all** the mighty	the mighty
xiv. 10	Hananiel	Hananeel, 1762

[1] Thus 1611 reads in all the other nine places where the name occurs, except in 1 Chr. vi. 39, "Berachiah."

Malachi	Reading of the Authorized Bible	Variation of later editions
iii. 4	**offerings**	**offering**, 1638
iv. 2	and shall go forth	and **ye** shall go forth, 1617, 1629, &c.

S. Matthew	Reading of the Authorized Bible	Variation of later editions
i. 5	Boos (*bis*)	Booz (*bis*), 1629
i. 9	Achas (*bis*)	Achaz (*bis*), 1629
ii. 1	Hierusalem Passim[1]	Jerusalem, 1629 (not 1629 L., 1630), 1638
iv. 13, 15	**Nephthali**	**Nephthalim**, 1638
v. 22	Racha	Raca, 1638
v. 22	**counsell** (counsel 1744)	**council**, 1629 L., 1630 (councel 1612, 1629, 1638). See 1 Esdr. iii. 15 note.
vi. 3	thy right doeth	thy right **hand** doeth, 1613 (not 1616, 1617), 1629, 1630
xii. 41	Nineve (Ninive 1616)	Nineveh, 1629 (not Luke xi. 32)
[xiv. 9 & Mark vi. 26	**oath's**, 1762 &c.	**oaths'**]. See p. 152 note.
xiv. 34	Geneseret	Gennesaret, 1629 C., 1638. Cf. Mark vi. 53; Luke v.1.
xvi 15	Thou art Christ	Thou art **the** Christ, 1762. Cf. ver 20.
xvi. 19	whatsoever thou shalt	**and** whatsoever thou

	loose	shalt loose, 1616 (1617), 1629
xviii. 28 *marg.*	7. *d. ob.* Cf. ch. xx 2	*seven pence halfpenny*, 1616 (not 1617), 1629.
xx. 29	Hiericho	Jericho, 1616 (not 1617), 1629
xxvi. 75	the **words** of Jesus	the **word** of Jesus, 1762
xxvii. 22	Pilate **said**	Pilate **saith**, 1629
xxvii. 46	Lamasabachthani (Lamm-, 1613)	lama sabachthani, 1629

[1]"Hierusalem" is the constant form in the N.T. except in Acts xxv. 1 Camb. Synd. A.3. 14, & c., 1612, 1613, 1617; not Oxf. 1611, 1616). I Cor. xvi. 3. Gal. i. 17, 18; ii. 1; iv. 25, 26. Heb. xii. 22. See 2 Esdr. ii. 10.

S. Mark	Reading of the Authorized Bible	Variation of later editions
ii. 4	for press	for *the* press, 1743. Cf. Luke viii. 19
v. 6	he **came**	he **ran**, 1628[1]
vii. 2 marg.	*Theophilact*	*Theophylact*, 1629
x. 18	there is **no man** good, but one	there is **none** good but one, 1638₁.
x. 46	**high ways** side	**high-way** side, 1629. Cf. Matt. xiiii. 4.
xl. 8	branches **of** the trees	branches **off** the trees, 1638 (ἐκ).
xii. 26 & Luke xx. 37	Isahac	Isaac, 1612 & 1617 (Mark), 1629. So 2 Esdr. iii. 16
xiv. 32	Gethsemani (Clementine Vulg.)	Gethsemane, 1616 (not 1617, 1630), 1638. Cf. Matt. xxvi. 36
xiv. 55	counsel	councell, 1630, councel, 1629 C. (not L.), 1638, council, 1743. See 1 Esdr. iii. 15 note.
xv. 34	lamasabachthani	lama sabachthani, 1629
xv. 41 & xvi. 7 & Luke iv. 44 & Acts xiii. 31 (Camb. Synd. A.3.14, &c.)	Gelile	Galilee, 1629 (1612 ter). See Tobit 1.2 note.

APPENDIX

[1] A variation taken from Matt. xix. 17. A like change might well be made in some other places, e.g. matt. xi. 27; ch. xiii. 32. In John x. 28 "any," 29 "none" of 1638-1762, are rejected by 1769 and later Bibles for "any man," "no man," of 1611-1630; "man" however being printed in italic type.

S. Luke	Reading of the Authorized Bible	Variation of later editions
i. 3	understanding of things	understanding of **all** things
i. 5, 7, 13, 24, 36, 40, 41 (*bis*), 57	Elizabeth	Elisabeth, 1638
i. 74	out of the **hands**	out of the **hand**, 1762
ii. 25, 34	Simeaon	Symeon
iii. 21	**and** it came to pass	it came to pass, 1629
iii. 25, 26	Matthathias	Mattathias, 1629
iii. 30	Simeon	Symeon. Cf. Appendix E § I, p. 244 and Acts xv. 14.
iii. 31	Menan (M ε νάμ Erasmus 1516, Aldus 1518, Tyndale, Great Bible)[2] see Appendix E. p. 244.	Menan, 1629, (Geneva N. T., 1557).
iii. 35	Phaleg (Clementine Vulg.)	Phalec, 1629
iv. 27	Elizeus	Eliseus[1], 1638
v. 1	Genesareth (Genn – 1638-1743)	Gennesaret, 1762. Cf. Matt. xiv. 34
vii. 11	Naim (Ναύμ Erasmus 1516, Aldus, Vulg. All Early Enlgish versions Naim, except Tynd. 1516 Naym)	Nain, 1638 (Ναείν Erasm. 1519)
viii. 5	the **wayes** side	the **way** side, 1743. Cf. ver. 12. Matt. xiii. 4; Mark iv. 4.
xi. 32	Nineve. Cf. Matt. xii. 41	Nineveh, 1699, American 1867.
xvii. 34	the other shall be left	**and** the other shall be left, 1638. Cf. vers. 35,

		36
xix. 2, 5, 8	Zacheus	Zaccheus 1638-1769¹.
xix. 9	the son of Abraham	a son of Abraham, 1762.
xx. 12	sent the third	sent a third, 1762
xxiii. 11	at naught	at nought, 1638. Cf. Acts xix. 27
xxii. 19	cast in prison	cast into prison, 1616 (not 1617-1638), 1743
xxiv. 13	Emaus	Emmaus, 1613
xxiv. 18	Cleophas	Cleopas, 1629

² In the same way all our books from Tyndale downwards (except Coverdale and the Genevan version) read "Heber" ver. 35 from Erasmus's Ἐβερ retained in Beza 1589, 1598), though "Eber" is the form used in the O.T. See Appendix E, p. 249.

¹ *Elissaus* might be preferable here, as Zacchaus is spelt in Oxf. 1835. Camb. 1858, and some recent Bibles. An English reader can hardly fail to confound the three separate terminations in –eus, (I) eu diphthong, as Menestheus, 2 Macc. iv. 21, Nereus, Rom. xvi. 15: (2) the dissyllable ĕ-us, e being short, as Timothĕus, I Thess. i. 1 & c.: (3) the more usual dissyllalbe –ē-us, e being long, as here. Such as Aggeus, 1 Esdr. vi. 1; 2 Esdr. i. 40: Asmodēus, Tobit iii. 8: Cendebēus, 1 Macc. xv. 38: Channunēus, 1 Esdr. viii. 48: Elisēus, here: Hymenēus, I Tim. i. 20: Maccabēus, 1 Macc. iii. 1 Y c.: Sabbathēus, I Esdr. ix. 14: Sabatēus, ibid. ver. 48: Timēus, Mark x. 46: Zacchēus, Luke xix. 2, 5 8. So also in I Esdr. ix. 21, 23, 30, 32 (*bis*), 33. These all represent the termination – αῖος. In 1 Macc. xii. 7 marg., 20, Αρειοπς should be rendered Arius, not Areus.

S. John	Reading of the Authorized Bible	Variation of later editions
i. 45-49 & xxi. 2	Nathaneel	Nathanael, 1629 (1612, ver. 47).
v. 18	not only because he	because he not only, 1629
vii. 16	Jesus answered them,	Jesus answered them, and said, 1634, 1638
viii. 30	those words	these words, 1629

APPENDIX

xi. 3	his **sister**	his **sisters**, 1629
xii. 22	**told** Jesus	**tell** Jesus, 1762
xv. 20	than the Lord (lord 1629-1743)	than his lord, 1762
xvi. 25	the time	**but** the time, 1756, 1762, 1769
xxi. 17 init.	He **said** unto him	He **saith** unto him, 1638

Acts	Reading of the Authorized Bible	Variation of later editions
ii. 22	miracles, wonders	miracles **and** wonders, 1638
iv. 17	no **farther**	no **further**, 1616 (not 1617, 1634), 1629, 1640. Cf. ver. 21: ch. xxi. 28.
vi. 5, 8 & vii. 59 & viii. 2 & xi. 19 & xxii. 20	Steven	Stephen, 1629
vi. 5	Permenas	Parmenas, 1629
vii. 10, 13	Pharao	Pharaoh, 1629, 1630 (1640, ver. 10), Cf. ver. 21.
vii. 16	Sichem (*bis*)... Emor (Ἐμόρ Erasmus, Ald., Tynd., Great and Bishops' Bibles, &c.)	Sychem (*bis*) 1638...
vii. 35	by the **hands**	by the **hand**, 1762
viii. 32	**the** shearer	**his** shearer, 1629
xiii. 18 *marg.*	ἐτροποφόρησεν	ἐτροποφόρησεν bore, or fed them, 1743₁.
xiii. 42 *marg.*	‖*Or, in the week*	† Gr. *In the week*, 1629
xv. 14	Simeon	Symeon, Cf. Luke iii. 30.
xvii. 22 *marg.*	‖*Or, court*	,rO ‖*the court*, 1638
xxi. 28 & xxiv. 4	**farther**. Cf. ch. iv. 17	**further**, 1609, 1762 (ch. xxiv. 4. 1639-1743).
xxiv. 24	which was a **Jew**	which was a **Jewess**, 1629. Cf. ch. xvi. 1
xxiv. 27	Portius	Porcius, 1638
xxvii. 5	Lysia	Lycia, 1629. Cf. 1 Macc. xv. 23
xxvii. 7	Gnidus	Cnidus, 1638

xxvii. 18	And being exceedingly tossed with a tempest the next day,	And we being exceedingly tossed with a tempest, the next day 1638. [2]

[1] After Deut. 1.31 in this marginal note modern Bibles which do not contain the Apocrypha (e.g. Camb. 1858) unwarrantably omit the reference to 2 Macc. Vii. 27. See above, p. 119.

[2] In 1616 (not 1617)-1630 the stop is transferred, but ἡμῶν is still over looked.

Romans	Reading of the Authorized Bible	Variation of later editions
iii. 24	Jesus Christ (So Beza's Latin only)	Christ Jesus
iv. 12	but also walk	but **who** also walk, 1762
vi. 12	reign therefore	therefore reign, 1616 (not 1617), 1629
vii. 13	Was that then	Was then that, 1616 (not 1617), 1629
ix. 29	Sabboth (Sabbath 1629 L., 1630)	sabaoth, 1629-1762 (Sabaoth[2], 1769)
x. 16 *text marg.*	our ‖ † report ‖*Or*, before † *Gr.*	† our ‖ report † Gr. before ‖ Or, 1629 (not 1629 L., 1630), 1638.
xi. 28	for your **sake**	for your **sakes**, 1762
xli 2	that acceptable	and acceptable, 1629
xiv. 6	regardeth **a** day	regardeth **the** day, 1629
xiv. 10	we shall all stand	**for** we shall all stand, 1638
xvi 10	Appeles	Apelles, 1616 (not 1617, 1630), 1629 c. and L.

2 In James v. 4 Sabbaoth, Camb. Synd. A.3.14, & c., 1613, 1617, 1629 L., 1630; Sabaoth, Oxf. 1611, 1612, 1616; sabaoth, 1629 C., 1638, &c.

1 Cor.	Reading of the Authorized Bible	Variation of later editions

APPENDIX

i. 12 & iii. 4-6, 22 & iv. 6	Apollo	Apollos, 1638
vii. 32	things that **belongeth**	things that **belong**, 1612 (not 1613), 1616, &c. See p. 110
ix. 9 & x. 2	Moyses	Moses, 1629 (1612, ch. ix. 9)
x. 28	The earth is	**For** the earth is, 1638
xii. 28	helps **in** governments	helps, governments, 1629
xiv. 10	none of them **are**	none of them **is**, 1638. Cf. pp. 109, 110
xiv. 23	**some** place	**one** place, 1629
xv. 6	**And** that	**After** that, 1616 (not 1617), 1629 C. & L. Cf. ver 7.
xv. 41	another of the moon	and another **glory** of the moon, 1629
xv. 48	such are they that are earthy	such are they **also** that are earthy, 1638
xvi. 22	Anathema Maranatha	anathema, Maranatha, 1629-1743[1]

[1] But 1762 and American 1867 have Anathema, Maran-atha, and 1769 even removes the necessary comma between the words; and so D'Oyly and Mant 1817, Oxf. 1835, Camb. 1858, and other moderns.

2 Cor.	Reading of the Authorized Bible	Variation of later editions
i. 19	Sylvanus	Silvanus, 1613 (not 1616, 1617), 1629 C. (not 1629 L., 1630). Cf. 1 Peter v. 12.
v. 20	earnestly, desiring	earnestly desiring, 1769 (ἐεπιποθουντεj)²
viii. 21	**that** ye be (that be ye Oxf. 1611) reconciled	be ye reconciled, 1612, 1616 (not 1613), 1617, 1629
ix. 5	but in the sight	but **also** in the sight, 1638
ix. 5	not of covetousness	**and** not **as** of

CLEANING-UP HAZARDOUS MATERIALS

		covetousness, 1638
ix. 6	sparingly…bountifully	**also** sparingly … **also** bountifully, 1638
xi. 26	**journeying**	**journeyings**, 1762
xi. 32	the city	the city **of the Damascenes**, 1629

² Professor Grote (MS, p. 16. See above, p. 23 note) states that this punctuation was adopted in a small 8vo. Bible by Field in 1660, but that in Field's 12mo. N.T. of the same year, and in all later editions of that period, the change was revoked. See above, p. 91.

Galatians	Reading of the Authorized Bible	Variation of later editions
iii. 13	on tree (Tynd. – Bishops')	on **a** tree, 1629

Ephesians	Reading of the Authorized Bible	Variation of later editions
iv. 24	**that** new man	**the** new man, 1616 (not 1617), 1629 C.
vi. 24	sincerity	sincerity, **Amen**, 1616 (not 1617, 1629 C.

Phil.	Reading of the Authorized Bible	Variation of later editions
iv. 2	Syntiche	Syntyche, 1629. 1638 (not 1699), &c.
iv. 6	**request**	**requests**, 1629

2 Thess.	Reading of the Authorized Bible	Variation of later editions
ii. 14	**the** Lord Jesus Christ	**our** Lord Jesus Christ, 1629
ii. 15	or our epistle	or **by** our epistle, 1613 only

1 Tim.	Reading of the Authorized Bible	Variation of later editions
i. 4	edifying	**godly** edifying, 1638

APPENDIX

		(Tynd.-Bps').
vi. 11	flie ($\theta \; \varepsilon \; \ddot{v} \gamma \; \varepsilon$)	flee, 1613 (not 1616, 1617), 1629 C. & L. Cf. 2 Esdr. xiv 15 note.
Subscription	Pacaciana (Bishops' Bible)	Pacatiana, 1629

2 Tim.	Reading of the Authorized Bible	Variation of later editions
i. 7	of love	and of love, 1638
ii. 19	the seal	this seal, 1617, 1629 C. & L., 1630
iv. 8	unto them also	unto all them also, 1629
iv. 13	bring with thee	bring with thee, and the books, 1616, 1617, 1629 C. & L., 1630.

Heb.	Reading of the Authorized Bible	Variation of later editions
iii. 10	their **hearts**	their **heart**, 1638
iv. 8 marg.	Josua	Joshua, 1638
viii. 8	and the house of Judah	and **with** the house of Judah, 1638
xi. 4	Kain	Cain, 1638. Cf. 1 John iii. 12; Jude 11.
xi. 23	and they (**thy**, 1617) not afraid	and they **were** not afraid, 1638.
xi. 32	Gideon…Jephthah	Gedeon … Iephthae, 1629. Cf. Judg. xi. 1 marg.
xii. 1	unto the race	the race, 1629 C. & L., 1630

James	Reading of the Authorized Bible	Variation of later editions
v. 2	motheaten	**are** motheaten, 1638

1 Peter	Reading of the Authorized Bible	Variation of later editions
ii. 1	evil speakings	**all** evil speakings, 1629 C.

ii. 5	**sacrifice**	**sacrifices**, 1629
ii. 6	Wherefore	Wherefore **also**, 1629
v. 12	Sylvanus	Sylvanus, 1629 C. & L (not 1630), 1638. Cf. 2 Cor. i. 19.

1 John	Reading of the Authorized Bible	Variation of later editions
ii. 16	the lust of the eyes	**and** the lust of the eyes, 1638
v. 12	hath not the Son[1]	hath not the Son **of God**, 1629 C. (not 1629 L., 1630), 1638[2].

[1] The Book of Common Prayer (Epistle for the First Sunday after Easter) follows the reading of 1611, as does the Gospel for Palm Sunday in Matt. xxvii. 52, "of saints which slept," not "the saints," as in 1762 and later Bibles. See Cardwell, *Oxford Bibles*, p. 14. [2] Even after 1638 this variation continued : "of God" is omitted by 1640-39, 1659 (fol.), 1677 (Camb.), 1678, 1679 (fol.), 1681; the words are retined by 1658 (Field) and its Dutch counterfeit (see above, p. 25 note 2), 1674, 1677 (4°), 1682, 1701, and by all later Bibles.

Jude	Reading of the Authorized Bible	Variation of later editions
ver. 11	Kain	Cain, 1630, 1638. See Heb. xi. 4.
ver. 25	now and ever	**both** now and ever, 1638

Revelation	Reading of the Authorized Bible	Variation of later editions
i. 4	Churches in Asia	Churches **which are** in Asia, 1638
i. 11	Philadelphia	**unto** Philadelphia, 1638
v. 13	honour, glory	**and** honour, and glory, 1638
vii. 5	Ruben	Reuben, 1616 (not 1617), 1629 C. & L., 1630.

APPENDIX

vii. 6	Nephali (Nephthali, 1629 C.)	Nephthalim, 1638-1762, Amer. 1867[1]. Cf. Matt. iv. 13, 15.
ix. 17 & xxi. 20	jacinct	Jacinth, 1762
xii. 14	**flee** ($\pi\acute{\epsilon}\tau\tilde{\eta}\tau\alpha\iota$). Cf. 2 Esdr. xv. 41	**fly** (flie, 1629-1699), 1743, 1762
xiii. 6	them that **dwelt**	them that **dwell**, 1629
xiii. 16 *marg.*	*to give*	*to give them*, 1769
xviii. 12	Thine (Thyne 1629 L.)	thyne, 1629 C.
xx. 13 *marg.*	‖*Or, hell* (‖ Or, well, 1612)	‖*Or, grave*, 1613-1630: ‖ Or, *the grave*, 1638.
xxi. 19	saphir$_2$	sapphire, 1638
xxi. 20	sardonix (even 1699)... topas	sardonyx 1634, 1640 .... topaz 1629.
Colophon	FINIS	THE END

[1] 1769, followed by our standard (Camb. 1858) and all other moderns we know of, reads Nephthalim."

[2] Elsewhere the forms employed in 1611 are sapphire and saphyre. See above, p. 97. N.B. All variations in the foregoing list, except those relating to the apostrophe, have been introduced into at least one previous edition. The changes described in the subjoined list (which relates chiefly to the Apocrypha) are peculiar to the Cambridge Paragraph Bible, and must justify themselves.

Genesis	Reading of 1611 and later editions.	Correction made in the Paragraph Bible
i. 20	creature that hath †life	† creature that hath life.
x. 16	Girgasite (Gergasite 1630)	Girgashite, passim.

Numbers	Reading of 1611 and later editions.	Correction made in the Paragraph Bible
xxvi. 58	Korathites	Korahites. Cf. 1 Chr. ix. 19[1]. (Gorle.)

[1] Less palpable is the error in 1 Chr. xxvi. 19 (cf. ver. 1), where Kore (קֹרֵא) is put for Korhite (קָרְחִי).

2 Samuel	Reading of 1611 and later editions.	Correction made in the Paragraph Bible
xvii. 26 [*marg.*]	*Ismaelite*, 1762	*Ishmeelite*. Cf. 1 Chr. ii. 17.

2 Kings	Reading of 1611 and later editions.	Correction made in the Paragraph Bible
iii. 9	†that followed	that † followed
xvi. 7 [marg.]	† Heb. *Tilgath-pileser*, 1762	† Heb. *Tiglath-peleser*.

1 Chronicles	Reading of 1611 and later editions.	Correction made in the Paragraph Bible
vii. 28	unto ‖ Gaza	azaG otnu ‖2.

² The annexed marginal note (omitted in Bibles which do not contain the Apocrypha, see above, p. 119) is almost unintelligible as it stands in 1611, &c. Inasmuch as the border of Ephraim did not reach to Gaza (Josh. xv. 47), our Translators suggest that עַד־טָה may possibly mean Adassa, the Ἀδαζὰ of 1Macc. viii. 40, 45.

Ezra	Reading of 1611 and later editions.	Correction made in the Paragraph Bible
ix. 8	a † little space	a little † space. Cf. Isai. xxvi. 20.

Nehemiah	Reading of 1611 and later editions.	Correction made in the Paragraph Bible
iii. 12	Halloesh, 1611-1630 (Haloesh, 1616; Halohesh, 1638, &c.)	Hallohesh. Cf. ch. x. 24.

Esther	Reading of 1611 and later editions.	Correction made in the Paragraph Bible
viii. 5	† the letters devised (the † l.d. Bagster 1856; in 1630 *marg. devised for the device.*)	the letters † devised

Job	Reading of 1611 and	Correction made in the

APPENDIX

	later editions.	Paragraph Bible
xxxii. 6 *marg.*	*I feared* (feared, 1638, &c.)	*I feared to.*

Psalms	Reading of 1611 and later editions.	Correction made in the Paragraph Bible
vi. 4 & xxxi. 16 & xliv. 26	for thy **mercies** (mercies', 1769)	for thy **mercy's** (תמדך:)[1].
cxxxvi. 8 *marg.*	*rulings*	*ruling.* Compare ver. 9 (Heb.).

[1] The noun *in pausâ* is no doubt singular, and so LXX., Vulg. have it in Ps. vi. 4; xxxi. 16. Our translators must have meant —mercies‖ to be singular, as they so spell "mercy" about four times out of ten. In that case 1769 would be the first to go wrong. See p. 152 note.

Canticles	Reading of 1611 and later editions.	Correction made in the Paragraph Bible
iv. 2	every one bear (bare, 1629 L., 1630)	every one beareth. Cf. ch. vi. 6

Isaiah	Reading of 1611 and later editions	Correction made in the Paragraph Bible
iv. 9 *marg.*	Hear ye ‖ indeed (‖† 1629) ,rO ‖without ceasing, & c. Heb. hear ye in hearing, & c.	† Hear ye ‖ indeed. † Heb. precedes ‖ Or, *Aliter sanat* Bagster 1846.
xi. 14	†and the children	and † the children.
xxvii. 8 *marg.*	*removeth it*	*removeth it with*
xxix. 1 *marg.*	*cut off the heads*	*cut off the heads of*
xliv. 14	he ‖ strengtheneth	morf .gram) htenehtgnerts eh ‖

Ezekiel	Reading of 1611 and later editions.	Correction made in the Paragraph Bible
iii. 20	† righteousness *primo loco*	† righteousness *secundo loco.*
xxxviii. 17 *marg.*	by the hands (Bagster 1846 adds *of*)	by the hand of. Cf. 1 Kin. xvi. 12

Daniel	Reading of 1611 and later editions.	Correction made in the Paragraph Bible
ix. 26 *text marg.*	but not for himself ,rO ‖*and* [*the Jews*] *they shall be no more his people*, ch. 11. 17, or, *and the prince's* [**Messiah's**, ver. 25] *future people*, 1762.	* but not for himself : ‖ and the people. * Or, *and* [*the Jews*]… ch. 11. 17 * Or, *and the prince's* [**Messiah's** ver. 25] *future people*.

Malachi	Reading of 1611 and later editions.	Correction made in the Paragraph Bible
i. 7	reffo ey ‖	Ye ‖ offer[1].

[1] The marginal —bring into‖ (b not B, 1611-1638) cannot be meant for the imperative, but renders *differentes super* of Tremellius.

S. Matthew	Reading of 1611 and later editions.	Correction made in the Paragraph Bible
xxiii. 24	strain **at** a gnat	strain **out** a gnat[1].

[1] So all the early versions from Tyndale to the Bishop's Bible, and even T. Baskett's 8 vo. edition of the Authorized, London, 8 vo. 1754, Brit. Mus. 1411. f. 5.

S. Mark	Reading of 1611 and later editions.	Correction made in the Paragraph Bible
vi. 53	Genesareth (Gennesaret, 1638-1769)	Genesaret. Cf. Matt. xiv. 34; Luke v. 1.

S. Luke	Reading of 1611 and later editions.	Correction made in the Paragraph Bible
i. 78 *marg.*	Malach. iv. 2; *follows* Isai. xi. 1	Mal. iv. 1, follows *sunrising*.

S. John	Reading of 1611 and later editions.	Correction made in the Paragraph Bible
x. 25	and ye **believed** not	and ye **believe** not.

APPENDIX

Acts	Reading of 1611 and later editions.	Correction made in the Paragraph Bible
vii. & xiii. 19	Chanaan	Canaan (1612 only, ch. xiii. 19). See Judith v. 9.
xxi. 1	Choos (Coos, 1638, &c.)	Cos. Cf. 1 Macc. xv. 24.
xxv. 23	**was** entered (Bishops' Bible). Cf. 1 Esdr. viii. 49	**were** entered (Tyndale, Great Bible, Geneva 1557). See above, p. 110 note 1.

Romans	Reading of 1611 and later editions.	Correction made in the Paragraph Bible
xvi. 9	Urbane	Urban.

Philippians	Reading of 1611 and later editions.	Correction made in the Paragraph Bible
ii. 7, 8	nem fo ssenekil ‖	likeness of men...‖ fasion as a man[1].

[1] That the margin, "Or, habit" refers to ὀχήματι, not to σμοιωματι, is plain enough in itself, not to add that for σμοιωματι the Vulg. has *habitu*, Tyndale, Coverdale, and the Great Bible apparel.

Hebrews	Reading of 1611 and later editions.	Correction made in the Paragraph Bible
i. 6	esohw, 2671, niaga dnA ‖ margin it is	And ‖ again
viii. 8	Judah	Juda. Cf. Matt. ii. 6; ch. vii. 14; Rev. v. 5. So Camb. 1863 in Ecclus. xlix. 4.
x. 23	**faith**	**hope.** See Appendix E, p. 247.

INDEX

1611, ix, xii, 7, 11, 17, 20, 27, 68, 93, 125, 146, 158, 204, 210, 211, 213, 214, 215, 222, 225, 235, 264, 268, 269, 278, 311, 334, 339, 341, 343, 344, 345, 349, 350, 353, 354, 357, 358, 359, 360, 361, 362, 363, 364, 365, 368, 369, 372, 373, 374, 375, 376, 377
1769, 7, 11, 18, 93, 158, 278, 336, 337, 338, 339, 340, 341, 342, 343, 345, 346, 347, 349, 350, 353, 354, 355, 356, 357, 358, 359, 360, 361, 362, 365, 367, 368, 369, 373, 375, 376
1800s, 215, 270, 271
Abraham, 43, 109, 110, 333, 366
acts, 103
ad hominem, 9, 33, 42, 65, 113, 120, 164, 190, 224, 240, 244, 246, 253, 257
Adam, 88, 102, 110, 152, 160, 317
adoption, 132, 230
ages, 54, 88, 135, 139, 231, 232, 280, 316, 331
Aland, 52, 57, 60, 75, 138, 140
Alexander the Great, 84
American Bible Society, 270, 308
American Standard Version, 36, 68, 186, 187, 188
analytical, 55, 67, 68, 95, 136
ancient, 17, 43, 51, 60, 62, 63, 66, 72, 74, 75, 84, 96, 99, 128, 133, 141, 142, 145, 154, 166, 168, 172, 173, 237, 240, 241, 249, 259, 262, 273, 282, 322, 324, 331

Andrews, 154
angels, 167, 319
anow, 158
apostles, i, ii, v, ix, x, 12, 26, 31, 109, 315, 317, 318, 319, 331, 334
apostolic, 13, 164, 317, 318
Armstrong, 31
Arndt, 50, 51, 52, 57, 58, 60, 75, 133, 137, 140, 185
Artemis, 281
ASV, 36, 42, 48, 120, 164, 165, 188
Athenian, 15
Atonement, 110, 245
Augustus, 84, 85
authority, xi, 9, 10, 11, 21, 22, 31, 33, 35, 42, 71, 80, 109, 112, 113, 158, 174, 185, 188, 195, 211, 212, 215, 225, 227, 235, 244, 245, 248, 254, 259, 260, 262, 265, 267, 295, 297, 312, 323
autographs, 4, 89, 90, 153, 164, 254, 255, 278, 279, 332
Baal, 173, 315, 339
back text, 192
back translation, 299
back-translate, ii, viii, 203, 207
back-translation, 208, 209, 211
backwards translate, 198, 203, 204, 205, 206, 207, 298, 306, 307
Baltz, 52, 60, 75, 140
baptism, 97, 317, 321
Baptist Bible Fellowship, 123
Baptist Encyclopedia, 270
Baptist Tribune, 123
BAPTIZO, 96

basis, xii, 21, 23, 31, 51, 79, 86, 111, 112, 120, 134, 137, 188, 196, 202, 207, 208, 211, 214, 221, 223, 225, 239, 265, 273, 277, 287, 305, 312, 319, 321
beliefs, 9, 164, 174, 183, 201, 238
Berry, ii, 42, 185, 227, 228, 229, 230, 231, 232, 234, 235, 243, 285, 286, 287, 289, 299
Beza, 20, 25, 124, 196, 197, 199, 201, 203, 204, 205, 206, 207, 209, 211, 212, 214, 215, 216, 220, 221, 222, 223, 224, 227, 264, 265, 306, 331, 366, 368
BIBLOS, 179
biographer, 174, 183
bishop, 323
Bishops Bible, 90, 124, 226, 269
blatant, 158, 207
Blavatsky, 39, 48, 120, 176, 183, 191
Bois, 216, 217, 237
Bomberg, 28, 29, 247, 248
Boyce, 17, 264
Brainard, 43, 183
brass serpent, 4
Breath, 275
Briggs, 116, 182, 201, 243, 244, 246, 254, 278
Brigham, 318
Britain, 236, 321
British Universities, 214
Brown, 116, 182, 201, 243, 244, 246, 254, 278
Bryn, 295, 297, 298, 303, 305
Bullinger, 38, 254
Burgon, 1, 2, 3, iii, xi, xii, xiv, 19, 20, 206, 235, 236, 279, 292, 303, 331, 332, 333
Burma, 8, 43
Burmese, 8, 43

Byzantine, 25, 64, 124, 143, 195, 239, 267, 286, 287
Caesar, 85
Cambridge, 11, 20, 40, 44, 93, 198, 199, 208, 210, 211, 212, 265, 310, 323, 334, 335, 337, 341, 373
Canaan, 314, 377
Carroll, 39, 176, 184
Catholic Church, 6, 23, 58, 65, 144, 145, 188, 219, 257, 262
Chadwick, 50, 63, 134, 143
chagrin, 17
challenges, 11, 18, 114
charismatic, i, ix, x, 320
charity, 146, 148, 319
Chaucer, 64, 143, 276
Chinese, 27
Christopher, 314
churches, 9, 21, 89, 116, 124, 164, 218, 258, 295, 314, 316, 317, 321
Churchill, 271
circumlocution, 322
Clement of Alexandria, 65, 144
Clementine Vulgate, 23, 273
Cloud, xv, 198, 300, 304, 311
Colinaeus, 223
college, vii, 9, 10, 48, 112, 120, 148, 177, 181, 182, 197, 245, 255, 257, 275, 318
Comma Johanneum, 195
commandment, 280, 312
committee, 17, 24, 48, 120, 123, 154, 164, 165, 178, 179, 184, 186, 191, 193, 197, 201, 202, 204, 209, 210, 212, 215, 222, 232, 237, 262, 272, 323
common, v, 19, 46, 59, 64, 68, 71, 76, 84, 85, 88, 90, 144, 149, 166, 175, 178, 182, 184, 238, 259, 262, 270, 282
compare(d), ii, 2, 5, 6, 19, 21, 22, 23, 44, 90, 111, 115, 152,

INDEX

169, 170, 178, 196, 209, 251, 262, 268, 271, 272, 285, 322
Complutensian, 25, 124, 194, 199, 204, 216, 223, 331
confess, 15, 74, 103, 219
Constitution, 4, 12
Coolridge, 181
Corinth, 316, 320
Corinthian, 13, 316, 320
Corinthians, 2, 12, 34, 79, 116, 151, 187, 217, 264, 316, 319, 320, 321
Creator, 73, 88, 253
D. A. Waite, Sr., 285
D.A. Waite Jr., 203
Daniel, 1, 38, 107, 110, 312, 359, 376
Danker, 50, 52, 60, 61, 63, 75, 128, 133, 140, 142, 146, 243
David, viii, 38, 43, 107, 110, 183, 198, 300, 304, 311, 315, 341, 342, 346
Dead Sea, 5, 253
Declaration of Independence, 4
denomination, 48, 114, 120, 318
devils, 165, 182, 315
dia, 158
Diadoti, 272
DIAMARTANONTES, 101
Diana, 281
Diocletian, 14
DISDASKALOI, 233
distortion, 25, 56, 113, 123, 137, 149, 168, 210, 264
distortions, 36, 88, 121, 158, 200, 203, 212, 250, 283
Divine-Human, 4
divines, 324
divisions, 209, 252, 253, 316, 322
doctrine, ii, iii, iv, v, 3, 70, 79, 86, 87, 91, 96, 104, 112, 114, 115, 179, 185, 242, 269, 315

documentation, 22, 31, 59, 139, 202, 216, 226, 251, 283, 286, 302, 312
documents, 4, 21, 147, 223, 278, 301, 303, 312
Dodgson, 38, 39, 171, 176, 184
Don Waite, 198, 204, 206, 207
Douay Rheims, 273
Driver, 116, 182, 201, 243, 244, 246, 254, 278
Dutch, 173, 182, 248, 249, 250, 251, 372
Dylan, 281
early, 3, i, x, 4, 5, 6, 14, 21, 26, 40, 45, 63, 65, 73, 74, 86, 124, 144, 147, 195, 215, 221, 225, 236, 242, 249, 250, 259, 260, 261, 263, 270, 271, 288, 290, 300, 316, 332, 376
ecclesiastical, 146, 188, 322
ecstatic, 317
Edward, 199, 302, 317, 331
egregious, xi
Egyptian, 79, 132, 166, 180, 314
element, 34, 313
Elijah, 1
Elisha, 1
Elzevir, 25, 26, 124, 228, 286, 287, 333
Elzevirs, 25, 124, 331
EMBRIMAOMAI, 96
encyclopedia, 167, 168, 314
England, 39, 188, 214, 271, 332
Enosh, 88
Epilogue, 11
Erasmus, 23, 25, 124, 195, 199, 204, 216, 223, 225, 264, 334, 365, 366, 367
errors, vi, xii, 9, 28, 29, 42, 49, 50, 51, 62, 90, 104, 112, 113, 115, 126, 133, 134, 152, 157, 163, 174, 200, 224, 230, 239, 248, 254, 285, 311, 312, 340
ESV, 129, 154, 188

etymological, 64, 72, 143, 277
Euripides, 63, 142
exegesis, ii, vi, 2, 3, 43, 114
facts, i, ii, vi, 15, 26, 29, 32, 53, 56, 120, 121, 125, 127, 134, 136, 137, 154, 205, 214, 224, 241, 261, 263, 264, 268, 270, 277, 286, 298, 299, 303, 305, 307, 312, 331
flame, 119
fornication, v, 161, 162
founder, 31, 66, 145, 304, 318
French, iii, 59, 155, 176, 182, 242, 248, 249, 250, 251, 267, 272, 317
frequently, ii, 201, 309, 312
fundamental, 45, 112, 189, 283
fundamentalist, 9, 177, 190, 253, 306
future, 40, 46, 50, 64, 116, 133, 143, 155, 232, 234, 376
gay, 64, 143
gematria, x, 38, 283
generate, 65, 144, 283, 319
generating, 319
genesis, 225
Geneva, 23, 25, 68, 90, 124, 224, 226, 249, 250, 267, 269, 321, 323, 365, 377
Germans, 58
Gesenius, 182, 201, 244, 254, 278
ghost, 245
gibberish, 319
gift, xiii, 13, 79, 93, 102, 116, 117, 130, 155, 186, 217, 218, 220, 225, 237, 238, 242, 258, 316, 317, 318, 321
Gingrich, 50, 51, 52, 57, 58, 60, 75, 133, 137, 140, 185
Ginsburg, 28, 29, 191, 247, 248, 249, 250, 251, 252, 253, 254, 255, 257
glossalalia, 318

glwvssa, 318
god, 41, 173, 181, 222
Goddard, 245
Good News Bible, 56, 137
Goodspeed, 56, 137
Gordon, 302
gospel, 14, 146, 232, 262, 280, 317
Gothic, 6, 13, 14, 22, 99, 174, 218, 225, 238, 241, 242, 257, 266, 267, 268, 311
Graham, 43, 177
grammar, 3, iv, v, x, 3, 7, 8, 32, 33, 43, 44, 46, 54, 61, 62, 63, 64, 67, 93, 95, 104, 135, 142, 143, 156, 157, 158, 159, 160, 161, 170, 182, 194, 245
Greece, 23, 64, 72, 83, 84, 85, 86, 143, 178, 332
Greek grammar rules, 277
Greek Orthodox church, 195, 218, 238, 273
Greek-German, 58, 242
Green, 28, 197, 198, 200, 201, 202, 203, 206, 207, 209, 211, 212, 227, 238, 249, 250, 255, 285, 286
Gulag Archipeligo, 160
gunpowder, 314
Gutjahr, 270
hades, 150, 154
Hampton, 321, 322
Harakas, 240, 241, 243
harpagmos, 128, 129, 130, 131
Harvard, 67, 148, 199
Hatch, 159, 245
head, 180, 184, 193, 270
heads, 324, 375
headship, 318
healing, 317
Hefner, 66, 145
Hell, 173, 232
Hellenized, 232
Hendrickson/Green, 28

INDEX

heresies, 65, 78, 144, 157, 164, 165, 177, 201, 240, 316
heretic, 4, 39, 153, 165, 170, 176
heretical, 125, 164, 316
heretics, 36, 47, 48, 65, 120, 144, 146, 190, 191, 212, 241, 316
hermeneutics, 99
Herodotus, 63, 142
HILASMOS, 111
Hills, 199
Holocaust, 226
Holy Ghost, 4, 12, 13, 14, 15, 26, 34, 74, 76, 90, 91, 112, 159, 161, 172, 176, 187, 217, 218, 225, 226, 237, 238, 257, 315, 316, 317
Holy Writ, 73, 170
Hort, 24, 26, 40, 48, 54, 55, 57, 120, 123, 125, 135, 136, 138, 177, 184, 186, 194, 202, 209, 254, 286, 287, 331, 332
Huios, 230
hurt, i, 81
hyperbole, 127, 149, 319
hypostatic, 4, 73
idiom, 68, 93, 96, 156, 160, 179, 231, 234
In Awe of Thy Word, xiii, 12, 13, 14, 15, 17, 80, 186, 311
India, 41, 68, 84, 182, 271
indicative, 116
inflected, 67, 68, 157, 242
inspiration, iii, iv, v, vi, ix, x, 1, 2, 3, 10, 11, 12, 13, 21, 27, 36, 44, 80, 84, 86, 89, 125, 132, 146, 159, 164, 169, 175, 188, 189, 222, 257, 258, 259, 262, 269, 275, 276, 277, 278, 279, 281, 297, 317
inspire, iv, 3, 6, 30, 52, 60, 83, 140, 152, 276
inspired, i, ii, ix, x, 6, 8, 10, 11, 12, 13, 15, 18, 19, 21, 22, 23, 26, 30, 32, 38, 52, 60, 66, 79, 83, 84, 89, 90, 105, 112, 116, 125, 140, 145, 146, 152, 153, 162, 164, 169, 171, 176, 199, 212, 217, 218, 222, 224, 226, 236, 242, 256, 260, 261, 263, 271, 272, 273, 275, 277, 278, 279, 321, 331
interlinear, ii, 55, 136, 202, 228, 232, 233, 234, 285, 286, 287, 288, 289
interpret, 8, 69, 70, 79, 80, 148, 151, 163, 170, 207, 320
interpretation, xi, 3, 8, 69, 76, 78, 79, 80, 109, 116, 170, 179, 226, 231, 239, 258, 270, 309, 317
Iraq, xii
Irving, 317
Isaiah, 1, 16, 38, 100, 110, 116, 150, 167, 217, 242, 291, 320, 338, 355, 375
Isis, 183
Israel, 1, 2, 109, 110, 116, 217, 258, 259, 280, 320, 321
Itala, 22, 217, 218
Italian Diadoti, 217
Ivan Panin, 37
Jansenists, 317
Jerusalem, 258, 315, 363
Jesuit, 164, 244
Jonathan Edwards, 43, 183
Jonge, 195
Jordan, 176
Josephus, 65, 144
Jowett, 39, 176
Judson, 8, 43, 270
Kabbalah, 38, 253, 257
Kabbalah-istic, 38
Kaleda, viii, 290, 297, 302, 304
Kethib, 5
Kimball, 318
Kingsley, 39, 176
Kittel, 50, 52, 60, 75, 133, 140

koine, 64, 143, 156, 175
Ku Klux Klan, 87
LaMore, 235, 236
lasciviousness, 163
Latin, iii, xii, 6, 13, 14, 15, 17, 23, 25, 26, 27, 33, 42, 52, 58, 59, 60, 62, 65, 68, 72, 75, 83, 85, 94, 124, 140, 142, 144, 145, 146, 166, 175, 182, 197, 199, 205, 206, 207, 211, 213, 214, 215, 216, 217, 218, 219, 221, 222, 223, 225, 238, 239, 241, 242, 246, 257, 258, 259, 260, 261, 262, 263, 264, 266, 269, 273, 274, 276, 306, 307, 312, 368
law, 43, 74, 75, 102, 108, 183, 187, 277, 298, 317
lectionaries, xi, 21, 26, 124, 238
Les Miserables, 155
Letteris, 28, 249, 250, 252
lexicographers, 3, xi, 50, 56, 66, 72, 133, 137, 139, 145, 146, 155, 167, 276
lexicon, 7, 8, 33, 34, 35, 36, 42, 43, 49, 50, 51, 52, 53, 54, 55, 56, 57, 58, 59, 60, 61, 62, 63, 64, 67, 71, 72, 74, 75, 76, 77, 87, 94, 95, 99, 111, 128, 131, 133, 134, 135, 136, 137, 138, 139, 140, 141, 142, 143, 145, 147, 149, 154, 157, 161, 165, 170, 171, 172, 174, 175, 176, 177, 178, 179, 180, 181, 183, 184, 185, 186, 189, 190, 215, 228, 230, 244, 245, 252, 286
lexicons, viii, xi, 8, 17, 24, 33, 36, 42, 47, 48, 49, 50, 51, 52, 53, 54, 55, 56, 57, 58, 60, 61, 62, 63, 65, 67, 71, 72, 73, 74, 75, 76, 77, 78, 95, 99, 112, 113, 120, 123, 125, 126, 127, 129, 131, 132, 133, 134, 135, 136, 137, 138, 139, 140, 141, 142, 144, 146, 맵147, 149, 150, 152, 154, 157, 160, 171, 175, 176, 179, 185, 189, 190, 201, 227, 234, 236, 246, 256, 270, 275, 299, 305
Liddell, 38, 39, 40, 50, 57, 61, 62, 72, 133, 138, 141, 170, 171, 172, 173, 174, 175, 176, 177, 178, 179, 180, 181, 183, 184
Lies, xv, 304
Logos, 3, 4, 19, 103, 131, 170, 198, 286, 287, 288
Lucifer, 48, 120, 150, 167
Luther, 15, 29, 90, 170, 247, 249, 250, 251, 267, 268, 269
Macedon, 84
MacRae, 164
magnify, 316
magnitude, 314
mainline, 318
Majority, 25, 124, 288
man-made, 12, 71, 257
marginal, 27, 196, 235, 250, 272, 322, 341, 368, 374, 376
mark, 101, 103, 115
marriages, i, vii, viii, 77, 120, 123, 289, 290, 291, 292, 295, 296, 297, 300, 301, 302, 303, 304, 305
married, 71, 120, 289, 290, 291, 292, 294, 296, 297, 300, 301, 302, 304
Mary, 4, 39, 40, 73, 176, 239
Massorah, 28, 247, 250
Massoretic, 28, 248, 249, 252
master, 97, 105, 184, 213, 233
masters, 79, 233
mat, 46, 65, 116, 144, 151, 157, 191, 203, 220, 234, 235, 243, 252, 268, 271
matrix, 13
Mayflower, 68

INDEX

meanings, 7, 32, 40, 42, 53, 56, 57, 58, 62, 63, 64, 65, 66, 72, 74, 76, 87, 89, 96, 110, 128, 132, 134, 136, 137, 141, 142, 144, 145, 147, 152, 161, 166, 168, 178, 181, 186, 244, 283, 322
Melanchthon, 170
methodology, 8, 56, 69, 80, 110, 137, 154, 161, 189, 193, 198, 276
Metzger, 57, 138, 163, 164, 333
Micah, 1, 4, 351, 356, 361
ministry, 3, 8, 9, 43, 91, 94, 112, 127
mishandled, 311
misinterpretation, 319
Missionaries, 6, 43
monastic, 239
monster, 172, 173
Morning Star, 167
Moulton, 40, 41, 50, 57, 130, 132, 133, 137, 196, 243, 275
movement, 268, 313, 318
Mowry, 164
Mt. Carmel, 315
Müller, 39, 159, 176, 182, 183
Muslim, 40, 71, 239
mystical, 36, 72, 169, 172, 179, 225, 283
myth, 30, 173, 312
NA, 121, 292, 293, 299
names, vii, 19, 20, 37, 42, 167, 170, 186, 197, 281, 282, 321, 322, 323, 331, 336
NASB, 54, 128, 135, 149
nation, 12, 13, 14, 39, 62, 72, 142, 155, 176, 217, 225, 237, 257, 258, 259, 273, 315
NEB, 149
Nebuchadnezzar, 89
Nehushtan, 4
Neopolis, 85
Nero, 84, 85

Nestle-Aland, 24, 54, 121, 123, 135, 157
New Age Bible Versions, 24, 122, 261, 304, 311
Newman, 56, 57, 137, 138
NIV, 54, 128, 135, 149, 151, 154, 201
noised, 316
Non sequitor, 113
Norse, 154, 173, 174
NRSV, 129, 164
NT, 3, 25, 130, 131, 205, 206, 306
Obadiah, 1
observance, 210, 323
observation, 157, 160, 200, 207, 305, 324
ocean, 5, 9, 317
official, 40, 123, 145, 176, 273, 303, 321
OINOS, 96
ordinances, 317
Origen, 65, 144, 256
originall greeke, 66
Orlinsky, 164
Oxford, 11, 41, 180, 182, 210, 309, 323, 333, 342, 356, 357, 372
pagans, 42, 48, 166, 174, 186, 315
Papias, 125
Papyrus, 180
parabasis, 102
paraptoma, 102
Pashto, 271
passages, v, x, 29, 89, 93, 107, 185, 195, 199, 315, 322
Passow, 183
pastor, i, 91, 92, 111, 112, 119, 185, 197, 288, 290, 291, 311
Paul, iii, 1, 5, 9, 13, 40, 79, 84, 116, 146, 155, 186, 217, 218, 230, 241, 280, 314, 316, 319, 320

PAUSONTAI, 116
Pentateuch, 238
Pentecost, 10, 12, 84, 116, 146, 217, 226, 237, 315
perfect tense, 99, 156, 234, 277
Perseus Project, 63, 142
Peshitta, 124, 222
Peter, iii, viii, x, 1, 26, 84, 100, 113, 125, 146, 238, 283, 300, 316, 320, 369, 371
phenomena, 36, 38, 315, 316, 318, 319
Philadelphia, 319, 372
philological, 64, 143, 159
philosopher, 314
pi, 172
plagiarist, 23
Plato, 39, 63, 72, 142, 155, 177, 178, 179, 181, 314
Poe, 181
Polly Powell, 277
Polycarp, 125
Polyglot, 25, 124, 194, 199, 204, 216
porn, 161
porneia, 162
powers, 23, 58, 139, 240, 317
praise, 44, 320
Pratensis, 29, 247
prayer, 107, 310, 319, 321
premise, 15, 60, 147
Prepositions, 158
Princeton, 301, 304
problems, viii, 9, 113, 115, 156, 279, 283
prophecy, 1, 26, 315, 317
prophesied, 315, 316
prophesy, 315
prophet, 1, 116, 312
prophets, i, ii, v, ix, x, 1, 279, 280, 315, 317, 321, 331, 334, 341
Propitiation, 110, 246

published, ii, vii, 21, 23, 25, 26, 31, 33, 40, 41, 45, 123, 124, 190, 191, 196, 197, 198, 199, 210, 215, 216, 228, 244, 254, 286, 293, 298, 304, 305, 331, 333
punctiliar, 277
Puritans, 188
Qere, 5
Quality, 58, 67
quotations, 22, 202, 212, 251, 322
quotes, 2, ii, vi, ix, xi, 22, 31, 32, 108, 119, 121, 126, 153, 167, 172, 201, 206, 208, 210, 223, 235, 237, 251, 261, 282, 283, 312
Quran, 166
Rabbinic, 28, 29, 247
rapture, 71
readers, 63, 69, 76, 142, 168, 170, 182, 223, 254, 310, 311
readings, 5, 20, 21, 22, 27, 31, 37, 38, 93, 179, 188, 190, 196, 197, 203, 205, 206, 208, 209, 210, 211, 213, 214, 216, 217, 218, 220, 222, 223, 224, 228, 236, 239, 241, 248, 252, 253, 265, 267, 273, 306, 323, 334
Recension, 28
recorded, v, x, 26, 125, 174, 314, 316, 317
rector, 318
reference, xii, 9, 24, 58, 95, 96, 108, 109, 115, 122, 138, 157, 162, 164, 177, 189, 198, 201, 202, 209, 211, 216, 219, 228, 238, 320, 322, 368
references, xiii, 87, 92, 96, 196, 254, 322
reformation, 317
regulation, 323
religion, 39, 41, 84, 183

INDEX

remission, 110, 246, 317
Renaissance, 23, 45, 170, 256
repent, vii, 147, 320
repentance, 148, 296, 312, 317
RETRANSLATING, 32
revelation, x, 1, 3, 30, 79, 108, 110, 113, 115, 116, 161, 192, 280, 321, 341
revelations, ix, 94, 317
reverse translation, 20, 29
Revised Version, 24, 36, 39, 40, 48, 57, 68, 119, 123, 138, 176, 177, 178, 184, 186, 187, 191, 196, 197, 202, 209, 210, 211, 212, 243, 244
revision, 7, 47, 50, 51, 52, 56, 60, 75, 93, 133, 140, 141, 174, 193, 196, 310, 323
revisions, x, xii, 7, 47, 50, 51, 62, 133, 134, 141, 175, 264, 322
ROBBERY, 131
Robertson, 47, 159, 160
Robinson, ii, xv, 206, 212, 285, 286, 288, 299
Roman, 6, 14, 15, 23, 25, 41, 58, 65, 84, 85, 96, 124, 144, 180, 189, 218, 230, 256, 257, 259, 262, 267, 311, 315, 316
Romanese, 14, 266
Romania, 176
Romanian, 176, 182
Romaunt, 14, 266
Rome, 14, 16, 58, 72, 83, 84, 85, 188, 219, 262
royal library, 214
Ruckman, iii, 125, 300
Ruckmanite, xi, 313
rules, 7, 46, 66, 81, 91, 126, 145, 167, 193, 213, 220, 321, 324
Ruskin, 39, 176, 179, 181
Russell, 31, 43

RV, 36, 42, 48, 120, 165, 178, 191, 202, 209, 210, 212, 220, 243, 244
sacrilege, 15
Salvific, 148
Samuel, 313, 315, 341, 342, 348, 374
Sanskrit, 159, 182, 183
Satan, 39, 157, 160, 167, 176, 312
Saul, 315
Schaff, 42, 164, 188, 191
Schneider, 52, 60, 75, 140
scholar, 19, 36, 60, 77, 121, 163, 228, 232, 245, 261, 301, 321
scholars, xiii, 9, 44, 50, 51, 53, 62, 67, 77, 84, 134, 141, 159, 166, 168, 175, 178, 235, 241, 242, 253, 255, 256, 259, 278
scholarship, 9, 31, 47, 68, 87, 97, 115, 174, 209, 312
school, iii, 39, 48, 76, 119, 152, 182, 229, 276, 331
Scott, 40, 42, 50, 57, 61, 62, 72, 133, 138, 141, 170, 171, 172, 177, 179, 180, 184
scripture, iii, iv, 1, 2, 74, 80, 86, 145, 222, 275, 277, 279, 322
scriptures, 13, 24, 107, 123, 159, 161, 163, 178, 183, 188, 217, 218, 237, 238, 239, 242, 279, 280, 281
Scrivener, 3, ii, viii, ix, xvi, 19, 20, 30, 190, 191, 192, 193, 194, 195, 196, 197, 198, 199, 200, 202, 203, 204, 205, 206, 207, 208, 209, 210, 212, 213, 214, 215, 216, 219, 220, 221, 222, 223, 224, 227, 236, 239, 264, 265, 266, 267, 286, 287, 299, 306, 307, 334
Scrivenerites, 222
Scythian, 15

Secret Doctrine, 183
semantic, 52, 60, 75, 140
seminaries, 76, 188
Septuagint, 59, 101, 111, 249, 250, 251, 272, 280, 281
Shakespeare, 44, 45, 63, 68, 143, 181, 310
sheol, 126, 150, 178
Shutt, 237, 295, 298, 305
sign, 50, 101, 116, 258, 262, 275, 321
significations, 322
signs, 291, 315
silence, 3, 17, 24, 28, 79, 112, 116, 122, 213, 241, 247, 270, 312
sins, 100, 103, 110, 111, 245, 246, 280, 317, 321
Slavic, 64, 143
Smith, 191, 200, 308
society, 25, 62, 142, 172
Sophocles, 63, 142
sounds, 109, 168, 315, 319
Spafford, 177
Spanish, iii, 166, 182, 242, 248, 249, 250, 251, 267, 273
Spanish Reina-Valera, 267
Spanish Reyna, 273
spirit, v, 34, 38, 73, 86, 96, 109, 171, 189, 241, 275, 277, 281, 315, 319
spontaneously, 60, 116, 319
Stanley, 39, 176, 178
Stephanus, 19, 20, 25, 124, 199, 200, 203, 204, 216, 223, 225, 227, 229
Stephens, 25, 124, 216, 227, 286, 287, 331
Strong, 35, 36, 42, 50, 55, 87, 88, 131, 133, 136, 165, 167, 168, 169, 188, 201, 243, 252, 263, 275, 286, 287
subjunctive, 235, 319
Summers, 158
sun god, 173
superfluidity, 163
supernatural, 79, 115, 117, 240, 315, 316, 319, 320, 321
Symonds, 184
Syriac, 194, 216, 222, 223, 239, 248, 249, 250, 251, 258, 261, 263
Syrian, 15, 124, 223, 261, 263
Syrians, 13, 263
targums, 238
Tatian, 316
TBS, 27, 28, 197, 203, 207, 209, 211, 212, 249, 250, 254
teaches, iv, xi, 3, 77, 91, 165, 317
temple, 89, 111, 156, 343, 361
Tertullian, 194, 219
testimony, ii, iv, 33, 42, 86, 273, 275, 285, 301, 332
textual, 7, 29, 37, 38, 44, 54, 135, 163, 193, 195, 199, 206, 212, 236, 249, 265, 267, 279, 285, 288, 312, 331, 334
Textus Receptus, 19, 25, 32, 54, 57, 124, 125, 135, 138, 157, 190, 193, 197, 198, 202, 203, 214, 222, 227, 228, 229, 237, 239, 272, 286, 287, 288, 331, 333
Thayer, 42, 50, 116, 133, 160, 170, 185, 186, 187, 188, 189, 191, 201, 228, 234, 255
theologically, 318
theology, 9, 10, 31, 47, 65, 94, 132, 144, 145, 149, 164, 171, 172, 174, 189, 253, 317
theses, 11
thesis, 10, 11, 12, 15, 43, 51, 83, 84, 112, 115, 119, 126, 128, 133, 174, 229, 230, 274, 282, 283
Thomas, 228, 229, 286, 288, 313

INDEX

thousands, 44, 59, 151, 231, 238, 239, 242, 297
Thucydides, 63, 101, 142
Timothy, iii, iv, vi, ix, x, 2, 3, 10, 32, 86, 107, 112, 267, 280, 300, 312
tongue, 15, 79, 125, 183, 219, 241, 242, 258, 269, 316, 318, 320
transgress, 101, 102
translator, xi, 6, 7, 8, 17, 20, 34, 39, 46, 59, 64, 66, 67, 87, 127, 132, 139, 143, 147, 148, 172, 176, 183, 190, 216, 219, 237, 252, 255
Tremellius, 222, 264, 357, 360, 376
Trench, 40, 83, 103, 152, 153, 201, 228
trespass, 101
Trinitarian Bible Society, 28, 198, 201, 205, 206, 254, 308
trinity, 71
Tufts, 63, 142
Turkish, 64, 143
Tyndale, 15, 23, 68, 90, 124, 148, 211, 220, 264, 269, 323, 365, 366, 376, 377
typeface, 212, 311
typographical, 20, 311
UBS, 54, 57, 121, 138, 157, 185
Unitarian, 42, 48, 120, 160, 187, 188, 228, 234
United Bible Society, 19, 24, 54, 121, 123, 135, 229, 262
universities, iii, 324
university, 275, 323
untempered morter, 115
utterance, 13, 315
utterances, 317
utterings, 319
variants, 5, 20, 31, 200, 223, 252, 279, 334
Vaticanus, 193, 195, 280

Vaudois, 14, 266
Vaughan, 24, 36, 123, 184, 191
Venice, 28, 29, 247
vernacular, 11, 14, 15, 21, 22, 99, 105, 108, 153, 216, 218, 227, 238, 249, 258, 260, 263, 266, 267, 269, 271, 272, 273, 274, 279, 281
virtually, xi, 35, 45, 47, 50, 55, 66, 113, 136
Vonnie Waite, 285, 286
vulgarly, 321
Vulgate, xii, 6, 199, 211, 213, 215, 216, 217, 219, 239, 249, 265, 269, 272, 273, 274, 312, 343, 344
Waite, 3, ii, iii, v, viii, xiv, xv, 2, 199, 200, 202, 203, 206, 207, 208, 220, 288, 289, 298, 299, 301, 302, 303, 304, 305, 306, 307
Warfield, 278, 279
Westcott, 24, 26, 40, 41, 48, 54, 55, 57, 120, 123, 125, 135, 136, 138, 177, 184, 186, 191, 193, 194, 202, 209, 254, 286, 287, 331
Westcott/Hort, 123
Westminster, 154, 199, 314, 319, 323
Whitchurch, 323
whore, 161, 162
Williams, 1, 3, xiv, 2, 3, 41, 334
woman, viii, 10, 88, 112, 178, 253, 276, 291, 292, 296, 297, 305, 312
275, 276, 277, 278, 279, 281,
written, i, iv, viii, xi, 1, 2, 5, 6, 7, 8, 11, 14, 15, 17, 22, 25, 31, 40, 43, 45, 51, 55, 59, 61, 64, 65, 67, 73, 76, 77, 83, 86, 89, 99, 105, 107, 113, 121, 122, 125, 134, 137, 141, 144, 153, 155, 160, 164, 168, 172, 174,

176, 188, 189, 190, 192, 204, 214, 229, 237, 242, 252, 255, 260, 261, 262, 275, 278, 281, 286, 291, 293, 298, 306, 317, 320
Wuest, 50, 111, 133
www.luminarium.org, 314
www.wayoflife.org, 306, 312
Wycliffe, xii, 12, 90, 94, 242, 257, 260, 269, 273, 312
Ximenes, 25, 124
Ximénes de Cisneros, 216
Yom Kippur, 111
Zeinner, 242
Zoroastrianism, 40

ABOUT THE AUTHOR

Dr. DiVietro was born in 1952 to Christian parents. He was in church faithfully from the time he was 2 weeks old. The two greatest influences in his life are his mother Shirley, now in heaven, who instilled in him a love for reading and learning, and his father Tony, who instilled in him a work ethic and Bible convictions and consistency. They remain each other's best friend.

He grew up in the country. Though his family were not farmers they lived on a farm, next to one of the best trout streams in Pennsylvania; on 100 acres of pine forest, orchards, and open fields. Church kids and school friends would travel miles to fish and play. It was most idyllic for a young boy.

No missionary or evangelist came through their church without spending at least one meal at their table. As a boy, he met Jack Van Impe, Hyman Appleman, Anthony Zeoli and many other famous evangelists of the time. His pastor and his wife were graduates of Philadelphia College of the Bible. His pastor's wife typed many of the pages of the New Scofield Bible. That is the kind of godly home he was raised in.

When he was 13 years old, he read a book that changed his life. It tore down the divine authorship of the Pentateuch and replaced it with the JEDP theory. Later that year he read the *Passover Plot*. These two books destroyed his confidence in the Bible and in God. From that day on, he became an atheist wanted to escape his fundamentalist roots. For high school graduation, his dad gave him a one way ticket to San Francisco with the words, If you want to go I'll pay your way. You will have to pay your own way to come back home. Three weeks after getting there, he saw someone eating out of trash cans and decided to buy that ticket.

Early in the morning of Palm Sunday 1971, the Holy Spirit of God broke through his drug befuddled mind and the lights went on in his soul. The things that he had been taught years before by his parents, his Sunday school teachers, and youth workers were not wasted. They suddenly made sense. At that moment he could believe and he did believe. It was almost as dramatic as Wesley's testimony who had written, "My heart was strangely warmed that night at Aldersgate. I trusted Christ and Christ alone."

He knew immediately that God had called him to preach. In the fall of 1972, he enrolled in United Wesleyan College. After 3 semesters, he was asked to leave because of his strong belief that the Bible was the word of God from cover to cover. Two other students and he were told that they were hindering the work of the Holy Ghost and keeping back revival (the school no longer exists). Then he enrolled in Liberty Baptist College and graduated cum Laude in June, 1977.

That same month he started the First Baptist Church of Belvidere, NJ which he pastored for 13 1/2 years. During that time, he continued his education, enrolling in Baptist International School of Theology in Oxon Hills, MD, headed by Dr. J. Roy Stewart. There he was introduced to computers. He earned a Master of Theology (1988) and Ph.D. (1990) in New Testament from BIST. Computerizing the Stephanus 1550 text became his doctoral project.

Dr. Stewart introduced Dr. DiVietro to Dr. D.A. Waite who introduced him to the Scrivener Text. Upon finishing the Stephanus text, he computerized the Scrivener Text. Dr. Waite introduced Dr. DiVietro to the developer of Logos Bible Software. His Greek New Testament continues to be used by Logos.

In 1992, he moved to Franklin, Mass., where he now shepherds the Grace Baptist Church. He served as an adjunct professor at Baptist Bible College East in Boston, MA, a BBF affiliated school for several years. During that time he returned to Liberty University and earned a Master of Arts in Religion (1998) and a Master of Divinity (2000). He parted with BBCE because of their leaving the King James Bible and because of other compromises. He was invited by two schools to come help start seminaries; however the Lord did not give him the liberty to do so.

Several years ago, he started a Bible institute in Woodlawn Baptist Church in Bowie MD where he continues to teach on a regular basis. He has made missionary trips to Romania, Jordan, and Iraq. While in Iraq, he was in an ambush that took the life of another pastor and left

ABOUT THE AUTHOR

Dr. DiVietro and another pastor wounded. He is planning to make a preaching missions trip to England.

At this writing he has been married 37 years to a girl he met on the school bus. They married the year after she graduated from high school have three children and eight grandchildren. His older daughter is married to the pastor of a Baptist church. His younger daughter and her husband are faithful active church members serving God through local church. His son is happily married and is also the pastor of a Baptist church. He had the privilege of ordaining his father to the ministry. He has a nephew in the ministry. Since coming to America there has been at least one preacher in each of nine generations of his ancestors. God's promise has proven true:

"Train up a child in the way he should go: and when he is old, he will not depart from it." (Proverbs 22:6).

Dr. DiVietro has written numerous books and articles which have been published through the Bible For Today ministries and the Dean Burgon Society. In addition, he has several works on various books of the Bible waiting to be published.

ABOUT THE EDITOR

Dr. Williams was born in Ft. Pierce, Florida. He was saved at the age of fourteen at his local Baptist church under Pastor J. R. White where he was active in the church youth group. His local church ordained him to preach the gospel. After graduating with honors from high school, he attended Stetson University where he met his wife, Patricia, and they were married in 1961. Starting in the ministerial program at Stetson and switching to pre-med in his junior year, he graduated with honors with a B.A. After Stetson, he taught high school at Eau Gallie, Florida for two years, and then continued his training at the University of Miami Medical School where he graduated with honors. Following his medical training, Dr. Williams and Patricia settled in New Port Richey, Florida where he practiced Family Medicine as a board certified family practitioner. He was active in his community as a hospital board member for twenty years, a chief-of-staff, president of the medical society, an advisory board member and president of Moody Bible Institute's Florida program, a board member of the Health Planning Commission, and a teacher at his local Baptist church. He helped develop and administrate a multi-specialist medical clinic with forty thousand patients and seventeen doctors. His Biblical training was obtained at Stetson University, Moody Bible Institute, and Louisiana Baptist University. After retirement, Dr. Williams has served the Lord Jesus Christ as an associate pastor, a teacher, and as vice-president and representative for the Dean Burgon Society. He received a Ph.D. in Biblical studies from Louisiana Baptist University. He has traveled to many foreign lands where he has represented the Dean Burgon Society, teaching pastors and participating in evangelistic events. He is author of the several books, *The Lie That Changed The Modern World; Word-For-Word Translating of the Received Texts, Verbal Plenary Translating; Hearing the Voice of God; The Septuagint is a Paraphrase; The Pure Words of God; The Attack on the Canon of Scripture; The Miracle of Biblical Inspiration; Origin of the Critical Text; The Covenant of Salt;* and *Wycliffe Controversies,* in addition to many articles and booklets.

He is President of "The Old Paths Publications," which helps authors publish their works by the modern method of printing on demand (POD) and a board member of "The William Carey Bible Society." Dr. Williams' Bible studies can currently be seen by archived or live streaming through Bible For Today ministries. Dr. Williams and his wife, Patricia have two sons, five grandchildren, and three great-grandchildren.

www.ingramcontent.com/pod-product-compliance
Lightning Source LLC
Chambersburg PA
CBHW060104170426
43198CB00010B/764